Pérez Galdós

SPANISH LIBERAL CRUSADER

Pérez Galdós
Spanish Liberal Crusader

><<>>>->>>->>>->>>->>>->>>->>>->>>->>>->>>->>>->>>->>>->>>

H. CHONON BERKOWITZ

LATE PROFESSOR OF SPANISH IN
THE UNIVERSITY OF WISCONSIN

><<>>>->>>->>>->>>->>>->>>->>>->>>->>>->>>->>>->>>

MADISON
THE UNIVERSITY OF WISCONSIN PRESS
1948

Preface

LIKE MOST PREFACES, THIS ONE is really an epilogue. Viewed in retrospect, the present biography of Benito Pérez Galdós tells something more than the story of a great Spaniard who is dead. At many points it parallels the currents of recent Spanish life and even merges with them. This is as it should be. Without the peculiar atmosphere of what Spanish historians call the Restoration, Galdós could not have developed his literary personality, and without Galdós the Restoration would not have acquired one of its sharpest features. From his era Galdós learned the immutable traits of Spanish character, and to his era he gave the courage to contemplate its own full-length portrait in a none too flattering mirror.

The Spain which Galdós knew so well has not yet passed into history. Nor has Galdós disappeared entirely from the contemporary Spanish scene. His spiritual vitality has manifested itself more than once since his death. And his survival goes deeper than the evidence which could be furnished by publishers' statistics. It is apparent in Spain's continued quest for a way of life appropriate to her own nature and temperament as they were defined by Galdós in novels and dramas. He strove to give his people a new national conscience; his people are still struggling to respond collectively to the voice of that conscience. Galdós urged his fellow Spaniards to learn to know themselves, and they are still seeking that knowledge.

The continued vitality of Galdós does not make the task of his biographer any easier. The issues which were raised by his particular interpretation of Spanish life still divide his countrymen today. Dispassionate appraisal of his efforts and achievements, whether as a spiritual leader of his people or as a significant literary figure, is not yet possible. This is especially true of Spanish opinion, which is uncommonly susceptible to fluctuating enthusiasms and condemnations inspired by ideological and artistic novelties of the moment. Today as yesterday Galdós is either everything or nothing to certain groups of Spaniards. Now as before a discussion of Galdós is apt to flare up into a heated controversy.

And so the present biography lays claim neither to definitiveness of content nor to infallibility of interpretation. Based on information gathered from a great variety of printed, manuscript, and oral sources, it is only an honest attempt to bring into focus one of the most impressive of modern Spanish figures. Had this been undertaken by a native of Spain, he would doubtless have preferred to use a color camera. I have chosen to sacrifice chromatic effects to sharp lines and clear detail. If the resulting likeness of Galdós should startle some, the reason would have to be sought in the fact—and it must be stated here with complete frankness—that all previous attempts at photographing Galdós have suffered from insufficient exposure and inexpert developing.

I should have fared no better than my predecessors had I not been tendered the invaluable aid of many kind persons. In Madrid, Santander, and Las Palmas I had the unfailing cooperation of members of the Galdós family and some of his friends and admirers. His daughter, María Pérez-Galdós de Verde, and her affable husband, Don Juan Verde y Rodríguez, were most generous with the materials and documents in their possession. The community of Las Palmas, with its Museo Canario and municipal archives and their respective staffs, may also be regarded as collaborators. Here I must single out for mention the genuinely sincere help of Sr. Agustín Martinón; and I wish to pause reverently and pay tribute to his memory if, as now seems likely, he lost his life in the recent Spanish tragedy.

It is no mere academic cliché to state that the present life of Galdós would have been impossible without the intimate collaboration of his nephew, the late Don José Hurtado de Mendoza y Tate. Throughout almost all his long life Don José had lived in close contact with Galdós. His knowledge and understanding of his celebrated uncle were extensive and penetrating. Only Don José could have written *the* biography of Galdós. This he chose not to do. Instead he willingly shared with me his knowledge and wisdom, helping me sift and winnow the accumulated mass of information and judgments in the interests of truth and accuracy. In the most literal sense this book could not have been written without the wise guidance of Don José.

Perhaps I should have put first things first. Had it not been for the generosity of the John Simon Guggenheim Memorial Foundation I should have been seriously handicapped in my studies. Likewise, without the aid of the Research Committee of the University of Wisconsin I could not have enjoyed at least a part of the leisure which the writing of this book has required. Finally, I owe an expression of deep appreciation to my wife. Through many years she has followed my "affair" with scholarship with amazing magnanimity and incredible freedom from jealousy. Her part in this scholarly enterprise has been truly heroic.

Contents

x   *Contents*

Illustrations

*Y es que la vida del hombre y el trabajo del artista van tan íntimamente ligados, y se compenetran de tal modo, que no hay manera de que por separado se produzcan, sin afectarse mutuamente.—*GALDÓS, *Arte y Crítica.*

I

The Pérezs and the Galdoses

IT WAS IN THE EARLY sixties of the past century. A group of undergraduates, obstructing the entrance to the main building of the Central University of Madrid, were gesticulating excitedly in a manner expressive of categorical denial. Someone had just asserted that the strangely timid lad from the Canary Islands, who looked like a prematurely retired carabineer in civilian clothes, was a poet; for days he had been shadowed on his way to the editorial office of a leading Madrid daily. Though the evidence seemed conclusive, few were willing to admit it. It was inconceivable that anyone bearing the prosaic name of Pérez—Benito Pérez—could be a poet. No Pérez had ever gained distinction in Spanish history!

Something akin to a conviction that Pérez and insignificance are synonymous must have prompted Spain in the years when Benito Pérez was emerging as a great literary figure to add dignity to Pérez by coupling it with Galdós, or even by suppressing it. By a curious coincidence, the diminishing emphasis on the paternal part of the surname actually reflects the minor role that Galdós' father played in the family history. One might almost say that, were it not for his biological indispensability, all reference to the father could well be omitted. The mother, on the other hand, dominates the scene completely. For the surviving Galdoses Papa Pérez is even today only a genealogical identification tag, but the mention of Mama Dolores floods their memory with details of a vividly etched personality. And although Mama

3

Dolores, for all her domineering nature, was unable to alter the laws of hereditary transmission, it is noteworthy that all her children, and particularly Benito, bore a much more striking resemblance to her than to her inconspicuous husband.

The available history of the Galdoses is relatively brief. Domingo Galdós y Alcorta, the maternal grandfather of Benito Pérez, was a native of Azpeitia, an ugly old town in the province of Guipúzcoa. Azpeitia was the birthplace of Saint Ignatius of Loyola, whose name appears with ironical persistence in the Galdós family. Two of Galdós' nephews, one uncle, and one brother were called Ignacio, and the last member of the peninsular branch of the family was a certain Ignacia Galdós, an old nun of Azpeitia, who died about 1890.

Domingo Galdós, characterized by his distinguished grandson as a worthy, virtuous man and a contemporary of the French Revolution, came to Las Palmas toward the end of the eighteenth century as Secretary of the Inquisition. He bore the official title of *Receptor* with distinction from 1797 to 1803. Since he did not belong to the priesthood and was not therefore committed to celibacy, Don Domingo married María Medina, a native of the Canary Islands. Persistent fecundity and constant financial difficulties were the lot of the couple for the better part of their lives. Doña María bore eleven children. All except Juan grew up and prospered in varying degrees; "Don Juan"—as Mama Dolores always called him with unaffected formality—lived only a few hours. Not many years later, between 1818 and 1822, he was followed to the grave by his father, who died prematurely, leaving a large and impoverished family.

Don Domingo's short life was filled with cares that increased as his progeny multiplied. Most of the males left Las Palmas in search of fortune. Some settled in Cuba; one, José María, a promising lawyer, took up residence in Trinidad, where, barring one scandalous amatory escapade, his conduct filled the family with pride. In the opinion of Mama Dolores, attorney José María was worthy of universal emulation. Another son, Pedro María, chose to serve the church with less authority but with greater zeal than his father. A tonsured cleric who had been competent in Latin and other humanistic studies from a tender age, Pedro María joined the official household of Bishop Luis de la Encina of Arequipa, Peru, at the end of a nightmarish journey that had begun in Montevideo more than six months before. Traveling on horseback and on foot, attacked by Indians, caught in a war between Uruguay and Argentina, and constantly exposed to inclement weather, he contracted tertian fever, which resulted in his death on February 16, 1813, when he was just past twenty. As a token of their profound esteem, Pedro María's associates dispatched to his parents a detailed account of his prolonged agony and tragic end.

The scapegrace of the Galdoses was apparently Benito Manuel. Seized by a spirit of adventure, he left for the European continent without parental consent. Domingo Galdós y Alcorta, who ruled his household with the austere dignity of his inquisitorial office, forthwith severed relations with his errant son, and for seven months adamantly denied his prayers for forgiveness. In 1818 Benito Manuel had an opportunity to secure free passage from London to Las Palmas, but he dared not return home without his father's permission. The rigorous climate in which the Galdós children were raised can be sensed in the closing lines of Benito Manuel's letter from London, under date of March 5, 1818: "Your Grace will be good enough to convey my respect and affection to my mother and a thousand caresses to my brothers and sister; command your ever obedient son, who embraces you from the bottom of his heart and who kisses your hand. Benito."

The desired reconciliation was not effected before Don Domingo's death. By 1822 Benito Manuel was temporarily established in Burgos, after a sojourn in the province of Vizcaya, where he had been engaged in pursuing "rebels." From Burgos he addressed his letters to his mother, who was already a careladen widow struggling with the problem of marrying off advantageously her daughter Dolores. As if anxious to make amends for the grief he had caused the family, Benito Manuel assumed personal responsibility for the solution of this problem. His mother ignored his intervention. Dolores was married in

1823. Two years later the news reached her wayward brother through the arrival in London of his boyhood friend, Luisito Navarro. This was the beginning of the reconciliation which was culminated at the birth of Dolores' first child. Doña María Medina de Galdós promptly informed her expatriate son of the event. Benito Manuel expressed his delight in a letter dated London, April 6, 1825: "I am very glad about Dolores' marriage, about her good health, about the blessed event. I am grateful for her greetings and I give her in return a thousand hugs and a thousand kisses for my Dominguillo, lots of love to her husband and I wish he may be so happy that he will have nothing to desire."

*   *   *   *

The sister of whom Benito Manuel was so patently fond was born at midnight of March 4, 1800. At the exact moment of her birth the family clock stopped on the mantel. Seven days later, in the austere cathedral of Las Palmas, the infant was baptized and christened María de los Dolores Josefa Galdós y Medina. Her godfather was a stern *teniente capitán*.

The name Dolores acquired a particular appropriateness in the long life of its bearer. Writing in her sixty-fifth year to cousin José Manuel in Madrid, Dolores spoke with unwonted frankness of the unhappy history of her family. She felt free to discuss intimate matters with this cousin, for only circumstances beyond human control had prevented her from marrying him back in the twenties: "Suffice it to say that my father and my mother were carried down to their graves by their troubles, and we too have suffered much; let us drop these memories which are quite sad."

It is conceivable that Dolores herself contributed substantially to the aggregate worries that sent at least her mother to her grave. She was an attractive girl, with a complexion so fair that she was teasingly called *"la negrita."* She was likewise amiable, primitively honest, strikingly independent of judgment, strong-willed, and deeply devoted to her mother, especially after the death of Don Domingo. Strongly attached to all the family,

Dolores was inordinately fond of José María, the successful Cuba attorney, and a bit grieved by the escapades of Benito Manuel, the brother who had so often lulled her to sleep in his arms when she was a baby. However, true to the family tradition of frowning on emotional exhibitionism, she never exteriorized her feelings or thoughts. Quietly but resolutely she made herself responsible for her mother's welfare, and when the time came for her to consider marriage this responsibility proved to be a serious obstacle.

It was no easy matter for Dolores to choose a husband. Suitors were not scarce and she was not hard to please, but her determination to include her mother in the projected love nest deterred more than one desirable party. The mother stayed in the background and viewed this family problem with utmost reserve and calm, but not brother Benito Manuel. From his vantage point in Burgos he unquestionably got a distorted view of the domestic issue, but he was determined to marry Dolores off soon and well, although without coercion, of course. His persistent concern for her happiness no doubt stemmed from a desire to reinstate himself in the good graces of the family. In his considered judgment the right man was cousin José Manuel, a clerk in the Crédito Público Bank of Burgos, with an impending increase in salary.

In a lengthy letter, plus an extensive "supplement," which he wrote to his mother from Burgos on September 4, 1822, Benito Manuel reported that he had sounded out José Manuel after he had been given a graphic verbal sketch of Dolores by a certain unidentifiable Ramona. The prospective bridegroom replied that "he would subscribe to nothing with greater pleasure," and that only the failure of the impending salary increase to materialize could delay his happiness. Being a practical business man, José Manuel set down in simple language, as addenda to Benito Manuel's letter, the complex and confused emotions stirred in him by love at first sight—in this case unseen. Among other things, the Burgos bank clerk said to Señora María Medina de Galdós: "Respecting Cousin Dolores you can tell

her on my behalf that if she thinks that my affection and hand
can constitute her happiness the decision rests with her, and so
let her tell me her thoughts."

The sincerity of her cousin's declaration must have impressed
Dolores no less than her brother's vivid description of him.
Pepe, said Benito Manuel, was a fine young fellow of twenty-
seven, tall, well built, very fair, and a most commendable character. In amiability and integrity he was matched only by
Dolores herself. Benito Manuel was convinced that she would
be happier as Señora Dolores Galdós de Galdós than as "Countess
de la Vega Grande." However, he had no desire to force her
will, nor did he suggest breaking a promise that she might have
given someone else.

An ordinary girl would have been delighted with so happy
a solution to a perplexing problem, but Dolores rejected it on
practical and temperamental grounds. She suggested that her
brother's hint that she was socially ambitious was unfair. A
"Count de la Vega Grande" would not necessarily be preferable
to a Galdós, but a Galdós with only a bank clerk's salary would
of necessity mean the continuation of the family's economic struggle, including the plight of her old widowed mother. Then too
she was loath to exchange balmy and delightful Las Palmas for
the cold barren plains of Castile. Did her brother merely suspect,
or did he actually know, that she had been attracted to someone
else? As a matter of fact, she had practically made up her mind
in favor of a very commendable person with whom she felt she
could be happy. The gentleman was neither as young nor as
handsome as José Manuel, and he was, to be sure, older than
she, but that appealed to her as an added attraction. It would
be challenging to dominate an older person, especially when
the promise of success was clear. But José Manuel, precisely
because he was so similar to herself morally and tempera-
mentally, might well be the cause of a constant struggle for
ascendancy. She really liked her Burgos cousin—perhaps she
even loved him—but she was going to marry the other man,
Sebastián Pérez, provided, of course, he agreed to receive her

mother into the new household for as long as it pleased the Lord to preserve her.

*   *   *   *

Sebastián Pérez y Macías was one of those individuals doomed by temperament and circumstances to an obscure existence. Only the subsequent fame of his son rescued him from complete oblivion. Don Sebastián was born on May 6, 1784, in the town of Valsequillo, in the northern part of Grand Canary. Of honorable peasant stock, he continued the family occupation and upheld its reputation throughout his long life. He received a limited and superficial education in the Las Palmas Seminary, which he abandoned early for a quasi-military career. Those were days when Spain had more need of soldiers than scholars. In his boyhood Sebastián had been attracted to the *blanquillos*, a sort of home-guard unit garrisoned in Las Palmas, and his enthusiasm for that organization soon led him into the army. A trained soldier, he joined in 1809 the Battalion of Volunteer Grenadiers organized in Las Palmas to fight against the French on the peninsula. Sebastián was the *subteniente* in command of the second of six companies that formed the column. A younger brother, Domingo, a priest, joined the battalion as chaplain.[1]

At five in the afternoon of April 5, 1809, the battalion embarked for Cádiz from the Puerto de Luz of Las Palmas. The eighteen days of the voyage were filled with peril and adventure. The small boats in the convoy failed to observe the signals that had been agreed upon, and for ten days they were out of contact with one another. Once a foreign vessel opened fire on them, but it proved to be only an English craft anxious to give the islanders a letter for delivery in Cádiz. The landing was made on April 23 amidst considerable excitement, the first transport having run aground.

The battalion remained in Cádiz until the end of August. There Domingo Pérez, the chaplain, roamed the streets in quest of human documentation, but Don Sebastián attended strictly to military duty. The very day of the landing he gave the measure of his ability as an officer. The military governor of

Cádiz, apparently using a brand of terminology unintelligible to the grenadiers, tried in vain to put them through some conventional parade drill in a ceremony of welcome. The insular officers were greatly embarrassed. Someone in the ranks called on Lieutenant Pérez to give the commands. He did so, and the expeditionary force paraded before the admiring crowd.

The islanders participated in some heavy fighting as part of the Army of Extremadura, whose triumphs and defeats they shared. Don Sebastián's most vivid experience of the campaign was the formation of a battery of grenadiers in the very mouth of heavy enemy fire. The soldiers were inspired to heroic feats by the cries of *"Viva la Virgen del Pino!"*—the patron Virgin of Las Palmas. They were all decorated for their valor. Lieutenant Pérez fought in other thrilling and dangerous engagements, but his modesty and frugal realism prevented him from recording them in his official report.

After approximately two years of pursuing the French, Don Sebastián and his chaplain brother proudly returned home. More concrete reward than praise and medals came to them in 1814, when Ferdinand VII was restored to the throne. In payment of accumulated wages each received a *data* in Monte Lentisca—plots of virgin volcanic land fit only for viticulture. The demobilized brothers plunged into work, and in 1819, after five years of persistent effort, gathered their first harvest.[2]

* * * *

The story of the courtship of Dolores Galdós and Sebastián Pérez is shrouded in mystery. Many serious obstacles had to be cleared before the marriage could be solemnized. Don Sebastián could have pressed his suit on the strength of his solid social and economic position, but he refrained from doing so because he was not naturally aggressive and because he feared violent reaction from strong-willed Dolores. He was always mindful of the fact that he was sixteen years older, and it would therefore have been ill-advised to urge a hasty decision. And so he waited patiently for at least two years, during which time some of the Galdoses negotiated elsewhere for a solution of the Dolores problem.

The union was finally solemnized late in 1823, not without
grave misgivings in certain quarters. Indeed, Don Sebastián's
married life got off to an inauspicious start the very first day.
His gentleness of the courtship period had to yield now to
rather violent pressure. When the wedding festivities were over,
Dolores refused to accompany the bridegroom to their new
home. She would not cross the threshold of the nuptial chamber
unless her mother came to live with them that very day! Don
Sebastián quickly perceived that he faced a real dilemma. As an
honorable gentleman he intended to fulfill his contractual obligations with the least possible delay. But Dolores' melodramatic
stand struck him as willful and inappropriate. He was not exactly
romantic or sentimental; rather he felt that his manliness was
challenged. Besides, a victory for Dolores in their first marital
conflict would be a flimsy foundation upon which to build their
happiness. The situation demanded quick and drastic action.
When night fell, Don Sebastián kidnapped the bride and carried
her to their new home.

Don Sebastián never had another opportunity to indulge in
marital heroics. Dolores Galdós—she never relinquished her
maiden name—quickly retrieved her dominant personality and
instituted a veritably dictatorial regime in her household. Her
husband, whom she henceforth called Señor Pérez, or just plain
Pérez, was assigned a role that can be adequately described only
as Dolores' husband. He was loyal and devoted, and worked
hard to support in moderate comfort his five sons and as many
daughters. His rural properties and sound investments in the
fishing industry of Las Palmas enabled him to educate his
children properly and to secure for his family a position of
esteem in the community. Nominally Don Sebastián was the
head of his household, but inwardly he knew that his part was
quickly being reduced to that of a resigned and unobtrusive old
man, surrounded by young and self-assertive individuals.

To his children, especially to the youngest ones, Don
Sebastián served as a symbol of grandfatherly serenity, mellowness, and indulgence. The limited space he occupied in the home
constituted a sort of sanctuary where they could seek refuge

from Mama Dolores' austere discipline. Papa Pérez felt grateful for this recognition of his usefulness, and whenever he could do so with impunity he rewarded his children with the one thing which in time he came to value as his most intimate possession— the story of his military exploits. But he always took pains to minimize his part in the War of Independence, emphasizing with infinite humility that he had been only one of a large cast of actors in the great national drama. These brief sessions with the youngsters were moments of true ecstasy in the declining years of Papa Pérez, when a few grandchildren came to replace his grown-up sons. The recital of his vivid memories gave him the thrill of a momentarily recovered personality. He sensed with delight that he was inspiring his youthful audience with ardent love of country. The old patriot lived to see his son Ignacio embark on a distinguished military career, but death overtook him in 1871, a few brief years before Benito Pérez Galdós acquired fame as the author of the monumental series of *Episodios nacionales.*[3]

* * * *

The house on 33 Calle del Cano was Mama Dolores' exclusive domain from 1823 to April 12, 1887, the date of her death. It was a compact little kingdom, ruled with stern dignity by a person who insisted on order and discipline as essential to individual and collective well-being. It was a microcosm, fortified against outside influences by the ruler's arbitrary concept of home and family and by her fierce sense of justice and propriety. Dolores' success was phenomenal. Her dead earnestness and deep sincerity made her "subjects" feel that they were living by the eternal and immutable laws of nature—a feeling strengthened by the rigid consistency and unswerving methodicalness with which Dolores regulated the family affairs and guided her own behavior. In a paradoxical way the Galdós household functioned like a tyrannical democracy.

Life in the modest Galdós home had its own rhythm, a rhythm never disturbed even by the arrival of a new child. The newly-born was merely fitted into the rigid domestic pattern.

For Mama Dolores the days were long and full. The family income was sufficient to provide servants, but these she only tolerated at best. For her the highest expression of family life was cooperative effort, and she herself set an example. Naturally she could not do everything singlehanded, but she did at least supervise the entire routine of the household. The energy that this required Dolores drew partly from her sturdy constitution and partly from her tremendous will power.

The day began early for the Galdoses, and the hour of rising was the same for all. In the shady patio of the house stood a deep, round wooden tub in which Mama Dolores bathed daily, immediately upon rising, in water cooled to a pleasant temperature during the night. She regarded personal cleanliness as a sacred duty, which she discharged punctiliously until the last weeks of her life. After her bath she assembled all but the youngest children and solemnly led them to the San Francisco church a few blocks away. There they heard mass with utmost devoutness and comported themselves with the decorum prescribed by Mama Dolores.

Nothing short of a cataclysm could have interfered with the religious routine of the Galdoses. In the late spring of 1867 Benito was expected home for a short visit. His boat was due to dock in the Puerto de Luz early one morning. Since rumor had already hailed Benito as Spain's most promising new writer, his anticipated arrival all but disrupted the household routine for several days. Excitement gripped his sisters, especially the oldest ones, who regarded "Benitín" as their own child. Someone suggested with trepidation that the daily schedule could perhaps be sacrificed to the extraordinary event. Would it be permissible to miss church that morning? Benitín would feel dreadful to step into an empty house. For a moment Dolores yielded sentimentally to the logic of the argument, then hastened to point out that duty to God was above logic or human sentiment. And the family marched off to church, sternly warned not to permit their behavior to betray their inner feelings. By way of compensation Mama Dolores put no limit on the effusiveness with which the sisters greeted Benitín after church.

The detachment from earthly interests with which Mama
Dolores listened to divine services in the morning yielded to an
all-pervading sense of everyday realities the moment she stepped
out into the soothing light of the little church square. Before
returning home for breakfast she invariably made the rounds
of all the shops where she traded. Although she trusted the
merchants and her servants, she nevertheless deemed it advisable
to look into the quality and prices of commodities herself. In
some instances she even took with her small samples of the
purchases which a servant later went to fetch. In this way Mama
Dolores blocked the path to temptation and made it impossible
for the domestics to loaf on the pretext that it took time to shop
around for bargains.

For time was a precious item in the Galdós family, and Mama
Dolores had to budget it carefully in order to carry on her
manifold activities effectively. She made all the clothes for the
children—even shoes for the younger ones—supervised their
education, watched their moral and spiritual growth, guided
them in their social development, harmonized their relations
with one another, and instilled in them a sense of mutual responsibility. Crowded as Dolores' life would have been in any
case, it might have been easier had all the children been boys. To
be sure, Benito's physical and moral rearing did present an
occasional problem, but even here it was the interference of the
sisters that usually caused the trouble. Carmen, the eldest, was
almost an unruly "rebel."

On one occasion Carmen attempted to disobey her mother.
As the house was becoming too small for the growing family,
Dolores decreed that the eldest girl should share her grandmother's bed. At first the new arrangement was a mildly
pleasant experience. But when the old lady became bedridden,
young Carmen hinted that physically and mentally she would
be more comfortable sleeping elsewhere. For Mama Dolores
there lurked behind that hint an inclination toward defiant
disobedience. She refused to alter the arrangement. Carmen
awoke one morning to discover her grandmother dead at her
side. She suffered a shock which resulted in a permanent nervous

disturbance. As her condition did not prevent her from ultimately marrying successfully—and Carmen was the only daughter who did marry—Mama Dolores probably never reproached herself for the evil effect of her harsh discipline.

The spinsterhood of the remaining four daughters was a vexing problem. They were attractive—Tomasa was decidedly beautiful—and by the standards of the day they were accomplished. Tomasa and her sister Dolores appeared frequently and successfully on public literary and musical programs. The home training of all the girls gracefully combined feminine virtue and charm with worldly accomplishments. Mama Dolores was thus puzzled and even irritated that no worthy suitors manifested an interest in her lovely daughters. True enough, her austere formality precluded easy social relations, but she reasoned that the worth of her lineage was well known, and it was not her place, therefore, to seek out strangers and admit them into the family sanctuary.

Manuela, the youngest daughter, infuriated Mama Dolores exceedingly with her aggressive interest in a young man of political promise, to whom she eventually became engaged despite her mother's instinctive dislike for him. The path of love was strewn with difficulties for the young woman. To escape maternal vigilance she was obliged to communicate with her suitor clandestinely and at long distance, from the roof of their house. In time this artifice was rendered ineffectual by the watchful eye of brother Sebastián, who shared Mama Dolores' austere views on many matters. But it was not easy to outwit Manuela, and she soon contrived to send notes to her suitor with such impenetrable secrecy that her mother never surprised her in the forbidden act. Eventually the engagement was broken off because of the fiancé's indiscreet conduct during his student days in Madrid.

At the half-century mark of her life Mama Dolores began to suspect that her forthright efforts to rear a happy family had not been entirely successful. The marriage of the first two children threatened her hitherto unchallenged supremacy. First Domingo, the eldest son, married Magdalena Hurtado de Men-

doza y Tate, a nervous, high-strung, and pathologically domineering woman. Then "rebel" Carmen became the wife of
Magdalena's brother, José Hermenegildo Hurtado de Mendoza
y Tate, an irritatingly liberal and tolerant young man. From a
social and moral viewpoint the children-in-law left nothing to
be desired, but Magdalena's domineering disposition and her
brother's excessive benevolence were gradually counteracting
Mama Dolores' sternness and austerity. In the case of young
Benito, the strict home training which had prevailed for more
than two decades often had to be relaxed because of the interference of the children-in-law. Madrina, as Magdalena was
familiarly called, and Señor Hurtado de Mendoza, as Mama
Dolores referred to her son-in-law, were molding little Benito's
character out of a curious mixture of stubborn will power, self-
assertiveness, humility, and kindliness. The mother feared that
with such conflicting traits the boy would never develop into a
worth-while person.

Anyone with less spiritual fortitude and without her keen
perception of realities would have weakened under the strain
of the conflict, but Mama Dolores was sustained by the hidden
reserves of her character. Her strategy was never to betray an
awareness of conflict but at the same time to fortify herself
against any challenge to her undisputed dominance. The crucial
test came when two persons arrived in Las Palmas from Cuba:
Adriana Tate and her daughter Sisita, a little girl of approximately Benito's age. For Mama Dolores the newcomers were the
sharp reminder of a shattered dream. In the tangle of sorrows
that marked the history of the Galdoses she had always discerned one bit of happiness—the professional success of her
favorite brother, Don José María. He was the prop of her
dignity and self-esteem. It had been her fondest hope that one
of her sons, preferably little Benito, would some day emulate
her brother. Then something dreadful happened. José María
became the father of a natural-born daughter—Sisita. The mother
was Adriana Tate, an American woman from Charleston, South
Carolina, who was also the widowed mother of Magdalena and

Hurtado de Mendoza. Adriana Tate and Sisita thus came to topple the figure of José María from the high pedestal on which his sister had placed it.

Dolores Galdós experienced the first moral defeat of her life. Yet in her mind it was Adriana and Sisita that she excoriated, and she set up a physical barrier between herself and them. She would have liked to banish them from Las Palmas, but she could not overcome the opposition of Magdalena and especially of Señor Hurtado de Mendoza, who loved his little half-sister like a father. Moreover, Carmen took Adriana and Sisita into her home and sheltered them affectionately. Mama Dolores had even thought of an open break with the disgraceful strangers, but she was afraid of converting an intimate family problem into a public scandal. She had to content herself with throwing a sort of sanitary cordon around Carmen's home. This was not very successful. But she was determined to stave off defeat, especially when she realized that Benito was being drawn closer and closer to Sisita. Once again Mama Dolores drew on the reserve strength of her character. She became more austere and more resolved—she became fairly tyrannical. Her children, now grown men and women, she regimented and disciplined like youngsters.

The presence of the "intruders" wrought a striking change in Mama Dolores' attitude toward Benito. Whereas she had always treated him with especial affection because he was the baby of the family, she now came to regard him as a sacred symbol of expiation. If she could raise him to be a perfect man, he would wipe out the disgrace that José María had brought to the Galdoses. The problem was how to shelter Benito from the harmful influence of his brothers and sisters, who felt that they should have a share in his training. This was no easy matter, but Mama Dolores managed to reduce meddlesome interference to a minimum and she was hopeful that the boy would some day occupy the pedestal from which indiscretion had removed José María. To realize her hope she planned to put distance between Sisita and Benito. In this she succeeded about 1862, when she

persuaded her son to go to Madrid to study law. For Mama
Dolores the good name of the Galdoses was well on the road to
redemption.

But her dream vanished when she finally learned that Benito
had spent his seven years at the university struggling to become
a journalist, not a promising young attorney. This disappointment added another sad chapter to the family history, which
Mama Dolores often characterized as "quite unfortunate." She
lived to see her son acclaimed Spain's greatest modern author,
but this thrilled her infinitely less than it did the other members
of the gradually diminishing family. Naturally Benito's repeated triumphs afforded her a measure of satisfaction, but she
received them with her customary sternness and austerity. The
course of her remaining years was not the one she had set. Outwardly Mama Dolores seemed tranquil and serene, but within
her continued the tense struggle to control the little world in
which she insisted on being the dominant figure. She still strove
to bend everyone and everything to her will.

Throughout her long existence Mama Dolores had matched
wits with life itself, without once admitting defeat openly. In her
last days she was a truly tragic figure. Of her five daughters
she wanted only "rebel" Carmen at her bedside. No tears and
wails and laments for Mama Dolores! She knew that Carmen
alone of all her children was capable of taking leave of her with
appropriate fortitude. Carmen's presence at her bedside would
symbolize, in a way, her own attitude toward life—unflinching
struggle for self-control. The family priest was also present. He
described eloquently the bliss of the hereafter for those who
live righteously. He bade Dolores Galdós forget the earth and
its sorrows and invited her to fix her mind on the joys of the
life to come. She looked at the cleric with an expression of
defiant skepticism and said, "Nonsense, my good man; the
mere thought of my departure fills me with infinite sadness.
I shall miss even the crude bench on which you are sitting."

María de los Dolores Josefa Galdós de Pérez died reluctantly
on the morning of April 12, 1887. Ten days later the details of
her death were communicated to Benito in Madrid by his brother

Ignacio: "Your letter at hand. I have nothing to tell you which you do not already know; the 12th at 11:40 the Lord took her away; the 13th at five in the afternoon was her burial. There is nothing left to do but to have patience and resignation."

There is profound filial respect in the superficially matter-of-fact wording of this laconic death notice. Had Mama Dolores been able to survive her own death, she would have transmitted the sad news with similarly severe dignity and complete absence of outward emotion. The concise objectivity of Ignacio's message testifies to the influence the mother exerted on her children.

*   *   *   *

In 1876 Benito Pérez Galdós had written the novel *Doña Perfecta,* whose protagonist immortalizes his mother, though only in part. He clearly limited himself to the readily discernible traits of Mama Dolores. Certainly the concluding phrase of the novel cannot apply to her: "This is all we have to say for the present concerning persons who seem good but are not." Possibly Galdós' mother was the reverse of the characters in *Doña Perfecta*—she may have seemed bad when in reality she was good. Her domineering nature, her strong will, her sense of the profound seriousness of life, her imperious demand for an ordered existence, her infinite respect for the fitness of things, and her keen perception of all basic moral values—traits which her son inherited in generous measure—these did not spring from a perverted conscience and a fanatical spirit. They were rather the inevitable impressions of grave experiences on a temperament that would not allow itself to be carried irresistibly by the current of life; a temperament that struggled to retard the current so that it might contemplate deliberately all the details of the landscape on both sides of the stream. María de los Dolores Josefa Galdós de Pérez forged her character and conscience out of the weapons which she found effective in her fight against frustration and despair. If her son failed to understand her, it was perhaps because he did not know her background intimately. Had she not told her cousin José Manuel in 1865 that Benito "is not well-informed concerning the most interesting part of our history, which is quite unfortunate"?

II

An Artist Is Born

IT WAS THE AFTERNOON of May 10, 1843. In the shady living
room of the Galdós home in Las Palmas, Sebastián Pérez and
his children sat in hushed silence. Over their heads, in a long,
darkish room, they could hear the heavy tread of servant Teresa's
canvas-slippered feet. Now and then the rhythm of her steps
quickened as she whispered acceptance of an order given in a
muffled feminine voice. This was followed by the rustle of her
skirt as she came running down the stairway into the patio.
Every time Teresa appeared, all eyes turned on her inquisitively.
But she merely looked comfortingly at Don Sebastián, who in
turn looked reassuringly at his children. There is no need to
feel anxious, he seemed to say to them; this has happened before.
Soon the air was filled with a cry which sounded like a voice
testing its range for the first time. The cathedral clock not far
away struck three.

Less than forty-eight hours later, the tenth and last child born
to Señor Pérez and Dolores Galdós was baptized in the San
Francisco church—the same church where his mother had received similar benefits forty-three years before. He was named
Benito María de los Dolores and was committed to the spiritual
care of his uncle, cleric Domingo Pérez.

Benito's infancy was a period of trial for the entire family.
He was not a sturdy child, and his physical development required watchful care. The procedures by which Mama Dolores
had successfully raised her other nine children had to be modified. Against her better judgment, she was even induced to
tolerate the intervention of the daughters, especially Carmen and

20

Birthplace of Galdós

Concha, because the child seemed to thrive better under the care of his sisters, particularly Carmen. At that Benitín's development was exasperatingly slow. Most disturbing was his abnormally protracted nursing period. How he would linger at the source of his food long after he had apparently had his fill! Benitín developed a pathological habit which persisted intermittently throughout his childhood. There was no way of shaming him, because he seemed to be seeking compensation for his low vitality in voluptuous contact with his mother's bosom. Could Mama Dolores have foreseen that some day Benito Pérez Galdós the novelist would dwell with delight on the description of a certain sculptural feature of the feminine body, she would not have permitted Benitín's perverted childhood indulgence.

But Benito's childhood was not all self-indulgence. In time he was forced to submit to Mama Dolores' uncompromising discipline. He yielded readily to domestic authority and was developing into a quiet, well-behaved boy. On the rare occasions when he was tempted to rebel against the hard routine of the home, sister Carmen would urge caution, thus forestalling evil consequences. Benito's rebellious impulses were limited to staying in bed beyond the hour set for the morning procession to church, or to bargaining for a special ration of sweets. Otherwise he was a bit better than well trained; he was decidedly inhibited.

To his playmates Benito was a timid, sickly, and ungainly little boy whom they cultivated patronizingly because he could be easily victimized. They proceeded warily, however, for fear of frightening him away. They did enjoy his presence at their heroic exploits because he was so appreciative a spectator. Yet it puzzled them that a boy who was so patently thrilled by manifestations of daring and aggressiveness could remain so meek and humble. There is no record in the annals of the neighborhood that Benitín ever hit back.

Benito Pérez did love heroes and deeds of valor. He spent many inspiring moments on his father's or his godfather's knee, fascinated by their vivid accounts of the heroic struggle for national independence. Papa Pérez's stories were so simple and so lucid that Benitín readily constructed his own version of the

War of Independence. Napoleon was a formidable enemy—
something like the leader of his own kid gang—who tried to
take away from his father and uncle something they prized
highly, something much more valuable than the thing little
boys fought for so hard. Surely the Virgen del Pino would not
have been on the side of his father and Uncle Domingo if that
national independence that they defended were not very precious.
For something like that he too could fight pluckily against all
the other children. It would not be a sin to fight for national
independence—would Uncle Domingo, a priest, have fought
against Napoleon if it were?

From the choice bits that Uncle Domingo read to him out of
his diary Benito drew the comforting idea that battles are not
always noise and shouting, blows and flying stones, bruises and
bleeding noses. He loved the graphic accounts of amusing experiences and scanned with admiration the words of the text.
Uncle Domingo had such a clear handwriting; it would be a
wonderful model for a little boy learning to write. When he
was old enough to go to school he would study penmanship in
his uncle's diary, and then he could write in his own words the
story of his father's heroic battle with Napoleon. Papa Pérez
said that those who went to war for their country's independence
were patriotic. Would he be patriotic if he only read his stories
about the war to the other children? Benitín wanted so badly
to be as good a patriot as his father and uncle!

The inspiring sessions with Papa Pérez and Uncle Domingo
yielded in Benito's preference only to the limited play hours his
mother permitted him. He had an extensive collection of figures
made out of paper and cloth; some were given to him, others he
fashioned himself under the supervision of sisters Dolores and
Tomasa. These sisters taught him many other pleasant pastimes.
Dolores played the piano and read poetry beautifully. Benito was
an apt piano pupil, but he never learned to recite a poem or tell
a story impressively. This was perhaps because of his shyness;
yet he was eloquent enough in the presence of his figures. With
these his conversations often seemed endless, possibly because he
endowed them in his imagination with the appearance and char-

acter of some of the people he saw at home. Sometimes they took on for him the personality of individuals he remembered from stories. And he was not always able to distinguish the figures that represented real persons from those that he himself invented.

Benito enjoyed playing with reality and its artistic limitations. One day he cut a man's figure out of paper and pasted it on the front door. It was a perfect likeness of Pepe Chirino, servant Teresa's sweetheart. Mama Dolores naturally scolded Benito for treating an older person disrespectfully, but his artistic skill plainly pleased her. She was even more delighted with something resembling an architect's model of a medieval town which Benito constructed when he was presumably only eight years old. It was made out of chalk, pasteboard, putty, glue, and pieces of glass. The model looked so strikingly like medieval Toledo that it was thought Benito must have been guided by a sketch of the city. But the youthful artist insisted that he had never seen a picture of Toledo—that the model was wholly the product of his imagination. Anyway, his first success in realistic art was so noteworthy that the family decided to preserve it for posterity.

Benito's childhood pastimes were so delightful and profitable that he was not cheered by the prospect of having to go to school. His parents, too, were inclined to question the value of the formal elementary schooling then available in Las Palmas. For the child's spiritual and social training the home was adequate, and even for his general education the combined knowledge of the family could probably have sufficed. But there were other considerations, principally the effect of the excessive indulgence he enjoyed as the baby of the household. Mama Dolores was of the opinion that Benito was developing into a spoiled youngster, badly in need of more disciplining. The "Migas" school, she was convinced, would provide the corrective influence that was needed.

The "Migas" school—officially called Las Amigas and conducted by two over-aged spinsters, the Mesa girls—has fortunately disappeared from the educational scene, but a record has been preserved of both the building and the institution itself. The building, whose principal room was a chamber of horrors to master Galdós and his youthful contemporaries, still stands on Calle Mendizábal, facing Calle Montesdeoca. Not far away one can hear the waves of the Atlantic splashing against the breakwater. The air is an odd mixture of aromas borne from the ocean and emanating from the fruits, fish, meat, and other commodities sold at the near-by market stalls. At midmorning the street is crowded with somberly dressed middle-class ladies in black mantillas and women of humbler station wearing the native white kerchief which drapes the head and covers the upper part of the body. Truant schoolboys, always careful not to collide with the impassive and dreamy-eyed officers of the law, mingle insolently with vendors and merchants. Overhead the sun is pleasantly warm and the sky is cloudless.

The former Migas school, now almost a shambles, is today the dwelling of a wretched family rich in progeny. A dark, narrow passage leads into a small, square patio crowded with a conglomeration of discarded household articles of uncertain identity. It is reminiscent of the patios in the Madrid tenement houses described by Galdós. At the right a stairway rises against a blank wall and disappears abruptly into the darkness of the interior. At the top of it is a grimy glass-enclosed gallery, from which one steps into the main "hall" of the Migas school. Like the patio it suggests crowded space, but unlike the patio it is dark. A shadow darkens the windows of the gallery. Then a sudden flood of grayish light outlines one corner of the "hall" where four or five ragged, filthy tots are crouching. Their bright, piercing eyes stare with roguish curiosity mingled with some fear. One of them begins to whimper. Are the Mesa girls still wielding the rod of authority?

A vivid description of the school, which might have been written by Galdós himself, has been left us by one Domingo José Navarro, a native of Las Palmas who survived the cruel discipline of the Migas and lived to be ninety:

> The school was popularly called "Migas," and perhaps rightly so; for, while there was nothing friendly [*amigas*] about it, it did have an excess of

the sting of garlic which is an ingredient of that substanceless food [*miga*].

The mistresses of the school were ordinarily involuntary spinsters who regretted having been deprived of an opportunity to contrive against men and who scarcely knew how to read. For their maintenance they resorted to the instruction of children of both sexes in the little learning which they possessed, and for their pains (or the pains of their charges) they received a very modest stipend.

Since they had not enjoyed the ineffable delights of motherhood, they could see in the tender creatures around them only youthful nuisances who aggravated their biliousness with their whimpers, sniffles, and pressing physical needs.

Seated in armchairs and forever knitting stockings, those harpies always had handy a long reed with which they rained right and left countless and merciless blows upon the soft little heads, either because one of the tots fell asleep, or because another stretched, or because a third talked or laughed, or because still another stopped repeating aloud the monotonous singsong: *b-a, ba; b-e, be*. Before, after, and during the class hour the anguished children were continuously tortured.

Only those children who daily brought them tidbits or other gifts escaped unscathed from the hands of the furies; everyone else was measured with the same yardstick.

On Saturdays in particular our possessed old maids, having gone through five days of maddening disappointment, were the little angels barbarously tortured with the review of what the teachers called Christian Doctrine. Pity the poor child who made an ill-timed sign of the cross, or suppressed one *por mi culpa* from the confession, or the Pontius Pilate of the credo, etc. On that day the tots were subjected to pinches, bumps on the head, boxed ears, and blows with the cane.

Let whoever cares to do so figure out the heights of learning scaled under the guidance of such mentors and how shamefully time was wasted by innocent children in such schools.[1]

Benito certainly did not exert himself unduly to scale the heights of learning in the Migas school. He played truant as often as he could evade the vigilance of Mama Dolores and enlist the support of his sisters. Nature too conspired with him. Because he was sickly and timid, fear of the physical prowess of his aggressive associates often served as an excuse for wanting to stay home. When this strategem failed, Benito contrived to meet with a variety of accidents which usually kept him out of school for a while. A frequent device was to fall into the muddy stream that he had to cross over a precariously insecure bridge on the way to the Migas. Since personal cleanliness was a mania with Mama Dolores, it was not always possible to make Benitín presentable in time for a second expedition. On the days he was unable to escape the educational torment of the Mesa girls he sought relief in the observation of persons, incidents, and things around him. Conceivably the critique of education enunciated by novelist Pérez Galdós had its inception in the big brain of little Benito Pérez during the dreary hours he spent in the chamber of horrors on Calle Mendizábal.

But Migas was only a tortuous corridor leading to the more spacious halls of learning. These were not the English school mentioned with persistent inaccuracy by Galdós' biographers; no such institution existed in Las Palmas, unless it was the private tutoring administered by a certain Miss Luisa Balls, a native lady of English paternity. It is extremely doubtful whether Benito was ever taught by this half-English mentor. It was Adriana Tate—Mama Tate, as the unhappy lady from Charleston was called—who taught him informally but effectively what little English he acquired before leaving for Madrid in 1862. Mama Tate's success sheds light on something more than Benito's educational history.

Benito was extremely fond of the Charleston lady for reasons other than her pedagogical skill. Since she lived in virtual ostracism, a visit to her house afforded him the keen pleasure of eluding the doglike watchfulness of his mother, for whom association with Mama Tate amounted to contamination of the soul. Benito naturally did not share Mama Dolores' scruple; not because he condoned Adriana's wayward behavior with his uncle, but because a mysterious force drew him to charming and pathetic little Sisita, who not many years later was almost to undo him emotionally. Added to this was Adriana Tate's informality as a teacher. The presence of Benitín did not interfere with her habit of taking frequent sips of whisky or brandy, mixed with water, out of a large glass on the table before her. In the mind of her naïve pupil, fluency in English must have become associated with the flow of the beverage and, wishing to imitate his teacher in every detail, he found himself almost unconsciously imbibing two things of which one went to his head faster than the other. But he liked it.

Of Benito's formal elementary schooling beyond the Migas there are no official records, but he undoubtedly completed the two preparatory years leading to the course of secondary studies in the Colegio de San Agustín.[2] At the time of his admission to the Colegio in 1857 his dislike of conventional learning and school routine was sufficiently strong to warrant the assumption that it resulted from an extended educational experience. According to his contemporary, Isaac Viera y Viera, he was a careless student during this period, shunning books until the end of the year, when he would retire into seclusion to prepare for the examinations. These he somehow managed to pass with average grades. Señor Viera's opinion is not borne out by extant official records.

The Colegio de San Agustín was a private secondary school competently directed by Diego Mesa, a relative of the Mesa spinsters who ran the Migas. It was housed in the San Agustín monastery, which is today the courthouse of Las Palmas. Benito entered the Colegio in the fall of 1857, at the age of fourteen, and completed the required studies in the spring of 1862.[3] The following September he was examined for the title of *Bachiller en Artes* by the insular board which met in Laguna, on the island of Santa Cruz de Tenerife.⁴ For the privilege of taking the examinations he paid a fee of one hundred *reales* in specie, because there was no paper money in the city. The diploma of *Bachiller en Artes* was issued under the seal of the University of Seville, on March 8, 1866. It is still in the archives of the Instituto de Laguna, unsigned and unclaimed by Bachiller Benito Pérez.

The years that Señor Pérez, as his classmates called him, spent in the Colegio were less significant educationally than artistically. During this period he gradually became aware of his latent powers and developed the first stages of what ultimately became his characteristic procedure. Although he was a better-than-average student, he was interested only slightly in his studies and derived little satisfaction from either books or masters. Instead, he used the classroom, his fellow students, and his time to further the development of his literary and artistic talents.

Miguel Sarmiento, one of Benito's classmates, testifies that he was neither a troublesome nor an inept student, simply a distracted one. Seated with a book before him, one elbow resting on the desk and his chin supported by his hand, he would spend many hours swaying from right to left, without uttering a sound or looking at the text, his spirit roving the Lord only knew where. Occasionally the authoritative voice of Don Diego Mesa would cut his flights of fancy with the admonition: "Señor Pérez, study!" And Señor Pérez would lower his eyes and read three or four lines, when a fly or a passing cloud would lure him once again into daydreaming.

He was not a refractory student, except perhaps in attendance. Nature and people often beckoned him, and for these he gladly forsook the classroom and his home. He was now a robust lad, and with like-minded friends he often set out in quest of contact with life. On these excursions he sought the human document with the same eagerness that impelled him years later to travel over the length and breadth of Spain. Similarly, traits which ultimately became markedly characteristic of him already began to distinguish him from his associates—his preference for silence and patient listening.

Although he loved to explore the city proper, especially the public market and the San Telmo church with its fascinating collection of miniature boats, Benito Pérez found the highways and mountain trails around Las Palmas more attractive and, from the standpoint of a truant, much safer than the town streets. His favorite haunt was the Risco de San Nicolás, where he often called on Maestro Juan in his cobbler's shop. When reminded by Maestro Juan that the classroom was the proper sphere of a *señorito*, Benito Pérez would argue that a skilled cobbler was socially more useful than a *Bachiller en Artes*. Such a scale of values puzzled Maestro Juan and others in whose presence it was expounded. They could not have known that it was part of a philosophy that Señor Pérez was evolving about professions and occupations against the day when he would surely have to argue with Mama Dolores over the choice of a career.

Much that Galdós observed and reflected on during his pleasant ramblings he undoubtedly stowed away in his memory for future use. (His native country is reflected in his works to a greater degree than is generally suspected.) But much, too, he exteriorized immediately via several artistic media. For this purpose he found the classroom and the school hours highly useful.

"As if it were today," reminisces classmate Francisco Inglott, "I can see Pérez Galdós before me with perfect clearness, seated on a hard bench in the study hall of San Agustín, the upper part of his body literally reclining on the black top of his desk, filling page after page with his scribblings, his daring and profane hand adorning the margins of his textbooks with sketches and caricatures. If these have been preserved, they surely reveal several silhouettes of teachers and classmates." During these onslaughts of artistic exuberance Benito was transfigured for his school associates into an object of wonderment and admiration. "It is not easy to forget," adds Señor Inglott, "those incredible positions which he adopted in the classroom, those inexplicable contortions; and, what filled us with particular admiration, and even envy, those seemingly elastic legs of his not merely crossed but terribly twisted and intertwined." In vain would the class teacher or the study-hall monitor exhort Señor Pérez to sit up straight. That was a physical impossibility![5]

Music, drawing, painting, architecture, literature—these were Galdós' artistic media during his student days, as indeed they were destined to be throughout his career. And he used them not merely to communicate his sensory impressions but also to transmute his sensations into their intellectual and spiritual essence. Already Galdós was both the faithful recorder and the interpreter of men, things, and events.

In 1861 Verdi's *Ernani* was produced in the Teatro Viejo of Las Palmas by an operatic company featuring Carlos Pelizzari and his sister. The performance delighted everyone except Benito Pérez and Jacinto Llanena, one of his schoolmates. For some time thereafter the two boys entertained themselves in the study hall of San Agustín with satirical parodies on bits of the opera. By moving their desks together and making a sound chamber out of their pads, Benito would imitate the contrabass by running his finger under one of the pads and manipulating a wax-surfaced ruler as a bow, while Jacinto, a skillful violinist, would warble the turns and trills of an operatic star. The cultural influence of this music criticism was probably confined to the students of the Colegio, but on another occasion Galdós sought a wider audience. The performance of the sopranos in the light-opera company that sang in the Teatro Viejo inspired him to write a satirical sketch in which he ridiculed the art of the singers and the enthusiastic reception accorded them by his compatriots. It is believed that this was Benito's first article in the local press.

Interest in music, it may be said, was in the tradition of the Galdós family, but in the plastic arts Benito was developing independently. What had begun as a childish pastime became an absorbing art in his Colegio days. Using his penknife like a burin on blackboard chalk, Benito patiently carved diminutive statues, to the speechless admiration of his classmates. He was then a lad of only thirteen or fourteen, but his exquisite work would have done credit to a more experienced artist. His supreme achievement was a miniature frame house which he built with the collaboration of a friend, Cardoso, and which circulated widely among persons of culture and refinement in Las Palmas. In the opinion of some, Benito never surpassed these artistic accomplishments of his youth; they bear favorable comparison with the perfect miniature of an ocean liner that many years later he carved out of wood with a penknife and sold to the Spanish Transatlantic Company for display purposes.

Most impressive of all was Benito's talent for painting and drawing. When something important occurred in the community he invariably took time from his studies to record it in ironical cartoons. Many of these fell into the hands of the school director, who saved them for posterity. But not all of them have been preserved. Very likely some which have disappeared portrayed the prototypes of many of his fictional creations, as is hinted by Juan Bethencourt, father of the well-known writer "Angel Guerra." On July 5, 1901, in a letter congratulating Galdós on the success of his drama *Electra*, he wrote: "When in my youth I read for the first time *La historia de un radical de antaño* (*El audaz*), I was able to collect several caricatures which as a boy you drew in the Las Palmas Colegio." Although the statement is vague, it suggests that the caricatures may have been of characters in that novel.

The most extensive evidence of Galdós' ability in the graphic arts is furnished by two collections of cartoons, one in the possession of his nephew, Don Ignacio Pérez Galdós, and the other in the Museo Canario of Las Palmas.

The second of these collections begins with pencil sketches— some traced over in ink—of six busts of grave, bearded men symmetrically arranged in two rows. One of the group appears in front view, the remaining five in profile. The sketches are crudely drawn, but they are sufficiently individualized to suggest six important personages. This suggestion is borne out by the succeeding cartoons and their corresponding legends, which identify the subjects as prominent figures in the press and local

politics of Las Palmas. Taken in their entirety, the cartoons may
be said to represent Galdós' first attempt at fiction—a graphic,
satirical novel in the *costumbrista* technique. The central theme
is the part played by the Las Palmas press in the prolonged contest between Grand Canary and Tenerife over the question of
administrative autonomy. The large number of incidents used
to develop the theme suggests that Benito must have followed
the dispute closely and intelligently.

As a cartoonist Galdós is imaginative, inventive, plastic, and
sharply ironical. His touch is light. While he shows an almost
complete disregard for detail of body, his heads are unusually
precise. The accuracy with which the six busts are reproduced
in their successive appearances speaks well for the retentive
power of the youthful cartoonist, and the ease with which a
stranger can grasp the theme is a tribute to his clarity of expression. The total effectiveness of the collection springs less
from incongruity or studied disfigurement than from originality
of perception and felicity of expression, particularly the former.
The content is more attractive than the form, as it so patently
is in Galdós' literary works.

Although cartooning was not a part of the Colegio curriculum,
Benito managed to integrate it with his formal studies and independent reading. The legends that accompany the cartoons
reflect a fair degree of familiarity with history, philosophy,
literature, the Bible, and other sources. Quotations, occasionally
in Latin and French, are drawn from Caesar, Napoleon, Alexander the Great, and other world figures. Science is also included: a passage from the second book of Humboldt is used
to explain an eclipse of the sun. In the light of this humble
erudition the conclusion is inescapable that although Benito
scorned textbooks, pedants, and the academic disciplines, he
did not hold education in contempt—an attitude repeatedly expressed in his novels and plays.

For all his humbleness and modesty, Benito naturally sought
more dignified artistic media than cartoons and more gratifying
plaudits than the admiration of his classmates and the citizens
of Las Palmas. For some time he had been painting with brush

and oil and had received encouragement from competent judges. In 1862, shortly before departing for Madrid, he entered three works in the Provincial Exposition. Two of his entries (*La Magdalena* and *Boceto sobre un asunto de la historia de Gran-Canaria*) received honorable mention in the section officially classified as "Dibujo al lápiz en sombras, y en contornos lineal y de adorno." The third entry was a painting in oil of a typical Canary farmhouse (*Una alquería*), and for it the artist was belatedly awarded, in 1864, a copy of the *Memoria de la exposición*.

* * * *

Although more evidence has been preserved of Galdós' skills in the graphic and plastic arts, his chief artistic preoccupation during his adolescence was literature. Among his classmates he was known as an assiduous reader; it was commonly believed that he knew by heart sizable portions of *Don Quijote*. In school he was more keenly interested in literary exercises than in anything else, and his comments and opinions were respected by pupils and teachers alike. Frequently his essays on rhetoric and poetics served as models and stimulated discussion. It was generally suspected that Señor Pérez was a widely read youth whose keen perceptions, refined taste, and facile expression would inevitably lead him to the cultivation of letters. He was not long in confirming this suspicion.

When did Galdós make his literary début in Las Palmas? In an interview reported in 1912 by his journalistic biographers, Del Olmet and García Carraffa, he stated that in his youth he had published a few articles in *El País* and in *El Eco de* . . . —he could not remember the rest of the newspaper's name. However, no Las Palmas periodical before 1865 contains anything signed by Galdós, although there are numerous sketches in the *costumbrista* vein, appearing over pen names, which resemble strikingly the first articles he published in Madrid three years after his arrival there. Some members of the Galdós family assert that he employed a pseudonym in Las Palmas, but no one can recall what it was. It is clear, nevertheless, that his literary talent manifested itself persistently in 1861 and

1862, his last two years at the Colegio de San Agustín. All his extant youthful writings date from that period.

Thinking perhaps of the dawn of his own career, Galdós once stated that every bright Spanish boy dreams of becoming a dramatist who shall write more realistic and practical plays. He himself yielded to an irrepressible urge in 1861 and composed in verse a violent historical one-act drama entitled *Quien mal hace, bien no espere*. It is a perfect specimen of Gothic literature, with a plot built out of feudal brutalities. Don Froilán, the sanguinary hero, succeeds in the course of one afternoon in killing his daughter, whom he does not know, and his brother-in-law in a feudal castle of 1304. When he discovers his frightful crimes, he roars his grief in metaphor-studded verse. The tone of the drama is typified by the closing lines:

> *Confound me, Lord, give me death;*
> *Death, yes; death and hell! ...*

In Las Palmas, however, this was regarded as suitable dramatic entertainment, and ambitious amateurs produced the play in an improvised "little theater" in 1861. Of the success of the performance there is no known record.

But violent passion was not even then Galdós' forte; his literary aims were simple: sincere realism, minute social observation, and satire. He had formulated his objectives during the school year 1860–61 in an essay entitled "El sol," assigned by Teófilo Martínez de Escobar, his professor of rhetoric and poetics. In four closely written pages comprising an exordium followed by a dialogue between a pedantic poet and the author, the adolescent critic condemns the poetization of reality as pedantry, since what poetry there is in our immediate world has been adequately expressed by the first genuine poet. It would be far more effective, he argues, to reproduce reality in natural and sincere images. The advice which Galdós addresses to others might well be taken as the expression of his own realistic creed. "Well then," he admonishes the poet, "while these marvelous things take place there above [*in the skies*], take a look out of the corner of your eye and you will see what is happening on earth." [6] And he himself, with only one recorded exception, concentrated on the faithful reproduction of the affairs of human beings during their earthly existence.

Benito Pérez's contempt for pedantic poets did not extend to the use of verse. On May 20, 1896, there appeared in the *Heraldo de Las Palmas* a maliciously satirical poem entitled "El Teatro Nuevo." The editor of the *Heraldo*, Leopoldo Navarro y Soler, a classmate of Galdós', announced it the previous day as "hitherto unpublished verses by Don Benito Pérez Galdós." Since the incident to which the poem alludes occurred in 1861 or 1862, it may be assumed that it was composed in the classroom of the Colegio and that it fell into the hands of a fellow student.

The object of "El Teatro Nuevo" must have been twofold. In its uniform *esdrújulos* Galdós playfully imitated his countryman Bartolomé Cairasco, famous addict of this rhyme form; in its content he satirized pitilessly the local city-fathers who had voted to erect a municipal theater almost on the edge of the Atlantic. Before writing the poem he had already expressed his reaction to the projected playhouse in a series of ironical cartoons depicting the actors, audience, and musicians in an aquatic environment, adorned with and surrounded by marine implements. But the good-natured irony of the cartoons yields to mock indignation in the satirical verses:

> *Who was the stupid patriot,*
> *Who was the patriot-vandal,*
> *Who designed the arches and vaults*
> *Of this aquatic theater?*

Thus queries Cairasco when he first beholds the "nautical colosseum," and the echo of his voice reverberates the answer through the air:

> *What barbarians, what barbarians!*

Thus far Benito's literary compositions were received with general admiration. But his poem "El pollo," which appeared in *El Omnibus* of Las Palmas on April 12, 1862, provoked a menacing reaction in one quarter. Francisco Inglott, who was one of the first surreptitious readers of the composition, testifies that it was written during a study hour in the Colegio. When it began to circulate openly among the students, one of them was convinced that he was the despicable *señorito* alluded to in the lines:

> *This stiff and grave sprout*
> *Who struts all decked out*
> *From morning till night,*
> *His best name is fop.*

Artist and model were on the verge of demonstrating that the fist was mightier than the pen when study-hall proctor Faustino Méndez intervened to rescue the author from ignominious defeat. He confiscated the poem and had it published in a local paper. By devious ways it reached the columns of *El Comercio de Cádiz,* whence it was copied by *El Omnibus.* Eventually "El pollo" was even reproduced by a Madrid journal. Señor Pérez was fast acquiring a literary reputation.

Indeed, Señor Pérez was beginning to take himself seriously as a writer. Sporadic satirical outbursts in verse no longer satisfied him; he now wished to bring all society within his purview and to cast his observations in a more artistic mold. Accordingly in 1861 he began to write "Un viage redondo por el Bachiller Sansón Carrasco," a pretentious work of Dantesque pattern and Cervantine style, describing a round trip to Hell. But it was not easy for the creative process to function in a study hall patrolled by a lynx-eyed proctor, and punctuation, orthography, stylistic niceties, and even the continuity of the narrative suffered. When he reached page fourteen the author could no longer elude the vigilant proctor, who confiscated the unfinished manuscript. It was surrendered to Teófilo Martínez de Escobar, priest-professor of rhetoric and poetics, who fortunately deemed it worthy of preservation. In 1904 Don Teófilo donated the "unfinished opus" to the Museo Canario, together with two other items of Galdosian literary juvenilia. There Benito's youthful writings remained until 1931, forgotten in a mass of miscellaneous papers belonging to Dr. Gregorio Chil, a Las Palmas naturalist.

For all its adolescent playfulness, "Un viage redondo" fore-shadows significantly the future Galdós. In the chapter head-ings and throughout the work there are stylistic touches that betray the influence of extensive reading in classical Spanish literature. The framework is reminiscent of Vélez de Guevara's *El diablo cojuelo,* and the social satire inspired by a visit to the underground regions recalls Quevedo's *Sueños.* And over the *Dedicatoria* the spirit of *Don Quijote* hovers palpably in matter and in manner. Like the Knight of La Mancha, the imaginary reader whom Galdós addresses attempts to enact in everyday life the romantic adventures he has encountered in books un-worthy of the dignity of literature. And just as Cervantes was inspired to ridicule the romances of chivalry out of existence, so young Benito Pérez is already imbued with the ambition to raise the artistic level of the modern novel. His present effort is not yet an application of his new conception of fiction; it is only a preview, as it were, of the raw materials that the new formula will prescribe.

The second chapter of "Un viage redondo" suggests very forcibly that content rather than form was to be Galdós' literary ideal. Already the adolescent social observer has concluded that society is losing sight of the inherent purpose of human values and institutions. Where should one turn for guidance in an ap-praisal of the essence of justice, morality, ethics, religion, science, literature, and the like? Not to the past, for history is willfully misinterpreted; and not to the church, which is ineffective be-cause of the cowardice of its leaders. Even science cannot be help-ful because its exponents have succeeded only in destroying the harmony of life. It is therefore the duty of literature to re-discover the truth and beauty of life that other means have failed to find. All this Galdós managed to express with naïve ardor and roguish slyness before the proctor recalled him to earth even before he had reached the end of his subterranean journey.

But a movement without an official organ is like an actor without a stage. In 1862 Benito Pérez founded a pretentious one-man journal which he appropriately named *La Antorcha.* It ap-

peared in manuscript in the Colegio de San Agustín and circulated among the students and even in important social circles
of the city. *El Guanarteme*, a similar publication, offered it some
competition, but without destroying its usefulness as the mouthpiece of its anonymous founder and editor. At least one Las
Palmas paper, *El Omnibus*, referred respectfully to *La Antorcha*
in its issue of August 6, 1862. The author of the reference, perhaps Galdós himself, bewailed the fact that the meritorious
articles and poems in *La Antorcha* had to circulate in manuscript.
He took that as evidence that in Las Palmas literature had no
worthy patrons, genius was doomed to die, and good taste was
wasted for fear of criticism which delights in destroying that
which it is incapable of building.

Regardless of the value that the adolescent Galdós may have
attached to the manifestations of his creative urge and skills, it
would be folly to overestimate the intrinsic importance of the
evidence that has been preserved. The absolute merit of his accomplishments may be slight, and this may explain why he himself chose to forget them. Yet for the study of his literary evolution they are significant. Certainly the fragment of "Un viage
redondo" may be regarded as the compressed content of Galdós'
ultimate vision of life and his artistic creed. Besides, his juvenilia
clearly refute his modest explanation that he excluded from his
memoirs everything relating to his childhood because it differed
in no way from the childhood of other diligent schoolboys. The
preserved proof of Galdós' skill with pen, brush, chisel, and
clay makes his modesty extremely regrettable.

* * * *

Benito's last years in the Colegio de San Agustín were a
period of some anxiety for Mama Dolores. With advancing
age she could not escape altogether the mellowing effect of time,
and this mellowness was reflected in her attitude toward Benito.
More than ever his future preoccupied her. She was no longer
sure that he would aspire to the professional distinction of her
brother, attorney José María, and thus demonstrate the superior
essence of the Galdoses. His progress in school and the praise of

his teachers were sufficient guarantee of his mental and intellectual powers. Physically he was growing sturdier, although his growth in height was so rapid that he was becoming very awkward, far more so than the normal adolescent. His shyness, modesty, and timidity pleased Mama Dolores, but his penetrating little eyes and his expression of imperturbability were definitely disquieting to her. It often seemed as if he were detached from his immediate surroundings, living in a highly compressed and sacred world into whose sanctity he would admit no one. In Las Palmas he was generally regarded as a misanthropic youth —much like his mother in this respect—but Mama Dolores rejected this characterization, attributing it to the common human failing of judging by external appearances. She disapproved also of the interest which people took in Benito's scrawls and scribbles. To her it seemed quite natural that, given his voracious reading, he should feel the urge to imitate what he read. That was something he would surely outgrow. Infinitely more disturbing was his pronounced interest in architecture as a profession. Yet Mama Dolores felt that at the proper time she could intervene energetically and successfully in the choice of a career for her son.

Time moved distressingly slowly for Mama Dolores. Benito never confided in anyone, but she suspected that his fondness for Sisita was more than adolescent infatuation. She did everything in her power to limit the association of the youngsters, but they contrived to outwit her. She knew she was causing Benito an emotional crisis, but she deemed it her duty to prevent his falling into a pitfall whose depth he was incapable of fathoming. Quite apart from Sisita's unfortunate origin, her opposition was justifiable; a serious affair of the heart at Benito's age would mean the disruption of the career she was planning for him, and this in turn would destroy her hope of consolation for the many sorrows that had been the lot of her unfortunate family. In Benito's professional success was centered all Mama Dolores' faith in the essential rightness of the laws that regulate human affairs, laws by which she had always been guided in her own life. Failure in this instance would mean a spiritual tragedy for her.

To Benito his mother was not a mystery. He understood clearly the complicated motives behind her insistence that he go to Madrid. In so far as these concerned Sisita he would have liked to assert himself against his mother, but it so happened that his own plans for the future included Madrid. He had definitely decided on a literary career, and for this the capital was indispensable. The legal profession he disliked thoroughly—had he not filled Hell in "Un viage redondo" with all those connected with the law?—but he was fairly interested in architecture. If his departure from home was to be in the nature of a banishment, he should at least be permitted to state the terms of exile. To become a successful writer he would have to serve a long apprenticeship; as a student of architecture he could have the necessary leisure for it.

Galdós did not reveal his literary ambitions to Mama Dolores, but he did argue energetically against law and in favor of architecture. Two strong wills clashed. Benito Pérez left Las Palmas in September, 1862, bound for the law school of the Central University in Madrid.

III

Life, Literature, and Bohemia

IN THE EARLY SIXTIES Madrid was like a growing family in which infancy, adolescence, and youth live in constant friction. Materially and spiritually the city was at the confused point of confluence of the old and the new. Tradition and innovation, conservatism and progress, provincialism and metropolitanism, nationalism and foreignism—all these fought their battles in the open. Life was tense, but much of the expended energy was not husbanded. Viewed outwardly the capital of Spain was a scene of chaotic activity, yet for its inhabitants life fell into a definite pattern. Outsiders fitted easily into this pattern, for Madrid was generous, hospitable, and democratic. In the midst of strife and tension it remained a pleasant city, and even periodic outbursts of violence failed to alter the rhythm of its life.

The nerve center of Madrid—and one might say of all Spain —was located in the famous intellectual club, the Ateneo, and in the numerous cafés. A few of the more select cafés served as a general clearing-house of all the latest developments in Spanish national existence. Pre-eminent among these were the Café Suizo and the Café Iberia.

The Café Suizo, located on the present site of the Banco de Bilbao, was nominally patronized only by writers and artists. Divided into *tertulias* they gathered here in the evening to discuss all manner of topic in an atmosphere of earnestness and sincerity tempered by good-natured humor. Here they im-

41

provised theories of art, launched artistic projects, built new reputations, and tore down old ones. Here timid, obscure, but artistically ambitious youths met and mingled with the great and the near-great in Spanish art and letters.

In the Café Iberia the pulse of Spain beat stronger than in the Suizo. Located under the Casino del Príncipe—the modern Casino de Madrid—it attracted especially the reputed political leaders in addition to artists and writers. Between nine and twelve in the evening the Iberia was uncomfortably crowded. Here, in the presence of small admiring groups, journalists improvised editorials, politicians delivered eloquent addresses, philosophers evolved complicated systems, novelists spun intricate plots, and poets recited sweet lyrics. Here too revolutions were planned and cabinets realigned, learning was generously dispensed, and imagination and fancy played freely.

Not all the activity in the Iberia was verbal. At its rear was a small garden with a little fountain. To the casual patrons it was only a delightfully secluded spot where ladies gathered over a dish of ice-cream. But the habitués knew that in one corner of the garden there was a concealed door leading to the humble Callejón de Gitanos—modern Calle de Arlabán—by which many a riotous revolutionary eluded the queen's secret agents. It also facilitated the rescue of more than one indiscreet lady from the wrath of her suspicious husband. Indeed, the Café Iberia was more than the intellectual and political center of Madrid.

The brains of Spain were comfortably lodged in the Ateneo, housed in a prosiac-looking remodelled building of middle-class architecture, located at 22 Calle de la Montera. The club was frequented by men of all ages, professions, political convictions, religious views, and social backgrounds. Politically the majority of the members were either liberals who stood for general progress or democrats who dreamed of a republic. Yet such was the atmosphere of tolerance in the Ateneo that these associated on terms of mutual respect with the "neos" who advocated the *status quo*—the camarilla rule of Isabel II. No group ever converted the other to its own cause or beliefs despite the mental energy and physical exertion that went into their prolonged but proper debates. The Madrid Ateneo was truly the popular palace of Spanish democracy and enlightenment.

The youth of Spain, especially the students, who frequented the café *tertulias* and the Ateneo listened respectfully to the political discussions of their elders but retained their own opinions and insisted on freedom of action. The vast majority adhered to the so-called *progresista* movement, bent neither on destroying the past nor on blazing new trails. Their primary aim was to make Freedom an unalterable reality, an instrumentality or agency whereby man could exercise without restraint his inalienable rights in the light of established law. Freedom so defined was regarded as attainable even under a monarchial government. However, as the reign of Isabel II became increasingly censurable, freedom came to mean not *Progreso* but *Democracia*, and the hope for its realization was centered in republicanism. But the possibility of a Spanish republic was discussed by students with extreme caution. The best outlet for their ideas was the daily press, but journalism was not always a safe occupation in those days.

While political discussion consumed much of the time of the students and most of their passion, they also treated other topics, although with more confusion and less sincerity. To hold an opinion on every important matter was considered a duty, which they discharged to the accompaniment of violent gesticulation and mighty blows delivered on tabletops. They expressed themselves categorically on romanticism, the contemporary stage, classical music, the new German composers, modern Spanish art, and all other manifestations of the human spirit everywhere. In intellectual skirmishes, which not infrequently developed into frontal attacks, religion and science often supplied the weapons and ammunition. The objective was not the annihilation of science or religion but a lasting peace between them. Here Krausism—or whatever each one understood as Krausism— served as a powerful ally. It was argued that a philosophy which wedded reason and faith in sweet union could certainly be counted upon to demonstrate the possibility of harmonizing science and religion. This conclusion was not reached without traversing vaguely charted stretches bestrewn with sophisms, solecisms, absurdities, platitudinous axioms, insolence, and egotism. One felt compelled to defend oneself against logic, common sense, forthright expression, independence of thought, and moderation in tone.

But even in Madrid man did not live by politics and intellectual discussion alone. There were many innocuous social pleasures, and some that were not entirely innocuous. The more sedate students sought relaxation with their elders in the concerts of the Campos Elíseos, the Royal Opera, the programs of the Circo Price, or the offerings of the Zarzuela and Variedades theaters. In the fall there were frequent premières of plays by famous dramatists. The more wayward students patronized institutions for friendly gambling and more serious indulgence of human frailty. On the whole student pastimes did not transgress the bounds of social propriety or conventional morals. Many an evening was spent in prolonged duels of wit and ingenuity, with intermissions only for food and drinks. The victims of these duels were usually famous national figures. Sometimes they yielded in interest to generic woman, whose nature was analyzed on a highly philosophic plane, or to specific women, whose virtues and weaknesses were submitted to a microscopic examination.

Such was Madrid, the "huge and motley city," as he called it many years later, when Benito Pérez reached it toward the end of September, 1862.

The voyage from Las Palmas to Cádiz in a hideous and illsmelling ship that pitched and rolled constantly made Galdós suspect that the phenomenon of equilibrium was a myth. And what a humiliating condition seasickness was! Oddly enough, it always attacked him dismayingly in the midst of a conversation with a charming fellow passenger, a beautiful young lady. She reminded him of Goethe's Margarita and Hugo's Cosette. Or was it perhaps Sisita? This thought first occurred to Benito when they parted in Cádiz.

The landing was a beautiful experience. Cádiz at dawn, after three days of water and sky, was even more rapturous than his uncle, Chaplain Domingo Pérez, had described it in his diary. He would have loved to stay there a while, but the train was waiting to take him to Seville and Córdoba. There the railway ended. It was thrilling to ride on a train for the first time, yet the trip from Córdoba to Alcázar de San Juan by stagecoach was more interesting. Somehow, on the train the chug of the locomotive, the rhythmic clatter of the wheels, and the shrill sound of the whistle that seemed to cry out to the vast spaces that it was lost, somehow all this made Galdós forget the recent past. It was different on the stagecoach. Perhaps because he had traveled in similar conveyances before, everything looked familiar. More than once he caught himself thinking about Las Palmas, the family, and others back home. And when he first beheld the vague outline of Madrid in the summer haze on the lead-colored horizon, a feeling of sharp anxiety came over him. Benito Pérez was homesick!

"Huge and motley," this is how Madrid first impressed Galdós. His brother Ignacio had preceded him there four years before and was now a brilliant young lieutenant. He still had a year in the capital, and during this time he would help Benito get adjusted. That reassured Mama Dolores, who insisted that Benitín was too young to be left to his own resources in the big city. When Ignacio first went to Madrid she had saved him from peril by commending him to the care of cousin José Manuel. She was sure that after Ignacio's departure José Manuel would be equally successful in guiding Benitín.

Benito Pérez was installed in a student boarding-house at 3 Calle de las Fuentes. It was a highly desirable location, close to the university, the Puerta del Sol, and the Royal Palace, and not too far from the picturesque Barrios Bajos. One wishing to become acquainted with the "huge and motley city" could begin with a study of the short, narrow, and intricately interconnected streets, alleys, and diminutive squares in the immediate neighborhood. Although geographically in uptown Madrid, Calle de las Fuentes had an air of middle-class shabbiness scarcely distinguishable from the outright poverty of the poorer districts. The building numbered 3 contributed generously to that air.

Benito's room on the second floor was reached by a poorly lighted stairway in need of a coat of paint and the use of a broom. Yet the boarding-house was of a superior category, always filled to capacity by students and miscellaneous government employes. A stranger who arrived there was made to feel at home without the formality of an introduction. Although shy and timid, Benito soon became one of the family with the aid of his schoolmate, Fernando León y Castillo, who also lived there. But before the end of the academic year he moved to 9 Calle del Olivo (modern Calle de Mesonero Romanos), allegedly because he wished to avoid a quarrel with León y Castillo, who, though the fiancé of Galdós' youngest sister Manuela, indulged in pastimes unbecoming to a betrothed young man. Whatever the reason for the change, Benito spent about six pleasant years at 9 Calle del Olivo, where Luisa, the landlady's daughter, was not the least attraction.

*   *   *   *

The files of the University of Madrid testify to the academic frailties of Benito Pérez Galdós. On September 30, 1862, he enrolled in the Faculty of Letters for one year of required pre-law studies. His program included universal history, geography, and Latin literature. At the end of the year he received two grades of *notable* (good) and a *sobresaliente* (excellent), the latter in geography. But the bare grades do not reflect the benefits Benito derived from his courses or teachers.

Two professors impressed the young student profoundly: the distinguished historian Fernando de Castro and Alfredo Adolfo Camus, teacher of Latin literature. Galdós' admiration and affection for Camus were lasting, and early in his journalistic career he paid him high tribute in a spirited sketch in *La Nación* (February 8, 1866). From Camus Galdós no doubt acquired the esthetic principles by which he came to interpret literature, painting, sculpture, and music. The teacher passed on to his pupil his dislike of crude realism, his abhorrence of conventional art, his severe judgment of contemporary French art, his worship of classical beauty, his preference for Rossini and Bellini, and his almost insulting estimate of French opera. Similarly, he transmitted to Galdós his irony and wit in the evaluation of contemporary Spanish writers, café erudites, homespun celebrities, and the great national figures trumpeted by the conservative press. Galdós listened with ecstasy to the Latinist's lectures, which evoked for him the very place and time of the Latin authors. Camus clarified for him the subtle relationship between life and literature, and impressed upon him how important it was for a writer to know humanity.

The profitable stage of Benito's formal education ended in the spring of 1863. The next fall, after a vacation in Las Palmas, he obtained permission to register late because, he alleged, he had been delayed by the unpredictable conditions of an overseas journey. He resumed his studies and barely managed to pass Roman law, political science, and economics. Although he was never to duplicate even this modest academic achievement, he continued registering every year through 1867–68, invariably requesting permission to enter late on grounds neither original nor ingenious. His excuses were sometimes startling. In the fall of 1864 he pleaded that the ship *Almogavar* was delayed by terrific gales on the way to Cádiz. Now it is a matter of record that the *Almogavar* left Las Palmas on September 13, and normally it should have reached its destination in three or four days. Even allowing for the most violent storm in the history of navigation, Benito could have arrived in Madrid in time for registration in late September or early October. In reality the delay was due to the fact that he spent several weeks in Seville with a fellow passenger, his former teacher of rhetoric, Padre Teófilo Martínez y Escobar. There master and pupil planned in collaboration a novel entitled "Un viage de impresiones." Twenty-two chapters were outlined but only two got written, one by each collaborator.

Beginning with the fall of 1864 Galdós' university record tells a monotonous tale. Every year he selected his studies and regularly absented himself from class. The most slighted subjects were canonical law and commercial and mercantile law. He earned his last grades in 1863–64; thereafter his record repeats uniformly the notation that "he failed the course because of lack of attendance." His file makes boring reading except for the exchange of correspondence between the university authorities and Benito's guardian in Madrid, cousin José Manuel.

Mama Dolores' cousin was puzzled by Benito's behavior. He impressed him as a serious, dignified, and intelligent young man, but with a disconcerting air of preoccupation. He seemed to be living in a world wholly out of touch with the present. During his periodic visits he was annoyingly shy and embarrassed. In a conversation he limited himself strictly to answering questions, mostly about the family, and spoke in an opaque voice, haltingly and cautiously, as if afraid of saying something improper. José Manuel suspected that Benito might be experiencing a deep crisis which he was careful not to betray. In his reticence and in his evident strength of character he resembled his mother strikingly. It would be futile to offer the young man advice, for it was apparent that another person's opinion would carry no weight with him. He was definitely a tenacious lad of unusual moral courage.

José Manuel thought that he found the reason for Benito's puzzling behavior when he discovered in 1865 that he was writing for *La Nación*. Could that be worrying cousin Dolores— Benito's concern with literature, art, music, and politics instead of his legal studies? Evidently something was worrying her, for in each of her letters she earnestly begged José Manuel to help her guide Benito toward the goal she had chosen for him. Apparently she knew that her son's interests were divided. But what made her fear that his literary activity might mean the end of his legal career? True, Benito's university record thus far did not indicate that he was heading for the highest court of the land, but he was still very young. Like many other Spaniards, he could conceivably combine literature and law successfully. His writings might even help him become an important political figure.

For the time being cousin José Manuel could only assure cousin Dolores that he was taking a fatherly interest in her children. For this he was graciously thanked. Mama Dolores was willing to believe that Benito's writings were merely a prolongation of his adolescent pranks in Las Palmas, yet the suspicion that he might be stealing time from his studies caused her grave concern. Her son was still in need of careful guidance, and to this effect she wrote to cousin José Manuel on March 28, 1865:

> My dear Cousin: with great pleasure I received your kind letter, to which I had not replied, and to thank you for the deep interest which you are taking in my sons, because I have been ill, I am better and I am taking advantage with pleasure of the sailing of the packet, to charge you to aid Benito with your good advice. I want to see him a worthy man and that he may some day be useful which is all I wish, so that he can profit by his work and I have the satisfaction of seeing him well placed and that he may not be as unfortunate as his uncle.

But reports that Benito's articles were appearing with increasing frequency in the Madrid paper were clear proof that he was neglecting his studies. Mama Dolores could not figure out how Benitín could attend the university and still find time to write about so many different things. Of course, she knew that he had a good mind, but he could not be getting all that knowledge out of his head. Besides, there were rumors that since his arrival in Madrid he had also been working intensely on novels, comedies, and verse. No one had seen any of these works, but it was known that his desk was filled with all sorts of manuscripts; he confided to some people that he was going through a period of concentrated preparation without knowing exactly for what.

When Benitín remained in Madrid all through the summer of 1865, publishing articles in *La Nación* week after week, Mama Dolores became almost alarmed. Back in April, when she had learned that he had participated in the bloody riot of St. Daniel's Eve (April 10, 1865), it had already occurred to her that his equivocal situation called for energetic action. But she refrained from taking immediate steps because Benitín had never intimated to her or to anyone else his utter lack of interest in a legal career. She could not make an issue of the matter without

calling into question his sincerity and even dishonesty in his
relations with the family. Perish the thought! Benitín was a
good boy who could do nothing base. What would she gain by
taking a bold stand? Daughter-in-law Magdalena would surely
take Benitín's side. It was with her money that her husband
Domingo contributed so generously to the boy's upkeep in
Madrid. And that half-Yankee was so bristly and irritable! It
would be impossible to involve her in a discussion about Benitín
without reviving the quarrel over his feelings toward Sisita
and Mama Tate, and that Mama Dolores sought to avoid by
all means. There were indications that Sisita was returning to
Cuba to marry a young man whom her father, José María
Galdós, had chosen for her. The prospect of the departure of
the unfortunate creature was so cheering that it was best not
to do anything that might interfere with it.

Mama Dolores was truly unhappy. Never before had she
found herself so checkmated. She drew little consolation from
the thought that no child of hers was capable of dishonesty.
To comfort her troubled spirit she repeatedly pleaded with
cousin José Manuel to continue his watch over Benitín. On
December 13, 1865, she unburdened her heart in the following
letter:

> Right now we are making sacrifices for Benito the
> smallest of all for three years he has been there in
> the Capital pursuing the study of law, Under this same
> date I am writing to him to pay you a visit; since you
> are taking so much interest in them, I commend him
> to you so that you may help him with your good
> advice, he is very young but he has a good disposition
> and is honorable, he will not commit a base act for
> anything; Nevertheless, I am not calm; when Ignacio
> was with him I was satisfied.

One might say that Mama Dolores' apprehension lagged
considerably behind the actual events. The fact is that when
Benito had joined the staff of *La Nación* the preceding February,
he had dropped his studies, although he did not withdraw from
the university. In the summer of 1866 he was obliged to take

some members of the family into his confidence. He had reached a serious stage in his literary career. *La Nación* was indefinitely suspended by the government on June 17, 1866. The brusque changes in the political climate of Spain were not conducive to the growth of hardy journalism. Besides, he aspired to something higher than being a columnist of a *progresista* paper. All he needed to realize his immediate ambition was adequate financial support.

There was mild consternation when Galdós revealed his situation to the family through Madrina, as he called his sister-in-law. Assuming that he did not intend to drop his studies, everyone was extremely skeptical about his ability to gain literary fame and legal prestige simultaneously. Brother Domingo, the only person who could come to his aid, argued that law and literature were an utterly impossible combination. Besides, what would Benito get out of writing books if not universal ridicule? The matter would have ended there had not a sympathetic friend intervened in behalf of Benito. Valeriano Fernández Ferraz maintained that Benito did not need legal training to be a stout defender of justice; his penetrating criticism of Spanish life gave proof of his forensic ability in a much broader sense. And when Don Valeriano met Don Domingo in Seville in 1867 he recommended adequate financial support for the young author. In his opinion Benito gave promise of becoming Spain's greatest writer of modern times, and it would be a pity to let him be exploited by commercial publishers. When Benito was writing verse, Valeriano told him that he was wasting precious time. But now he was concentrating on prose, a field in which he was destined to become a European celebrity.

Although Don Valeriano's plea did not bring Benito the means for the publication of his rapidly accumulating manuscripts, it bore fruit in another direction. The Adriana Tate faction of the family was apparently convinced that he deserved encouragement and should be offered a trip to France instead of money. Could a literary amateur wish for a greater opportunity than a visit to Paris? The idea was approved even by Mama Dolores, who was perturbed by reports that excessive reading and study were making Benito "as thin as a rail" and that he was becoming "queer" as a result of his constant wanderings in the regions of fancy and imagination. She readily accepted the offer of her son-in-law, Don José Hermenegildo, to finance the trip.

Thus it came about that in May, 1867, Don José Hermene-gildo, accompanied by his son, José, Jr., made a surprise call on Benito Pérez in his none too orderly room on the second floor of 9 Calle del Olivo. Benito was slow to be convinced that the object of their mission was not a figment of his imagination. Of course he could get ready for a trip even on that short notice! Several minutes before train time he appeared at the Norte Station with a book under one arm and a few personal articles wrapped in newspapers under the other.

Paris with its Universal Exposition, museums, monuments, visiting royalty, and especially the bookstalls along the Seine threw him into ecstasy. At the end of the first week he knew the city almost as well as Madrid. The urge to record at once his most vivid impressions inspired him to keep a diary in French. But his knowledge of the language proved inadequate and he soon suspended this literary exercise. In his leisure moments he devoured the works of Balzac, who cast a spell over him.

Upon his return to Madrid Galdós took stock of his work thus far and decided to chart a new course for himself. Without knowing how it happened he found himself working effort-lessly and in earnest on his first novel. As in previous years, he registered in the university only as an excuse for remaining in Madrid. He had no time for study anyway. Between work on his novel and on articles for *La Nación,* when it resumed publica-tion in January, 1868, he spent full and profitable days.

When summer came the family took Galdós on a more exten-sive trip to France. They returned to Spain in the last days of the reign of Isabel II. When they reached Barcelona the revolu-tion got under way in earnest. A family council was hastily sum-moned and it was agreed that Las Palmas would be a safer vantage point from which to watch the downfall of the Bourbon dynasty. The *America,* a packet bound for the Canary Islands, happened to be in port. At dawn of September 30 Galdós and

Model of a Town Constructed by Benito at the Age of Eight

The youthful artist used whatever he had at hand: chalk, pasteboard, putty, glue, and pieces of glass. Although the model bore a striking resemblance to medieval Toledo, Benito insisted that he had never seen even a picture of the city.

his relatives were on board this boat heading for its first stop
at Alicante. A fine way to watch a glorious revolution! Galdós
pleaded for permission to go to Madrid. When other arguments
failed he insisted with all the eloquence at his command that
the political upheaval should not interfere with his school duties.
He silenced all opposition and was permitted to land in Alicante.
He ran from the pier to the railroad station and reached Madrid
in time to witness the triumphant entrance of Prim and Serrano
on the Puerta de Sol midst the delirious applause of the populace. In the tremendous developments of the ensuing days Galdós
naturally forgot the solemn promise he had made on board the
America. He did not register in the university.

While Spain was groping for a new mode of living Galdós was
busy planning his immediate future. His first and most difficult
task was the clarification of his situation with respect to the
family. Matters at home were not in a happy state. Sisita had
been removed to Cuba to live with her father. Madrina had
suffered two severe blows: the death of her only child, Chanito,
and subsequently the death of her husband. As a measure of
relief from the sorrow which had been her lot in Las Palmas
she now asserted herself more than ever against the Galdoses
in whatever pertained to Benito's literary ambitions. In a sense
she adopted him emotionally, and when she came to live in
Madrid she set out to dominate him completely. For Mama
Dolores this self-assumed guardianship over her son spelled
danger. She was afraid that it might lead to a renewal of relations between him and Sisita. This she was determined to prevent, even though she now regarded Sisita with compassionate
tolerance. And something else made Mama Dolores unhappy.
For seven years the hope of Benitín's professional success had
buoyed her up, but in view of his growing literary activity this
seemed now quite uncertain. In her unhappiness she even tried
to draw comfort from cousin José Manuel's observation that
in Spain it was possible to be a good lawyer and a writer at the
same time.

The situation at home brought Galdós to Las Palmas in the
summer of 1869. *El Eco de Gran Canaria* welcomed him on

July 21 as "our esteemed friend, Attorney Don Benito Pérez Galdós." The "attorney" did not remonstrate against the title, and Mama Dolores elatedly informed her brother in Cuba that Benito had happily concluded his studies. Her elation was so great that she sent effusive greetings to "Sisi." Just what means Benito took to disillusion his mother is not known, but it is certain that before leaving Las Palmas he revealed his literary ambitions to the family. To his friends the revelation was a confirmation of a fact, not a promise for the future. Accordingly, when Galdós sailed for the mainland *El Eco de Gran Canaria* announced (September 29) that "our esteemed friend and well-known writer, Don Benito Pérez Galdós, left for the Peninsula on board the packet *America.*"

What Don Benito Pérez Galdós neglected to do in order to win the title of "attorney" is by now clear. What he accomplished to deserve the characterization of "well-known writer" constitutes the story of his literary apprenticeship.

* * * *

When Benito Pérez reached Madrid he fell at once under the spell of student Bohemia. He wore the conventional dress of a student—high, flat-brimmed hat, cravat, Prince Albert coat, mother-of-pearl-colored trousers, high-heeled shoes, and the classic Spanish cape. Only his physical appearance distinguished him from the crowd. He was not at all bad-looking: tall, broad, robust, and well-proportioned. His forehead was high and smooth, and his straight thick hair, parted on the right side, was banked on his rather large ears. Darkish down shaded his upper lip, but his cheeks and chin were still hairless. His whole face had an expression of immobility and the static quality of old age. Whether indoors or on the street, he was always seen with a hand-rolled cigarette, which he smoked energetically until it burned his lips. In a crowd he usually remained silent, but he followed closely the animation and chatter of others. His companions sought his presence because he was an appreciative spectator. In time they discovered in him talents and skills which contributed greatly to their noisy entertainment.

Benito Pérez's room served as a sort of salon for boisterous literary, artistic, and musical *tertulias*. In those days students read the novels of Victor Hugo—*Les Misérables* was a best-seller— Sir Walter Scott, and Manual Fernández y González, and the serial stories of Pérez Escrich, Ortega y Frías, Tárrago y Mateos, and others, but they discussed glibly and heatedly the works of Balzac, Goethe, and Schiller. Galdós admired the ease with which the young fellows from the provinces mastered the fluent, witty, and mordant chatter of the native Madrilenians. He was particularly interested in the catch-phrases and clichés which formed the intellectual arsenal of his companions. There was little originality or independence of opinion in most of what they said. In the drama they insisted upon the traditions of the Golden Age, and in the novel they seemed to uphold Fernández y González's condemnation of the social novel of moral tendency as *ñoña* (feeble-minded). Their conception of the value of literature in modern times was lamentably narrow, and they frowned upon Galdós' suggestion that the role of the writer, especially the playwright, should be that of an educator. On this point, as on the need for honest interpretation of reality, he clashed with his friends, but his arguments fell mostly on deaf ears. The lack of enthusiasm for literary reform among young people really puzzled him.

The musical séances in Benito Pérez's salon were more enjoyable and less controversial. Everyone knew that he rarely missed an opera in the Real or a concert in the Campos Elíseos. In the Real, perched high up in the *paraíso* (gallery), slouching in his seat, his long legs crossed under the bench in front of him, his head thrown back, and his penetrating little eyes closed, he seemed as much a part of the place as the vitiated and dust-laden air. These striking positions were regarded by some as having contributed to the development of his remarkable ear for music and his highly retentive memory. Occasionally someone would suggest that he sing an operatic passage—for example, the curfew aria from *The Huguenots*—with orchestral accompaniment and all the rest. Unwilling to sing because of his opaque voice, he would nevertheless give an impressive imitation of the orchestra. By manipulating his lips and tongue in a mystifying manner he would reproduce the sounds of the violin and the oboe amidst the loud applause and uproarious laughter of his companions. As a reward, and while coffee was being served, he would be regaled with an extensive repertoire of anecdotes of varied colors. From these anecdotes Benito was able to infer the popular conception of many national figures, and he developed a taste for that painless pungency which is the essence of Spanish humor.

Competing with the gatherings in his room for Galdós' preference was the Spanish daily ritual of café life. His first introduction to this pleasant pastime was at the seemingly endless *tertulias* of his fellow Canarians in the Café Universal on the Puerta del Sol. Before very long he began to frequent also Fornos, Suizo, Iberia, and other cafés. Although by nature neither forward nor aggressive, he nevertheless made the acquaintance of many prominent personages and was well received by them. But he naturally felt more at ease among his friends in the Universal. There he spent many evenings listening with an obliging smile to the violent discussions, outbursts of wit, and sallies of nonsense. His own silence was almost proverbial, and the waiters claimed he did not open his mouth even to order coffee. Bored by the impassioned political discussions with their bombastic rhetoric and dearth of ideas, he entertained himself drawing caricatures in pencil on the marble tabletop. These were invariably the source of prolonged hilarious amusement, and although they often satirized someone present, nobody ever took offense at the artist.

Benito Pérez owed his popularity with the café public to still another skill. As if to shut out the noise that interfered with his musings, he would frequently tear up a newspaper page into small squares, out of which he would fashion with unusual dexterity either birds or feminine figures. The latter were readily recognizable as notorious professional worshippers in the Temple of Venus. Benito seemed to enjoy communing with these figures, drawn up on the table before him in a formation whose significance he alone understood. The birds he would catapult into space, following with rapt attention their fantastic maneuvers in the smoke-filled air of the Universal. These aeronautic displays earned him the title of "The Little-paper-birds Man." Some years later, when *La fontana de oro* was published (1870), one of the numerous admirers of Galdós' skill, Cánovas del Castillo, remarked to the author, within earshot of Emilio Castelar: "Oh, my friend! This little bird has certainly turned out fine—it flies by itself."[1] For his feminine figures Benito was nicknamed "The Harlot Kid." It often embarrassed him to be thus identified, especially in the presence of those familiar with his occasional amatory escapades. As late as 1873, when *Trafalgar* was published, many readers of the novel knew the "Harlot Kid" better than they did its author, Benito Pérez Galdós.

Galdós' paper birds and figures may have been merely an application of the principle of "art for art's sake," but in his pencil caricatures he often revealed himself as a political thinker. At a *tertulia* in the Universal, a friend was haranguing him on the current political situation, proposing a new cabinet combination which would maintain the "intolerable lady" on the throne and at the same time guarantee the enforcement of the Constitution of 1812. Being a more reasonable person than his eloquent friend, Galdós had not yet discovered a sure cure for the ailments of the millions of inmates in the political madhouse that Spain was in those days. For the time being, he felt, healthy irony was the only sane attitude to adopt. Acting on this thought, he began to sketch what at first looked like a violoncello but which turned out to be a caricature of Don Salustiano Olózaga, distinguished orator and foe of the Bourbon dynasty. Establishing communication between the head and feet of the statesman were the strings, each one representing a well-known politician of the period. Obviously Galdós had selected his own cabinet of ministers for the ultimate salvation of Spain. His political acumen was probably not recognized, but his cartoon was admired by many. It remained on the table for a number of days and drew greater crowds than the staff of the Universal could serve efficiently.

*   *   *   *

Galdós' days were so crowded that to indulge in what he called "spiritual hygiene" he was obliged to snatch time from his school work. By "spiritual hygiene" he meant the intellectual and emotional stimulation he derived from strolls through Madrid and its outlying districts. He justified and rationalized his cheerful surrender to the allurements of the great city in terms of the much discussed educational philosophy of Sainz del Río and Giner de los Ríos: that direct observation and articulate reaction lead to a higher type of education than can be obtained from books. Since Galdós' primary aim was a deep understanding of Spanish humanity, he reasoned that he could arrive at it only by studying the landscape and people of Madrid. By applying his inventiveness, imagination, and moral energy to the knowledge and wisdom gathered through direct observation and detailed analysis, he would produce literature of a new high order. Without any scruples Galdós sacrificed his studies to the much-needed "spiritual hygiene."

For the study of the fascinating types and bizarre landscapes of Madrid he preferred the morning hours and the outskirts of the city. He loved to go down to the Manzanares River, where he indulged in baffling banter with the bright-eyed and sharp-tongued women who did their washing there. Their crude wit and sly expressions often routed him, but not infrequently his own mental agility triumphed over their naïveté. Such triumphs sometimes led to amorous conquests of short duration. Galdós' experiences on the banks of the Manzanares served him well in his contacts with the gypsies in the Ronda de Embajadores. Without overlooking the picturesque shabbiness of the settings and the intricate pattern of activities, he concentrated on the peculiarities of gypsy speech. Equally instructive were his frequent visits to the military barracks. There was nothing martial about the soldiers who loitered on the grounds, but their skirmishes with servant girls and nursemaids were worthy of tried and proven strategists. To Galdós these skirmishes afforded an opportunity of studying at close range the art and speech of love-making in the Spanish army. He discovered that language was the spice of life for the humble people—and he never forgot that discovery.

The study of language was perhaps Galdós' principal motive in seeking "spiritual hygiene." Hitherto he had derived his notions about appropriate popular language for literary purposes from Cervantes and Ramón de la Cruz, but the compound that resulted from imitating these two authors lacked the spontaneity of living, vibrant speech. This missing element he discovered after diligent search in the humble districts of Madrid. It was not an easy discovery, for he was baffled by the constant invention of new words and idioms. In the skits of Ramón de la Cruz he had observed a tendency to preserve the pure traditional forms, but the residents of the Barrios Bajos were extremely individualistic in their treatment of existing forms and unrestrained in their invention of new expressions. They were inclined to mutilate the most common words; as he subsequently put it, they tended toward a "telegraphic style, economy of saliva." [2] Galdós concluded nevertheless that the speech of the Barrios Bajos without the peculiarities of the "telegraphic style" was the most suitable for literary purposes.

For one destined to become one of Spain's great anticlerical leaders Galdós displayed a remarkable interest in religious buildings. He made a careful study of the architecture, artistic treasures, special ritual, music, history, and social standing of all the places of worship in the capital. The vast specialized knowledge he thus acquired meant less to him than the keen esthetic pleasure that accompanied the process. He spent many hours listening to sermons, choirs, and organs, and many more chatting with priests, friars, nuns, attendants, and *beatas* (feminine hypocrites). Nor did he overlook the beggars, whom he regarded as minor agents in the arduous process of earning salvation.

The Sacramento and San Sebastián churches had a particular fascination for him. Often, after watching the change of guard in front of the Royal Palace—a ceremony which his imagination transformed into something like an auditory and visual transcription of Spanish history—he liked to drop in for a rest in the Sacramento church. There he occupied himself examining the altars, the choir, and the specimens of the grotesque art of the prosaic eighteenth century. He was especially entertained by an amusing quatrain inscribed in huge letters under the figure of San Bernardo that was painted in monumental dimensions on one of the four squinches supporting the cupola. Years afterwards he liked to recite this quatrain with loud mirth.

In the parochial church of San Sebastián the image of the arrow-pierced martyr-saint seemed to call to Galdós from its vaulted niche. He rarely failed to answer the call, for he enjoyed the contemplation of Nuestra Señora de la Novena, patron saint of all who make their living by the stage. As one who nurtured secret dramatic ambitions he felt impelled to worship at the altar of the Virgin, but he was often distracted by the profusion of flowers, which must have been placed there by actresses, he thought, in gratitude for the occasional applause they received. On leaving the church by the little patio that served as a flower market he reflected more than once that many actors and dramatists deserved to be sainted after experiencing the thrill of the footlights, the fickleness of audiences, and the scalpel of the première reviewers.

In the heart of the city, window displays and photographers' showcases held out the greatest allurement to the realistic observer. The shopping district alone, Galdós thought, offered more information about commerce, industry, agriculture, sociology, geography, and other human enterprises than a whole university faculty could teach in a lifetime. As for the photographers' exhibits, they were a useful means of learning what the celebrated national figures looked like. Galdós "met" in this way some of Spain's famous authors whom he later included in his *Galería de figuras de cera*. The first time he saw the bulky figure of López de Ayala in the flesh he was so impressed that he unconsciously extended his admiration for the dramatist's physical charms to his energetic verse and the sculptural perfection of his plays.

In moments of strong creative urge Galdós was irresistibly drawn to the humblest streets of the Barrios Bajos. The Plaza de la Cebada, tumultuous and bustling, enticed him only a little less than Calle de Toledo, which he regarded as the prettiest and most picturesque street in the world. Again and again he covered it from one end to the other, overwhelmed by its gay animation and the baffling variety of its shops—including eighty-eight taverns with red-painted fronts. Only the thrill of another visit to the Rastro could tear him away from unique Calle de Toledo with its memories of pathetic historic scenes. That peerless open-air market, existing as a microcosm within the capital, was worth to him a whole course of liberal studies. There he observed what he called "the evolution of the last shred of life into death." [3] The Rastro's multitude of enterprises, all engaged in converting into something useful what society had cast off, proved to him that in industry, as in nature, nothing dies, everything evolves.

Somewhere near the Rastro, Galdós had his most profound experience in "spiritual hygiene." He made the acquaintance of a tenement-house manager whom he accompanied one Sunday on his round of rent collection in the wretched dwellings of the district. The scenes he saw and the angry remonstrances and wrathful sighs of the ragged tenants saddened him to the point of grief. He would have given all he possessed to become the good landlord in Ramón de la Cruz's skit *La Petra y la Juana*—that extraordinary landlord who let his tenants go rent-free. With this thought he found himself heading toward the Plaza de Lavapiés. As he sat down on a bench to rest, Ramón de la Cruz and his immortal picture of eighteenth-century Madrid came to his mind. Don Ramón was more than a painter, he reflected. He actually recreated the picturesque humanity of Madrid's humblest zones. There was an artist worthy of emulation by anyone aiming to grasp the substance and spirit of the Barrios Bajos. Lucky would be the author who could approxi-

mate Ramón de la Cruz's native genius, sharp realism, and
pungent wit.

Galdós had discovered an admirable literary model.

*   *   *   *

Cautious and uncommunicative by nature, Galdós was able
at first to keep from his companions the ultimate aim of the
rigorous literary training he was undergoing, but in time he was
obliged to take some of his best friends into his confidence.
Fellow students perceived that he was undergoing a change.
Still silent and preoccupied, he now showed greater eagerness
to mingle with them and to observe them actively. His constantly shifting and penetrating little eyes scrutinized everything, and his dilated nostrils seemed to perform the duties of a
ferret for his eyes. When pressed for an explanation of his
puzzling behavior he would reply with a shrug of the shoulders,
a deep blush, or a few unintelligible monosyllables. Sometimes
he would even leave the *tertulia*. This naturally inspired ingenious speculation. It was suggested, for example, that Señor
Pérez Galdós—as Professor Castro called him in the history
class—might be a police investigator. A government spy! The
more perspicacious argued that his strangely unobtrusive alert-
ness probably meant that he was observing his friends only as so
much literary material. An answer to the puzzle was finally
found by Manolito Moreno, Madrid's notorious academic gossip-
monger. One day he excitedly assembled his mystified colleagues and announced:

> Hey, come here! Last night I saw "him" in the office
> of ... It seemed to me that he offered a manuscript
> to the editor. So the old man is impudent! Poet, ha,
> ha, poet! Did you ever see a poet who doesn't know
> how to make a speech, or greet the ladies, or get into a
> discussion with us? A seer whose name is Pérez!
> Benito Pérez![4]

Manolito Moreno's report was correct in so far as it implied
that Galdós had literary ambitions. He had hardly settled down
in Madrid when he was seized by a vague but persistent yearning

to express his observations and reflections. He began to pursue feverishly some elusive and imponderable form—what he later called "that spiritual copula by which art and beauty reproduce themselves and create families, generations, races." [5] His specific problem was to discover the most effective mold for the realization of his ambition to revolutionize Spanish literature. The novel seemed to him in more urgent need of reform, but the drama had the greatest attraction for him. Perhaps it was because he realized that as a beginner he could prevail little against the rampant bad taste and practice in fiction. The drama, on the other hand, was indisputably superior to the novel, and if he cultivated it he would be in worthy company. Even if his contribution could not be revolutionary, it would nevertheless be in the direction of progress. In addition to these considerations was the fact that, like other young Spaniards, he conceived of literary glory in terms of dramatic success only. He dreamed of the thrills of premières and of that instantaneous success which spells lifelong and even eternal fame.

Indeed, he would reform and regenerate national dramatic art. With the faith of a mystic Galdós believed in his calling and in his specific talent. He confided this to a few of his closest friends. Some regarded him as a dreamer deserving of moral support; others thought he should be promptly disillusioned. The samples of the dramas he submitted now and then for comment only tended to accentuate this division of opinion. But regardless of the reaction of his friends, Benito Pérez turned out prose and verse dramas and comedies with impressive speed, each successive accomplishment giving him new encouragement. Themes and problems came to him readily, although their elaboration was a slow process. He took pains above everything else to impart to his writings the inner warmth of his imagination.

But for all his diligence and fecundity, Galdós knew he had not discovered his peculiar dramatic vein. By and large he was strongly influenced by the current moral and social comedies he had read or had seen on the Madrid stage. The recent success of Tamayo and of Ayala were evidently converting him into one of their many imitators. That was not the road to reform and glory. All he had written thus far was only valuable training in the mechanics of dramaturgy. He must begin to work more consciously and more energetically toward the elaboration of a personal formula. And if a novice could not avoid imitation, he should at least select his model judiciously.

Galdós found the object of his quest in 1864, when from a seat in the gallery of the Teatro Español he watched ecstatically the first performance of García Gutiérrez's *Venganza catalana*. What a marvelous play! What grandiose drama! That night he rushed home and scrutinized critically his accumulated manuscripts. He was strongly tempted to make an *auto de fe* of them. How lumberingly conventional his plots, how insipid his themes of adultery, how futile the financial jabber of his bankrupt aristocrats, how pale and self-conscious his characters, how obvious his devices, and how puerile his pontifical moral pronouncements! Not until he could rise to the grandeur and vigor of *Venganza catalana*, so superbly interpreted by Matilde Díez and Manuel Catalina, should he risk approaching an impresario. With a worthy model like García Gutiérrez a good part of his success was assured.

Benito Pèrez took the first confident step on the road to fame and fortune; he began to write *La expulsión de los moriscos*, an historical drama in verse.

His classmates and friends became aware of a sudden profound change in his behavior. Without shunning them entirely he made it clear that he preferred undisturbed seclusion. He welcomed the quiet of the early morning hours, free from the useless political and literary chatter of his associates. Work on the drama progressed slowly but gratifyingly. Having discovered the weaknesses of his former plays, he was now able to proceed with self-discipline and objectivity. He wrote with feverish excitement. He was hurried and impatient. The sonorous verse of his drama kindled his imagination, and his characters stood before him living and real. The settings, too, were so vivid that they seemed to him like familiar places. It was all an exhilarating experience; never before had he felt so poignantly the joy of creation.

The satisfaction of having created something significant enabled Galdós to face calmly the difficulties that followed. He knew that the stage was an impregnable fortress to the untried dramatist armed only with faith in his talent. The slight fame he already enjoyed among journalists would carry little weight with impresarios. Yet he preferred to negotiate with them unheralded, relying on his firm determination to mark a new stage in the history of the Spanish drama. He had his heart set on Matilde Díez and Manuel Catalina for the production of his *La expulsión de los moriscos* and a prose comedy of manners, possibly *Un joven de provecho*. Catalina was the director of the Príncipe, and to him Galdós submitted his two works in 1867. Catalina had a spacious cabinet where he accumulated unread and rejected plays. Into that cabinet went Galdós' dramatic works, and there they remained for about three years.

Although by 1870 Galdós had definitely decided to cultivate the novel, he did not entirely neglect his interest in the drama. Possibly his program of literary reform now included both genres. Irked by Catalina's procrastination, he now sought the intervention of his friend Federico Balart. The famous poet and critic invoked the aid of Eusebio Blasco, author of *El pañuelo blanco*, which had recently been produced by Catalina with notable success. Galdós, looking both modest and unconcerned, delivered to Blasco a letter from Balart in which he was introduced as the writer's very talented young countryman (Balart was a Murcian!). Blasco promised to intercede with Catalina immediately. The impresario must have read the two plays carefully, for he recalled them clearly. *La expulsión de los moriscos* he characterized as a very bad historical drama, and the other piece as a violently dramatic comedy doomed to failure because of its intrinsic bad qualities and its author's obscurity. Blasco himself maintained a polite silence about the historical drama, but he dissented from Catalina's opinion of the comedy. He thought it was a beautiful intimate drama, distinctly superior to the productions of the day. Naturally Catalina's estimate prevailed, however, and neither play saw the boards. Galdós, it may be assumed, took his failure seriously, but he liked to attribute it exclusively to his obscurity as a dramatist. Yet he was sufficiently disillusioned not to undertake the regeneration of the Spanish theater again until 1892.

Of Galdós' presumably extensive repertoire of unstaged plays the only one that has been preserved intact is *Un joven de provecho*, which was recently discovered and published. *La expulsión de los moriscos* has never appeared in print, although as late as 1912 Galdós claimed he still had the original manuscript. Besides these two works there are the few scenes from *El hombre fuerte* which were reproduced in 1902 by Eduardo Lustonó, who erroneously asserted that this was Galdós' first play.

On the basis of *Un joven de provecho* one is constrained to admire the frankness with which Galdós concluded in 1867 that all his dramas and comedies deserved to burn in an *auto de fe*. Oddly enough, it reveals a fair mastery of the stereotyped dramatic technique then in vogue. Evidently the vicarious dramatic experience he derived from attending *estrenos* (premières) enabled him to handle adroitly the very conventional patterns and formulas which in 1892 he ventured to defy and, if possible, to destroy. Perhaps the realization that he was not a dramatic innovator induced him in 1867 to limit his dream of a literary revolution to the novel. Quite clearly, the inspiration of *Venganza catalana* turned out to be a form of self-deception.

Galdós enjoyed better fortune as a journalist, despite the precarious conditions of the profession in the sixties. Contrary to his frequent complaints, which friends and biographers have repeated sympathetically, his articles in newspapers and critical journals netted him more than "tired feet." He may not have derived much inner satisfaction from his achievements in journalism, but he certainly received gratifying recognition. This is particularly true of the period following his journalistic apprenticeship on the staff of *La Nación*.

This paper had been founded by Pascual Madoz early in 1865

as the organ of the *Progresistas* under the editorship of Santín de Quevedo. Galdós, who had been in Madrid only about two years, had impressed his friends as a promising young writer, though his reputation rested on the extensive practice writing he had been doing rather than on published work. It was apparent to his most intimate friends that he was methodically casting into literary molds his impressions of Madrid life in all its implications, and they were greatly impressed with his power and scope of observation and his felicitous style.

One such friend, Ricardo Molina, a relatively obscure young newspaper man, prevailed on Pascual Madoz to accept Galdós on the staff of his paper. His first article, dealing with music, was published in the issue of February 3, 1865. Thereafter he contributed regularly—at least once a week—until *La Nación* ceased publication in the fall of 1868 after the overthrow of Isabel II. His last article appeared on October 13, 1868. Two long lapses were occasioned by government suspension of the paper from June 17, 1866, to January, 1868, and by Galdós' absence from Madrid during the summer of 1868. Altogether he contributed a hundred and twenty-eight articles on art, drama, literature, music, politics, prominent contemporary figures, and feature stories about Madrid. In addition he published the series of *Aventuras de Pickwick,* a complete translation of Dickens' *Pickwick Papers,* which was the first introduction of the English novelist to the Spanish public.

In "Recuerdos de una fiesta," his last article in *La Nación,* Galdós naïvely reflected the prevalent belief that the despised Bourbons had been forever banished from Spain. A new era was dawning, and he was eager to watch its rise at close range. Since anti-dynastic *La Nación* lost its raison d'être with the dethronement of the queen, he decided to devote himself exclusively to the observation of the turbulent political scene in the days ahead.

The opening of the Cortes Constituyentes inspired Aníbal Alvarez Osorio to found the newspaper *Las Cortes.* It was staffed by some of Spain's most brilliant writers, among whom Galdós felt honored to be included. He accepted enthusiastically the difficult assignment of covering the parliamentary sessions and writing a series of pen sketches of the deliberating deputies. For some time now he had been thinking seriously about the national problem, but mostly in abstract terms. In his new capacity he would be in a favorable position to build up a body of opinions and attitudes based on fact.

Galdós took up his duties with keen interest and intense devotion. He attended all the sessions of Cortes and was profoundly stirred by the eloquence of Spain's famed political orators. Emilio Castelar's celebrated oration "Grande es Dios en el Sinaí" electrified him. But Castelar's oratory no less than the pronouncements of Echegaray, Pí y Margall, Salmerón, Figueras, Cándido Nocedal, and others only strengthened his belief that Spanish politics was a weird mixture of rhetoric, idealism, theory, confusion, and intransigence. Between speeches and after sessions he mingled in the famous *pasillos* (corridors) with colleagues and politicians great and small. His fame grew as his friends and acquaintances multiplied. In the noisy office of *Las Cortes* he wrote feverishly and effortlessly about the congressional deliberations and sketched with firm strokes the physical and moral likenesses of the deputies. His readers admired his stylistic ingenuity, his unerring political judgments, and his penetrating analysis of human values. His feature column, "La Tribuna del Congreso," was read avidly and brought the paper fame and subscribers. It was a fairly long distance from the editorial office to his home on the third floor of 8 Calle de Serrano (old series), and Benito Pérez Galdós covered it at two A.M. or later every night, physically tired but exhilarated and eager for the next day's work.

When finally the function of the Cortes Constituyentes was reduced to the selection of a foreign prince as the liberal constitutional monarch of Spain, Alvarez Osorio's paper reached the end of its mission and Galdós lost his job. But this caused him little concern. He now felt that his record as journalist and his forthcoming first novel, *La fontana de oro*, entitled him to a more dignified position than that of political commentator and feature writer. Indeed, he was confident that as peer of the best of the guild he would have no trouble in getting what he wanted and deserved.

On the recommendation of José Ferreras, an ace journalist, Galdós was invited in 1870 to join the staff of *La Revista de España,* a literary review founded not long before by José Luis Albareda. Within a few months he was promoted to editor-in-chief, a position he held for several years. Before the end of 1870 Albareda also founded *El Debate,* a daily pledged to support Amadeo, and sponsored and in part financed by General Prim. Galdós was appointed editor, and he assumed his duties a short time before the mysterious assassination of Prim and the ill-fated arrival of the Italian prince to rule constitutionally the unruly Spaniards. It was not easy to edit an embattled newspaper directed by a man of exacting standards like Albareda, but Galdós faced the task bravely and acquitted himself creditably. Besides serving as editor he wrote numerous articles, all unsigned, on politics, literature, and art. Among his distinguished associates were José Ferreras and Gaspar Núñez de Arce. The latter succeeded Albareda as director in 1874, after the Pavía *coup d'état* effected the Bourbon restoration.

Altogether the years Galdós spent in association with Albareda were the most valuable of his apprenticeship for creative writing. Naturally they lacked the dynamism and thrills of modern journalism, but on at least one occasion he feared a conflict with the authorities because of one of his articles. This was a sketch entitled "Un baile en el Faubourg," written in collaboration with Albareda and satirizing with poignant wit the famous mantilla parade staged by the aristocratic ladies of Madrid as a protest against the reign of Amadeo. In reality this was Galdós' second journalistic faux pas. The first he had committed in 1866, when in a sketch of Carlos Frontaura in the series *Galería de figuras de cera* he had drifted into caricature by dwelling on the ugliness of his subject. He met Frontaura's remonstrances by insisting that the accentuated strokes resulted from an esthetic impulse and not from personal animosity.

What had fitted Galdós for newspaper writing? Two agencies: life and books. For the first all Madrid served as a field of observation, and from the very start Galdós displayed a keener interest in the human document than in photographic records. His sharp eye and retentive memory combined with his vivid imagination and reflective mind to invest his writing with social, spiritual, and esthetic significance. From books Galdós derived his imaginative substance and his weighty wisdom. He was extremely well read, especially in literature, history, mythology, music, and the other fine arts, past and present, national and foreign. Because of his youth, particularly during the first years of his journalistic career, he could not always escape a tone of sophomoric seriousness and dignity, but in the main he mixed life and learning pleasantly and stimulatingly in narration, description, exposition, and criticism. The material for his articles he had in a sense acquired before 1865, but their artistic form he developed in the columns of the periodical publications with which he was associated.

Since Galdós the journalist survived to a large extent in Galdós the novelist—for some five years he had been both simultaneously—it may be well to appraise him at the end of his literary apprenticeship. Such an appraisal must necessarily be based upon his contributions to *La Nación,* since these were the only ones that did not appear anonymously. From what is known about Galdós' articles in *Las Cortes* and *El Debate* it would appear that when *La Nación* ceased publication at the end of 1868 he had already reached the most characteristic stage of his journalistic career.

Perhaps Galdós' most notable quality is his broad humanitarianism. Barring an occasional outburst of youthful severity, he is tolerant and even compassionate in his criticism of human foibles. His fundamental preoccupation is with the distortion of values, with the distressing distance between things as they are and things as they should be in the light of justice and logic. Quite naturally, as a youthful idealist he is sometimes amusingly insistent upon strictly rational behavior, but such ingenuousness did not manifest itself too frequently.

Although Galdós' immediate scene of observation is Madrid
—and he treats it with unprejudiced fondness—his ultimate aim
is the interpretation and evaluation of Spanish life in the main.
He loves Spain deeply, but his love does not always transcend
bourgeois patriotism, pride in the national heritage, and impatience with blind imitation of foreign modes and practices.
Like the *costumbristas* (writers of sketches of local customs) of
the preceding generation, he is ever ready to defend his country
against the slanders of the black legend, but he finds defamation
by foreigners less odious than the scorn of natives. Although
he himself is given to denouncing traditional vices, he ridicules
the Spaniard who condemns all manifestations of the national
temperament and genius. In general he decries the gradual surrender of indigenous virtues and modes to an external foreign
(French) veneer. As in later years, he advocates modification
and regeneration from within.

In his worship of the indigenous and the popular Galdós
often finds sublimity where someone less prejudiced might see
only bad taste. He applauds, for example, the populace of
Madrid, "drunk with pleasure and wine," celebrating a national
holiday at the base of the Dos de Mayo monument. For him
the sight of a people observing its festivals around the tombs
of their heroes is a spectacle of imposing grandeur and a sublime
canvas. Here he is not merely waxing rhetorical; he speaks rather
as the future chronicler of the history of the nineteenth century,
convinced that the "forgotten man" of national events deserves
a prominent place alongside the consecrated heroes and leaders.
Yet on occasion he is distinctly anti-popular. He would favor,
for example, the suppression of the bullfight for the material,
spiritual, and even artistic benefit of the nation. He would be
willing to replace the national sport with something foreign
like turf, tea, or Italian opera, since he would rather appear
like a foreigner in Spain than like a barbarian in Europe. But
he is no more hopeful about the disappearance of the bullfight
than about the Spaniard's capacity for enterprise and sustained
effort in worth-while endeavors.

Although caution marks Galdós' discussion of politics, he reveals a highly developed political consciousness. Without being an embattled rebel he upholds the principles of democracy and liberalism which in 1868 gained temporary ascendency in Spain. His general philosophy is that a political party rooted in history, tradition, and precedent has no future; to be vital, political principles and procedures must derive from the needs of contemporary society and from its ability to satisfy them. By contrast with this ideal he condemns the peculiar workings of practical politics in Spain, where personalities replace principles and awakened ambitions often lead to venality and corruption of character. But he is not discouraged by the obvious inability of the politically uneducated Spanish masses to use their new freedom with dignity and intelligence. On the contrary, he stoutly defends the constitution on the ground that it is far better to allow a hundred Spaniards to misuse freedom than to take it away from one who might use it for some concrete benefit to the entire nation. Even the masses, he believes, will in time learn to appreciate liberty in its true essence.

The restraint with which Galdós discusses politics is totally absent from his criticism of Spanish religious life. He speaks with unrestrained hatred about neo-Catholicism, which he regards as Spain's most serious problem, and about formalism and institutionalism with their lack of appeal to the spirit and the soul. Church processions, particularly those of Holy Week, he regards as sheer grotesqueness. Curiously enough, certain other plastic expressions of religion, such as the *nacimientos*, he defends solemnly and even ecstatically because he views them as childhood souvenirs and symbols of the Catholic faith. Obviously Galdós has also a positive concept of religion. In general he professes an intimate, personal, and purely spiritual faith free from superstition and formalism. Uninfluenced by the metaphysical discussion of the Krausists, he expresses his religious ideas in conventional terms. He conceives God to be love, and resents the doctrine of sin and retribution. He frowns upon organized public prayer, preferring private and intimate communion between the individual and God. The spurious elements in religion, such as belief in the devil, he berates as incompatible with modern enlightenment, and he calls on all Christians, Catholics in particular, to banish these from the mind of humanity.

In short, Galdós reveals a deeply religious nature, though not in the ordinary sense of the phrase. He is an ardent Catholic, but not of the uncritical practitioner variety. Those aspects of religion which he respects he defends with youthful sincerity, sometimes with vehemence. And out of his attitude toward religion springs his personal conception of the good life. He defines it in terms of contemplation, virtue, diligence, study, the cultivation of science, and the perfection of the spirit. But individual intellectual and spiritual perfection are sterile without concern for the propagation of these virtues among one's fellow beings. Those who are endowed with some special talent are in duty bound to extend its benefits to the masses. The gifted must descend from the heights of reflection and contemplation to the lower levels of instruction and enlightenment.

In his own case Galdós very definitely did not identify journalism with the good life. His reserved nature, his pure and austere conscience, and his propensity to dream and to exercise his imagination were at variance with this profession. He had embarked upon his journalistic experience largely because it was an indispensable step toward his ultimate goal. In the months just before the national upheaval of 1868 he had already been tempted to relinquish it, but two considerations restrained him: first, he had not yet discovered a better road to literary achievement; second, the turbulent national scene precluded contemplative detachment on the part of any conscientious Spaniard. Journalism was his way of participating in Spanish life. It enabled him at least to understand more clearly the strains and stresses responsible for the national chaos. But it did not solve his personal problem. His ultimate objective was to give his countrymen a coherent vision of their collective destiny. In what way could he best utilize his intellectual, spiritual, and artistic resources for the realization of this objective? Journalism was clearly not the answer.

IV

On the Way

IN THE SPRING of 1865 the air of Madrid was heavy with
rumor. The national treasury was sadly depleted, and the Spaniards' purses were flat. Queen Isabel II, skeptical of the effectiveness of new taxes, proposed an astonishingly simple remedy. Why
not sell part of the Royal Patrimony—which was the nation's and
not her personal property—for the rehabilitation of the ex-
chequer? By way of reward for this life-saving solution she
would retain for herself only twenty-five per cent of the amount
of the sale. Prime Minister Narváez promptly had Cortes pass
a bill incorporating the queen's suggestion. The deputies were
so delighted to be rid of the vexing problem that they gave the
monarch a rising vote of thanks.

Spanish liberals did not share the lawmakers' admiration for
the queen's ingenuity. Galdós, who had entered the journalistic
arena only recently, shot arrows of irony at the ruler and her
cabinet from the columns of the *progresista La Nación*. The
more radical *La Iberia* lashed out against the government in
an explosive article, "El rasgo," by Emilio Castelar, then professor in the University of Madrid. The queen met the attack
with a royal decree ordering Rector Juan Manuel Montalbán
to "separate from his chair" the revolutionary professor so lacking in restraint—that is, to suspend him from the faculty. Rector
Montalbán deemed the royal decree arbitrary, and rather than
carry it out he resigned, as did Nicolás Salmerón and Miguel
Morayta, distinguished scholars and leaders of the young republican movement. The Marqués de Zafra was forthwith appointed
to fill the vacant rectorship.

The crown-and-gown controversy was seized upon by the student body as an excuse for a political demonstration. In those days Galdós overcame his aversion to academic precincts and mingled unobtrusively with the excited groups of students milling about the ugly university building on Calle Ancha de San Bernardo. There was a plan afoot to serenade the resigned rector at his home. It was to be carried out in orderly fashion and with legal sanction; Madrid's Civil Governor Gutiérrez de la Vega granted permission for the musical demonstration, and a suitable band was engaged. The general public was kept informed about the forthcoming "manifestation."

All was set for the procession to Señor Montalbán's modest residence on Calle Santa Clara. Good Spaniards without academic standing joined the orderly if noisy crowd in front of the university. But just as the command to march was about to be given the civil governor ordered the serenade cancelled on grounds of public order. Hundreds of voices invoked long life for the rector and instant death for the queen's cabinet and all the other reactionary "neos." The crowd, swelled by the arrival of more non-academic citizens, followed the instinct of Madrilenians in days of political stress and streamed spontaneously and in confusion toward the Puerta del Sol. There the serenaders struck up an explosively revolutionary note, but they were promptly dispersed by the threatening maneuvers of the Guardia Veterana. Madrid became tranquil once more and remained so the rest of that night of Saturday, April 8, 1865. Benito Pérez Galdós retired to his room to reflect on the meaning of the painful incident.

The students looked upon the victory of the Guardia Veterana as merely temporary. Sunday they worked feverishly to reform their lines. Monday night, St. Daniel's Eve, they stormed the Puerta del Sol with the aid of strong contingents of plain citizens. Spain's famous political citadel was well fortified against a frontal assault. Prime Minister Narváez and Minister of Interior González Bravo, symbols of government frivolity and ruthless enforcement of law and order, stood confident and defiant in front of Gobernación (Ministry of Interior). But

nothing could now silence the surging, indignant, and outraged
multitude. The Guardia Veterana flashed its sabers savagely.
Horses galloped in circles around the Puerta del Sol. Confusion
developed into panic and riot. Stampeding citizens jammed the
streets radiating from the square, pursued mercilessly by the
infuriated Guardia Veterana. Galdós, with many other students,
instinctively sought safety in the near-by Ateneo. He had received several saber blows on his shoulders and back, but the
pain was not severe. A number of persons lay dead and a hundred
wounded.

The general public could merely hope that the bloody clash
would soon be followed by a more violent and victorious battle,
but the students sought immediate compensation for their defeat.
They converted the inauguration of the new rector into the
most elaborate, noisiest demonstration on record in academic
circles. Despite the heavy police guard, strident and shrill whistling punctuated the learned remarks of the Marqués de Zafra.
One appreciative student pelted him with an egg. The professor
of history who replaced "separated" Castelar had greater foresight than the new rector. To protect himself against the hostile
visitors who ever since St. Daniel's Eve had been overcrowding
his lecture hall, he ruled that admission would be only by an
official enrollment card. Galdós, who had been in something like
a trance since that memorable night, was not present at the
inaugural riot nor did he exert himself to be certified to Castelar's
successor. Somehow, nevertheless, he managed to report in *La
Nación* (May 11, 1865) all the latest developments at the university. By October normal academic routine was re-established,
although, as Galdós predicted, another flare-up was inevitable
should the authorities see fit to move rectors and professors
again like pawns on a chessboard.

The riot of St. Daniel's Eve was only the prelude to the
imminent showdown between the two forces. Moderate liberals
were gradually joining the ranks of the republicans. The *progresista* press still brandished its verbal sword, though not in
open defiance of the zealously vigilant government. Galdós was
obliged to resort to subtle stylistic subterfuge in presenting

political opinions. After the suspension of his paper for approximately a month early in 1866 he grew ever more cautious, and his weekly articles were increasingly devoted to music, drama, literature, and biography. In June *La Nación* was indefinitely suspended, and he was forced to consider seriously the next step in his literary career. The rising tide of revolution came to his aid.

The liberals of Madrid had been carefully planning a military uprising on June 22, 1866. There was general confidence in the strategy that called for the San Gil artillery barracks and the Montaña infantry to start the mutiny, which would be joined by other military units throughout the land. On the designated day citizens and students made common cause behind barricades protected by sharpshooters strategically posted on the roofs of neighboring buildings. Victory was in sight. The San Gil sergeants were to roll out the artillery pieces the night before while their officers were asleep. The sight of those weapons near the barricades would surely intimidate the government troops; it might even inspire them to come over to the revolutionary ranks. Enthusiasm ran high. The republic was on the horizon.

Whether through misunderstanding or willful disobedience, the San Gil sergeants decided to shoot their officers before seizing the guns. The officers returned fire and the slaughter was heavy on both sides. The detachments manning the barricades grew uneasy when the artillery failed to arrive. When finally they saw cavalry and infantry troops approaching, terror spread among them. Yet there was no thought of fleeing. Revolutions were not won that way. But General Serrano in command of the loyal troops was as eager for victory as the revolutionaries. In the ensuing battle the latter went down in heroic defeat.

Benito Pérez Galdós watched the bloody spectacle from his boarding-house on Calle del Olivo. The air echoed to the thunder of cannon. From the street below and from others near it rose "the groans of victims, raging oaths, bloody exhalations, hateful voices."[1] Madrid was an inferno. Late in the afternoon Galdós went out with some friends to view the ravage of human life and property, and was filled with horror by what he saw. Even more terrifying was the scene he watched the next morning. A line of public coaches, each carrying two artillery sergeants, rolled in tragic procession up Calle Alcalá toward the old Plaza de Toros, where the victims were to be shot against the wall of the arena. He was so grieved and horrified that he could not follow the coaches to the place of execution. He ran home and sought solace in his books and manuscripts.

The riot of St. Daniel's Eve and the San Gil insurrection affected Galdós and influenced his literary temperament immeasurably. Bitter reflections raced through his mind as he sat in the hushed silence of his room on the afternoon of June 23, 1866.

He thought that the two violent conflicts which had occurred within little more than a year were in reality a repetition of earlier riots. They might well be regarded as part and parcel of the abominable legacy inherited by the reigning ruler from her ineffable father. Who could guarantee that agents-provocateurs did not operate among the liberals just as they had in the era of Ferdinand VII? But no nation could develop and prosper amidst constant strife and strain; frequent repetitions of violence and bloodshed only impoverished the people morally and spiritually. And the remedy for the national ailment was still distressingly remote. There was little hope in political theories and systems. With its arbitrariness, obstinacy, and passion, Spanish politics propagated a germ which infected all those who exposed themselves to it. The urgent national need was to discover some form of immunity from this political virus.

What was he, Benito Pérez Galdós, doing actively for the solution of the national problem? He was patriotic. But all Spaniards professed profound patriotism, even those responsible for the nation's plight. To be sure, his patriotism was of a different kind. It seemed to be a subtly fused compound of several sharp sensations. Sometimes he felt it as an all-pervading memory of the exultation with which as a child he had listened to his father's tales about national glory and honor, or the avidity with which he had read Chaplain Domingo Pérez's delightful diary. More recently he had been experiencing it as

countless rays of light radiating from the pages of national
history and suffusing him with warmth and sympathy. At all
times his patriotism, or national conscience, was compounded of
sentiment, emotion, knowledge, and understanding. He often
yearned to communicate this to others, but he did not know
exactly how to do it. Once it had occurred to him to write a
drama about the defeat of the Spanish navy by Nelson, but he
soon realized that the theme did not lend itself to dramatic
treatment; the drama was so artificial and conventional. Nor was
the daily press suitable for his purpose because it was chiefly concerned with topics and interests of the workaday life. Of all the
literary genres the novel was perhaps the only one in which
so vast a theme as a national conscience could be treated effectively. Why not explore the possibilities of fiction?

Somewhere between June, 1866, and the fall of 1867 Galdós
took the first steps in what he once called "the rascally art of
novelizing." He wrote *La sombra,* a work which is less a novel
than an attempt to formulate the author's concept of fiction
and perhaps also a test of his ability to integrate in one relatively
extensive work the various styles and types of content he had
been cultivating.

Barring the settings, which are real—although of an extravagant reality—everything in *La sombra* moves on a symbolic
and ideological plane sustained by abstract reflection and speculation. Don Anselmo, the principal figure, is a quixotic creature
whom Galdós exploits experimentally for the analysis of mania,
fixation, and hallucination. He also serves as a sounding-board
for the author's loud thinking on a variety of psychological and
social topics. The theme is the conventional one of *pundonor*
(conjugal infidelity) elaborated in a series of stereotyped incidents presented in flashback fashion. The author is always present
as an interlocutor, and by the opportune interjection of comments
and questions he develops a penetrating discourse, among other
things, on the nature of reality and imagination and the tenuous
line which separates them.

What were some of Galdós' preoccupations at this time with
"the rascally art of novelizing"? The question is answered by

La sombra. A novelist's essential endowment is his imagination, which must be consciously restrained by reason and common sense. In art imagination should function as a faculty and not as an aberration or an organic vice. A rebellious and unbridled imagination can lead only to futile ecstasy and hallucination, transporting the artist to an incongruous world. This is permissible with purely poetical and personal creations, but where the direct reflection of life is the goal, fancy must not be allowed to so obscure the natural that it can be seen only in hazy outline. The natural, or the real, cannot be defined in absolute terms save in the physical realm. What seem to be spiritual and moral realities are often deceptions and hallucinations which the novelist will do well to explain in terms of their physiological origin or their root in the human conscience. In general, the novelist's chief concern is the study of human behavior as a resultant of man's inability to distinguish the real from the imaginary. Such a study naturally involves an examination of social, ethical, and moral values as they are manifested in dynamic and complex characters judiciously selected and placed in vivid settings.

While *La sombra* unquestionably served the purpose for which it was written, it did not wholly satisfy Galdós, and he delayed its publication until 1871. His true fictional vein he discovered in Paris in the summer of 1867. The first book he bought there was a volume of Balzac—*Eugénie Grandet,* edition Librairie Nouvelle, for which he paid one franc. Notwithstanding his bland assertion to the contrary, this could hardly have been his first acquaintance with the French novelist, although it probably marked the beginning of his almost religious veneration for him. The reading of Balzac fortified his newly discovered interest in the novel, enriched his ideas about the art of fiction, and perhaps also influenced him to abandon the dazzling dream of dramatic glory. Shortly after returning to Madrid he began intense work on *La fontana de oro,* a quasi-historical novel of revolutionary tendency. "A mechanical impulse," he said, "which sprang from the very depths of my being urged me toward this work." [2] The creative process functioned effortlessly and pleas-

antly. He continued writing methodically until the summer of
1868, when he was taken on a second trip to France. In 1867
he had left for Paris with a book under his arm; in 1868 he took
with him the unfinished manuscript of his second novel.

Galdós apparently did discover his true vein, but neither suddenly nor as a result of a mechanical impulse. The historical
background of *La fontana de oro*—the years 1820–1823 in the
reign of Ferdinand VII—required patient research in the history and social life of the period. Much of this Galdós accomplished in the Ateneo, which he joined on November 30, 1865.
He soon became almost a feature of the club. Instead of seeking
association with the distinguished national figures among its
members, he spent long hours daily in the well-stocked library
and reading-room, gathering material according to a well-defined
plan. His historical research—he was already a serious student
of Spanish history—inevitably led him to observe the striking
similarity between the events of the sixties and those of the
earlier decades of the century. For some time he had been preoccupied with the part that he should play in the struggle for
national regeneration; now he saw his duty clearly. If he
stopped to weigh the chances of success, he probably had few
misgivings. The historical novel had a great vogue, thanks
largely to the prodigious fecundity of Manuel Fernández y
González. What Galdós had in mind was something quite different from the fictional monstrosities of the picturesque poly-
graph—but *La fontana de oro* seemed to him well worth a
gamble.

The second sojourn in France was even more delightful than
the first had been. On the way back to Spain Galdós and his
traveling companions stopped at Bagnères de Bigorre in the
Pyrenees, where he resumed work on his novel. After a tour
of the picturesque Midi, including a fatiguing and dangerous
overland journey, the party reached the border town of Figueras
toward the end of September. From there Galdós went by train
to Gerona. Something prompted him to cover in detail all the
points of interest in the city, about which he was to write one
of his historical novels. The next stop was Barcelona. There he

witnessed the first steps of the Revolution of 1868, which was destined to influence his own life more than the nation's.

Galdós reached Madrid a few hours before General Serrano, who had been an exile in the Canary Islands, was welcomed with delirious noise in the Puerta del Sol. Several days later General Prim, popular hero of the uprising, was received with frenzied enthusiasm. When Prim and Vice-admiral Topete of the revolutionary navy spoke from the balcony of Gobernación, the roaring multitude drowned their eloquence. Galdós was disappointed that he could not hear what the leaders said to their followers on so important an occasion. He recalled another mass demonstration in front of the same building—the riot of St. Daniel's Eve. In 1865 it was the people who addressed their leaders, Narváez and González Bravo, and the leaders manifestly did not understand the people. Did the multitude now understand Prim and Topete even though they could not hear their speeches? Or did the roars of approval really matter very little? Anyway, it was evident that the Bourbons had been permanently removed and that an era of progress, liberalism, and national dignity was in sight. This the revolutionary leaders promised, and the people had faith in their promise.

An extraordinary stroke of good fortune came Galdós' way. The city of Zaragoza invited the glorious generals of the Glorious Revolution to be the honored guests at a local exposition of art and industry. One October morning a colorful caravan of politicians, writers, and journalists left for the heroic Aragonese city. It was the Revolution on parade. Affairs of the new state detained General Prim in Madrid, but General Serrano and Vice-admiral Topete went as representatives of the provisional government. Galdós was thrilled to be included among the gentlemen of the press.

It was a festive and ebullient crowd that filled the speeding special train. At Sigüenza there was a bit of amusing excitement. The population had turned out en masse to hail the heroes of the Glorious Revolution. The municipal band rent the air with the strident strains of the Riego hymn. At the head of the committee of welcome came Bishop Benavides, an intimate friend of Serrano's. The general ordered the train to stop after it had sped past the station. The crowd roared its appreciation of the courtesy shown to Sigüenza. Serrano and the bishop fell into a warm embrace. It was a touching symbol of perfect harmony between church and state, disrupted only by the jarring medley of the Riego hymn and the Marseillaise which the municipal band jangled. A deafening roar from the crowd punctuated the solemn scene. Galdós fell into a fit of skepticism: the incident was tumultuously pathetic.

The reception in Zaragoza was noisy and varied, but spontaneous and sincere. Speeches were delivered from balconies and lamp-posts, from the pedestals of statues, and from every other point where a speaker could rise to a higher physical level than the appreciative listeners. The air was as heavy with rejoicing, hope, and good will as the city was crowded with celebrants. Special evening performances were given in the theaters and banquets in the hotels, at all of which highly seasoned political verses were improvised and recited. The sense of it all was that the Bourbons had at last earned eternal damnation, whereas the people were assured of redemption by the Glorious Revolution.

This was only the beginning of the festivities, but Galdós detached himself from the official party after the first day. The historic memories of Zaragoza and some vague reflections inspired by the tumultuous celebration of the revolution prompted him to go out and become intimately acquainted with the heroic city. He spent many hours roaming streets and squares, visiting famous buildings and sites of the city's two sieges, and in general observing the most typical aspects of the life of its inhabitants. He had made a similar study of Gerona the month before. In both instances his motive went deeper than curiosity. It was akin to the urge that still impelled him to wander in and around Madrid in quest of the raw materials of literature. His tour of Zaragoza exhilarated him more than the political celebrations. Perhaps Galdós was unconsciously preparing himself for a literary enterprise of magnitude.

The return trip to Madrid lacked official pomp because Serrano, Topete, and other dignitaries had preceded the crowd on an express train. The rest of the delegation traveled in highly typical Spanish fashion on a "mixed" train. At Alcalá de Henares the boisterous journalists stopped for lunch at the station restaurant. They were joined by Salustiano Olózaga, deadly foe of the Bourbon dynasty, and Cristino Martos, later the speaker of the Cortes Constituyentes. The occasion had a political tinge. Olózaga gravely warned his audience not to expect the establishment of a republic. At first Señor Martos took sharp issue with Olózaga, and for a while it seemed as if the two politicians were giving a preview of the next stage of the Glorious Revolution. However, Cristino Martos yielded to the temperate words of the patriarch of the *Progresistas*, and the unscheduled political session ended in harmony except for several impassioned but inconsequential pronouncements by other orators of indeterminate stature. From the stream of familiar oratory Galdós salvaged only one concrete idea—that the monarchy would be retained, with a frankly democratic and popular dynasty replacing the Bourbons. Such was the wish of General Prim, whom none desired nor dared to gainsay.

* * * *

After the Zaragoza junket Galdós felt like a pessimistic night reveler on the morrow. For some time he shared the popular enthusiasm that was carrying Spain onward to an uncertain political future, but as weeks lengthened into months he felt increasingly skeptical about the ultimate benefits of the national upheaval. With the din of the oratorical cascades in the station restaurant at Alcalá de Henares still in his ears, he could not erase the impression that this was not a radical but a domestic revolution. Yet he shared the general conviction that the spurious government of the Bourbons was irrevocably gone; he had said so in his last article in *La Nación* ("Recuerdos de una fiesta," October 13, 1868). For the time being he could do nothing more than observe closely the national scene and continue work on his novel *La fontana de oro*. Although he was pleased with the procedure of combining historical evocation and pure fiction, he felt that his second book, like *La sombra*, was little more than a practice exercise. In his first work he had concentrated his recently acquired knowledge of neuropathy on the analysis of a psychopathic case almost to the exclusion of its structural aspects; in *La fontana de oro* he was still interested in abnormal behavior, but was also taking pains with the elaboration of the plot. This novel unquestionably had more substance and could safely be offered to the public.

As the decade of the sixties drew to a close, Galdós surveyed carefully the road he had traveled thus far and concluded provisionally that the novel held greater promise of enduring achievement than the drama. He had no illusions about scoring an instantaneous success. Although *La fontana de oro* had some of the stereotyped technical features of the romantic fiction in vogue, he feared that its novel content and purpose might very well hinder its acceptance. Most serious of all was the problem of publication. Would the established publishers view favorably a novel which was, in a sense, blazing a new trail? Besides, the prevailing practice was to publish *novelas por entregas* (novels distributed in instalments to subscribers), and with this method he would have nothing to do. The only alternative was to print his novel privately, arrange with bookstores for its distribution—and trust the rest to fate.

To take this bold step Galdós had to solve the problem of financing the publication. His own earnings were insufficient for even his personal needs, and he was receiving aid from the family. When in 1867 he had asked for money to put out *La sombra*, he failed to convince anyone that it would be a wise investment. This time he was successful. Sister-in-law Magdalena willingly undertook to finance the enterprise. The other members of the family raised no serious objections, for they realized that it was no longer a question of disciplining a listless student but of launching Benito on a career from which no one could dissuade him. And so, near the end of 1870, *La fontana de oro* lay in state, as it were, in the windows of the Madrid bookstores, without eliciting pity or respect from passers-by.

It had taken courage to publish the novel privately, and now it required faith to await with equanimity its reception by the press and the public. Galdós had both—his assertions to the contrary notwithstanding. But it was naturally a slow affair. Although he was fairly well known in literary circles and was even acquainted with a number of public figures, he was a relatively obscure name to the rank and file of readers. It thus seemed to him at first that his new novel had dropped into a bottomless well. It was praised and admired by his friends, but the larger reading public was exasperatingly slow to accord it recognition. Galdós was on the verge of concluding that there were no fiction readers in Spain when the tide of fortune changed.

Sometime in April, 1871, Gaspar Núñez de Arce addressed an open letter to the editor of *El Debate* concerning *La fontana de oro*. He made a careful analysis of the novel and praised it highly on many scores, taking objection only to the prolix descriptions and exuberance of detail. He cautioned Galdós to see less and to feel more in his future works. Confidently predicting a bright future for the novice author, he warned him that it required courage and patience to cultivate letters in a country so indifferent to the creations of the human spirit.

There is every reason to believe that the philosophically minded poet's review was spontaneous and genuine. Galdós' gratitude was deep and lasting. Don Gaspar's laudatory remarks created readers for the novel, and his stimulating advice gave fresh inspiration to its author. Before long the substance of his criticism was repeated by other writers, including some of Galdos' closest friends and fellow journalists. A number of these opened the floodgates of eulogy. With so distinguished a sponsor and such unstinted praise the new novelist faced the future with confidence.

For approximately a year *La fontana de oro* was lauded in the Madrid and the provincial press. The high tide of the swelling stream of reviews came twice. Francisco Giner de los Ríos, who did not know Galdós personally, hailed his work in the *Revista Meridional* of Granada as the inauguration of a renaissance of the genuine Spanish novel and praised the author for having ushered in a new era in Spanish literature. Since others spoke in similar terms about the transcendental significance of his book, Galdós was encouraged to nurse more hopefully his slowly maturing ambition to effect a revolution in national fiction. No less inspiring than Giner's reasoned judgment was the estimate of the distinguished academician Don Eugenio de Ochoa. In a long letter to the editor of *La Ilustración de Madrid* he praised the social and moral purpose of the novel and commended its literary qualities. He was most profoundly impressed with the author's evocative power and the unerring sense with which he discovered in the recent past the eternal verities of Spanish life. And in Las Palmas, where the triumph of *La fontana de oro* did not lag behind its success in Madrid, local pride led an anonymous writer to the conclusion that "Señor Pérez Galdós is without doubt the most worth-while thing that has come out of the Grand Canary Island in many, many years." [3]

As Galdós summed up the appraisal of his new novel he had just cause to feel aglow with success. Most of the adverse criticisms concerned technical features which he could consciously control and remedy. It undoubtedly flattered him that several reviewers compared him to Balzac and Dickens, his favorite and constant masters. From a relatively unknown quantity his name had become a topic of conversation in the most prominent literary circles, where he was now received with sincere enthusiasm. Most interesting of all was the recurrent suggestion that, like Erckmann-Chatrian in France, Spanish writers should create a national novel dealing with the epic and dramatic content of Spanish life since the beginning of the century. By a strange coincidence this had been his own thought as far back as 1865 and 1866—as far back as St. Daniel's Eve and the San Gil mutiny.

The suggestion was first made by Galdós' new colleague and friend, José Alcalá Galiano, grandson of the famous Alcalá Galiano portrayed in *La fontana de oro*. Conceivably Galdós himself had let the idea escape inadvertently in the course of a conversation, for Pepe (José) was one of the few with whom he occasionally exchanged ideas and discussed artistic problems. They had first become close friends on the staff of *Las Cortes* and subsequently as the journalistic wards of José Luis Albareda. But Pepe was not the only critic who urged him to continue cultivating the modern national scene. Even more specific was Don Eugenio de Ochoa, who suggested the disaster of Trafalgar as the starting-point and the contemporary period of political wrangling as the end. Galdós shared the conviction of the learned academician that Spaniards must learn to evaluate the past in its true light and cease to regard it with reverence merely because it was a part of national tradition. Don Eugenio put it aptly when he said: "... the past is a sepulcher; we should venerate it, but as for burying ourselves alive in it—never!"⁴ That was the modern lesson which Spain must learn. Where? How? Certainly not in the political arena, and most assuredly not in the soulless and uninspiring history books.

It must have struck Galdós as remarkable that most critics should have perceived so keenly his reasons for writing *La fontana de oro*. Even the few who, unlike Ochoa, resented his alleged political and religious bias stressed the need for presenting in pleasant and popular form the basic causes of the periodic political and social crises in Spain. Galdós was naturally encouraged by the general endorsement of his belief that the novel could be converted from an agency for mere artistic pastime into a powerful instrument of social and moral education. The novel was the most popular genre of the day, but it was largely exploited by writers without talent or skill. More than that, the contemporary novelists were not imbued with a mission. Had destiny chosen him to fulfill a mission?

*   *   *   *

The thought of a mission was flattering but also disquieting. How was he to harmonize the conflicting ideas racing through his mind and the discordant voices calling out to his conscience? Characters of profound human significance—Balzac. Descriptions that rival reality—Dickens. Serene, compassionate humanity tinged with irony—Cervantes. Racy, kaleidoscopic "pueblo"—Ramón de la Cruz. Huge, motley, bantering Madrid —Mesonero Romanos. *La fontana de oro*—bright future. Rebirth of the national novel—critic one. From the battle of

Trafalgar to the present—critic two. Transcendental historical novels—chorus of critics. Shattered dreams of dramatic glory— Manuel Catalina. Cascades of words and clamorous applause— Cortes. The regeneration of Spain through the awakening of a new national conscience—Benito Pérez Galdós. Action or imagination? Politics or fiction? Happiness?

Benito Pérez Galdós was living in a trance.

V

The Great Decision

YES, BENITO PÉREZ GALDÓS was living in a trance. The next two years, to which he subsequently referred as the cataleptic period of his life, were truly critical. The reasons were not entirely literary ones, and he was ultimately restored to consciousness and impelled to renewed action by a profound emotional experience.

As he took stock of himself he could not escape a feeling of listlessness and disorientation despite his superficial achievements. He was an impressionable and idealistic person, given to living in a world of dream and imagination. Often he unconsciously projected himself into a vague future crowded with dramatic incidents of a purely novelistic nature. Hazily he saw himself playing the principal part in enterprises of magnitude. With a vanity of which he was not quite aware he sometimes even imagined himself as the only figure in these fanciful undertakings. At such moments he was stirred by deep passions and was aglow with exultation. Like most of his young contemporaries he breathed the spirit of revolution, sectarianism, and proselytism. Incapable of dynamic, heroic action, he was nevertheless conscious that he was destined to become the apostle of new ideas. The thought that he had a new mission to perform gave him a strong sense of personal dignity, even though he had no clear notion of the nature of that mission or the best means for its realization. For a time he did not even attempt to define concretely the great enterprise for which destiny had chosen him. It was so pleasant to dream that he was reluctant to come into contact with reality.

But the new ideas—it was really one great vague idea—could not be indefinitely sustained as a latent passion, a hazy ambition, and a glorious dream. It was in part the relentless pressure of the great idea for definition and expression that resulted in *La fontana de oro*. Galdós created this novel out of the essence of his heart and mind and spirit. Rather than a story it was the echo of his inner voice and the sublimation of his conscience. In Lázaro, its protagonist, he endeavored to mold the idea, to convert it into reality and dramatize it. In his projection of himself into Lázaro he proceeded without restraint. To Lázaro he surrendered all his personality, even to sharing with him his emotional experiences. It was painful to disturb Sisita from her enshrinement in his heart and to transform her into the heroine—delicate, pathetic little Clara—but he was resolved to reveal himself sincerely and loyally. Except for the conventional fictional features, everything in *La fontana de oro* grew out of the inner logic of its theme and protagonist. Its conclusion, though disillusioning, was honest. Obviously, plots and conspiracies and oratory—even revolution—would not bring about the realization of the great idea.

The stark, ugly realities of the unfolding national scene substantiated for Galdós the validity of his negative conclusion in the novel. General Prim, the idolized prophet of liberal constitutionalism, was assassinated even as the newly chosen monarch, Amadeo of Savoy, was embarking for Spain in Spezia. The sovereign people watched in silence and with foreboding his official welcome in Madrid on January 2, 1871. It was a sad day. The capital was blanketed with snow and heavy leaden clouds moved slowly across the sky. In the ensuing months the sublime ideal of the Glorious Revolution degenerated into an extended petty conflict of persons and procedures. Those who formerly had sung loud hymns to loyalty and self-sacrifice now wrangled over rewards in government bureaus. Sensitive Spaniards became strongly pessimistic. Against this mood Galdós fortified himself with enthusiasm and faith—not faith in the human capacity for lofty living, but faith in the enduring attractiveness of the ideal. There were even moments when the ugly realities became sublimated in his mind. At such times he fell into prolonged musing over the hidden sources of Spanish vitality that might still be tapped for national regeneration. His belief in the indestructibility of the great idea filled him with ecstasy and restless yearning for some form of action by which he might transmute it into a new beautiful reality.

Writing *La fontana de oro* was so inspiring a spiritual experience that even before the critics took notice of it Galdós was busily working on *El audaz*. This novel, which appeared serially in *Revista de España*, is in a sense a sequel to the preceding one, except that it deals with the ideological forces of an earlier period of Spanish history. In *La fontana de oro* Galdós learned the peculiar nature of the Spanish struggle for liberalism; in *El audaz* he discovered the forces responsible for Spanish absolutism. The two works made him realize that human institutions are fundamentally only concepts and abstractions, and that the basic reality of society is the individual. Like some of the more advanced thinkers of his time he came to believe that social reforms cannot be brought about by revolutionary changes in institutions, but only by a spiritual and intellectual reorientation of human beings. These are the only reality of life; against these all abstractions and ideologies dash themselves tragically to pieces. The pressing need was for a process of human reform; the transformation of social institutions would follow naturally. That was really the great idea. Which was the way leading to its realization?

Now that he saw the problem clearly, Galdós believed that its solution would offer him a way of satisfying his urges and ambitions. He became aware of a latent capacity for action that could be applied to the execution of a great task. As in the days preceding the revolution, he imagined himself as the motive power of deeds of enduring value. He was no longer the follower of an ideology; he was the discoverer of a demonstrable truth. The Glorious Revolution had accomplished practically nothing because its leaders mistook an idea for a fact—they substituted one political system for another. He was going to tackle the one great reality of Spanish life—the people. By reforming the national conscience he would realize the great idea. His part in the regeneration of Spain was to revolutionize Spanish fiction. It was a worthy role for a man of action.

Something of his self-confidence Galdós communicated in 1871, while *El audaz* was being published, in a letter to Agustín Millares in Las Palmas:

> I am going to continue writing novels, and now I am preparing the third one. I believe that if I have earned the public's favor it is not because of the merit of what I am writing—for it is scant indeed—but because in writing novels I have raised the standard of reality in protest against a depraved and affected realism. I propose to continue on this road to see how far I can get.

But Galdós was relatively slow in answering roundly the call of destiny. He needed time to prepare himself. True, in a sense he had been preparing himself ever since his arrival in Madrid, but the period of intense study and training was between 1870 and 1873, the years of his prolonged trance. During this time he frequented the old Ateneo regularly. His appearance at the club in midafternoon became a daily event. As the habitués gathered in the "Senate," or lounge, were tuning up, as it were, for a medley of wit and pleasantries, and as the reading room was slowly waking up like a city street in the early morning hours, they invariably heard measured footsteps squeaking in the direction of the library. Screak, screak, screak—tiptoed a pair of shoes with heels raised above the floor.

The wearer of the noisy shoes was a young man of about thirty, who looked somewhat older. He was tall, bony, robust, erect, but not very limber. His clothes were simple and, except for his derby, revealed little of the style of the day. They seemed to be merely a compliance with a social custom. With his cropped thick hair, heavy mustache, and ever-present hand-rolled cigarette between his fingers, he might have passed for an artillery officer wearing a civilian disguise. He had slightly prominent cheekbones, small and deep-set eyes sheltered by lightly folded lids, and a dark, sallow complexion. Only his tall forehead and the expression of tender irony in his eyes saved his face from being wholly unimpressive—even ordinary. His shyness and reserve gave him an air of childish embarrassment. He always looked preoccupied, severe, sad.

Known to only a few members of the Ateneo, Galdós acquired a measure of fame for his long sieges in the library and the periodical room. Rarely did he interrupt his work to mingle with the groups of vociferous disputants that gathered as the afternoon wore on. And just as rarely did he leave his books and reviews to pace up and down the corridor where the "Senate" was in session. Occasionally he was seen conversing briefly and with languid speech with some interesting elderly member. It was evident to all that the reticent and diffident young man was studying something systematically and with great concentration. He was taking copious notes, among which, his neighbors furtively observed, he often interspersed odd drawings. Nor did anyone suspect the intent student of dawdling when he was meditating and musing abstractedly.

But literary and spiritual preoccupations were not alone responsible for delaying Galdós' answer to the call of destiny. His personal life had been in something of a turmoil ever since 1869. His mother, though she was gradually becoming resigned to his literary career, was nevertheless disappointed. Moreover, her incompatibility with Madrina was growing ever more pronounced even after Sisita's departure for Cuba. The new difference that arose between them was over Benito himself. It was not Madrina's moral and financial support that Mama Dolores resented but her obviously preponderant influence on the young man. Matters became worse after Madrina took up residence in Madrid. Then the bond between her and Benito seemed literally indissoluble. He became the principal object of her affection and the great source of comfort in her childless widowhood. His devotion to her was tenderly filial. Mama Dolores was not jealous, but she was frankly puzzled by her son's submissive attitude toward Madrina and his strong-willed attitude toward herself.

Galdós clearly perceived his mother's distressing preoccupations, but he did nothing to comfort her. Although his respect and love for her remained undiminished, he could not help viewing critically her struggle for ascendancy in the family. His appraisal of her attitudes and actions did not spring from a filial relationship but from the same sense of values that governed him as a writer in the judgment of human nature. He looked upon his mother as a complex strong character that challenged his power of analysis. He ruefully reflected that her intolerance and lack of generosity had sometimes alienated people. In a sense he was himself a victim of her spiritual and moral rigidity. He knew that she was largely responsible for Sisita's return to Cuba and that she was motivated by a maniacal obsession concerning his salvation. Somehow she seemed to regard his love for the stigmatized child—if love it really was—as fatal to his career and as a painful reminder of Uncle José María's disgrace.

Mama Dolores had of course no way of knowing that Sisita's departure from Las Palmas almost cost Benito an emotional crisis. In reality her radical solution solved nothing; it only made him melancholy and more listless. Although Madrina helped him maintain a tenuous contact with Sisita, basically his relation to the girl was now more awkward than ever. In Las Palmas he had failed to assert himself because of the fear with which everyone bowed before the will of Mama Dolores, and during his early years in Madrid he had somehow permitted his many new distractions to reduce Sisita to little more than a constant sweet memory. He did not regard this as evidence of disloyalty or diminishing affection. On the contrary, Sisita was so intimately a part of him that to treat her otherwise would have been novelistic and melodramatic. But now the situation was extremely embarrassing. Uncle José María probably knew nothing about Benito's interest in his daughter, and in view of the circumstances of her birth there was no way of asking for her hand without risking a conflict of wide melodramatic possibilities. Rather than bring out into broad daylight what Mama Dolores was pained to regard as the family's blackest shame, Galdós chose not to alter the status quo. Nevertheless he clung to a dim hope of future happiness.

No one will ever know how severely shocked Galdós was when he learned that Sisita had married in Cuba. He may not have felt the full weight of the blow, since his father died at about the same time. The two griefs merged into one immense sadness which for a while crowded out everything else. Don Sebastián left this earth as inconspicuously as he had lived on it. His death threw Galdós' personal problems into sharper relief, for the economic affairs of the family were in a much worse state than anyone had realized. Besides the aged widow there were four spinster sisters to support. Of the male heirs only Ignacio was competent to administer the modest estate, but he was stationed in Cuba, risking his life for the military glory of Spain in sanguinary local fighting. It was a trying moment for Galdós, the more so since his personal misfortunes coincided with his literary and spiritual prepossessions. He could no longer depend entirely on family or relatives. It was high time that he became economically independent.

Benito Pérez Galdós was living in a trance. His life was a tangle of problems which he found impossible to solve in his emotional and spiritual state. The success of *La fontana de oro* was still inconclusive. Although the plaudits of the critics were gratifying, the sale of the book was rather discouraging. His enthusiasm for the great enterprise had not diminished, but he still lacked the spiritual energy to launch it. Until the hour of decision should arrive he sought distraction in study and in miscellaneous writing. He also did a little traveling. In the summer of 1871 he took his first trip to Santander, where he met Pereda. The city as well as the rest of the *montaña* region fascinated him and he resolved to establish his summer residence there. The early months of 1872 were a period of great productivity, but they brought him no closer to a decision. That came suddenly in the middle of the year.

Word reached Galdós that Sisita had died, leaving an infant daughter. The shock of the news roused him from his trance. In his own words, he returned to life. He now realized that during his prolonged daze he had been subconsciously formulating a plan of action and preparing himself for its execution. Now he saw clearly that bit by bit he had been marshalling his spiritual and artistic resources for the great enterprise. His aims were precise: he wanted to revitalize and modernize the national Spanish novel and at the same time provide an outlet for his desire for action. The great idea which the Glorious Revolution had failed to convert into a living reality; the great idea which was being stifled by ignorance, demagoguery, fanaticism, violence, intransigence, and all the other forms of moral and spiritual hideousness responsible for the deformed national conscience—this great idea would regain its force and vitality in a series of short, pleasant historical novels. Benito Pérez Galdós was called by destiny to lead a truly glorious revolution! He would give Spain not another government but a new national conscience.

*   *   *   *

In the middle of 1872 Galdós returned to life spiritually and withdrew from life in every other sense. Aside from intermittent contact with several publications, a few friends, and the Ateneo, he inaugurated an existence of monastic seclusion and dedicated himself to his mission with amazing zeal and energy. His whole being was absorbed in the great enterprise, and he shunned all else—politics, café *tertulias*, the theater, opera, music—like a horrible experience he was trying to forget.

In the solitude of his modest apartment he spent long hours, day and night, reading, meditating, dreaming and planning. His companions were for the most part the human creations of his fancy or of his evocative imagination. The silhouettes of historical figures of the nineteenth century mingled in kaleidoscopic fashion with vaguely outlined sketches of men and women he had known or run across in Madrid and Las Palmas. Two pressed themselves on him with particular persistence. One looked partly like Clara, the heroine of *La fontana de oro*, and partly like Mama Tate's little girl, for whom he used to pick orange blossoms from the tree in the patio of his home. The other figure vaguely resembled his father, but was much younger. The sight of the boy and the girl stirred many melancholy memories in him, and he felt alternating joy and sadness. It was a strangely soothing feeling which he wanted to retain as long as possible. Why not include the boy and girl among the characters of the novel he was planning?

What should be call that novel? *Trafalgar* would be a most appropriate title. It was to be the story of that terrible but glorious naval tragedy, an excellent starting point for the vast panorama of the nineteenth century he hoped to paint. After Trafalgar would come Bailén, Madrid, Zaragoza, Gerona, Arapiles, and many other places famous in Spanish history. Papa Pérez, renamed Gabriel Araceli, would be the narrator. It would be a fitting role for a heroic but humble patriot in a series of historical novels depicting heroism and patriotism. But what title should he give the series?

In those days José Luis Albareda was Galdós' literary father-confessor. With him he counseled about a number of details in connection with his gigantic literary plan. Don José Luis, with his unusual resourcefulness, suggested the descriptive and euphonic title of *Episodios nacionales*. Neither man suspected that the title would one day become almost a household term, yet it would not have been unnatural if privately Galdós hoped for just such a success.

Fortune accompanied Galdós on his first sally into fictionalized history. In the summer of 1872 he returned to Santander, where he began work on the first novel. In that delightful Cantabrian city he had a good friend, Amós de Escalante, a local writer of greater fame than merit. Galdós must have thought that the angels descended from heaven to collaborate with him when Escalante casually informed him during an afternoon stroll that the last survivor of the battle of Trafalgar lived in Santander. The very next day a meeting took place in the Plaza de Pombo between Galdós and the Trafalgar veteran, whose name was Galán. He was a very pleasant old man, short of stature, and he wore an antiquated afternoon coat and a high silk hat. In the famous battle he had served as a cabin boy on the then gigantic battleship *Santísima Trinidad*. That had been some seventy years back, but his memory was unimpaired and he supplied Galdós with many details about the life of sailors in war and peace—all of which were recorded faithfully and picturesquely in *Trafalgar*.

When the novel was published Galdós experienced none of the misgivings that had beset him upon the appearance of his other works. This time he knew well the spiritual and literary climate it would encounter. He had few doubts about the critics' reception of his first historical episode. They would be insincere and illogical if they failed to interpret his purpose as accurately and praise his accomplishment as unstintingly as they had done in the two previous instances. As for the public, whose reaction would determine the economic rather than the artistic success or failure of the venture, Galdós was inclined to credit it with good sense and sound judgment. Still he supplemented his optimistic opinion of the reader with an energetic advertising campaign. Albareda was again most helpful. Before *Trafalgar* went on sale he inserted a sixteen-page sample of it in *Revista de España* (number 120), describing it as the first of a series to be called *Episodios nacionales*. Other literary friends were not quite so generous, but all stressed Galdós' indisputable merit and right to reward. Aside from these supplementary measures, Galdós relied on the faith which leaders are wont to have in their own ability. If the public were to fail him this time, it would support him on the next occasion and on the many others to follow. If necessary, he was prepared to train a special reading public. It was a pretentious if not an inordinate ambition, but his determination and will were equal to its realization.

Early in 1873 *Trafalgar* was strategically displayed on the shelves and in the windows of the Madrid bookstores. It did not bear the general title of *Episodios nacionales;* that was to appear on the second volume of the series. The first returns were slow but not discouraging. As it was a long-range project, the early returns indicated to Galdós that he could confidently count on a moderately enthusiastic endorsement of his patriotic, artistic,—and financial—enterprise. The fortunes of *Trafalgar* were sufficiently gratifying not to discourage the prosecution of his original plan for ten volumes embodying the heroic history of Spain from the naval tragedy of Trafalgar to the battle of Arapiles. But regardless of results, he was resolved to fulfill the promise he made at the end of chapter one of *Trafalgar*.

Thus committed, Galdós worked enthusiastically and without respite, as if in response to a physiological urge. By the end of the first quarter of 1875 he had completed the first series—ten full-length novels in approximately two years! Now he was certain that the decision whose formulation had thrown him into a trance for almost three years had been a sound one. Few of his readers knew anything about him personally, but Benito Pérez Galdós, author of the *Episodios nacionales*—those popular-looking novels with the national colors on the front cover—was rapidly becoming a national figure and even a national myth. The great idea which had been dimmed by the Glorious Revolution was beginning to radiate some faint light. Benito Pérez Galdós had discovered his stride as a man of action.

The critics recognized Galdós' greatness with commendable freedom from the alleged Spanish vice of envy. They received *Trafalgar* and the succeeding novels with something like a violent explosion of long pent-up enthusiasm. The reviews were not numerous but they were nearly all panegyric. Emilio Huelin, mining engineer and honorary member of German and French academies, writing in *La Ilustración española y americana*, dusted off his manual on the art of poesy—possibly Hugo Blair's *Lecciones* in four volumes, 1804—compiled an exhaustive list of literary virtues, examined Galdós' work in the light of this list, and found it necessary to add a few that had not occurred to the eighteenth-century rhetoricians. At the height of his enthusiasm Don Emilio confidently predicted that *Trafalgar* would ultimately become the patrimony of European literature. He called on all good Spaniards—even the untutored—not to forego the delight and instruction inherent in this unusual work. And lest anyone question his authority as judge of literature, he referred the reader to the lofty pedestal on which Benito Pérez

Galdós had been placed by critics of the greatest learning and wisdom.

Benito Pérez Galdós would not have been human had he protested against the critics whose enthusiasm outdistanced their vocabulary. He must have been pleased when several of Madrid's leading dailies reproduced Huelin's eulogy. It was probably at his own suggestion that *La Nación,* his own literary cradle, inserted after the word *Trafalgar* in the title the following bit of advertising: "The forthcoming volumes will be: *La corte de Carlos IV, El Motín de Aranjuez, Bailén,* etc. etc." (Yet in later years Galdós often asserted that he had written *Trafalgar* without a complete plan, and that the other novels had occurred to him "unconsciously"!) Perhaps he was defending to himself the use of this device and others like it on the principle that the end justifies the means. The *Episodios nacionales* proved so attractive that other publications dangled them as bait to subscribers. As early as 1874 *La Guirnalda,* a fortnightly magazine "devoted to the fair sex," with which Galdós was associated as contributor and business partner, offered as a unique service to procure for its subscribers at reduced rates all the *episodios,* avowedly the most popular Spanish novels, unsurpassed in literary beauty, patriotic intention, and national inspiration.

The *episodios* were indeed popular. In the medical school of San Carlos they periodically claimed a greater share of the students' attention than did their studies. Too poor to buy individual copies even at the popular price of two pesetas, they formed *episodios* clubs. The members would enter the classroom with the latest novel snugly tucked away between vest and shirt, whence it was removed and read with delight as soon as the lecture got under way. If the lecturer got through before there was time to finish a chapter or a volume, the reader did not hesitate to miss the next class, sometimes more than one. A professor of clinical surgery once noticed among his inattentive students one who had a copy of the latest novel sticking out from his vest. "Look here," the professor jovially called the student to order, "you, the young gentleman with the national colors!" The class solemnly signified its approval of the professor's pleasantry. The "young gentleman"—Dr. Tolosa Latour—in time became one of Galdós' closest friends.

The spreading fame of the historical novels aroused considerable speculation concerning the age of the author. For some recondite reason the name Benito Pérez Galdós apparently suggests to the Spanish ear all that is associated with mature and even old age. Thus before meeting Galdós personally in 1871 Pereda had always imagined him to be a man of at least forty. Similarly, when Clarín first saw the name Benito Pérez Galdós on the cover of *El audaz* he instinctively assumed that the author was probably a contemporary of the first Spanish constitution of 1812. The readers of the first *episodios* reacted in the same way. There was a widespread impression in Madrid that Galdós was one of the oldest residents, an eye-witness of the events he so vividly evoked, who was spending the days of his retirement in pleasant literary reminiscences. His age rapidly became a topic of conversation and even impassioned discussion in the cafés.

The publication of *Cádiz* in the last quarter of 1874 inspired a serious wager as to Galdós' age among a number of *indianos*, members of the Casino Español de Méjico, who were visiting in Madrid. They decided to settle the controversy sensibly and subsidized a rich Cádiz merchant—it was naturally assumed that Galdós was a native of that city—to investigate the matter scientifically. Neither the amount of the stakes nor the names of the *indianos* have been recorded, but the interesting wager set agog more than one *tertulia*.

Galdós was unquestionably pleased with the anecdotal aspect of his mounting success. He was keenly delighted and even sentimentally moved by the reception of his novels at home. Mama Dolores doubtless had very sharp personal reactions, but she never made them public. In keeping with her peculiar sense of values she still regarded story-telling as an undignified occupation for a Galdós, but as a realist and fatalist she deemed it her duty to accept Benito's books as an unalterable fact and to appraise them honestly. She thus permitted the family to solemnize the appearance of each of the *episodios*. In fact, she instituted a new tradition in the household. When a novel arrived, she fixed the days and hours for its reading. All the Pérezs and Galdoses, their kin, and a few intimate friends were invited to assemble in the inner patio under the orange tree. Sister Dolores, the most accomplished of the four spinsters, was designated the official reader. The listeners were expected to maintain an attitude appropriate to the austere and dignified occasion. It frequently happened that a humorous passage moved the audience, including Mama Dolores, to a mirthful reaction that drowned out the voice of the reader. The latter had been enjoined never to interrupt the exercise; and when someone suggested that the laughter-provoking passage be repeated, inflexible Mama Dolores would promptly remind the assemblage that the occasion permitted no frivolity. Galdós' humor was appreciated solemnly at 33 Calle del Cano.

*   *   *   *

Much water had run over the political dams of Spain since the launching of Galdós' great enterprise for the redemption of the great idea. Amadeo lost his throne but saved his dignity and his conscience. His abdication on February 10, 1873, signified the failure of liberal constitutionalism. With incomprehensible political logic the Spaniards set up a republic which four successive presidents were unable to prevent from collapsing in less than two years. By December, 1874, a Bourbon—one of the family that in 1868 had presumably left Spain never to return—was restored to the throne. Alfonso XII was welcomed in Madrid as king of the Spaniards even as Prim, Serrano, and Topete had been welcomed six years before as the torchbearers of the Glorious Revolution.

This political whirlwind blew over Galdós' head and left him unaffected. He had charted his own course firmly and minutely, and the flotsam and jetsam of the Spanish ship of state could not impede his progress toward the goal he had set. Possibly he welcomed the restoration of the monarchy because it promised peace and tranquillity—two conditions he regarded as essential for the cultivation of the new novel. In the calm days ahead he would point the way to regeneration and redemption. He had made a great and irrevocable decision.

VI

The Creative Process

It is doubtful whether the career of any other Spanish author has been recorded in the press more fully and more intimately than that of Benito Pérez Galdós. He was always cordial to newspaper men, but as he was not given to expansive personal revelations, the conversation frequently turned on art and literature. His opinions received extensive publicity in the liberal newspapers and reviews, and they were elsewhere discussed with marked deference. From these opinions, which were always deliberate and carefully weighed, one could readily formulate a Galdosian esthetic of literature, but they suggest only remotely his notions about the creative process. Galdós, whenever he was asked a question on this point, was as evasive as most authors; in fact, he preferred not to discuss it. Sometimes he conveyed the impression that artistic creation was too intimate an experience to be analyzed in so many words. Once he came close to doing the impossible, however, and defined it as a state in which the imagination surrenders itself with complete abandon to vague and pleasant wandering, unimpeded by arid reason and uncontrolled by a directing will, in the difficult elaboration of a unified, logical, literary product of predetermined form and special structure. But beyond this he either told his questioners little or merely described his method of work.

The curious will derive little satisfaction from Galdós' account of the genesis of individual works. The novel *Gloria*, he told Clarín, was the result of a fortnight of enthusiastic application. The central idea occurred to him as he was walking on the Puerta del Sol, and it came to him suddenly, with the first part of the story completely outlined. The second part was spurious and *tourmentée*—he wished he had never written it—because he yielded to the opinion of "Señor X," who insisted that the theme and the thesis required fuller treatment. His monumental *Fortunata y Jacinta* presumably had a similarly fortuitous inception. While strolling through the Barrios Bajos he chanced upon Fortunata's prototype under circumstances very like those described in the opening pages of the novel. She was standing in the doorway of a tenement house, drinking a raw egg. His interest in the woman developed into an intimate relationship which eventually yielded much of the rich human content of the four-volume masterpiece.

First-night reviewers were importunate in their attempts to wrest from Galdós his artistic secrets, and he was fairly annoyed at them. One such, after the premiére of *Celia en los infiernos,* was determined to discover the origin of the theme and plot. Galdós dismissed the reviewer with what had become a stock answer, namely, that the idea had come to him unconsciously. And with ill-concealed irritation he added that he could not understand how other writers were able to keep telling their public about the inception of their works. He himself would undertake to describe the procedure he employed to develop an idea, but he could not honestly give an explanation of his inspiration.

Thus it is obvious that a factual investigation of Galdós' creative process can only lead to a reconstruction of his method and routine. For this the materials are readily available.

*   *   *   *

When blindness overtook Galdós in the last decade of his life, he complained bitterly about the difficulty of dictating to a secretary, because, as he expressed it, "the pen is nothing more than the prolongation of the spirit of the writer, who leaves a part of his being on the pages of his manuscript." [1] There is a suggestion in this observation that, objective though he was, he could not always prevent his personal experiences from intruding upon his fictional world. And his own life, notwithstanding his reputedly hermit-like existence, was varied, rich, and picturesque.

Even as a student Galdós had found the streets of Madrid more educational than classes and books. Until the day when physical ailments confined him to his room he continued to roam over the city, seeing everything with his small but penetrating eyes, and storing everything in his remarkably faithful memory. Day after day he strolled through the central streets and up and down the Barrios Bajos observing striking individuals, picturesque crowds, and colorful incidents, and scrutinizing interesting buildings and unusual vistas. Only Mesonero Romanos knew the capital better than Galdós. He cultivated the acquaintance of different social types and studied their speech with keen interest. He frequented popular and even disreputable bars, civic institutions, churches, and government buildings. Whenever in need of specialized knowledge he managed to gain entrance into an establishment not normally open to the public. In connection with *La de Bringas*, for example, he was allowed to inspect the picturesque parts of the Royal Palace which, during the early years of the Restoration, formed a sort of tenement district within the building for numerous bureaucratic parasites. To document *Misericordia* he obtained permission to pose as a municipal doctor making the rounds of the patients in the shabby dwellings of the poor, and he also found it necessary to camp among the gypsies and horse thieves on the outskirts of Madrid. To write authentically the opening scenes of *La desheredada* he examined the famous insane asylum of Leganés.

Galdós was not entirely secretive about his sources. Occasionally he took some of his closest friends into his confidence and even invited them to accompany him on his tours of observation. As a result, some of his secrets circulated privately even before his death, sometimes embarrassing those who were involved. The family was seriously annoyed because Laura, the heroine of the play *Alma y vida*, was so unmistakably a reconstruction of Madrina. The lady had been dead for several years and it did not seem to be a very delicate way of perpetuating her memory. Pepa Fúcar, that interesting character in *La familia de*

León Roch, was in time identified as the wife of a well-known general. The unique family of Bueno de Guzmán, essence of the absorbing novel *Lo prohibido,* lived under a different name on the Paseo de Recoletos; and María Juana, Eloisa, and Camila were in real life María, Luisa, and Micaela, daughters of a civil engineer who lived on the Plaza de la Independencia. The graphic viaticum scene involving Mauricia la Dura in *Fortunata y Jacinta* had really taken place in a tenement building called La Corrala on Calle Mesón de Paredes. The day of the actual incident Galdós had a bonanza. In the room with Mauricia sat a modestly dressed lady of a distinguished family—Ernestina Manuel de Villena. Rechristened Guillermina Pacheco though otherwise retaining her personality, she became the indefatigable lady of charity in the four-volume novel. She fully deserved the immortality thus bestowed upon her.

With regard to sources other than those of his characters Galdós was freely communicative. It would have availed him little to conceal the fact that he attended assiduously all the leading murder trials. The court proceedings did not always satisfy him, and he often interviewed the prisoners and the important witnesses. In the famous case of Father Galeote (1886), accused of shooting a bishop, he called on the priest in his cell and on his housekeeper, Doña Tránsito, at her home. The direct evidence he thus obtained, together with what he gleaned from popular discussion, enabled him to test the impressions he gathered during the trial. Father Galeote's case furnished material only for a lengthy story in a Spanish-American newspaper, but the sensational Calle de Fuencarral murder trial in 1889 yielded him two interesting novels, *La incógnita* and *Realidad.* His sedulous presence at all the sessions was widely commented on in Madrid. When the two novels appeared, the public understood that he had been interested in something more than the plastic court scenes and the due process of law. At this trial he learned great lessons about reality. The slow emergence of the truth out of the confusing evidence and the manifest lies of the criminals was compensation for the spiritual suffering he endured from the parade of so many horrors.

In gathering material for the *Episodios nacionales* Galdós found the traditional historical sources inadequate, since his purpose was the intimate portrayal of the masses rather than the recital of public events. What he needed was access to memoirs and private correspondence that would furnish personal documentation. But this was difficult, for the Spaniard is averse to recording intimate experiences sincerely, and he screens the memory of the dead from the public with exaggerated reverence. The press of the period which Galdós sought to reconstruct revealed little about the average citizen. The authoritarian governments then in power followed a policy of suppression, not revelation. But in the advertisements in the *Diario de Avisos*, Spain's oldest newspaper, Galdós discovered a mine of miscellaneous information. From these he extracted the wealth of color, period atmosphere, and national accent that characterizes the first ten volumes of the series. His task was somewhat easier in the next ten novels. Although he still had to lean frequently on imagination and inference, there were contemporaries of the period with whom he could converse and counsel. Mesonero Romanos and others furnished information unobtainable elsewhere. Also, works of Larra, Miñano, Gallardo, and Quintana, the comedies and farces of obscure authors, non-political newspapers, and even fashion magazines proved exceedingly useful.

As the artistic and educational merits of the historical novels were more widely recognized, access to source material became easier. Galdós often repeated with pride that the Conde de San Luis, founder of the *Heraldo de Madrid*, made available to him for an indefinite period his private file of that paper. The national and provincial governments, too, recognizing the significance of his works, opened to him the archives of the ministry of war and other official records. But Galdós preferred living documents, and these were most accessible in the conference room of Cortes, which he called his "living archive." There he spent hours listening to the recollections of elderly eye-witnesses of great events, and through them he became acquainted with associates of such historical figures as Prim and Amadeo. Meeting prominent persons was usually a strain because of his shyness, yet in

1900 he went to Paris to ask his friend Ambassador Fernando León y Castillo for an introduction to ex-Queen Isabel II. The interview was eminently profitable despite Galdós' bashfulness, and he did not soon forget his success with the former monarch. Other journeys in quest of data were less thrilling but even more enjoyable. He traversed the length and breadth of Spain many times, mostly in connection with his work. In his travels his keenest pleasure was to live, sometimes for weeks, with the humble survivors of humble historical happenings and go over with them the scenes of famous events.

Once the historical content of a novel was painstakingly assembled and the plan drawn up, the actual writing proceeded rapidly. Reporters gasped when Galdós told them in 1876 that he had written *La segunda casaca* in two weeks. That was of course the period of his most feverish creativeness, but twenty-two years later journalists were no less astonished over the genesis of *Zumalacárregui,* the first novel in the resumed series of *Episodios nacionales.* On Friday, March 18, 1898, he had returned to Madrid after an extensive research trip through Navarre, Vizcaya, and Guipúzcoa. Saturday he rose at six and began to arrange his copious notes and to make a skeleton outline of the story. That took two days. Monday, the twenty-first, was the day of his patron saint, San Benito. In years past he had rarely failed to observe the occasion with appropriate solemnity, frequently in the San Clemente convent in Toledo, where he attended a special service with almost mystic rapture. In 1898 San Benito Day went by unobserved. At eight in the morning Galdós began to write *Zumalacárregui.* On Friday, April 1, the printer was setting up the first hundred pages. Early in May the novel was placed on sale and was bought up by thousands of readers who eagerly welcomed the resumption of the *episodios* after a lapse of nineteen years.

*   *   *   *

Although very much the painter of Madrid life, Galdós nevertheless presents even in his non-historical works a cross-section of Spanish life. His characters, too, bear a national stamp which

critics have frequently stressed—they are Spanish and Madrilenian at the same time. The discovery of this national quality,
this common denominator of Spanish personality, Galdós made
in the course of his travels, whose extent and method came to be
talked of in quasi-legendary terms. Traveling was for him in the
nature of a physiological necessity, as pressing as his constant
urge to create.

He preferred to travel in third-class coaches and with a minimum of baggage. As a literary observer he found first-class
passengers devoid of individuality—standardized *señoritos* and
older aristocrats not much different from their social counterparts
in any other country. In third-class compartments, on the other
hand, he could see Spanish life in all its colorfulness, variety, and
individuality. He invariably sat inconspicuously in a corner of
the coach, closely observing his fellow travelers and listening to
their conversation. Whenever he could do so without arousing
suspicion he noted down unusual turns of speech or interesting
manifestations of popular psychology. Occasionally he even overcame his shyness and joined the passengers in their conversation,
but mostly as an attentive listener only. Generally he preferred
to remain in the background lest he be identified. On those
occasions when he was recognized as the author of the popular
Episodios nacionales he was all but terrified by the extemporary
homages and tributes he received at the railroad stations.

In regions not accessible by train Galdós resorted to mules
and donkeys. Indeed, he liked the less-traveled paths better than
the main roads, and for intimate glimpses of indigenous Spanish
life he favored villages and hamlets. The primitive inns and
roadside houses, with all their physical discomforts, appealed to
him more than the best-appointed hotels of the larger settlements. In general, he enjoyed traveling the hard way.

He set out on most of his trips with hardly any previous planning, much to the dismay of whatever personal servant happened
to accompany him. In later years it was usually faithful Manuel
Rubín. Galdós' greatest difficulty was to keep his movements
secret from the press, but generally he succeeded even in this.
When absent from Madrid he kept very few of his friends in-

formed of his whereabouts, but he was almost punctilious in his periodic reports to the family that he had no news. His usual message was the phrase *"sin novedad"* ("nothing to report") written on a cheap picture postcard and signed "Benito," or "Don Benito," or "B. Pérez Galdós." In this respect he treated everybody alike, including the scattered feminine friends with whom he maintained other than formal relations. These frequent junkets were of the essence of his creative process, and he was intolerant of any intrusion upon his privacy.

Galdós was exceedingly proud of his travels and retained lasting impressions of the delight they afforded him. In his old age, whenever younger writers foregathered in his den to comfort him in his lonely blind existence, he never wearied of relating his experiences and extolling the places he had visited. He liked to challenge his callers to mention the Spanish town with the quaintest name. It was a childish game which the venerable master was allowed to win every time. The pleasure of such victories was rivaled only by the joy of dwelling on the numerous admirers and friends he had won in his travels. He was proud of his correspondence with many of them and treasured their letters. They were evidence, he repeatedly claimed, of the mutual attraction between him and the people.

But Galdós' correspondence with the anonymous masses was more than a source of sentimental satisfaction. It afforded him a rich fictional vein. He was, generally speaking, a poor correspondent, but he always answered an interesting letter promptly and enthusiastically, especially if it came from a woman. With his remarkable intuition he was able to spot a promising writer where a less penetrating analyst might have dismissed him as merely one of the host of fawning, inarticulate admirers and unctuous, self-appointed critics. Those who were critical of his works intrigued and challenged him, and he often invited them to call on him. It was in this way that he met the cultivated woman who became his one great love. Many women wrote to Galdós, often in terms so sincerely personal that he could not resist the temptation to meet them. Since it would not always have been politic or practical to have them call on him, he frequently arranged to meet them in their own homes. Among these women he discovered prototypes for his characters as well as some of the creatures who gratified the demands of his physical nature. Those were the women who, like a powerful magnet, drew Benito away from home almost daily during the afternoon hours—a routine which mystified his doting sisters and suspicious nephews for many, many years.

Obviously, then, Galdós came to his work documented, informed, and experienced. Many of the characters that vitalize his novels and plays had their prototypes among his acquaintances, and the actions by which they are defined correspond to experiences both observed and lived. Galdós did not, as has occasionally been asserted, always carry a notebook and pencil to jot down what he saw and heard. Though he had a mania for saving, even hoarding, maps, railroad guides and steamship schedules, hotel bills and banquet menus, invitations and announcements, posters and advertisements, he left to posterity few notes relating to his work. The almost total lack of such documents certainly deprives the student of valuable if not indispensable sources.

Some of the Galdosian material that has been preserved throws interesting light on his creative process. He was in the habit of drawing pencil sketches of his characters, which he kept before him as he wrote. A number of these sketches, elaborated into pen-and-ink drawings, he used for the illustrated edition of the *Episodios nacionales*. As his gallery of characters grew and he found it increasingly difficult to remember in what works some of them appeared and the role they played, he constructed a set of intricate family trees. In most other respects he depended more often on his imagination than on concrete memory aids, but he did have lists of picturesque expressions, notes on technical items of commerce, street and place names, dress and occupations, and lists of proverbs of decidedly anticlerical flavor. He rarely resorted to outlines, except in the case of the dramatic version of *Marianela;* of this he made a very careful sketch, which he revised repeatedly. Even the rigorously documented *episodios* were apparently written with a minimum of reference to notes. A list of bibliographical items, a map, an original document such as a letter or a manifesto, an occasional sketch, a list of answers to specific questions addressed to a competent eye-witness of an historical event, a diagram of the interior of a building, a few books profusely and heavily underlined and marked up with dates, question marks, and innumerable *ojos* (the Spanish equivalent of N.B.)—this is a fairly comprehensive record of the sort of thing Galdós kept before him for consultation during the composition of novels that required a staggering amount of study and research.

Galdós' personal library, strikingly poor in works of science, erudition, and philosophy, was probably not exceedingly useful to him. It can best be described as the collection of a cultured person who manifestly specialized in drama, fiction, and poetry. To what extent he read the purely belles-lettres works on his shelves is hard to say. He certainly paid slight attention to the numerous books he received from obscure colleagues. Their effusive dedicatories did not even move him to cut the pages of many of them. That task he reserved for his young literary callers. However, the curious and comparatively rare histories, encyclopedias, dictionaries, and general reference works that he possessed were all used frequently and extensively. This may be inferred from the numerous strips of paper which he used as bookmarks and rarely removed from the volumes consulted. But Galdós' library unquestionably reflects only a negligible fraction of the vast knowledge, often highly specialized, which he gathered for his needs somehow and somewhere. The question of how learned he was is largely an academic one. Conceivably his reserve of wisdom was greater than his knowledge, but for a creative writer this can hardly be regarded as a handicap.

*   *   *   *

How and when did Galdós write?

He rose very early, usually at dawn, and soon thereafter entered his study. His personal servant or one of the two sisters who lived with him both in Madrid and Santander had preceded him with a glass of strong black coffee and a pitcher of hot boiled milk. On his table there were two small wooden stands, one for paper and the other for the manuscript. The paper was in half-sheets, evenly cut and carefully paginated.

Sipping his coffee, to which he gradually added milk until its strength was reduced to the conventional Spanish *café con leche*, Galdós began to write. He rarely went over the manuscript of the previous day; that had already been done for him by his spinster sister Concha, who read all his works, as it were, in serial form. Doña Concha invariably obliged her brother, even before he settled down, with a summary and criticism of the previous "installment." To make sure that he would resume the thread of the story properly, she sometimes looked over his shoulder for a while. Such interference, however, was not allowed very often. In the heat of creation only two beings were permitted in the study: the author and his muse.

The beginning of a book always came rather hard. For the relief of his nerves Galdós had at hand a supply of scratch paper. Random sketching and concentrated figuring in all the four operations inevitably provided relief. Once the vein was discovered, the precious metal came steadily and abundantly. Cursive, clearly formed, diminutive letters filled page after page, which changed stands in rapid succession. Galdós wrote with fervor and enthusiasm. Occasionally, when his exuberant imagination required a moment of rest, he would stop writing, stare at the narrow space between the lines or at the margin, and distractedly begin to sketch a figure suggested by the last figment of his imagination. It might be a delicately drawn head of a girl, a landscape or marine scene, a boat in fine detail, a cross, an architectural sketch, a cartoon, or some fantastic mosaic. If worldly cares were besetting the creator, it might be a rapid succession of arithmetical exercises casting up the coffee consumption for the week, the cigar bill for the day, the taxes and mortgage still unpaid on his summer home (San Quintín), or the royalties the new novel might be expected to net. Ill-chosen words or awkward phrases were often covered up with similar aberrations of the imagination. Generally speaking, however, Galdós made few changes or corrections. Almost always the first thought was the happy one, and the original expression the appropriate one. Now and then he compressed. Occasionally he substituted a popular turn of speech for a venerable phrase. Sometimes he rearranged several paragraphs. The completed manuscript was so neat that it hardly looked like a first draft. But it always was. Galdós never once rewrote a whole page.

While he wrote, no one disturbed him. He rarely interrupted his work to contemplate from his study window the beautiful vista of the Cantabrian Sea in Santander or to sweep the Madrid skyline with a glance. His favorite position was extremely awkward—desk pad on lap, knees raised, and his long legs pushing against the drawer. In winter—as a Canarian he felt the cold—he had a cape thrown over his right shoulder, a fine Mexican blanket wrapped around his legs, and a Basque beret covering his head and pulled over his right ear. If he suspected the arrival of a caller he would exclaim in a nervous, impatient voice: *"No estoy para nadie—ni Cristo Padre ni Dios bendito"* ("I am not at home to anyone—not even Christ the Father or the Blessed Lord"). This wish was always scrupulously respected by the household. At one o'clock he stopped writing, and after a frugal lunch consumed in silence with his family he would leave for unannounced destinations, on literary and mysteriously intimate missions.

Galdós' creative process functioned silently and methodically. Upon the completion of a work there was a brief spell of exuberance and exultation, then a period of sharp and constant anxiety over the reaction of the critics. This feeling was slightly mitigated by the dim recollection of the joy that had filled the hours of creation. Then came the irksome job of reading proof. Galdós disliked going over his own work. Revising a novel for a new edition he regarded as a form of divine punishment. But he was not one to shirk responsibilities. Since he could not delegate the task to someone else, he tried to derive as much pleasure as possible from doing it himself.

His pockets bulging with galley proof, he would call on some fascinating "woman of the people," in whose company he did the correcting. He possessed the unusual ability to combine meticulous proofreading with participation in the charming chatter of his companion. For the most part he made changes only to eliminate awkward repetition and correct errors of orthography and punctuation. Above all, he regarded repetition as an unpardonable stylistic sin, and to avoid guilt on this score he often requested someone in the family to check the galleys scrupulously and replace all repeated words with suitable synonyms.

In general, style preoccupied Galdós more than any other aspect of the novelistic art. In his younger days he wrote spontaneously and with fair assurance of his stylistic power, but the older he grew the less confident he was of his ability to use the Spanish language effectively. Whenever he had to write a formal piece, such as a political speech, he was plagued by the fear of putting every word in the wrong place. Once he dictated a message to the people of Argentina. When it was read back to him, he was horrified by the frequent repetition of the name of the country and asked his secretary if there was not a satisfactory synonym for it. More serious than stylistic details was the matter of verbosity and diffuseness. Galdós was aware of his tendency to give his imagination free reign, which often resulted in stylistic incontinence. This artistic sin had forced him to abandon the short story fairly early in his career and it led him, while proofreading, to prune narrative passages mercilessly. It was otherwise with dialogue. Here he felt that he was forging something new, and his chief concern was not brevity but appropriateness and naturalness. Moreover, convinced that conversation was the most effective means of revealing personality, he regarded amplitude as a virtue in this instance.

When the proofreading had been completed, fear of the critics returned to plague Galdós. He knew that in most cases their judgments were inspired either by unwarranted generosity or by an indefensible and studied objectivity. He was convinced, too, that posterity would radically revise their opinions. He himself had been a literary critic in his younger days, and he realized how easy it was to find fault and to rule pontifically. Despite all this he never learned to regard with equanimity this stage of the creative process. Though his successive works were received with increasing enthusiasm, he never ceased to be apprehensive lest some arrogant and self-constituted literary judge should misunderstand his purpose and misinterpret his finished product. He was not inclined to underestimate his talents and skills, but he retained a degree of genuine modesty about the general merit of his works. Paradoxically, the man who had embarked upon his career fully confident of his ability to effect a literary revolution rarely felt sure about his ultimate position in Spanish letters.

In 1883, after the stupendous testimonial banquet at which he was hailed as Spain's leading literary figure, Galdós wrote the following in accepting a distinction conferred upon him by the Gabinete Instructivo of Santa Cruz de Tenerife:

> I cannot rid myself of the idea that certain tributes which are tendered to living authors who are still enveloped, one might say, in the heat of battle, present this danger: that posterity, which is always infallible, may revoke them in time, modifying or even nullifying the quite premature judgment of contemporaries.

In 1904, when the production of *El abuelo* raised his stock as a dramatist to a point which it had reached only once before and he was invited by *Le Temps* to write an article on the Spanish stage, he first forwarded his essay to his young friend Manuel Bueno in Paris. Manuel Bueno was to decide whether it deserved to appear in the French newspaper.

Galdós' lack of self-confidence was particularly conspicuous in the field of the drama. While he resented the ex-cathedra judgments of the reviewers—in 1894 he denounced them with surprising arrogance—he accepted without a murmur of protest the suggestions made by actors. His greatest difficulty was compression and compactness—he tended to proceed at the leisurely pace of the novel. During the rehearsals of *Mariucha* in Barcelona, actress María Guerrero announced categorically that she was going to cut three pages from the last scene of the second act. Galdós replied calmly but seriously: "They will be well cut. Let us have lunch now, and after that you can tell me when and where three more pages will have to be cut." [2]

One can only speculate how Galdós viewed his monumental output in retrospect. His dramas apparently lingered in his memory as children taking their first steps under solicitious supervision. He remembered vividly the première of each one and recalled how he sat in the wings of the stage, his eyes moist with tears, following with emotion the unfolding of scenes and acts. Of his novels it would seem that *Marianela* was his favorite. It was the only one that he reread—and he did so frequently— and the only one he was determined to see dramatized. For a number of years he negotiated with Valle Inclán for its dramatization, and at one time he undertook to do it himself. The Quinteros finally did the job, and Galdós rewarded them with his personal copy of the novel. It is an interesting bit of evidence of his intense fondness for *Marianela*—its margins are profusely covered with comments in his own hand. For his other works his preferences varied periodically. However, to inquiring reporters he mentioned most frequently *La campaña del Maestrazgo, Fortunata y Jacinta, Electra,* and *Mariucha.* In the case of the historical novel his preference was based upon the perfection with which he thought he had developed his initial idea. He was attached to *Fortunata y Jacinta* because of the circumstances attending its genesis, and he thought highly of two plays because of their success with the reading public.

*   *   *   *

This is all that can be said of Galdós' creative process. It was in reality the process of a highly methodical person who planned far ahead, at times as long as four or six works. His claim that his inspirations were spontaneous and unconscious were probably sincere. The first impulse seized him like a passion. In this as well as in his creative energy and power of improvisation he was typically Spanish. For his speed of composition and for his fertility—between 1873 and 1918 his pen rested only once, in 1917—he takes his place among Spain's literary immortals. All in all, Galdós' impressive output of novels, dramas, short stories, articles, and essays was the result of a typically Spanish creative process.

VII

The Dawn of Glory

WHILE GALDÓS AND HIS STEADILY multiplying readers were vicariously reliving in the *Episodios nacionales* the heroic events of the first third of the nineteenth century, the Spanish political pot was simmering monotonously. Now that the Republic had been succeeded by the restored monarchy, both conservatives and liberals, and even republicans, rushed to feather their nests under the new restful regime. Only the Carlists, stubborn defenders of the letter of the Salic Law, maintained an intransigent attitude, but their intermittent uprisings in the northern fastnesses had long been accepted as the logical sub-plot of the Spanish political tragi-comedy. Henceforth there was to be only one gospel for all the faithful—"functionarism"—and its apostles were to be alternately the conservative Antonio Cánovas del Castillo and the liberal Práxedes Mateo Sagasta. Since Cánovas was the first to reach the altar of the rededicated temple of the monarchy, Sagasta temporarily performed the duties of acolyte in the unholy ritual calculated to earn salvation for the tormented political soul of Spain.

Sagasta, a former revolutionary, became the leader of the liberal monarchists, a heterogeneous assemblage of politicians ranging all the way from old supporters of Amadeo to a few republicans. Ostensibly unified by Sagasta's new "dogma" of support for the king and the so-called national interests, they were in reality moved by the desire to retain what they held and, if possible, to increase their holdings. Their leader easily convinced them that while making common cause with Cánovas, who upheld the Bourbon dynasty, they would not necessarily lose their identity as zealous guardians of individual rights and freedom of conscience. Sagasta was convinced that the maintenance of national order—the only animating principle of Cánovas' political philosophy—was not incompatible with personal liberty and the rights of man. He felt sure that somehow he could harmonize the strident notes of the revolutionary Riego hymn with the grave psalmody of the Royal March. His Constitutional Party would combat the excesses of demagoguery as well as the atrocities of conservatism. To put it bluntly, if absolute sovereignty was unattainable, the politicians could at least enjoy the national budget.

With the inalienable rights of the political leaders and their followers thus harmonized, the national election of 1875 brought happiness to all factions. For the first time in many years the country was organized on a basis of normalcy. But it was a vapid and drowsy normalcy of flatulent common sense and bombastic verbiage. The Cortes of 1876, assembled to frame a sensible constitution—one that would skillfully adapt advanced principles of government to the peculiar temperament and traditions of the governed—flooded the land with torrents of stereotyped concepts, banal ideas, and outmoded hyperboles. The sessions were a continuous marionette performance, manipulated by string-pullers representing both the conservative majority and the liberal minority. Between scenes a few unaffiliated performers were shoved forward on the stage as if to convince the audience that not all the actors were mechanical figures. Even the great republican leader Castelar was occasionally permitted to recite his favorite thrilling numbers from the days of the Republic.

Not within the memory of any of the deputies had there been so dazzling a display of verbal pryotechnics: recrimination, threats, denunciations; but all of it was hopefully directed toward union and tranquillity. Alejandro Pidal y Mon predicted a dire future for the regime that failed to conciliate the Carlists, and he blamed Cánovas for failing to enlist their cooperation. Venerable Claudio Moyano, determined to extinguish even the faintest revolutionary spark, excoriated the Glorious Revolution and in lurid colors painted its supporters as frivolous and criminal demagogues. Castelar and General Pavía came to grips over the dissolution of the republican Cortes by force of arms on January 3, 1874. Sagasta, as if to cool the overheated air, waved energetically the flag of national sovereignty, and Cánovas, for whom the art of government was a game of ministerial permutations and combinations, swept away the differences of the rhetorical gladiators by opening the dikes of his eloquent logic and bidding them all lay down their swords at the base of the altar of Alphonsine legality.

Peace and tranquillity came as suddenly as violence and tumult. Prompted by disillusionment, or perhaps by a universal desire for relief from the harrowing experience of recent years, the nation settled down to a routine existence characterized by apathy toward everything that did not concern the immediate material welfare of the individual. The surging passions and stirring enthusiasms of yesterday gave way to spiritual torpor and mental stagnation. It mattered little that in the north the Carlists still rattled their sabers and pointed the mouth of their cannon at the throne. When the rattling grew too loud, the king's glorious army executed a few heroic gestures and returned triumphant from the field of battle. What if constitutionalism was a mockery so long as the restored throne gave back to the country splendor, pageantry, and festivity? It was far more pleasant to watch military and regal parades on the Puerta del Sol than to dodge bullets. And at the café *tertulias* only fools preferred plotting against real or imaginary enemies of progress to choosing a consort for the young monarch. After all, the paramount duty of a regime is the happiness of the people—and under the Restoration the people enjoyed the relaxing drowsiness that follows a savory meal.

The Restoration distributed its blessings among all save the uncompromising republican plotters in exile and the recalcitrant Carlists in the north. In the years since the Glorious Revolution there had grown up an army of impoverished *cesantes* (dismissed government officials) in whose favor the wheels of fortune were now turning. Conservatives and liberals alike were elevated to high positions through the studied generosity of Cánovas and

Sagasta. Their tasks were light and pleasant, even if their reward was not always commensurate with their talent and merit. They were indolent and irresponsible as a class, delegating their duties but not their authority to those below them on the official scale. One ambition stimulated them all—to incarnate and personify the cumbersome bureaucracy of the Spanish state.

Those seeking social honors and titles of distinction had a veritable heyday under the restored monarchy. The ranks of Spain's old aristocracy of blood were swelled by recruits from the numerous slave-trafficking *Indianos*, enriched merchants, and successful stock-market speculators. King Amadeo had elevated many of them to the topmost rung of the ladder of nobility— and Alfonso XII was not to be outdone by his predecessor. The rapidly multiplying counts and marquises of the new vintage vied among themselves in servility to the Palace and in purely formal respect to the Church. The older ones limited their ambition to social recognition, but their offspring, the *señoritos*, aspired to munificent government appointments. They were foppish, empty-headed university graduates who evolved new standards of elegance and deportment. Vain about their appearance and manners—these were their only values in life—they held in contempt those outside their class, those whom they condemned as the abominable proletarian mass. Although the *señoritos* regarded themselves as the source of national vitality, they took little pride in their country. France was for them the only civilized land, and after a brief sojourn there they found everything Spanish worthy only of derision. Indeed, high society under the Restoration so distorted the norms of Spanish life as to retard progress and permit the slow generation of forces that were destined to bring about violent national explosions.

The lower social reaches, too, carved out their particular groove in the new scheme of things. Their behavior was largely motivated by a desire for easy living, fashionable dress, and money effortlessly acquired. Baldomera Larra, daughter of the famous essayist of the romantic period, satisfied the public's and her own craving for easy wealth by founding a so-called Popular Bank in Madrid. Lured by the promise of heavy profits, numerous Madrilenians trusted her to invest their savings in American mines of gold, silver, and other precious metals. Some even sold their modest possessions and property in order to have a share in Doña Baldomera's attractive investments. The enterprising "banker" eventually had to flee to Switzerland, taking with her the savings of her depositors and leaving to posterity an interesting index of the mentality and spiritual state of the age.

The tranquillity that came with the Restoration instilled in the masses an abiding faith in the permanent stability of everything and a sort of limitless credulity. It was thus easy for quacks, known as "apostles," to sell at high prices to the residents of the Barrios Bajos cure-all medicines consisting of none-too-clean water. As in the case of Doña Baldomera's promised financial millennium, the government was unaccountably slow in delivering the dupes from the hands of the miracle-workers. Perhaps the government could not with a clear conscience penalize the practitioners of an art that resembled the one it practised itself so profitably. Was not Cánovas a stupendous magician who had mesmerized the most turbulent generation of Spaniards?

*   *   *   *

In those days of the Restoration—days of spiritual drowsiness and creeping stultification for Spain—Galdós struggled against sadness, depression, apathy. He still adhered to the quasi-monastic routine he had inaugurated in 1873. He shunned the halls of Cortes, the rarified atmosphere of the political circles, and the *tertulias* in the cafés. Even the Ateneo attracted him less and less, and if it had not been for the imperious necessity of maintaining contact with the literary world, he would probably have avoided it altogether. But he could not afford to slight old acquaintances nor to miss the opportunity of cultivating new ones. In the Ateneo were Manuel de la Revilla, Luis Alfonso, Leopoldo Alas (Clarín), and Palacio Valdés—the last two recent arrivals—whose services were of inestimable value to him.

Association with these men gave Galdós much-needed encouragement for the continuation of the historical novels. There was, of course, no question of suspending his work now; the response of the public had been too magnificent and the income from the *episodios* too gratifying. Yet, by and large, he was losing the deep faith and exultant enthusiasm with which he had embarked upon the enterprise. So much in the contemporary scene turned out to be more disillusioning than he had anticipated. Although he had convinced himself long before the Restoration that the salvation of Spain could not be won through politics, it was nevertheless impossible to accept the painful reality with equanimity. The banal actualities depressed Galdós spiritually. Day followed day with dull, gray monotony. Yesterday, today, tomorrow seemed like a barren stretch over which rolled heavy, dark clouds, following one another in meaningless pursuit. Memories were blear and hope was dim. He felt that he was slowly lapsing into a trance similar to the one he had experienced between 1870 and 1873.

For Galdós with his keen historical sense of Spanish life and his power to discern the eternal strains of the national character even in the most superficial incidents, the early years of the Restoration were a period of anguish and anxiety. On March 20, 1876, he watched the entrance of Alfonso XII into Madrid at the head of the troops that had scored the latest triumph over the Carlists. The incessant civil wars, despite the successive victories of the so-called liberal forces, made him sick at heart. He found it pathetic that Spaniards should periodically feel elated over the cessation of hostilities which failed to insure peace. In his opinion the time to eradicate the malady had been back in 1834, when Don Carlos María Isidro first entered the country at Elizondo and planted the germ. What did it avail now to suppress the occasional uprisings? Since 1834 the issue had transcended the simple question of dynastic succession. The civil wars reflected the resolute determination of the forces of bigotry to control Spanish life at the center, to poison the heart and kill the body of the nation.

The gestures made by the Restoration to create the impression that Spain was governed by a liberal constitution struck Galdós as ludicrous. The return of the Bourbons did not restore the country's natural dignity, nor did it set her on the path of progress; it only reinstated arbitrary government in which Altar and

Throne joined forces for the oppression of the masses through continued poverty and ignorance. Old familiar specters were once again stalking in Cortes, in the Palace, and in the spiritual institutions of the land. Despite the liberal constitution, army generals multiplied, multitudes of old and new functionaries jostled one another for preferred positions at the "national manger," politicians ruled by the formula of inertia, empty formulas of the past were revived. The Restoration did more than restore a dynasty—it literally brought back the past.

As the months dragged on, public affairs were reduced to the boring trivialities debated in Cortes and the monarch's trips to exhibit himself to his subjects. Nowhere did Galdós discern an attempt to solve the nation's religious, economic, or cultural problems. The conservatives did nothing, and the liberals thus had nothing to oppose. In the midst of this do-nothingness the monarchy was secure, and so too were the bureaucrats and *caciques* (political bosses) and the spiritual advisers of the crown. Most disappointing to Galdós was the State's failure to restrain the revived influence of the Church in the private life of the Spaniards. He thought that, paradoxical though it might seem, Spanish tradition demanded vigorous protest by the throne against the intervention of church authority. That was the stand that had been taken by Charles V, Philip II, and Charles III against the popes from Clement VII to Clement XII. But Alfonso XII was not the sort of monarch to assert himself against the Vatican. To be sure, the pope no longer interfered in the affairs of the Spanish state after he lost his temporal power through the unification of Italy, but he achieved the ends of the Church more effectively through a more tightened dogma and stricter control of the Spanish Catholic conscience.

Two events served to deepen Galdós' disgust with the new regime. The baptismal ceremony of the daughter born to Alfonso XII and María Cristina accentuated the ludicrous nature of palace honors. Military, religious, political, and financial dignitaries squabbled over the preferential places at the ritual in the royal chapel. In vulgarity and grotesqueness the occasion rivaled the hair-pulling scenes staged by fisherwomen in the Spanish seacoast towns. Frivolity reached new heights when the monarch distributed commemorative honors and favors. Spain's public figures sought and grabbed decorations and titles with an avidity that bordered on farcical delirium. An orgy of banquets was held at which ministers sat as guests of honor and eloquence flowed more freely than the champagne which was served liberally as a matter of protocol. The press virtually burst with lengthy accounts of the celebrations and generous reproductions of vapid speeches. The nation seemed deliriously joyous over the birth of the princess, though there were some among the pilots of Spain's destiny who recalled 1834 with a shudder. Would the tender princess some day plunge the country into a fratricidal war as her grandmother Isabel II had done?

Even more serious in the opinion of Galdós was the descent upon Spain of numerous friars expelled from France. They came swarming in from all directions. But he felt that it would be premature to declare open war on the Jesuits. In ironic mood he told a friend that he would gladly become a deputy of Sagasta's Fusionist Party if he was also appointed Inspector of Nuns with full charge of institutions where the cloistered of both sexes could be united in contemplative life. More seriously he suggested that the religious would bear watching as they exerted their influence upon national life. He was willing to let them assume their definitive position in order to test their ingenuity and battle strength. The fact that Spanish ladies of means and position rushed to extend a welcome to the guests did not worry him unduly, since it was not prompted by a spiritual impulse or a religious upsurge; the ladies were only following an established Spanish social practice. They were carrying on the tradition of "the elegant sanctimonious swarm" [1] which made up the ruling class of Spain. They adopted the Jesuits because they knew it was impossible to realize social or political ambitions without pretending to befriend the spiritual descendants of Loyola.

Nevertheless the influx of the foreign Jesuits was a grave national problem not easily solved. Galdós harbored no illusions about what the politicians could or would do. They were busy alternating in control of the nation's interests for their personal

gain and permitted many other important problems to go un-
solved. Agriculture was not progressing, the working class was
neglected, the army was expanded, schools were scarce, and legal
pomp flourished at the expense of commerce and industry. Obviously a government that showed such slight concern for the
country's welfare could not be expected to interfere with the
Church in general or the Jesuits in particular. In time these
would absorb education, wealth, civil power, and even national
independence.

For Galdós, Spain of the Restoration was a dead country without ideals and without interest in its destiny—a country in the
process of decomposition. Worst of all, there was no remedy in
sight. It would be idle, he believed, to turn to the old revolutionaries of 1868 or to the Sagasta liberals. The weight of tradition
was so heavy upon the Spanish body and soul that free movement
in the direction of progress and civilization seemed impossible for
the present. It would take years—perhaps even decades—before
the existing regime, suffering from an attack of "ethnic tuber-
culosis," [2] would be replaced by one with new blood and new
"foci of mental light." [3]

But time is a slow healer, and relief, however temporary, was
urgently needed. It finally occurred to Galdós that although
revolution was a terrifying word, it might be used at least as
a term to conjure with in order to overcome the atrophy of the
national will. A revolutionary attitude, firmly asserted now and
then, might serve to stimulate the nation into action and life.
Once before he had heeded the call to create a national conscience.
His task was not yet completed. It was his duty and destiny to
be the voice of virile, romantic protest.

                    *   *   *   *

The restoration of the Bourbon dynasty influenced Galdós
even more profoundly than the Revolution of 1868. Since he had
come to identify his literary career with the nation's spiritual
welfare, he was led to pause and examine his achievements
as a national writer and perhaps to revise his conception of his
role. In addition to the contemporary scene, there were purely
literary considerations that obliged him to seek a new orientation,

one that would satisfy him artistically and hasten his contemplated revolution in the Spanish novel.

Three years of incessant labor had brought gratifying results in terms of popular appeal and financial returns. Considering the small number of Spaniards who read native novels that were not published serially, Galdós had good reason to be pleased with the sale of the *episodios*. The success of the first ten encouraged him to continue with the second series. One by one the novels came off the Guirnalda press almost as regularly as the installments of a serial story, gradually forcing the *novela por entregas* out of circulation and even offering serious competition to its successor, the peseta-apiece novel which was being peddled unobtrusively in the cafés. Contrary to his repeated assertions that he was not writing for profit or popularity, Galdós took a keen interest in the commercial aspect of his enterprise. His was the idea of the national colors on the outside cover, the uniform length, the low price of two pesetas, and the regularity of appearance. His, too, was the strategy of the advertising campaign managed by the publishers—he was, in point of fact, associated with Guirnalda as his own publisher. And it was his literary contacts that secured for the historical novels even the limited attention they received in the press.

The literary success of the *episodios* was something more difficult to define. Reviews of them were few and by obscure writers, mostly personal friends of the novelist and perhaps inspired by him. Of the competent critics Manuel de la Revilla was the first to take notice of these novels in 1874. About three years later, Clarín and Palacio Valdés, whose friendship with Galdós was new but strong, began to sponsor them enthusiastically, albeit not very objectively. Had it not been for the fact that literary criticism was in its infancy in Spain during the seventies, Galdós might have been tempted to say with Fígaro that "to write for the public in Spain is like reciting a monologue in solitude." [4]

There were little guidance and few helpful suggestions in the occasional reviews. The most constant and consistent critic was Emilio Huelin, who was primarily a mining engineer and not a writer. His wanton praise would have been excessive even for an author thirsting for applause. Galdós probably considered Don Emilio's enthusiasm malapropos when, in the review of *El 19 de marzo y el 2 de mayo*—written in the era of modern Spanish republicanism—he placed a scepter in the author's hands and seated him on the throne of the kingdom of Spanish novelists. The same reviewer's appraisal of *Bailén* was hyperbolically fulsome. With obvious *non constat* reasoning unworthy of a German-trained scientist, Huelin said that Galdós' varied and convincing characters were paintings worthy of the brush of Goya, genre pictures from the palette of Velázquez, descriptions with the coloring of Titian and the chiaroscuro of Rembrandt! In a purely literary sense, he insisted, the *Episodios nacionales* contained pages as good as those in George Eliott (*sic*), narrations reminiscent of Cervantes, and qualities superior to those universally recognized in the novels of Berthold Auerbach.

Other critics were more moderate, but not entirely unbiased. Some were influenced by moral considerations of the author's courageous task or by their ideological preferences; others were pedantic and dogmatic in the manner of the Renaissance and eighteenth-century preceptists. The most intelligent was Revilla, but he was given to dressing up trivial reactions in abstract and pseudo-philosophic verbiage which gave them a tone of false profoundness. Even in his less austere moments he spoke condescendingly, as if he were stretching the quality of mercy. Only two ideas stood out clearly in Revilla's criticism: that Galdós rarely overcame the principal difficulty of the historical novel—the duality of historical and fictional action—and that he lacked warmth of passion and lyricism. Flattered as Galdós no doubt was to be treated with deference by Spain's ace critic, he must have been irritated by Don Manuel's feigned generosity and ill-concealed pedantic arrogance. Having for a number of years masqueraded as a literary pundit himself, he knew how much presumptuous authority could parade beneath a critic's toga.

But the paucity of formal criticism was offset by the informal discussion of the *episodios* wherever members of the Spanish intelligentsia met to kill time. Opinions were naturally varied, and in most instances they sprang from considerations only remotely related to literature. For those who, with amazing elasticity of conscience, called themselves the intellectual youth Galdós was already a celebrated author, the peer of the most famous in England and France. To give his artistic achievement the exalted position it allegedly deserved, the works of other novelists were contemptuously swept up into a dark corner. He was a lone star in the Spanish literary firmament, the only clear thinker of all those who offered a welter of ideas for national regeneration. It was frequently claimed that not since Cervantes had an author displayed such talent in speaking of the people, to the people, in the language of the people. Other writers were admittedly more formally artistic, but none were comparable to Galdós in creative power, spontaneity, fertility, gravity of matter, and lightness of manner. He alone revived the native literary traditions, and he alone led the Spaniards to see themselves as they really were. It was a pity, moaned the panegyrists, that in Spain so few people knew how to read and fewer still had the habit of buying books of such wholesome and enlightening entertainment.

The older intellectuals—more particularly the writers among them—were far from willing to place the laurel wreath on Galdós' brow. Quite the contrary, their instinct of self-preservation forced them into defensive methods against his rapidly rising reputation and much talked-of worth. And when Clarín, in his self-assigned role of police-critic, concentrated his protective power almost exclusively on Galdós, the old generation took the law into its own hands. Against their conscience and better judgment they stubbornly refused to concede to Galdós any of the artistic and philosophic powers claimed for him by the young intellectuals. There were, of course, exceptions. Men like Castelar and even Cánovas received the historical novels with commendable magnanimity. *Cádiz*, with its brilliant evocation of the infancy of Spanish liberal constitutionalism, led Castelar, the last president of the fast-dying republic, to discover in Galdós a worthy emulator of his own apostolic zeal, and he publicly predicted for him a place among humanity's immortals.[5] But other elders could not keep envy out of their opinions, which by their own admission were formulated on the basis of what others said about the *Episodios nacionales*. In this instance, as in others, they insisted on the right of authors not to read what others wrote. And lest they be accused of an insincere pose, some frankly told Galdós himself that they still had to discover his historical novels. A friend of his reported that when she expressed to a member of the Royal Academy her delight with these fascinating evocations of the past she was admonished to read no more of them, for they were unworthy of her attention. Truly, among the older generation it became the fashion to profess intentional ignorance of the popular *episodios*, and by such a profession one presumably reached the top of the Olympian heights.

Regardless of his reaction to the native critics, Galdós was both pleased and roiled by an extensive study on the *Episodios nacionales* which appeared in 1876 in the *Revue des deux mondes*. That his work should have attracted attention outside of Spain so soon manifestly flattered him, but he was irritated and grieved that the writer Louis-Lande had interpreted his attitude toward the French as hostile. He was tempted to reply to the French critic *in extenso,* but he considered the time inopportune for a controversy with a foreign commentator. M. Louis-Lande himself admitted that his evaluation of Galdós was in part prejudiced, although he justified his prejudice on the ground that his patriotic sénse was offended. Besides, the unbiased portion of the study coincided in large part with the consensus of Spanish opinion. That Galdós found encouraging, for it suggested that his novels possessed inescapable qualities. All in all he accepted M. Louis-Lande's criticism graciously. Particularly he agreed with him that one could not derive much guidance from Spanish criticism, since, strictly speaking, there was none. He was convinced more than ever that whatever literary course he chose to pursue, he would have to chart it himself in the light of his personal conception of the essence of the novel and under the impact of the forces of Spanish national life with which no honest, intelligent Spaniard could fail to reckon.

*   *   *   *

In 1870 Galdós had written a reasoned essay entitled "Observaciones sobre la novela contemporánea en España." It is more

than an abstract dissertation. It may well have been intended as
a statement of his personal literary creed and as an announcement of a program for whose fulfilment conditions were not yet
propitious.

In this essay Galdós expressed the conviction that regeneration
of the Spanish novel was urgently needed, and that it could be
effected only by cultivating the novel of contemporary urban
customs, with particular emphasis on the middle class. This class,
he argued, because it completely symbolized the man of the
nineteenth century and formed the basis of modern society, constituted the great model and inexhaustible source for the realistic
novelist. It was untrue, argued Galdós, that the character of the
Spanish bourgeoisie was not sufficiently distinctive to justify a
national novel of manners. Quite the contrary, contemporary
Spanish society had all the necessary vitality and originality to
serve as a model in the inauguration of a literary epoch like the
one introduced by the modern English novel. The skillful observer could choose one of two aspects of the middle class: its
external life as reflected in politics, commerce, and the struggle
for progress, or its intimate domestic life. The latter aspect
opened to the novelist the vast panorama of the universal and
eternal manifestations of the human heart and the everyday incidents of life, as well as the peculiarly Spanish and the char-
acteristically modern conditions of the middle class.

The outstanding feature of the Spanish scene, according to
Galdós, was the religious problem with its frightful contradic-
tions and disturbing effects upon the life of Spanish families.
Whether it manifested itself in religious disbelief or in fanaticism
and false devoutness, the result was invariably the weakening or
destruction of the moral and civil ties that held the family together. Another serious disruptive force was adultery—a problem
for which there were three possible solutions: religious, purely
moral, or simple civil reform. The proper solution for these or
any other problems was not the immediate responsibility of the
modern novelist, but it was his duty to reflect these profound
social agitations—the constant struggle between principles and
facts which constitutes the marvelous drama of modern life.

The great Spanish novel of manners—that vast, complex, inevitable artistic expression of modern life—had not yet appeared in Spain. Conditions had not been favorable for its appearance, since the modern social observer, Galdós suggested, required serenity, peace, and tranquillity to accomplish his mission. The absence of these requirements could not be counterbalanced by the mere will or skill of the novelist. Yet the time was becoming increasingly propitious. All great periods of novelistic literature must be preceded by stages of slow, laborious practice and experimentation, first in the *cuadro de costumbres* (sketch of local customs) and then in the short story, which was in some respects a more highly dramatic and amplified version of the *cuadro*. In Spain those preliminary steps had been successfuly taken.

Obviously Galdós thought of himself as the standard-bearer of the literary movement inaugurating the modern novel of middle-class life. Having conceived the new gospel, he would naturally be its leading, perhaps sole, apostle. Thus far he had really done nothing about this important mission. The *Episodios nacionales* had grown out of a concept and an urge not exclusively artistic, and they bore only a remote relationship to his theory of 1870. They were not the result of direct observation; they could not and did not emphasize the importance of the middle class; and they did not, as they could not, bring into relief the transcendental problem of religion. Moreover, for all the favorable impression they created, they did not gain literary adherents. They did blaze a new trail, but their author was the only one who followed it toward a goal that was not necessarily accompanied by literary fame.

Galdós decision to turn to the contemporary scene did not rest solely on a conviction that the conditions he regarded as essential were adequately met in 1876. The question of his personal prestige and leadership in the new literary movement was also an important factor.

While it unquestionably flattered him to have Revilla state that with *La fontana de oro* and *El audaz* the regeneration of Spanish fiction had already begun, compelling men like Valera and Alarcón to write serious novels on the theme of religion, he was not satisfied that these writers had fully grasped his views or had applied them effectively. Alarcón in *El escándalo* and Valera in *Pepita Jiménez*, by taking cognizance of the religious problem, had merely revealed that they recognized the need for dealing with transcendental themes in the new Spanish novel; their accomplishment could scarcely be regarded as satisfactory. Alarcón's novel was actually a victory for the "neos," precisely the element of Spanish society that was chiefly responsible for the continued aggravation of the problem. His treatment of religion was limited and elementary, reduced to the practice of the confessional booth. Despite the scattered philosophic and theological discussions in *El Escándalo*, nowhere did the author probe the deep significance of religion in modern Spain. As for Valera, his treatment of the theme on the lofty plane of mysticism was exceedingly nebulous, with never an indication of its tremendous social importance.

In short, Galdós was convinced that there was still room for a courageous and artistic presentation of the religious question. As a matter of fact, even before 1876 he had conceived "a valiant and very Spanish novel of struggle," [6] but thus far he had not had the fortitude to write it. Now he was emboldened by the last civil war, which Alfonso XII ended triumphantly, and by the return of the Church as a power behind the throne. Additional encouragement came from his friend Fernando León y Castillo, who suggested that he write the "valiant and very Spanish novel of struggle" for the *Revista de España*. Galdós accepted the suggestion without even having a definite plan in his mind.

Doña Perfecta began to appear in March, 1876, as a serial story, and at first it came rather haltingly. Two weeks elapsed between the first two chapters. It was a serious step Galdós had taken, and he was not going to be rushed. Much of his literary future and his position in Spanish national life depended on this work. Friends and critics had faith in him, and he lacked none in himself; but caution was neverthless desirable at this important stage in his career. Above all, he needed time for reflection, since the trancendental terms in which he conceived the Spanish religious problem surpassed anything previously attempted.

With the publication of *Doña Perfecta* in book form by the Guirnalda press, Galdós inaugurated the series which he called *Novelas contemporáneas* instead of the later title of *Novelas de la primera época*. Simultaneously it was announced that the new series would resemble the *Episodios nacionales* in some unspecified respects. Evidently, in the mind of the publishers—and possibly also in the author's—the new novel was merely an extension of the historical novels into the contemporary scene. Indeed, in conceiving *Doña Perfecta* Galdós was mindful of the historical moment with which it deals, a moment when—to paraphrase the hero—the peace of the land was recurrently disturbed by bandits, "for bandits are those who in the name of a political or religious idea rush into adventures every four or five years." [7]

The reception of *Doña Perfecta* could not have displeased the author. Professional critics, to be sure, took slight notice of the novel, for reasons which need not be retailed again. Conceivably Galdós was even grateful for this relative silence, inasmuch as the few reviews that did appear were so nearly identical that they might have been written by the same person. They contained the same immoderate praise and the same ex-cathedra pronouncements on the so-called esthetic aspects of the novel. It must have irked Galdós again to be told pontifically that such and no other were the means of achieving artistic effects. Manuel de la Revilla once more took him to task for his slight concern with turbulent emotions and tumultuous passions. Quoting a friend, the critic remarked that it was high time for some of Galdós' numerous lovers to decide to sin at least once. All in all, however, the critical estimates were favorable, even flattering. Although none attempted to analyze the theme, the more intelligent ones at least pointed out the opportuneness of treating religious fanaticism in generally comprehensible terms, and that Galdós had succeeded in writing a novel that was both serious and interesting. And all agreed that the author was progressing surely and steadily to supreme fame among modern Spanish novelists.

Such a conclusion was not unfounded. *Doña Perfecta* precipitated extensive discussion about the author and his other works.

Many of his faithful readers to whom he was merely the author of pleasantly instructive historical novels now wanted to know him personally. There was great speculation about him when it was revealed that he remained aloof from national politics and was not ambitious to convert his literary capital into political small change. To the average intelligent Spaniard of the day it was almost incredible that a writer should devote himself exclusively and zealously to literature. Such a writer deserved high esteem. The author of *Doña Perfecta* began to acquire the stature of a national figure.

It was characteristic of Galdós, as of his mother, to be firm and uncompromising in his decisions. He had conceived it to be his duty to regenerate the national conscience, and he was now resolved to carry it out. The scene unfolded by the restoration of the monarchy revealed alarming symptoms of apathy and spiritual lethargy. The specter of the hateful past was stalking across the land; it must be destroyed and that called for violent measures. The impression produced on the public by *Doña Perfecta* convinced Galdós that he had raised a vital issue for whose settlement he could count on vigorous though limited support. But this novel was only a preliminary skirmish to test the enemy's strength and the effectiveness of his own tactics and weapons.

It was a profitable skirmish, and it gave Galdós courage to rush into thick and bloody battle. In deference to his conscience, his financial needs, and his readers, he still managed to publish three new *episodios* in 1876. But the most absorbing task of the year was the writing of *Gloria,* the first volume of which appeared in December. When Alfonso XII entered Madrid triumphantly, Galdós was reading the proofs of the work in which he rose from the relatively restricted zone of fanaticism to the loftier plane of religious intolerance and conflict. The symbolism and violence and tumult of the first novel yielded in *Gloria* to analysis, reason, and philosophic reflection. The agitator who had written *Doña Perfecta* had turned thinker and searcher for truth.

The first volume of *Gloria* made Galdós the man of the hour among Spanish liberals. Its appearance created in intellectual circles almost as great a furore as a major cabinet crisis. It was generally asserted that at last Spain could point to a novelist who equalled the best in Europe. The regeneration of national fiction was now assured. *Gloria* rang the death knell of the *novela por entregas* and other types which, masquerading as literature, degraded the art of the novel and debased the reader's taste. Still more significant was the implication of *Gloria* for the spiritual redemption of Spain. Liberals discovered in Galdós the courageous voice of a repressed and tortured conscience. In a land of sectarian spirit the appeal to tolerance was tantamount to a summons to revolution.

Gloria remained for a long time the topic of animated conversation and discussion wherever several Spaniards met. Among writers and politicians, students and professional men, artists and generals, in the Ateneo, newspaper offices, theaters, academies, and cafés, the artistic qualities of *Gloria* were analyzed and argued. Few questioned that Galdós' success was complete and that the problem, characters, and situations were most opportune. *Gloria* was a literary event of cataclysmic magnitude.

The critics—even the most distinguished of them—reflected the enthusiasm and exultation of the public at large. It would have required great courage to do otherwise. Reviews were more numerous, more extensive, more reasoned than they had been in the past. The writers strained themselves philosophically, esthetically, and stylistically to rise to the novel's high plane of rarified transcendentalism. Some got lost in the climb and wandered off into dense forests of verbal abstractions and adjectival underbrush. For the first time the critics laid aside their conventional yardstick and made an honest effort to evaluate the novel in terms of its far-reaching purpose and artistic innovation. This was no literature of mere pastime, and everyone now forgot the ordinary technical skills an author must employ in order to beguile and fascinate the average reader.

Even Manuel de la Revilla was sparing in his hackneyed suggestions for the attainment of esthetic perfection. This time he was most seriously concerned over the effectiveness of the ending, but he was pleased to state that in the second volume, which came out early in the summer of 1877, Galdós skillfully overcame the almost insuperable artistic and philosophic difficulties inherent in his particular solution and that at long last he had acquired the power to portray emotions and to allow human passion a reasonable degree of free play. For the rest he exceeded his vaunted generosity toward Galdós and hailed him as the first Spanish author to enter gracefully the vast field of the psychological-social novel and as the only modern novelist anywhere who was both a profound thinker and a meticulous observer. He deemed him worthy of dwelling on the heights where artist and philosopher rub elbows and where works of art are perfect manifestations of beauty as well as sources of transcendental wisdom. *Gloria,* according to the philosophically minded Revilla, recorded the tragic history of the human conscience oppressed by one of the most terrible tyrannies which spring from the individual himself—religious intolerance.

Clarín entered the arena to break his first critical lance in behalf of Galdós. With his review of *Gloria* he laid the foundation of a lifelong friendship with the author, a friendship to which Galdós' contribution was far lighter and less disinterested.

Clarín went further than Revilla and asserted that *Gloria* was the first truly modern Spanish novel. The flexible logic which arises from the truth of the animating idea, he predicted, would cause painful but wholesome struggles in the conscience of many if they stopped to reflect on the lesson of the novel. This note, incidentally, was stressed by almost all the critics. Galdós was hailed as the Spanish standard-bearer of the social and religious revolution then in the making on the European continent, as the builder—perhaps the sole one—of a new era in which scientifically discovered truth would reign supreme.

With almost pathetic faith, Spanish liberals believed—as did Galdós himself—that what political revolutions had failed to accomplish the author of *Gloria* would achieve through the mere regeneration of the novel. There was hope everywhere that a writer who so skillfully and so plastically gave utterance to the aspirations of his generation would endow his nation with a new conscience and would bring about the triumph of the idea that had been agitating Spain since the beginning of the century. The spirit of the age—progress, liberalism, and human freedom —was descending upon Spain.] It was sad but not disheartening that Gloria, the heroine of the novel, symbol of everything pure and noble in religion, died tragically. It was sad but not disheartening that her Jewish lover, Daniel Morton, ended in madness through his search for a new universal faith—the faith of the future. But Gloria and Daniel were happily joined in Heaven, whence they could hopefully watch the growth of their little boy Jesús, born out of wedlock but conceived in love and sympathy and understanding. Nazarenito—they called him so in his native town of Ficóbriga—"the son of conflict, the most beautiful personification of a humanity emancipated from religious antagonisms by virtue of love, the symbol of the fusion of two consciences" [8]—little Nazarene was destined to accomplish great deeds. The battle had not yet been won, but at least a champion and a leader had been discovered. Young Spain, hopeful Spain, dreaming Spain, idealistic Spain was ready to follow Galdós on the road to national spiritual salvation.

Precisely as the liberals adopted *Gloria* as their manifesto, so conservative Spaniards, especially the so-called "neos," interpreted it as a bold challenge to their principles. It was a stab at what they considered to be the heart of Spain. The novel fell on their camp with the force of an explosive, and passion ran high.

Galdós could not long remain the man of the day with impunity. Hitherto the forces of opposition had merely kept a discreetly watchful eye on him. The liberalism of his *episodios* rose to the surface only in the second series, and it was overlooked in deference to the lofty patriotic tone of the first ten novels. Even *Doña Perfecta* had aroused only scattered antagonism; the traditionalists interpreted it as a particularized aspect of misguided religiosity. The author, to be sure, had not been at all priggish in the exposition of fanaticism, but he had leveled his attacks against unscrupulous persons rather than against the principles of religion. It was otherwise with *Gloria*, argued the defenders of conservatism. Here the very foundation of the Catholic church was mercilessly attacked. A bishop, a priest, a genuinely religious heroine, and other intelligent characters were presented as utterly helpless to defend their beliefs against the onslaught of the Jew Morton. Formerly Galdós had been merely leaning toward a heretical point of view, but in *Gloria* he had completely succumbed. There could be neither compromise nor conciliation. The battle lines were sharply drawn, and the war would be fought to the finish.

The indignation and passion with which the "antis" sought to scourge *Gloria* affected Galdós far less than did the eloquent resentment with which his good friend José María Pereda reacted to the first volume. Their friendship was put to the acid test, but fortunately it emerged stronger than ever.

On February 9, 1877, Pereda lashed out against his friend in a long, impassioned letter which he was more pained to write than Galdós to receive. Pereda's conscience was so troubled that six days later he sought relief in a letter to their mutual friend Marcelino Menéndez y Pelayo, who was at the time in Italy. In his communication to Galdós the Santanderine novelist said he was deeply hurt to see him toppling over into what he called "the mire of the Voltairean novel." As a literary work *Gloria* was precious, but what did Galdós hope to gain from heaping ridicule upon Catholicism? In time he would certainly regret it, but his repentance might come too late. If Voltaire achieved nothing but sterile scandals, what could Galdós accomplish by posing in a novel a problem that no amount of dispute could resolve? Aside from its deleterious effect upon Catholics whose faith was already weak, *Gloria* could only win the doubtful distinction of a place on the *Index*. What a lamentable triumph for the novelist who alone possessed the inspiration and the talent to effect a renaissance of Spanish fiction! It was a pity that so intelligent a person as Galdós should presume that by establishing a religious *"Unión Liberal,"* comparable to the political one which had failed so miserably, he could reconcile Catholicism and Judaism. Such a union, in which the advance guard would be obliged to retreat and the rear guard would have to advance, could only result in the abandonment of the principles on which both elements were based. In religion it would surely lead to chaos.

Galdós, who was, one might say, a congenitally poor correspondent, answered Pereda promptly, and exceeded by four his customary one folio per letter. Pereda regarded this as a personal triumph and as evidence of the serious respect with which Galdós considered his harsh but sincere criticism.

In his reply Galdós stated that Pereda's opinions had come down on him like a shower of cold water and went on to justify, with deep sincerity, the theme of *Gloria* and its artistic treatment. His choice of a Jewish hero, he explained, was born of dramatic exigency, not the desire to idealize Judaism or to detract from Catholicism. Certainly, protested Galdós, it was unfair to call him a "Volteriano." He had no intention of undermining the Catholic faith; on the contrary, he hoped to arouse Catholics to the need for a new, more beautiful religious edifice. It would have delighted him to treat religion in a fashion that would have pleased everyone, but one must be exceedingly vain even to harbor such an ideal. Unfortunately, in a world of issues and problems, common sense and honesty called for partisanship. Moreover, it had never entered his mind to write for the pleasure of both Tyrians and Trojans—not even in the *Episodios nacionales*. But that did not mean he was willful or blindly biased. Surely *Gloria* suffered from none of the prejudice with which Pereda had ridiculed politics in his *Los hombres de pro*. As for the possibility of a place on the *Index*, he was not seeking such notoriety, although it might be said that the best works of the nineteenth century were thus distinguished. He would consider it a compliment if Rome took cognizance of his writings.

Touching on more fundamental points, Galdós argued that Catholic unity was not an article of faith, and that insistence on that attitude had been a greater corruptive influence in Spain than the liberal movement since 1812. Moreover, there was no basis for the conservatives' belief that liberals were rascals and fools. To convince Pereda that they were neither one nor the other, he would gladly sacrifice the twenty volumes of his novels if Pereda deserted to his camp—and in view of his great admiration for the Santanderine novelist no one could say that he wished to see him in undesirable company!

Pereda lost no time in answering Galdós. As was to be expected, each man fell into an occasional misinterpretation of the other's meaning or intention, but on the whole their dispute was on the same lofty plane as their friendship, which dated from 1871. If anything, they came to know and understand one another better—like newlyweds after their first serious quarrel. Both men retained a lasting memory of their literary controversy and often referred to it. Twenty years later, in his speech before the Royal Academy, Galdós recalled the incident:

> When in my novels of 1875 and 1876 [*the dates are slightly inaccurate, as are usually those which Galdós cites*] I presented cases of conscience which displeased him [*i.e., Pereda*] or were not in accord with his ideas; he scolded me with genuine anger, and I was delighted to be scolded. I have preserved as a precious treasure among the letters of our extensive correspondence his bitter criticisms of some works of mine which I need not mention, judgments of great severity which are the best proof of the consistency of his doctrines and of the affection which he professed for me.[9]

With *Gloria* Galdós took the first timid step toward recognition outside of Spain. Not at all discouraged by the hostile reception of the *Episodios nacionales* in France, he contrived to have *Gloria* translated into English and published in London in 1879. The following year, despite an unfavorable review in the *London Saturday Review*, a German translation appeared in Berlin. In the opinion of his ardent admirers, Galdós was now a European literary figure of magnitude. They felt reassured about their generous appraisal of his novel and their insistence on its transcendental quality. As for the dismal impression it made on the English critic, it was attributed in part to the deplorably wretched translation and to the ignorance and bad taste of the reviewer. As one Spanish comment put it, the measure of the Englishman's stature in matters pertaining to Spanish letters might be taken from his statement that Galdós was a disciple of Manuel Fernández y González, but less brilliant and less entertaining than the master. The English critic described Galdós as a devout Catholic and the characters in *Gloria* as religious marionettes who shut their eyes, tremble, and turn pale when they see a Protestant or a Jew. The entire work had a narcotic effect on him, and the second part with its weakened characters seemed rather absurd.

The newly discovered star of Spanish letters and his fervent admirers were irritated by this review, but since others in England discussed Galdós more seriously, they dismissed the writer of the *London Saturday Review* as one of the large category of British eccentrics. Galdós' next novel in the contemporary series, *Marianela* (1878), has been called his lyrical interlude. Its marked sentimental note has led critics to speculate concerning the author's purpose. Taken at face value, *Marianela* reveals none of the violence of *Doña Perfecta* nor the ponderous ideology of *Gloria*. In it Galdós presumably set out neither to pose a national problem nor to suggest solutions for the conflicts that exist between human beings and their institutions. It is rather a simple tale of the idyllic love of a pathetically ugly orphan girl for a physically and morally attractive blind boy whose guide she is—a love which ends in the pathetic death of the girl when the boy regains his sight and discovers how wide of the mark is his concept of Marianela's physical beauty. *Marianela* has relatively few characters, and the author has expended his power of observation on the physical rather than the human background. It was definitely written from the heart and was calculated to appeal only emotionally. Possibly it was intended merely as a romantic story.

Perhaps no one will ever discover why Galdós struck this one intensely lyrical note of his career. There have been various interpretations, convincingly presented, of the symbolic significance of *Marianela*. For some it signifies Galdós' preoccupation with the struggle between the old and the new in Spain, for others his attempt to be guided by the prevalent philosophic thought of his age, particularly that of Auguste Comte. These interpretations are of fairly recent origin. Galdós' contemporaries accepted the novel as a moving and delicately wrought tale. The critics who formerly had regretted Galdós' lack of tender and delicate sentiment were pleased with this evidence of his poetic capacity. Accustomed as they were, however, to seeing philosophic subcurrents in his contemporary novels, they did not limit themselves to esthetic observations. Ponderous Revilla, for example, saw in *Marianela* an artistic demonstration of the modern principle of esthetics that beauty is sensuous, and that only experience can perceive it. He argued that Pablo, the blind hero, was wrong to assume that Marianela's physical beauty corresponded to her moral beauty.

It is conceivable that the ultimate meaning of *Marianela* has little to do with the motives that inspired it. Several factors may have influenced Galdós to desert transcendental themes temporarily. As a matter of fact, abstract speculation and all that smacks of metaphysical acrobatics were always abhorrent to him. In this instance he may have decided to demonstrate that the absence of lyricism from his previous works was not to be taken as an artistic shortcoming but as the logical consequence of his literary esthetic; in other words, that perhaps his concept of lyricism did not require the use of conventional sentiment and emotion, but that he could satisfy the most sentimental reader or critic if he chose. It may also be that he wrote *Marianela* as a means of clearing the heavy atmosphere precipitated by the controversy over *Gloria*. Had not Pereda advised him to write for Tyrians and Trojans alike? *Marianela* was just that sort of novel, and it might temporarily appease those who were hostile to *Doña Perfecta* and *Gloria*. Then, too, ever since he had begun to cultivate realism in earnest—even before he had finished his first novel—Galdós often liked to rest from the strain of contact with concrete actualities by writing works of fantasy. Such works came hard to him, but he greatly enjoyed them. Finally, the pathetic tale of the waif may be an artistic recasting of a story based in fact or in local legend of the Cantabrian region which the author frequently visited.

By now Galdós' sympathizers were beginning to make a concerted effort to secure fuller and more vocal recognition for him. They contended that in Spain he was supreme, and that in the universal republic of letters, too, he ranked with the most distinguished citizens. To offset the adverse impression created by *Gloria* in certain quarters, they reiterated that Galdós was greater than his reputation, measured in terms of the space he got in the press. Was this literary giant to be another victim of the Spanish practice of lavishing esteem upon the small during their lifetime but withholding it from the great until they are dead? How differently he would be treated, it was argued, if he were not so modest and if he did not shun the political arena like a house of pestilence! In no other country would talented writers and the intelligent public abstain from reading such novels as *Doña Perfecta* and *Gloria,* yet in Spain many preferred mediocre foreign works to gems of native origin.

This was the note on which Galdós' small but articulate army of disciples harped when *Marianela* appeared. More and more newspapers printed articles dealing with the rapidly growing stature of the one and only Spanish novelist. *El Imparcial,* Spain's leading daily, virtually became the organ of the *galdosianos* who identified the liberalism of his works with the movement for Spanish regeneration. Although these *galdosianos* were mostly anticlerical, they pursued their aim in accordance with their enemy's principle that the end justifies the means. Among these Galdós enthusiasts Fernaflor (Isidoro Fernández Flórez) put on the best one-man advertising campaign. He painted such an attractive picture of his idol in *El Imparcial* that some of the novelist's friends—persons with whom he had frequent contact—asked him if he was actually the celebrity depicted in epic terms by Fernaflor.

With the publication of the three-volume novel *La familia de León Roch* (1878) Galdós closed the so-called religious trilogy and made the transition to the extensive series of contemporary novels which he was to inaugurate more definitively in 1881. It was the first time that he localized the action of a non-historical novel in Madrid and painted a gallery of types and characters. The religious problem was still one of his concerns, but he did not allow it to overshadow his interest in the salient features of the Restoration society.

La familia de León Roch was the inevitable next step in

Galdós' plan. The second series of the *episodios* was nearing completion. He had announced at the beginning that it would not be extended beyond the period of the first civil war. After that he had intended to enter upon what he liked to call his second or third manner. In this new phase he would begin to apply in earnest his conviction about the essence of the modern novel of manners. He would abandon the realm of speculation, abstraction, and idealism and would concentrate on direct observation of the role played by the middle class in contemporary society. The "human comedy" of Spain was pleading for a chronicler, and he would heed the plea. But before launching the great new enterprise Galdós felt that he must complete his analysis of the religious problem by studying its implications for society and the family. His treatment of this transcendental theme in *Gloria* satisfied him less than it did the critics. It was more the result of meditation and fancy than of direct study of life. In a sense it was the outgrowth of absorbing conversations with the most attractive lady who had entered his life thus far —Juanita Lund, an extremely intelligent Scandinavian woman. She had written him pointed observations about his novels, and he had contrived to meet her. The delightful meetings that followed served Galdós as a proving ground for the many reflections on religion in *Gloria*. In fact, Juanita Lund was his model, physical, mental, and spiritual, for the heroine of the novel.

But what immediately impelled Galdós to write *La familia de León Roch* was the desire to sketch broadly the features that were gradually setting the physiognomy of Restoration society. Eventually he would enlarge this sketch into a complete canvas of the period.

Galdós believed that the return of the Bourbons, with the relative calm it brought the nation, really signified neither innovation nor reaction. It merely marked the freer flow of the principles and practices whose operation had been somewhat impeded but not halted during the period of revolutionary agitation and political instability. In his opinion the difference between the two periods was one of degree rather than kind. In the drowsy atmosphere of the Restoration a spurious variety of positivism governed Spanish society. There was a general desire for advancement, but only in the petty, material sense of the term. Many were animated by a vain ambition for distinction in wealth, dress, manners, and social position. The woefully restricted brand of positivism against which dramatists like Tamayo y Baus and López de Ayala had moralized and declaimed in their plays now informed the life of large segments of the Spanish people. A vigorously ambitious middle class was encroaching on the old aristocracy and titled nobility, whose defense of its prerogatives could at best be rather weak.

Of the spiritual ideals and progressive aspirations of the revolutionary period little had survived, and these were cherished intimately by a minority who for the most part lived in dignified seclusion. In the absence of a carefully coordinated protest, Spanish society was acquiring layer upon layer of the fat of degeneracy. Both private and public morals were characterized by a laxity born of a childish desire for display rather than a new standard of right and wrong. The *señorito* and his inane forbears, governed by a perverted sense of freedom and privilege, often set the pace and gave the tone. Religion did little more to maintain life on a high spiritual plane. Exploited by society to satisfy petty ambitions, it became routine religiosity marked by purely external formalism. Instead of an urge rising from the depths of one's spiritual being, religion became a part of the artificial social etiquette, having little influence on one's ethical conduct, yet capable of serious distortion of character and personality.

Such was the Restoration canvas which Galdós meant to paint in his latest novel, and he chose for its protagonist his friend and enthusiastic critic—Mining Engineer Emilio Huelin.

The reaction of the critics again followed the fixed pattern. Intelligent reviewers took due notice of the emphasis on the moral and social implications of the so-called religious problem in *La familia de León Roch,* and for this they praised the author without stint. The only new note the critics struck—they could have done it with equal force on former occasions—was the tendentious nature of the novel. Ordinarily, it was argued, a writer must not offer philosophic or social disquisitions under the guise of literature unless, like Galdós, he can create a work that is both artistic and ideologically significant. As a matter of fact, continued the argument, the true artist cannot extract beauty from fragmentary bits of life; these must be interrelated in terms of some specific finality—they must be cemented with some ideological matter. This Galdós did in his last novel, demonstrating that tendentious literature is capable of realizing the aims of modern esthetics.

Some critics regarded *La familia de León Roch* as inferior to *Gloria* in poetic power, but superior to it in moral and social conception. It was destined to enhance the author's popularity everywhere except among those who insisted on judging him with the very intolerance which he treated in his recent works. Conceivably the average reader would not be attracted by *La familia de León Roch*, for it was a bulky work. But for the cultured Spaniard, capable of appreciating the vastness of its conception and the range of its social gallery, it was a great achievement, a rare combination of beauty, human progress, truth, and virtue.

In view of Galdós' artistic integrity it must be assumed that the critical drone which followed the appearance of his works must eventually have palled on him. He discounted almost everything that the literary arbiters uttered by way of approval or advice, though he appreciated their contribution to the promotion of his works. He had his own esthetic, but he was none too confident that he had realized his purposes. Often he felt that he was groping in the dark toward a goal whose validity could be determined only by the reaction of the readers. The professional critics he was inclined to include in the category of the neoclassic rhetoricians whom he had abhorred in his younger days. He reacted ironically to the pseudo-scientific pretensions of modern literary criticism, and he took its authority lightly. His own experience as a critic had inoculated him against the species. The humility with which he apparently accepted critical dicta was only a screen for his personal criteria, which admitted no challenge. Without impugning the authority or the influence of professional critics in the abstract, he set more store by the spontaneous reaction and the honest comment of the intelligent readers of the rank and file. Like a genuine Spaniard, Galdós had slight respect for laws that were neither natural nor divine.

Thus far in his career he had listened with respect to only four men: Núñez de Arce, Eugenio de Ochoa, Pereda, and Francisco Giner de los Ríos. He particularly valued the opinion of Giner because of his intellectual honesty and esthetic sobriety. Giner symbolized for Galdós a vital force in the slow process of the spiritual regeneration of Spain. He believed that the new man who would some day build a new Spain would have to be the intellectual and spiritual descendant of Giner.

Galdós was therefore deeply affected by Don Francisco's rather unfavorable review of the first part of *La familia de León Roch*. To be sure, the bitter was mixed with sweet, but it was the taste of the bitter that lingered. After reading a lengthy enumeration of flaws in character conception, plot, emphasis on moral aim, stylistic impurities, and the like, he was not much cheered by Giner's encouraging predictions regarding his future. Nor did he feel flattered to be declared the only equal of Valera and the superior of Pereda, Trueba, and Alarcón. A fine rating for one who was being universally proclaimed the father of the modern Spanish novel!

Galdós' disappointment was especially keen because of his instinctive faith in Giner's sincerity and esteem. He did not commit the folly of airing his feelings in public, but he expressed them privately to his friends, who hastened to inform Giner of them. Don Francisco was grieved that he had unintentionally offended Galdós, and although the severity of his criticism was prompted by his honesty, he waited impatiently for the opportunity to bestow unqualified praise upon the author of *La familia de León Roch*. Galdós' resentment did not entirely blind him to the value and possible soundness of Giner's opinions, and in time he was to solicit his judgment and advice.

The year 1879 was a lean one for Galdós. He published only two *episodios*, and with them closed the second series and presumably abandoned the genre forever. There were other enterprises in the offing, chiefly the inauguration of the contemporary series, but these required careful planning and preparation. *Un*

faccioso más y algunos frailes menos was the last historical novel.
Galdós ended it with a statement to his readers. Because of its
documentary value, his declaration deserves to be quoted:

> Here the narrator ends his task, certain of having
> performed it very imperfectly; but sure at the same
> time of having ended it opportunely (we are thus
> quits), and at a time when its continuation would have
> resulted in unpardonable imperfections and faults.
> The years following 1834 are too close to us, they
> touch us, rub elbows with us and are on familiar terms
> with us. Their men are almost confused with our men.
> They are years which cannot be dissected because there
> is in them something alive which hurts and jumps
> when touched by the scalpel. And so let this long work
> come to a stop here, a work on whose last page (which
> I beseech to serve me as a Bible) I solemnly swear to
> abuse no more the kindness of the public by adding
> more manuscript pages to the ten thousand that make
> up the *Episodios Nacionales*. Here they end defini-
> tively. If some well-intentioned person does not think
> so and wishes to continue, he has before him at his
> disposal historical facts and political and social curiosi-
> ties in great quantity. But the fictional personages that
> have survived during this very extensive journey, I
> keep for myself, as my legal possession, and I shall
> preserve them for a race of contemporary types, as
> the reader will see who will not abandon me as I now
> abandon forever and with entire resolve the so-called
> *historical genre*.[10]

Thus ended the dawn of glory. Then followed the brief
moment of intense darkness which precedes the sunrise. It was
not long before the sun that shines high in the skies of Spain
shed its light generously upon Galdós. Soon he was to emerge
from the dawn of glory into the bright daylight of national fame
and universal recognition. Galdós was fast becoming Spain's
man of the nineteenth century.

VIII

National Recognition

IN HIS PARTING REMARKS to the readers of the *Episodios nacionales* in 1879, Galdós invited them to accompany him in the exploration of the contemporary scene. The next year went by, however, without the publication of a single work. Besides making preparations for the launching of the contemporary series, Galdós was busy with the circulation of his works outside of Spain and the publication of an illustrated de luxe edition of the *episodios*. The realization of these two projects involved obstacles none the less difficult because they had been foreseen.

The unpleasant experience with the English translation of *Gloria* did not deter Galdós from seeking recognition abroad. The desire for Continental fame seized him early, and it remained with him to the end of his days. Even before *Gloria* was translated into English he had succeeded in having *La fontana de oro* appear serially in Italian in *La Ragione* of Milan. Somehow he let himself be persuaded by the critics that his destiny transcended the revival of Spanish fiction and that the significance of his works placed him well in the current of European literature.

Of his non-historical novels, *Gloria* seemed to him to hold the greatest universal appeal, and he left nothing undone to make it available in the principal Continental languages. As a matter of record, its complete English version was preceded by a partial translation into Dutch, published in *De Gids* (February, 1879), an Amsterdam review of slight repute. In 1880 the novel was translated into German, and that same year *Doña Perfecta* appeared in English in London. An Italian translation of *Marianela* ended Galdós' quest for foreign fame in 1880. But more abundant results marked the years immediately following. *La familia de León Roch* was published in Swedish in 1881; the next year *Gloria* came out in New York and *La fontana de oro* was printed serially in the Russian review *Dielo*. American versions of *Doña Perfecta* and *Marianela* appeared in New York in 1883. At about the same time *Doña Perfecta* was translated into Dutch and—according to Dr. Tolosa Latour, one of Galdós' best friends—also into German. Latour also made an unsubstantiated claim that by early 1883 *La familia de León Roch* had appeared in German and *Gloria* in Italian and Hungarian. Altogether, then, Galdós had by the early eighties made an auspicious beginning toward the establishment of a European reputation.

Less difficult but more complicated and hazardous was the enterprise of the illustrated *Episodios nacionales*. Prominent among the motives for this undertaking was the hope of monetary gain. Despite the literary success of the contemporary novels, their popular appeal—and sales—lagged far behind the enthusiasm of the critics. The *episodios*, on the other hand, had attracted a substantial following upon whose support Galdós could count, notwithstanding the mild resentment aroused by his treatment of the religious problem. Now that he had abandoned the historical genre he must retain and consolidate his clientele as much as possible. The projected illustrated edition, he was convinced, would achieve that. His friends who thought otherwise endeavored to dissuade him.

Galdós, only a little less stubborn than his mother, made light of all predictions of disaster. A peculiar quirk in his nature made him hanker strongly for commercial enterprises despite his utter lack of business acumen. This time the venture was rather urgent. For some years now he had followed a mode of living that taxed his capacity for economic independence even in his celibate state. As his imaginative activity grew more intense, he found it increasingly difficult to distinguish the pattern of his own intimate life from that of his fictional world. He frequently confused his own experiences with those of his characters, and money was the most effective means of extricating himself quietly from confusions of this sort. He knew the risks of the project he had conceived, but he was obliged to run them. Time was to prove how sound had been the admonitions of his good friends.

Galdós laid his plans with characteristic meticulousness. It was important to ascertain in advance the approximate number of subscribers to the illustrated edition. Here his friends were extremely helpful by informally launching a country-wide advertising campaign. The liberal press, where Galdós had become something like a masthead emblem, spared neither space nor enthusiasm. Considerable interest was aroused by the announcement that Galdós himself would be among the well-known illustrators of the new edition. Some of his older friends recalled his student-day sketches on café table-tops and his famous paper figures, but it was not generally known that he could draw seriously. With aid from several sources, Galdós was convinced that his undertaking would be fairly successful, and he plunged into it with limitless enthusiasm.

The most difficult problem was financing the enterprise. It involved approximately fifty thousand pesetas, and Galdós had never had that much money. The situation was reminiscent of the publication of *La fontana de oro*. Again he turned for assistance to his whimsically generous sister-in-law. She responded unhesitatingly, confident that Benito was now even more deserving of her faith in him. Capricious Magdalena continued to regard Galdós as her particular protégé, and it pleased her immensely that even as a mature and famous man he yielded most readily to her influence.

By the end of 1880 the printing of the special edition was begun. Thirteen of Spain's most famous contemporary painters, along with the author, formed the staff of illustrators. Among them were the brothers Enrique and Arturo Mélida, José Luis Pellicer, Apeles Mestres, and Aureliano Beruete. There were to be ten volumes in all, each comprising two *episodios*. Delivery to subscribers began in 1881 and continued through 1885. The last volume appeared with a lengthy epilogue by Galdós, setting forth the nature of the genre and the difficulty of gaining access to historical sources in Spain. He also took occasion to answer the charge of chauvinism that the French critic had leveled against him in 1876.

*   *   *   *

For almost a decade now Galdós had lived in a state of un-interrupted artistic feverishness which completely blotted out the immediate past and only occasionally permitted the present to impinge upon his consciousness. Except for inevitable pre-occupations of an intimate nature, his mind had been entirely devoted to the realization of his mission as a novelist. In 1880, however, he not only interrupted his productivity but resumed contact with the literary workaday world. Although he had no intention of abandoning the goal he had set for himself, he could not avoid surveying the distance he had covered and the stretch of road still ahead of him.

In the process of self-evaluation Galdós took notice of the work of other novelists and the new literary ideas that were being controversially discussed. Without belittling the achievements of his contemporaries, he felt he had so little in common with them that he was bound to continue alone on his chosen path. Only one author insistently claimed his attention, and he was not a novelist. José Echegaray's stage successes impressed him deeply and even revived his own dramatic ambitions. He had seen none of Echegaray's plays, but he read them all, not alone because of their author's steady triumphant march but also because of the prevailing critical opinion that Echegaray and he were the outstanding figures of the post-revolutionary period in their respective genres.

Although Galdós could not escape a vague temptation to re-turn to the drama—possibly as a means of maintaining his hold on his public—his immediate concern was the evolution of the contemporary series. Much of the program he had outlined in 1870 still remained unrealized. Except in *La familia de León Roch* he had not yet made full application of his own conception of the middle-class novel. This could be done in one of two ways. One might concentrate on the superficialities of Spanish life as expressed in politics, but Galdós regarded these as unworthy of literary treatment. He preferred to focus his attention on the internal life of Spain—on the art and science of life and on the norms and models of human passions. That would be the content of his future novels. As for their artistic mold, he was aware that here and there critics were talking excitedly about the new French doctrine of naturalism, but he saw little novelty in the ideas that were being bandied about.

For Galdós, naturalism was not the exclusive invention of Zola, whom he regarded as an author-propagandist. Basically the new literary creed impressed him as merely a modification of realism, with no startling innovations even in France. Certainly in Spain it had worthy antecedents in the picaresque novel. He admired Zola, whose novels stirred him deeply and gave him food for thought, but it never occurred to him to imitate the Frenchman consciously. He believed that every artist has his own temperament, a personal vision of life and an individual philosophy of art, and only those who lack such endowment can conscientiously set out to adopt another's procedure. Moreover, he had little faith in so-called literary schools. Even what was currently referred to as realism he defined not as a principle delimited in time and in practice, but as the absolute formula for all art.

In Spain literary realism had suffered a temporary eclipse, and he, together with Pereda, was trying to revive it. But he had no intention of specializing in repugnant physical and moral deformities; his aim was to paint faithfully a particular aspect of human nature in the light of the eternal ideals of justice and beauty. His forthcoming novels would indeed differ from their predecessors in their simplified composition and construction and in additional stress on the social overtones and ethical undertones of his canvas. Galdós firmly believed that an artist should avoid becoming mannered and standardized. He favored constant renovation, but he frowned upon the idea that the artistic conception could be basically modified. The prevailing capricious distinctions between realism and naturalism he branded as "deceiving vaguenesses equidistant from practice and from the idea of art," [1] in which he would have no part.

La desheredada, a novel in two volumes, ushered in Galdós'
new manner in 1881 and was the first in the series officially called
"Contemporary Novels." According to his own confession, it was
his most painstaking effort thus far and his greatest accomplishment. As if to call attention to his new point of departure and,
moreover, to soothe those troubled by his previous stress on
so-called transcendental themes, he issued the first volume with
the following dedicatory:

> Without knowing how or why, I have brought out in
> the open certain social ailments which are the result of
> a lack of nutrition and the slight use that is being made
> of the most beneficent tonics called Arithmetic, Logic,
> Morality and Common Sense. It would thus be fitting
> to dedicate these pages—to whom? To the unhappy
> patient, to the quacks and pharmacists who under the
> title of philosophers and politicians prescribe for him
> day after day? . . . No; I dedicate them to those who
> are or ought to be his true doctor: to the school-
> masters.[2]

The meat of *La desheredada,* it was apparent, was too raw for
the literary teeth of Spain's readers and critics. They reacted
with cold aloofness, if not frank hostility, toward this restrained
narrative of a poor Madrid girl who stoops to prostitution in her
attempt to make real a delusion of social grandeur. The splendid
lifelike canvas of Madrid's Barrios Bajos, the superb reproduction of natural popular speech purged of coarseness and vulgarity, the faithful evocation of the ambient of the early seventies, the sincerity and wholesomeness of the author's social vision
—all these qualities failed to win the favorable reception Galdós
had anticipated. Only his prestige prevented a storm of protest.
Fear and respect prompted conservatives and liberals to adopt a
prudently silent attitude, which was nevertheless expressive.
Everyone seemed dismayed that Galdós should have declined—
as they thought—into a wretched version of Zola. Only Clarín
thundered against the silent condemnation of a work which, in
his opinion, marked a new stage in the author's evolution, a

praiseworthy Spanish adaptation of French naturalism. With
caustic sarcasm he exclaimed:

> Galdós has thrown himself into the stream; he has
> published his program of incendiary literature, his
> naturalist's program; he has written in five hundred
> seventeen pages the history of a prostitute! Let us ex-
> communicate him, for it is fitting that we excommuni-
> cate him. I will say more than this—I will say with St.
> Thomas: *Juste occidi.*—Let him die![3]

Clarín was lightly and warily supported by Luis Alfonso, staff
critic of the rather conservative *La Epoca*. The naturalistic vein
in *La desheredada* did not surprise Alfonso, since presumably he
had already detected it in *La familia de León Roch*. On the contrary, he thought that Galdós had very sensibly adapted naturalism to the Spanish brand of realism—to his own variety of it.
Thus he praised the work, but in guarded terms and without
enthusiasm.

Galdós drew little comfort from Clarín's lone voice rending
the respectful silence which enveloped his latest novel. He was
frankly discouraged and even tempted to change his course. It
is not known in what direction he might have turned. It may
have occurred to him to begin work in earnest on a life of Christ
he had had in mind for some time and about which he had
written and talked to his friends.[4] That would conceivably have
earned him forgiveness for his naturalistic sin. He may even
have entertained more seriously the vague dramatic aspirations
stirred in him occasionally by Echegaray's successes. But his dis-
couragement was of short duration, and by the end of 1881 he
had fully planned his next novel, *El amigo Manso*—possibly his
most profound character study up to that time. Given Galdós'
high speed of composition, this work progressed slowly. The
theme of the contrast and conflict between ideas and reality
fascinated him, but its elaboration proved extremely difficult, in
part because he was still disturbed by his experience with *La
desheredada*. He was firmly resolved to pursue his new path, but
he was also eager not to displease his readers—provided it could

be done without offense to his convictions and concept of art. Although the tenets of art were always his first consideration, he was unwilling to write merely to satisfy his inner urge. The reader's reaction was an integral element of his literary esthetic.

In this mood of momentary depression Galdós tactfully turned to Giner de los Ríos for encouragement by sending him a set of *La desheredada*. The educator's reply was like an answer to a fervent prayer. As if he had cast aside his customary moderation, he praised the novel as the best of the period by any author and hailed it as marking a new stage in the evolution of Galdós' art. Moreover, he ventured to predict that all Galdós' former triumphs would be overshadowed by this one and that he would be identified exclusively as the author of *La desheredada*. Even with its minor shortcomings—were Dickens, Balzac, and Cervantes always perfect?—it was the only modern Spanish novel on a par with the best produced across the Pyrenees, and for this he offered sincere thanks to the Lord.

Replying to Giner, Galdós politely protested against his generosity and interpreted his opinion as a command to carry out his plan for the contemporary series. Giner's words, he said, strengthened his will and fortified his spirit. Nothing that all the critics in the world might say for a long time to come would weigh with him as much as Don Francisco's judgment. With such encouragement he would redouble his efforts to overcome the difficulties of the theme he was in the process of elaborating, and he hoped that Giner might be good enough to criticize *El amigo Manso* when it appeared.

And when it did come out in the middle of 1882 it retrieved some of the ground Galdós had recently lost with certain critics. Though few reviewers took official notice of it and these offered varied interpretations, no one made the criticism the author feared most—that he had not developed the theme adequately. To one critic it was clear that this time Galdós had caught admirably the spirit of the age—a lack of enthusiasm or *abulia*, as it later came to be called; to another it was equally obvious that he had successfully presented "a course on the anatomy of the soul." As for defects, naturally there were some, but no one cared to discuss them because they were allegedly so trifling. In the words of the eulogistic reviewer for *El Liberal*—whose attitude toward Galdós was undoubtedly typical—"Puny are the defects which have to be looked for with the power of a microscope in order to make them visible to the masses. . . ! Even if there are spots on the sun, they do not take away from it either fire or light." [5]

The fact that Manuel de la Revilla was now dead may explain in part the total absence of negative judgments in the appraisal of *El amigo Manso*. But this time the critics probably impressed Galdós even less than on previous occasions, for, barring José Ortega y Munilla, they were all relatively obscure individuals. For some reason neither Clarín nor Luis Alfonso nor Palacio Valdés—nor any of the other so-called "authoritative pens of Spain"—put down in writing their appraisal of the novel. Nevertheless its reception measured in terms of informal and unpublished comment was quite gratifying. Galdós was apparently absolved of the sin he had committed in naturalistic *La desheredada*. With this absolution—indeed, even before it had been publicly granted him—he left Madrid on an extended tour through northern Spain: Santander, Bilbao, Vitoria, and other points.

*   *   *   *

It is well to stress the fact that after the suspension of the *Episodios nacionales* and the completion of the religious trilogy the cause of Spanish spiritual regeneration became identified in the minds of many liberals with Galdós' literary success and his popularity. There was wide dissatisfaction over the scant attention he received in the press. Everyone knew that this was mainly due to the traditional Spanish indifference toward everything not related to politics, but it was felt that Galdós merited better treatment. There was a growing conviction that Galdós' literary activity might serve to arouse the public to an awareness of Spanish cultural and artistic strength and weakness; that the author of the *Episodios nacionales*—as Galdós was most frequently designated—might well become a civilizing agency in the life of Spain. Thus even the liberal press was often chided for failing to give adequate prominence to Galdós' new productions and their significance.

Protest against this neglect rose high with the publication of *La desheredada.* Clarín undoubtedly spoke for the liberals when he sarcastically remarked:

> If Señor Galdós, instead of writing some thirty excellent novels before this one—perhaps the best that have come out in Spain in this century—had written one poor average comedy, another good one, and still another bad one, and if he had immediately gone over politically to the party of the Duque de la Torre, then to Cánovas, and then to Sagasta or to the devil in person—if he had turned politician, criticism would have sung a different tune; then he would have seen that the moment he wrote a couple of lines the entire press would at once be full of wonderment, admiration and enthusiasm.[6]

And when Galdós' translated works began to attract attention outside of Spain, the demand for greater recognition of him became insistent. It was virtually *de rigueur* for commentators to complain mournfully about this neglect whenever his name was mentioned. Such preoccupation with an author's popularity is perhaps without precedent in the history of Spain.

Galdós' position in this campaign in his behalf was at best equivocal. He himself did little or nothing to become personally known to the public, less because of modesty than because of overmastering timidity. Socially awkward by nature, he was embarrassed in the presence of strangers and felt at ease only among his intimate friends. It required a hitherto unexercised brand of heroism to meet the persons to whom he was referred for information in connection with his historical novels, and if the prospective informant was a figure of national stature, he would usually delegate others to obtain the data for him. When his controversial novels made his name known to thousands of

Spaniards, editors had to resort to subterfuge—not always successfully—to obtain his photograph. Few outside the capital's literary circles had ever laid eyes on the author whose every new work was anticipated with almost as much agitation as a significant political development.

And yet Galdós was not entirely free from a brand of vanity begotten by a consciousness of superiority and by confidence in the ultimate worth of his achievement. His fairly scornful attitude toward the critics stemmed from his belief that only posterity is the final judge in matters of art and that it was likely to decide in his favor. He was even capable of a form of pride which on occasion approached arrogance. Gradually he developed the attitude that he could not be judged by ordinary standards and that the recognition accorded him fell far short of his due. Without exactly hungering for fame he was eager for wide acceptance, not alone for its sentimental value but also for the financial reward it entailed. And his insistence on material gain as an important factor in artistic success was not due entirely to money-madness. It was in a recondite way an integral part of his ambition to instill in Spaniards a proper respect for cultural and spiritual accomplishment. It was one of the principles of the literary and spiritual revolution he was quietly promoting single-handed.

Because of his deep-seated timidity Galdós did not readily exteriorize his attitudes and feelings, and that is why he was mistaken for an inordinately modest and irritatingly humble man not only by his chance acquaintances but by his blind and untiring supporters. Had he possessed the social personality with which nature often endows great men, or which they manage to acquire, he would have claimed recognition in dramatic fashion. As it was, he had to rely on the aid and influence of the literary and intellectual liberals. These supported him with genuine generosity, which he accepted and encouraged unostentatiously.

Even official Spain—its government and its institutions—took cognizance of Galdós. Honors and favors came his way, albeit stintingly. In 1876 he was awarded with appropriate solemnity the Cross of the Royal and Distinguished Order of Charles III.

To his fervent followers this was not honor enough—so many Spaniards wore the Cross of Charles III. Galdós, it was felt, already deserved something more conspicuous—a commandery or the plaque of the Grand Cross. That almost happened two years later when, in 1878, he received "an ordinary commandery in the Order of Isabel la Católica." The circumstances of these awards are rather obscure. Someone with political influence must have intervened in Galdós' behalf, and official Spain responded less grudgingly than might have been anticipated.

It was otherwise when cultural institutions were solicited to honor the novelist. As the first volume of *La desheredada* was coming off the press in 1881, Galdós was proposed for an "honorary literary post" in the Ateneo. The proposal was voted down in a secret ballot, and the press reported the incident in tones of resignation to the stupidity that characterized the deliberations of all Spanish *ateneos* and academies. The next year, as if to rectify the injustice, the Ministry of Public Instruction named him a member of the board that was to appoint a professor of Spanish literature at the University of Madrid—an honor he was to enjoy repeatedly in the following years. But the minister's confidence in Galdós' literary competence was apparently not shared by the majority of the forty immortals of the Royal Academy of Language. When his named was proposed in 1883, victory went to the strong opposition led by the conservative politician Antonio Cánovas del Castillo. The irony of the Royal Academy's decision was not lost on the liberal press. The triumph of the conservatives was interpreted as a defeat for the institution and a perversion of its aims. It was argued that, however Galdós' general literary norms might be viewed, only blind prejudice could refuse to recognize his contribution to the forging of a literary language without the coarseness and vulgarisms of popular speech, the mannerisms of journalistic style, and the artificial rhetorical quality of the so-called elevated style. Galdós, creator of a new style, was denied the company of the guardians of the Spanish language!

Of the Royal Spanish Academy of Language it may be said that many have knocked but few have entered. It has been traditional with Spanish writers to speak disdainfully of the institution in public but to covet the honor in private. Now Galdós had treated the academicians ironically, scornfully, and sarcastically even in the earliest days of his journalistic career. When he was finally elected in 1889 he thought so little of the distinction that he tarried some nine years before officially accepting it. In 1883, however, he would have been pleased to become an immortal at forty. It would have enhanced his prestige, and it might have recovered for him some of the ground that his so-called materialistic novels had lost with conservative readers. Indeed, among his ardent supporters the Academy's action precipitated a storm of protest and highly uncomplimentary reflections. They too would have been elated had their idol received the honor, for they were seriously disturbed over the waning publicity he was receiving in the press. The feeling was that Galdós had reached a stage of artistic maturity that called for a definitive appraisal of his literary stature and for official consecration of his leadership in Spanish cultural progress. The man who was educating the younger generation, who was keeping alive the liberal spirit of the nation, whose historical novels were fast becoming a household commodity, and who had won the respect of foreign critics —certainly such a man ought to be rescued from obscurity even if it meant that some violence had to be done to his timid and retiring nature.

* * * *

Of the various Madrilenian literary *tertulias*, the one that camped daily in the Cervecería Inglesa on the Carrera de San Jerónimo was among the noisiest. Its nucleus was a group of young Asturians who had come to the capital for the doctorate and literary renown, among them Armando Palacio Valdés and Leopoldo Alas, alias Clarín. The latter furnished most of the intellectual and artistic ferment for the sessions. Not all the members were natives of Asturias. Anyone with a taste for beer, a mind for Krausism, and—in the early seventies—a stomach for Zola's naturalism joined the "Oviedo fellows" in their strident protests against the existing order and in their enthusiastically conceived plans for a sane and spiritual future.

The *esprits forts* of the Cervecería Inglesa did not neglect politics, and the times fortunately provided them with abundant opportunity for cultivating this all-absorbing Spanish interest. Their absorption reached a climax with the bloodless establishment of the Republic in 1873. How blessed were they to be living in an historic moment! And the moment was historic also in the realm of literature. Young Tomás Tuero, countryman of Clarín, had completed the translation of Zola's *Nana,* and naturalism stirred deep passions in the youthful intellectuals. Naturalism, Krausism, and political liberalism co-existed in ill-defined zones of their minds as ingredients of their common and all-embracing ideal of revolution and progress. Whatever and whoever could be even remotely associated with this ideal was welcomed by this *tertulia,* whose judgments and decrees came to be feared if not respected, especially after Clarín began to convert them into printed darts which he shot at the public from the columns of *El Solfeo*. The *tertulia* continued to mature until it reached a point where its anonymity was considered incongruous with its importance. José Ortega Munilla christened it the "Bilis Club," and thus it was called throughout the years of its existence by all who remained on the outside and looked in on its awesome sessions.

In the early eighties the membership of the "Bilis Club" changed somewhat, but not its program nor its constitutional principles. New members had come in—Luis Taboada the humorist, Leopoldo Cano and Eugenio Sellés the daring social dramatists, Manuel del Palacio the festive poet. The passing years also furnished new targets for the bilious sharpshooters. Restoration politicians and men of letters had their vanity pricked and their fame deflated. Such operations were not always governed by principles; friendship often inspired convictions which nothing else could have sustained. In the realm of literature the novels of Galdós were the gospel for these high priests of innovation. In view of the fact that the "Bilis Club" functioned mainly as a fault-finding body, its unqualified endorsement of his successes and its magnanimous condonation of his failures represented an admiration bordering on reverence, almost religious fanaticism. It was the "Bilis Club" that saw in Galdós' relative obscurity evidence of the low cultural level of Spain, and it started an agitation in behalf of his public glorification. In keeping with Spanish practice, the agitation passed through a period of verbal incubation, but such was the determination of Galdós' promoters that before very long a course of action was charted.

At a dinner in celebration of the première of Sellés' *Las esculturas de carne* was born the idea of rendering public homage to Galdós in a manner reminiscent of the coronation of the poet Quintana and the glowing tribute to the prolific Lope de Vega. It was admittedly a unique way of glorifying a novelist, but Galdós' novels were unique in Spain. Sellés was father of the idea and took upon himself all the details of organization. Clarín regretfully abstained from participation because of his duties at the University of Zaragoza.

The specific scheme proposed by Sellés was a vast banquet to be tendered not by the government nor by duly constituted organizations, but by the voluntary subscription of Galdós' admirers. Thus the honor would be a spontaneous gesture, popular and national—all very much in keeping with the glory that had come to the Spanish nation from the author's artistic achievements. Sellés' suggestion was accepted without a dissenting vote, and on March 4, 1883, the press of Madrid carried the following appeal penned by Armando Palacio Valdés:

> As a homage of admiration to an illustrious novelist who, a glory of Spain ever since he first made public his works, is today known and acclaimed throughout Europe, there was born among several of his devotees and enthusiastic admirers the idea of tendering him a banquet similar to those held in other cultured countries in honor of men who have achieved eminence in letters, arts and politics.
>
> Such a demonstration of respect and enthusiasm could never have been made with greater reason than now. Don Benito Pérez Galdós, by his incomparable genius and his amazing fecundity, which stand out so

vividly against his singular modesty, is one of the
Spaniards who bring the greatest honor and glory to
their country. By gathering here today to honor
him, we who fervently admire him are prompted not
alone by our own sentiments, but also, we are sure,
by the sentiments of the great majority of cultured
people who have savored with delight his beautiful
creations.

To all these persons we appeal and from all of
them we expect effective support for the realization of
the demonstration that is being prepared.

Not only writers and artists are duty bound to
honor men who are distinguished in letters and arts,
but likewise those who love these without professing
them.

The undersigned, then, will gratefully receive the
support of all who care to be present at the banquet
which will be given in honor of Pérez Galdós on a
day and at a place which will be properly announced
in the press.[7]

The response to this appeal exceeded all expectations. An
important political event would hardly have stirred up more
interest than the forthcoming banquet. The press featured it
prominently up to and even beyond the date set for it—March
26, 1883. It was as if all the editors and feature writers had
resolved to make amends for the respectful silence they had
generally maintained about the man to be honored. So many
illustrated biographies of Galdós were published that certainly
no one remained ignorant about his life and appearance. The
numerous articles and editorials that appeared in less than a
month had all the earmarks of a high-pressure publicity and
sales campaign. Only the Catholic press, generally speaking,
maintained a cautious reserve about the forthcoming homage.
It was good strategy to keep its powder dry for an attack when
the enemy might not appear so formidably armed and supported.

The rapidly growing demand for participation in what promised to be a veritable apotheosis of Galdós came from such

widely divergent elements of the population that it was deemed advisable to organize a morning banquet—admission three pesetas—at the Café Inglés in addition to the official evening banquet—admission five duros—at the Círculo Ayala. The over-flow celebration would accommodate the humble Spaniards whose admiration for Galdós exceeded their financial assets and who preferred their own company to that of the prominent national figures.

Public curiosity was centered in the identity of the great men who were to honor Galdós by their presence. The lists of the subscribers and patrons in the daily press were scanned and dis-cussed in café *tertulias*. Particularly was there speculation over the attitude Cánovas del Castillo would take. The part he had recently had in excluding Galdós from the Royal Academy was recalled in terms unflattering to the famous politician. There was considerable satisfaction when Echegaray and the pre-eminently famous Castelar announced their participation in the homage, and there was much guessing about the identity of a justly popular man of letters who made a reservation in the name of "*un desconocido*." The "unknown one" turned out to be the serious-minded poet Campoamor. In short, so high were the enthusiasm and interest that had King Alfonso's cabinet planned a daring coup between March 4 and March 26, it could have been executed without attracting much public notice.

The days immediately preceding the banquet were days of great anxiety for Galdós. His frame of mind was like that of a person who, on the eve of assuming a grave responsibility to which he had been looking forward, is seized by the fear that he cannot discharge it competently. He was unquestionably flat-tered to be the topic of conversation and the inspiration of boundlessly eulogistic comment. He realized he was to be brought together with his public in a way that had few parallels in any country and certainly none in the recent history of Spain. His conscience was quite easy with respect to the spontaneous origin of the homage, for he had done nothing overt to build up his popularity or to suggest the celebration. If on occasion he had shown disappointment over the limited attention paid to his work, it was because it grieved him that his countrymen were incapable of intense interest in anything above the plane of petty and prosaic actualities. The recognition he coveted was not for himself personally, but for his ideal of national spiritual regeneration. Yet the method his friends adopted for dramatizing his achievements and merit struck him as excessively theatrical. He questioned whether such a manifestation of esteem was of much significance.

Galdós revealed his state of mind to his most intimate friends and expressed his opposition to the forthcoming event. He did not make the outright suggestion to cancel it because of a mixture of human and professional motives. But on the eve of the momentous day he grew panicky over the prospect of having to face and address two large crowds, and suddenly decided to escape the ordeal by fleeing to Toledo. He would add a dramatic touch to the solemn occasion by not witnessing his own consecration! But in order not to appear rudely ungrateful, he printed a humble reply to all the after-dinner speeches and made secret arrangements for its distribution at the proper moment. Unfortunately the conspiracy was foiled just in time. When somehow Galdós' disappearance from Madrid became known, a company of scouts was sent in pursuit of him. The night of March 25 the fugitive was located in Toledo and brought back in the custody of a committee of writers. The accumulated emotional strain of several weeks, climaxed by the trying experience of the flight, prevented Galdós from participating in the splendid gastronomic program of March 26, 1883. The guest of honor was unable to take food that day!

The morning banquet in the Café Inglés—admission three pesetas—made up in expansiveness, enthusiasm, and artistic fervor for what it lacked in culinary delicacy, solemnity, and studied dignity. At eleven in the morning more than one hundred and fifty guests, mostly young people, overcrowded the dining-room and staged a scene of unprecedented enthusiasm. There were no scheduled speeches, but no one present was denied the opportunity to unburden his heart and mind about the honored author. Marcos Zapata, a second-rate popular comedian, proved himself worthy of his art and fame. When he entered the Café Inglés, he made a remark that might well be regarded as a complete, if laconic, account of the celebration. Said Marcos Zapata: "We are going to eat only twelve-reales' worth here, but we are going to show two-hundred-duros' worth of enthusiasm."

Indeed the humble luncheon was a frenzied festival. Shortly before dessert was served, Galdós entered, not too majestically. He had a headache and was not an inspiring sight. But the crowd ignored that. They rose and greeted him with fifteen minutes of deafening applause. Marcos Zapata again honored his calling. First to glimpse Galdós in the doorway, he threw his hat at the novelist's feet and exclaimed: "Bravo! A blessing upon your mother, and blessed are those who can read your books!"[8] Thus welcomed and sanctified, the guest of honor traveled along a veritable *via crucis* through the applauding and cheering crowd, amidst expressions of genuine affection, in a sea of hands eagerly seeking to clasp his, profoundly stirred by that spontaneous ovation. Physically weakened and emotionally exhausted, Galdós left the luncheon as soon as he could politely do so and walked over to the Ateneo to recover. The cheering crowd left its dessert and followed him in one of the most picturesque processions that had ever traversed the streets of Madrid. In front of the Ateneo, Galdós, with tears of joy and fright in his eyes, begged to be excused, thanked the crowd in brief, inaudible words, and entered the building. The celebrants returned to the Café Inglés to continue the homage and to fulfill Marcos Zapata's prediction.

But the banner event was the night banquet in the Círculo Ayala—admission five duros. Estimates of the attendance range from one hundred and thirty to two hundred and forty, but there is no divergence of opinion about the hierarchies present. In the words of one reporter: "What a spectacle that was! . . . It is indescribable. Suffice it to say that Madrid's most outstanding notables in arts, letters, the army, science and finance were present, mingled and merged in friendship and cordiality with the many admirers of the novelist's talent."[9] The wall back of the speaker's table was decorated with Galdós' drawings for the

illustrated edition of the *Episodios nacionales*. A huge bouquet
of flowers sent by the Valencia press added a bright touch.

The guest of honor did not have his customary serene expression, which some had come to regard as revelatory of the great
thinker who judges everything with calm detachment. He was
pale; his small black eyes looked even smaller; his lean frame
seemed leaner. His simple clothes contrasted with the elegance
of the formal attire and the splendor of the military uniforms
of near-by guests. Gone was his light and somewhat ironical
smile. His sparse moustache stood out conspicuously on his
upper lip. He appeared nervous, more retiring than usual—even
frightened. At his right, somewhat symbolically, sat Cánovas
del Castillo. Castelar and Echegaray were also at the speaker's
table. The quality of the menu was commensurate with the
admission charge of five duros, but this Galdós was unable to
ascertain for himself.

If it is true that because of their envious nature Spaniards are
sparing with their appreciation of the worth of others, they
successfully repressed that trait on the night of March 26, 1883.
According to the press accounts, "public enthusiasm, which had
long been scattered and held in, came rushing like a river swelled
by heavy rains and fell thunderously like a heavy torrent, en-
gulfing the famous novelist in its foam of triumph." [10] Salvos of
applause greeted the reading of numerous telegrams from clubs,
newspapers, and individuals in Madrid and in the provinces.
Some admirers sent greetings more substantial than congratulations. Galdós wept when the representative of the Canary colony
in Madrid made him a gift of a beautiful mudéjar plate, and
he was only a trifle less moved when he received a de luxe edition of Goethe's *Faust* in Spanish from the Círculo Nacional de
la Juventud and a complete set of Sir Walter Scott's works in
English—and in an artistic bookcase—from the Córdoba bookstore.

But the speeches were the *pièce de résistance* of the program.
Such a galaxy of orators, among whom were Castelar, Echegaray, and Cánovas, would have been a delectable treat even in
the halls of Cortes! Cánovas' speech was listened to with an

interest not justified by its content. The guests were wondering
if the politician would rectify in public the injustice he had
committed in the private chambers of the Royal Academy. He
did not. An unforeseen incident made Echegaray's speech even
more memorable than his histrionic skill. Because of his low
stature the triumphant dramatist mounted the speaker's table
and with his arms described sweeping arches in the air to accompany his waves of eloquence. During one of these gestures his
arms lashed the chandelier—and a gas lamp came crashing down.
Someone called out: "Señor Echegaray is so theatrical that there
are catastrophes even in his speeches." [11] The playwright replied
in words that might have come from the lips of one of his heroes:
"There you are; we have barely missed adding a shower of
light to the illumination which radiates from our honored
guest." [12] Galdós—the source of the radiating light—remained
somber. His mind was probably on the speech he would soon be
called upon to make. He had a strange surprise in store for his
admirers.

The man who—in the words of Eusebio Blasco—"carried the
whole world in his vestpocket" lacked the courage to rise and
read his printed address. Excusing himself on the grounds of
physical indisposition, he asked José Castro y Serrano to perform
in his stead. Don José obligingly read the following simple and
humble words from the pen of one who had written more than
one eloquent address for his fictional characters:

> Gentlemen: The fear of not being well heard be-
> fore so large a gathering, because of the small volume
> of my voice and because of the natural emotion that
> perforce overwhelms me as I address you, moves me
> to introduce this unconventional but effective way of
> expressing my gratitude, although at the same time I
> am constrained to lodge a protest.
>
> Yes, gentlemen; I protest against the singular
> honor your kindness renders me. I protest in the name
> of privileged talent here present, whom I have long
> revered and admired. I protest in the name of others
> not here present but who, wherever they may be,

deserve not only my fondness but also my attachment and enthusiasm. I protest in the name of kindly friends and dear colleagues who, whether they hide their glory in the modest corner of a province or parade it through the splendor of the capital, have always had me as their disciple and whom I shall always count as my model. I protest in the name of literary celebrities whose loss we have sustained a short while ago; celebrities, gentlemen, who have not yet received the tribute of a solemn tomb: Bretón de los Herreros, father of our modern drama; Hartzen-busch, father of our language and contemporary criti-cism; Mesonero Romanos, not alone the father but the preceptor of all of us in the profession of fine literature, master of written grace and wit, master in pictorial truth and richness, master in themes of meaning and transcendence; lastly, Fernán Caballero, whose admirable narrations, imbued with a spirit as national as it is Christian, have found an honorable place for contemporary Spanish literature in the con-cert of European literatures.

All these should have earned before me and very much in preference to me honors like the present one. I say this in truth and without false modesty. If, then, on this day you open the path of public distinctions to literary talents and you transfer this one of which I am the pretext to all those who deserve them, and if you will permit me to adjudicate them to them in your name, reserving for myself the smallest part to which I am entitled, then, indeed, I can say with satisfaction and pride: gentlemen, guests at the ban-quet of March 26, I thank you. I thank you very much. Benito Pérez Galdós.[13]

Thus ended the official program. Castro y Serrano's last words had hardly died away when the banqueters burst forth in a salvo of *vivas* for Galdós, many of which were accompanied by an energetic Spanish embrace. Galdós emerged emotionally crushed and physically bruised from this exuberant display of affection and escaped in time the danger of a complete collapse. On the way out, at the door, someone remarked to him: "It seems that we are leading you to the gallows of glory." [14]

Galdós was not the only one to pay the price of his consecration. In Las Palmas, Catalina Robayna had been the family nurse beyond the memory of its oldest member. She was the wife of a fisherman whom she often helped at the port. One morning, early in April, 1883, Catalina was at the pier when a boat from the Spanish main delivered a bundle of Madrid newspapers. These carried the accounts of Benitín's banquet. Catalina grabbed a copy and, overcome with joy, ran several miles up Calle Triana into town. Her mantilla slipped off her shoulders to the ground, but Catalina did not stop to pick it up. All out of breath she reached the Galdós house and fairly exploded with enthusiasm. Mama Dolores, who had just lined up the family for the morning procession to church, sternly rebuked Catalina for stirring up such a fuss over an insignificant incident. What did one more bit of vain glory mean to Benitín? For the first time in her life Catalina dared disobey Mama Dolores and impetuously poured forth her version of the banquet as it had been read to her at the pier by her husband's associates. Mama Dolores bade her hold her peace, under pain of instant dismissal. Catalina lost her job that morning. Thereafter other members of the family surreptitiously cared for the aged servant.

In 1897, when Catalina Robayna had been dead for a number of years, she was resurrected by the last Galdós she had nursed. Catalina Robayna came to life again in the soul and spirit of the unusual Benina, heroine of *Misericordia*. Catalina and Benitín are partners in glory.

IX

The Widening Horizon

THE PREDICTION OF SPANISH critics in 1877 that *Gloria* would bring Galdós universal recognition came true sporadically and very slowly. This is not necessarily a reflection on Galdós' works. Possibly because of Spain's humble international position, students of Continental literature naturally took scant notice of what the Spaniards hailed as a veritable rebirth of their national novel. In fact, even the limited attention that Spanish literary developments received in Europe and elsewhere came largely from professional translators in search of marketable merchandise. Although the standards of these literary traffickers were not too high, their interest in a given author could serve as an index of his worth and appeal outside his native land.

It was the banquet of 1883, and not *Gloria*, that added a bit to Galdós' European fame. He was still obliged to be the peddler of his own wares, but the market was now less restricted. By comparison with his contemporaries he had been impressively successful even before 1883, but now, as the nationally consecrated novelist, he approached Continental translators and publishers with a confidence not possessed by his colleagues.

Four translations of Galdós' novels appeared in 1884, two of which were in French. It was his first conquest of France, and he regarded it as the highest point his success had reached. The next four or five years witnessed the steady publication of his works in English, French, German, Dutch, and Swedish. He was particularly pleased to have his non-controversial novels introduced abroad. *Marianela*, his so-called lyrical interlude, enjoyed three different translations in French in as many years, and one in German. The first two *episodios* were translated into English, and *El amigo Manso* came out in French. True, some of the translations appeared serially in obscure journals, but it gratified Galdós that in Europe and even in America the range of his translated works extended from *La fontana de oro* through the contemporary series. The financial returns were still slight, but the bread he was casting upon the waters would surely return to him some day in a pleasantly profitable form.

With Spain, Europe, and North America fairly conquered, Galdós turned his attention to the Spanish-American continent. He had many admirers there, especially among the Spanish immigrants who had crossed the ocean in quest of the very progress and liberalism of which he was the exponent. Because of their distance from the homeland, they naturally overestimated the extent of Galdós' regenerative influence. They wrote him enthusiastic letters which revealed that they mistook his efforts for accomplishments and which urged him to be steadfast in his crusade against obscurantism. Their wanton praise of his novels, especially the *episodios,* surpassed even the bias of the liberal Madrid critics.

Galdós was vainly proud of his Spanish-American admirers and treasured their correspondence. In his meditations on the regeneration of Spain he assigned them a prominent part because of their spiritual unity with the homeland and their superior revitalizing energy. He had a strong desire to visit the Hispanic republics in order to strengthen his ties with the people. For the present, however, he could do nothing more than toy with the idea of a trip across the ocean. He loved the sea, but he was a better land traveler.

Other considerations, too, drew Galdós toward those distant lands. The code of business ethics practised by Spanish-American publishers did not redound to his financial welfare. His works circulated across the Atlantic on a large scale, but mostly in unauthorized editions, of which some were printed in Germany. At this distance there was little he could do legally to restrain unscrupulous exploiters. As a measure of compensation he established contact with the Spanish-American press and became

European correspondent of *La Prensa* of Buenos Aires shortly after the banquet of 1883. He held the assignment for approximately a decade, contributing frequent articles on political, social, and cultural events in Spain and the rest of Europe. In a very real sense he became the connecting spiritual link between Spanish America and Continental Spain.

* * * *

Galdós' quest for wider horizons was not, of course, limited to circulating his books abroad. Beginning in 1883, he became the most widely traveled Spanish writer of his century with the possible exception of Valera, whose diplomatic appointments took him to many lands. The date is perhaps significant. Galdós may have felt that as a consecrated national glory it devolved upon him more than ever to become acquainted with his country and the world beyond it. As a matter of fact, however, his passion for travel had manifested itself long before he became established as a novelist. Even in the days of his literary apprenticeship he had spent his free time in excursions to cities in the vicinity of Madrid, and after his first visit to Santander in 1871 the *montaña* with its imposing mountains and idyllic valleys beckoned to him almost every year. So much importance did he attach to travel that he rarely planned any specific work for the summer months. He himself has described the spiritual and artistic experience that traveling afforded him:

> My greatest pleasure is to travel in Spain and to be the guest of its glorious cities, going through them from one end to another in pursuit of intense historical poetry; to cover next the towns and villages, the desolate places that in the past were the scene of memorable events, true or imaginary; to live in the midst of the humble people who are today a precious relic of the original settlers of those lands and hamlets; to see at close range men and rocks, and to converse with both, searching in the old fountainheads of Spanish life the elements of a new and splendorous vital current.[1]

All this he "would not exchange for the riches which the miner extracts from the bowels of the earth." [2]

Because of his historical sense and interest in architecture, Galdós had a decided preference for the cathedral cities of Spain, and he made frequent pilgrimages to Burgos and more particularly Toledo. Whenever he felt the need of detaching himself from prosaic actualities, he would journey to the city on the Tagus and spend hours and days in ecstatic contemplation of its artistic monuments. The mystic atmosphere of Toledo cast a spell over the author who in *Angel Guerra* treated mysticism with critical objectivity. The splendid Gothic cathedral had charmed him back in his student days, and he revisited it frequently. On some of these visits he was overcome by its sublime beauty to the point of physical exhaustion. On such occasions he would be particularly annoyed at the official guides, whose endless chatter and mechanical recital of the cathedral's features and history he regarded as blasphemies against the divinity of art.

In moments of physical fatigue Galdós preferred to rest quietly in front of the main altar, or in one of his favorite chapels, for a few moments of reverie and prayer. Once, in his later years, he was attracted by a commotion near the principal door. A foundling had been brought to the cathedral. Galdós quickly turned away from the scene with moist eyes, and his lips moved in silent prayer. Perhaps the sight of the foundling brought contrition to his heart for the carnal creatures he had so irresponsibly engendered and brought into the world. However that may be, Galdós must have been stirred to the very depths of his soul, for he fell into a profound slumber from which his nephew José Hurtado de Mendoza, who accompanied him, dared not rouse him for some time.

Toledo had for Galdós an intimate and hidden meaning which will forever remain a mystery. In this mystery lies the principal reason why he localized the story of *Angel Guerra* chiefly in Toledo. No other city outside of Madrid enjoys such distinction in his canvas of contemporary Spanish life.

Besides its cathedral, Toledo lured Galdós with the haunting beauty of the churches adjoining its fifteen convents. He always regretted that the rules of the institutions prevented him from examining the interior of the cloisters. He would have given the world for a glimpse of the life of the nuns! In this desire there was nothing facetious. His interest in these humble servants of God was sincere, and in his novels he always treated them with genuine sympathy and generosity.

To see the interior of the convent churches it was necessary to get up very early, and more than once Galdós attended morning mass with a handful of aged beggars—the only congregation the nuns had. The service over and the mendicants scattered at their posts, he would linger in the church until the clanging of the sacristan's keys reminded him that it was time to leave the premises. Many a morning he spent sitting on the doorstep of a building opposite the convent of Santo Domingo el Real, fascinated by its Renaissance portico, which faces a little square—the most solitary and deserted spot in the city of Toledo. Never once had he seen even the shadow of a human being darken that little square at so early an hour.

In Galdós' memory the San Pablo convent occupied a place of preference alongside Santo Domingo el Real. He always remembered fondly the impoverished nuns of San Pablo and their inordinate pride in the possession of the precious knife with which Saint Paul had allegedly been beheaded. He made his first visit to this convent church in the company of Arredondo, a famous Toledo painter whom the nuns befriended. As a tribute to his escort, they allowed Galdós to examine the precious but murderous weapon, which was kept in a case of red velvet. With manifest skepticism concerning the use to which that shiny damaskeened blade had been put in centuries past, he desecrated it by sharpening his pencil with it during a moment when the trusting nuns had left him and his companion alone.

When a few years before his death Galdós was prevailed upon by the popular illustrated magazine *La Esfera* to publish his memoirs, he devoted more space to Toledo than to any other topic. Back in the days of his journalistic career his first serious effort had been a mature study entitled "Las generaciones artísticas en la ciudad de Toledo," which he published in *Revista de España* (1870). In 1923, three years after Galdós death, a group of young Spanish writers and intellectuals, headed by Gregorio Marañón and Ramón Pérez de Ayala, organized the society of "Los Amigos de Galdós," dedicated to the perpetuation of interest in the works of the great author. Very appropriately the "Friends of Galdós" chose Toledo for their first solemn meeting on April 15, 1923. One can forgive this group for having failed thus far to keep their first promise—the compilation of a census of Galdós' characters—in return for the sincerely eloquent tablet, magnificent in the simplicity of its text, which they unveiled on the façade of the building on Calle de Santa Isabel, where Galdós lived and wrote part of *Angel Guerra*. The legend reads:

> In the year 1891 of the Era of Christ, living the Toledan life for immortality, here dwelt Benito Pérez Galdós and here he wrote, with ever young words, the Spanish poem—religious, tragic and burlesque—of our times: *Angel Guerra*
>
> Traveler:
> do not pass in front of me indifferently.
> Numen inest.

*　*　*　*

Clarín has observed that Galdós, like some of the characters in his novels of the late eighties, was a Spaniard English style— *"un español a la inglesa."* [3] This is in part a valid characterization. During his childhood Galdós had been to some extent exposed to the English language—in the private school of the Balls spinsters and through his association with Mama Tate. Moreover, in the Las Palmas of those days Englishmen constituted a considerable element of the population, living as an independent British community on Spanish soil. But how well Galdós mastered their language in his boyhood and to what extent he became acquainted with English life and literature is a question. The profusion of interlinear translations in his copy of Oliver Goldsmith's *The Vicar of Wakefield* suggests that at some undefined date he had to use the dictionary for the meaning of even some of the commonest English prepositions. It is therefore likely that with the exception of Dickens, to whom he applied himself with "mad eagerness" [4] after Balzac in the late sixties, his knowledge of English literature in the original was acquired mainly in the decade between 1880 and 1890, particularly after his first trip to England in 1883. As regards his oral mastery of the language, he admitted that in 1888 he could only converse in "jabbered English" (*"inglés chapurreado"*) with some young British misses who accompanied him up Mt. Vesuvius. Nevertheless, in 1868 he felt sufficiently competent to make a Spanish translation of Dickens' *Pickwick Papers,* which he introduced to the public serially with an article full of admiration for the author. It may thus be assumed that one abiding influence of Dickens upon Galdós, who as late as 1916 called him "my most beloved master," [5] was an irresistible urge to see the land and the people he found so fascinating in the master's novels.

And so something more than chance impelled Galdós to visit England first when, in 1883, he decided to glimpse the horizons beyond the Spanish frontiers. That summer he went from Santander to London, where he spent most of the season, living in a modest hotel on Golden Square patronized by other Spanish guests. Reviving the sight-seeing technique he had successfully employed in France in 1867 and 1868, he quickly became acquainted with the British capital to a degree that even an official guide might have envied. With knowledge gleaned from Baedeker and from history and literature, and with his penetrating power of observation, he familiarized himself easily not only with the physical features of the city, but also with the character, psychology, and life of its inhabitants.

Overlooking literally nothing, Galdós dwelt with particular interest on the London of Dickens and other literary reminiscences. He liked the city as a whole—its immensity and its disproportionate beauty as well as its ugliness—and even preferred it to Paris, notwithstanding the physical regularity and harmony, the gaiety and greater pleasantness of the French capital. Everything he observed deepened his already great admiration for the English philosophy of government and the principles of common sense regulating the life of the people.

Westminster Abbey, after Parliament, moved Galdós to prolonged meditation. On his numerous trips to London he never failed to revisit it, and every time he experienced the sensation of "one who shares in the bringing of an offering to the Gods or to the mortals who rub elbows with the Gods." [6] His recurring impression was that nowhere else in the world had a nation gathered into one shrine all the glory and grandeur of the race. On his visits to the Abbey he paid homage to Newton, Darwin, and others, but in Poets' Corner he would linger in mystic rapture before the graves, busts, and statues of the immortal writers, composers, actors, historians, and critics—the "vast celestial throng" [7]—of the English genius. The first time he approached the grave of Dickens he was filled with reverence and moved to mystic adoration. In the presence of the spirit of his literary patron saint he felt the intimate joy of two souls in fervent communion, and with every visit he rededicated himself to the veneration of his favorite English novelist.

The deep impressions his first trip to England made upon Galdós found immediate though sporadic expression in his next novel, *Tormento* (1884), and more palpably in *Lo prohibido* (1884–85). For some time after his return he regaled his friends with accounts of his travels and spoke of a plan he had for a book on London. But many years passed before he published any of his impressions of England. In the meantime his interest in the country evolved imperceptibly into something like an annual summer ritual, which he anticipated more than any other diversion. His starting point was Santander and, after 1883, his destination was invariably Newcastle and the home of José Alcalá Galiano, his one-time colleague on the staff of *Las Cortes*. Pepe, who was Spanish consul in Newcastle, and his charming Irish wife, Mary, gave Galdós a taste of English hospitality. Together the two men made many extended tours of England and Scotland, and sometimes they met to plan trips on the Continent.

Because he believed that "art has always been more beautiful than history," [8] Galdós, who always strove in his travels to discover the connecting link between the past and the present, felt the essence of eternity only at the sites immortalized by universal fictional figures and their genial creators. Dickens, Goldsmith, Thackeray, Milton, Garrick, Shakespeare, Dante, Michelangelo, Cellini, Leonardo da Vinci, Velázquez, Rubens, Hamlet, Portia, Macbeth, Ophelia, Juliet, Shylock, Beethoven, Handel, and scores of others moved him more deeply than the names of rulers, princes, potentates, and popes associated with the historic monuments he saw in every country of Europe. If the published accounts of his journeys are more visual than emotional, it is perhaps because he wrote them more out of need than in response to an inner urge. And because he was not given to expansiveness, he was not under the compulsion, as are most famous men, of communicating his intimate travel experiences to his public.

Yet Galdós' homage to art and artists, however brief, abounds with deep sincerity, delicate sentiment, and admiration verging on adoration. In the presence of the creation of the human genius he was invariably lifted far above reality, and he literally found words inadequate for the expression of their grandeur and transcendence. In Shakespeare—"the sovereign creator of human lives," [9] as he called him—he saw the essence of divinity and regarded his birthplace as sacred soil. In the eighties Galdós was an accomplished student of Shakespeare, and one might say that he knew his plays better than his own novels. Down to the last years of his life callers frequently found him engrossed in one or another of Shakespeare's works. They were his favorite recreation during the months he spent in his summer home. In his library he had complete sets and odd volumes of the English dramatist in Spanish, French, and Portuguese as well as in the original language. Among his most prized books was *Bell's Edition of Shakespeare's Plays* in five volumes (London, 1774). And his own novels abound with direct allusions to Shakespearean characters and incidents.

Thus Galdós' visit to Stratford-on-Avon in September, 1889, was the realization of a long-cherished desire. Shakespeare's birthplace was for him unquestionably the most soul-stirring point of pilgrimage in all Europe. In those days it was no simple task for a foreigner to make the trip from Newcastle to Stratford with only the aid of a Bradshaw and the laconic directions of the British railway employees, but Galdós cheerfully suffered a few inconveniences and embarrassments in exchange for the ineffable joy ahead. One of his early thrills was the discovery that he was probably the first Spaniard to sign the register book.

He reached Stratford at nightfall. Immediately he had an impression of well-being, tranquillity, and rustic simplicity. He felt transported to another age, communing with the great artist who was the object of his pilgrimage. He tried to visualize Stratford in the days of Shakespeare, or the dramatist strolling at his side in the gas-illuminated streets of modern Stratford. Nothing interrupted his imaginings, not even his arrival at Shakespeare's Hotel.

He was assigned a room bearing the name of "Love's Labours Lost," not far from "Macbeth" and "Hamlet." This incident extended for him the illusion that he had suddenly entered the only enduring world—the eternal world of artistic creation. A sweeping glance at the hotel with its modest comforts, tranquillity, and cleanliness brought to his mind descriptions in Dickens and Macaulay. His first impression was strengthened by other pleasant details. Hosts and guests mingled in friendly harmony, and if the food was typical of English culinary sobriety, nothing in the world could compare with the roomy, clean, soft English beds. Galdós had never slept in such comfort before. Otherwise he felt quite at home, especially in the dining-room. The English guests looked so very much like old acquaintances. He had first seen them some twenty years before in the novels of Dickens. Externally they had changed very little. He looked under the table to see if they wore leggings like Pickwick!

Altogether Galdós spent a delightful holiday in Stratford. He missed nothing of interest and took minute notes on everything he saw. Holy Trinity Church, the burial place of Shakespeare and his wife, led him to reflect gloomily on Spain's neglect of its great men, living and dead. It may have occurred to him that his own remains would some day share the fate of those of Cervantes and Velázquez, resting unidentified in some common grave. He was haunted by the thought that Shakespeare had enjoyed respect, fame, and wealth in life. How different were England and Spain in their treatment of the great! But he had not come to Stratford to muse about himself and his country. Holy Trinity Church was most interesting: its interior had none of the cold bareness so typical of Protestant places of worship. The most absorbing sight, of course, was Shakespeare's bust. It fitted so perfectly into the construction and atmosphere of the church that it might easily be taken for the shrine of some saint placed there for the worship of the faithful.

So lifelike did the bust seem to Galdós that he stood before it in prolonged contemplation and dreamed that he was conversing with the dramatist. His reverie over, he noticed the inscription on the plinth:

Judicio Pylium, genio Socratem, arte Maronem.
Terra tegit, Populus maeret, Olympus habet.

This seemed to him an understatement of Shakespeare's talents, and he recalled that the word *Socratem* was probably the engraver's mistake for *Sophoclem*. He then made a translation of the six English verses under the inscription and also of the famous quatrain inscribed on the stone over the grave. For him Shakespeare was beyond doubt the author of this quatrain. He had always liked the vigor of its expression, and so he was very pleased to acquire a replica of it. He also obtained a number of artistic tiles depicting famous Shakespearean scenes, which, not many years later, he used as inlays in the fireplace in San Quintín. Out of respect for the dramatist he never lighted a fire in it.

Galdós' lasting impression of his visit to Holy Trinity Church —of his communion with Shakespeare—can best be stated in his own words:

> It is a mystical impression, a spiritual communication, akin to those which in the religious realm are derived from devout exaltation in the presence of sacred mysteries or venerated relics. The literary enthusiasm and fanatical admiration which the works of a superior talent awaken in us take on in such a place and before that tomb the character of religious fervor which

quickens our imagination, subtilizes and confounds our
senses, causes us to become as one with the spirit of the
being there represented, and makes us feel him within
ourselves, as if we had absorbed him by means of
mysterious communion.[10]

*   *   *   *

In the spring of 1885 Galdós made a hurried tour of Portugal
in the company of Pereda and a wealthy Santander merchant.
Naturally enough, Galdós was led to draw comparisons between
that country and Spain, particularly as regards the character of
their inhabitants.

He found Lisbon a sad and silent city, contrasting sharply with
noisy, even tumultuous Madrid. The Lisbonese were more dignified and better behaved than the Madrilenians, but they were
also less animated and less friendly. He saw nothing in the
Portuguese capital comparable to the lively Madrid crowds that
in favorable weather stream in steady procession to the Prado
or the Retiro. Portuguese sobriety of action and speech accentuated for Galdós the excessive loquaciousness and animation of the
Spaniards, but he wondered whether the decorous behavior of the
Lisbonese crowds, as he observed them on a Sunday, did not
bespeak a lack of imaginative vigor, capable of creating a serious
deficiency in the country's general culture. He missed the music,
songs, laughter, and banter so characteristic of the streets of
Madrid on that day. He reflected, however, that his own countrymen might gain something highly desirable if they could exchange a part of their noisy Andalusian gaiety for a bit of the
composure and spiritual tranquillity of the Portuguese.

Besides the capital, Galdós' Portuguese itinerary included only
Cintra, Coimbra, and Oporto. The call of his muse and the outbreak of a serious cholera epidemic in Spain impelled him to
shorten his trip. The more urgent of these considerations was
the call of his muse. The gestation period of his supreme novel,
Fortunata y Jacinta, was nearly over, and the desire to begin
writing was irresistible. By June 4 Galdós was back on Spanish
soil in Vigo. The last Portuguese city he visited was Oporto,

where his stay was pleasant and profitable. There he and Pereda made the acquaintance of many prominent literary and scientific figures, and they were especially delighted to meet Oliveira Martins, who presented Galdós with an autographed copy of his *History of Iberian Civilization*.

Reflecting on his impressions of Portugal, Galdós concluded that it was unnatural for the two Iberian countries to hold themselves aloof from each other. Two nations so closely related racially, culturally, historically, and geographically should be brought together more intimately. In his opinion the fault lay with the Portuguese, who loved the Spaniards infinitely less than the Spaniards loved them. Spain had made repeated overtures of rapprochement, which had been received with indifference. This was probably due to the fact that the Portuguese, conscious of their inferiority, were more sensitive. True, relations between the two countries were growing more cordial, but they were still incommensurate with the efforts exerted by Spain. This was clearly exemplified in Portuguese ignorance of Spanish literature. Galdós ruefully observed the popularity in Portugal of the worst products of Parisian boulevard writers. He regarded this as unfair, particularly since contemporary Portuguese literature was relatively well known in Spain. Least understandable of all was Portugal's exertion to achieve economic independence. It did not make sense, since Spain also had to struggle to preserve a semblance of a big nation. Why could not the two nations pool their resources without necessarily renouncing their sovereignty? Galdós would not suggest an outright political union because of Portugal's extreme sensitiveness, but, like many another Spanish intellectual, he favored pan-Iberianism and sanguinely hoped that some day Spain and Portugal might form a powerful sovereign bloc in the international affairs of the European continent.

*   *   *   *

In the summers of 1886 and 1887 Galdós visited Germany and adjacent countries. The first trip was unpremeditated. He had just arrived in Paris, where he chanced upon a moderately priced excursion to the Rhineland. For the first and only time in his life he joined an organized travel tour. It was a pleasant excursion, but not a particularly impressive one. After the cathedral of Strasbourg, his main interest was in the boat trip up the Rhine. Most of the famous landmarks he only glimpsed from the decks of the splendid steamer. He was keenly disappointed that he could not disembark at Bonn to visit the home of Beethoven, his favorite composer. In Cologne he was puzzled to discover the sepulcher of the Magi Kings in the cathedral. Why were those warm-hearted Oriental rulers laid to rest in the cold north? He thought it curious too that the bones of the eleven thousand virgins—whose memory is so often evoked by Spaniards in a mild oath—were housed in another Cologne church. But he found no explanation for these oddities, not even in the home of his good friend Dr. Johann Fastenrath, with whom he had a delightful visit before ending the Rhineland tour.

From Cologne Galdós proceeded by rail through Belgium to France, and in Le Havre he embarked for Santander. He was happy to be back home. Like parents away on a vacation, he was lonesome for his spiritual children. He had been working for some time on *Fortunata y Jacinta,* and its characters had become so real for him that he missed them. It was a highly emotional reunion, and Galdós plunged feverishly into his work.

The hurried tour of 1886 failed to satisfy Galdós' curiosity about Germany. Traveling with an organized group was not satisfactory, for it had irritated him to have to do everything as if he were a member of a military unit. In the summer of 1887, when he was again in Newcastle, he and Pepe planned an extended tour of Germany, including a visit to Holland.

The German stretch of the trip from Amsterdam to Berlin impressed Galdós indifferently, and Berlin itself appealed to him much less than other European capitals. Its size was imposing, but otherwise it struck him as a gloomy city without personality. When he reached Hamburg, however, he began to enjoy himself, particularly in the San Pauli district. He preferred the cosmopolitan atmosphere of Hamburg and its great commercial activity to the military rigidity and Prussianism of Berlin. He had never been an admirer of Germany, and in 1887 he was probably still under the influence of the anti-German wave which had swept Spain in 1885 as a result of the threatened seizure of the Caroline Islands by Berlin. Like most Spaniards of his day, he respected German scientific and technological progress and had a high regard for Goethe and Schiller, but he never felt strongly attracted to the country.

In Galdós' memory the summer of 1887 remained associated with his very brief glimpse of Denmark and not with the German tour. At Copenhagen he made the acquaintance of his translators and enjoyed a visit to the Thorvaldsen Museum. But the highlight of the trip was the apocryphal tomb of Ophelia. That it was merely legendary mattered little to him, and he felt as if he were in the presence of the greatest reality in the world. He was equally stirred by the ruins of Elsinore Castle, and since he knew *Hamlet* virtually by heart it was easy for him to rehearse in his imagination the opening scenes of the drama he regarded as the world's greatest. That experience fairly blotted Germany out of his memory.

*   *   *   *

Galdós' lengthy accounts of his Italian travels lack the enthusiasm and intimacy of his impressions of England. They are the record of a trip made by a well-informed and cultured traveler rather than the interpretation of the beauties of nature and of human genius by a sensitive and poetic soul. What chiefly distinguishes them from the conventional guidebook is the heavy emphasis on artistic treasures and the personal reflections inspired by the reminders of Dante in Florence and of *Romeo and Juliet* in Verona. And yet there can be little doubt that Galdós' experience in Italy yielded in richness and significance only to his frequent visits to England.

Galdós spent two months in Italy in the fall of 1888. His traveling companion was Pepe, who joined him in London. On this trip Galdós was in almost constant communication with his sister Concha in Madrid, but his frequent postcards to her were too laconic to be informative. Almost invariably they carried the familiar text—"*sin novedad*"—and the signature "B." Some were not even signed. Occasionally Galdós became prolix to the extent of reporting the weather and informing Concha that the city he was in was more beautiful than some other. And he must have been exceedingly distracted or spellbound in Italy, for he capriciously addressed the postcards to "Spagne," "Espagne," and "Espagna."

One episode of the Italian trip, however, obliged Galdós to depart from his epistolary frugality. On the occasion when he attended Sunday Requiem mass in Saint Peter's, an unusually complicated matter, he reported minutely his extensive negotiations for the prized admission card through Alejandro Groizard, the Spanish ambassador in Rome. The most vexing detail was the requirement of formal dress. Galdós, who disliked formal attire, spent an entire day searching for it. He was amply rewarded after the profoundly moving ceremony with a photograph of Pope Leo XIII bearing the apostolic benediction and plenary indulgence *in articulo mortis*, granted to "Benito Pérez Galdós de Canarias" and to all the consanguineously and otherwise related members of his family up to the third degree. This papal document has often been produced by Galdós' survivors as evidence of his good personal relations with the Church of Rome.

Reporting his general impressions of Italy in *La Prensa* of Buenos Aires, Galdós dwelt on the results of national unification and on the relations between Rome and the Vatican. In general, he observed that political unity—the persistent obsession of all Italians, including their poets from Dante to Leopardi— had brought about material progress and prosperity. Unfortunately the influence of the brusque political renaissance upon the arts was unfavorable. The old dismembered Italy, Galdós thought, had been artistically more impressive. He was confident that a veritable efflorescence of the great native talent was inevitable, but for the time being, even in sculpture—for him the genuinely Italian mode of artistic expression—the sporadic manifestations of brilliancy were overshadowed by extensive mediocrity. As regarded literature, there was little that the unprejudiced student could characterize as conspicuous, possibly because the all-absorbing interest in politics diverted literary talent to journalistic channels. This observation led Galdós to wonder whether constitutional freedom, especially following a period of oppression, was the best patron of art. But he was not despondent, for he believed that the mainsprings of art never run completely dry.

It seemed to Galdós that Spaniards and Italians were similar and even alike in many respects. Indeed, he felt quite at home in Italy. His difficulties with the language were fewer than he had experienced with Portuguese; despite his limited knowledge he acquired a fair accent. Southern Italy reminded him of Andalusia—the houses, the farms, the trees, the dress of the people, their vivid imagination, and their precipitous and excited speech. In Naples some of the streets aroused memories of Málaga, Cádiz, and Valencia. The old Via Toledo—modern Via Roma—resembled Madrid's Calle de Toledo, and the noisily gay Neapolitans looked like Madrilenians streaming toward the bull-fight arena.

When he arrived in Rome after a tiresome journey, Galdós had the sense of having come to an ordinary provincial city, and nothing between the railroad station and the Hotel Americano on Via Trattina changed that impression. Before very long, however, the Italian capital—especially its sculptural treasures—began to impress him profoundly. Its grandiose monuments—the two hundred churches, the many palaces, and the imposing ruins—suggested to him that Rome was an ideal setting for splendid popular festivals on a vast scale. But nothing in Rome, nor in the Vatican, stirred him more deeply than the genius of Michelangelo. The contemplation of his works left him literally speechless, and not until his return to Spain was he able to give adequate expression to his feelings. Next to the ceiling in the Sistine Chapel, which impressed him as a beautiful page of theology composed in honor of dogma, Michelangelo's *Moses* moved him most strongly, filling him with amazement and inexplicable terror, and lingering in his mind for a long time. It seemed to him that the severe expression so energetically carved in marble belonged to real life, and that those cold lips were about to burst open with words of wrath. Never had art simulated the essence of spirit and the expression of life with greater intensity. The statue was truly alive for him, and its immensity and grandeur gave him the sensation that if it rose from its seat it would touch the ceiling with its head.

Michelangelo's *Moses* and the city of Verona often crowded one another in Galdós' memory. He had seen more impressive monuments and greater works of art elsewhere in Italy, but the city of Juliet haunted his mind. As on many previous occasions, he could not refrain from reflecting that poetic idealization could give its creations more enduring fame than the greatest figures in history have enjoyed. Romeo, Juliet, Don Quixote lived in the spirit of the people with greater reality than Julius Caesar, Alexander the Great, the Cid.

For Galdós all Verona was reduced to the setting and substance of Shakespeare's drama, and he relived its scenes as he strolled through the city. He visited Juliet's grave, and although he was convinced that it was apocryphal, he accepted it as a truth superior to reality and, indeed, worthy of his tribute. The streaming throngs did not surprise him; he thought their fervor not unlike the faith of pious Catholic pilgrims on the road to the shrine of a miracle-working image. A troupe of pretty young English girls who trailed him and Pepe impressed him with their expression of sincere reverence, and it seemed to him that they muttered a prayer and that their thoughts soared to the plane of Romeo and and Juliet's pure love. He left Verona with the thought that material reality grows dim in time and fades, but dreams and ideals live eternally in the human memory.

The principal delight of Florence, of course, was its association with Dante. Just as in Stratford-on-Avon Galdós had lived with and in Shakespeare, so in Florence he constantly had the illusion of intimate contact with the great Italian poet, and for the first time he had a poignant realization of his greatness. Dante stood out in his mind as the greatest poet of the sorrow and the sublime aspirations of the human spirit, and Giotto's portrait of him—with the lily in his hand symbolizing the lasting freshness of his profoundly human and eternal creation—seemed eminently fitting. On the other hand, the sepulchral statue of Dante in the Santa Croce church annoyed Galdós a bit. A mausoleum without

the remains of the one for whom it had been created struck him
as a monstrance without the consecrated host. But he thought
better of the monumental statue in the church square—it was the
Dante he knew and had often imagined.

As Galdós contemplated the *sasso di Dante* in front of the
cathedral, evoking the scene of the poet and his friends gathered
there in the cool air of the evening, he wondered why the *Inferno*
was the most widely read of the poem's three parts. In his opinion
the *Purgatorio* is a more splendid expression of Dante's inspiration and of the perfect harmony between his moral and intellectual nature. The entire work, however, palpitates with reality,
and is singularly free from rhetorical chaff and obvious poetic
artifices. Apparently Galdós was especially struck by Dante's concentration on man to the exclusion of everything else in nature.
That was almost like his own process of selection—man viewed
from the standpoint of passion and ideas. How different was
Dante, thought Galdós, with his lofty sense of what is truly
great and eternally significant, from all other poets and their
concern with the accidents of nature. The sobriety of the poem,
encompassing the entire moral world in such narrow limits, must
have humbled Galdós if he reflected on the dimensions of his
own works.

Reflections of a surprising nature occurred to Galdós as he
stood before Machiavelli's tomb in Santa Croce Church. Without
approving the unscrupulous political principles propounded in *Il
Principe,* he was inclined to interpret them as the natural product
of a particular social state. He saw them not as a set of abstract
theories, but as the product of an inescapable realism. A ruler
must derive his ideas and practices from the moral and social
conditions of the land he governs, not from ancient philosophic
maxims. It would be sheer folly for an artistically inclined
Mediterranean people torn by passions, partisanship, and anarchy
to attempt to govern themselves according to the austere ideas
of the puritanistic north. A nation's form of government must
be determined by the people themselves in the light of their
own character and temperament.

Thus viewed, Machiavelli did not seem to Galdós to have

deserved the censure and execration that his political philosophy had evoked. It was encouraging that people were beginning to evaluate him more objectively as they came to understand the true intellectual and moral state of the Florentine environment which produced him. For Galdós *Il Principe* was a profoundly sincere work, and its author an ardent patriot and efficient statesman. Those who bandied about the opprobrious epithets derived from the name of Machiavelli were merely indulging in banal mannerisms without any appreciation of the great Italian's sagacity and sense of realism. Obviously Galdós had traveled far from the political principles he had voiced in the days of the Glorious Revolution of 1868.

Padua, Naples, Bologna, Venice, and other cities were included in Galdós' Italian itinerary. In each he found objects of interest, and each made a lasting impression. In Bologna he visited the famous Spanish college founded in the fourteenth century by Cardinal Albornoz. Faculty and students were vacationing, but Galdós was able to inspect the school and the student quarters. Alcalá Galiano had known in Madrid two young men of high social standing who were students in the Colegio de Albornoz. The janitor obligingly permitted the travelers to see the rooms occupied by these young fellows, Alvaro and Rodrigo Figueroa. Galdós could not help reflecting how different were his own student quarters, with their atmosphere of complete comfort, excellent furniture, maps and games, fencing implements, and— crowding everything else—photographs of gay and pretty actresses on the walls. He was pleased to learn that the young aristocrats were not outstanding students, but indeed intelligent, alert, and attractive. Neither he nor Alcalá Galiano suspected then that some day Alvaro Figueroa would, as Conde de Romanones, be the leading figure in the troubled reign of Alfonso XIII.

After Rome, Naples afforded Galdós a welcome respite from monuments, churches, and ruins. Strolling in the popular district of Santa Lucia, he put history, art, literature, and philosophy out of his mind and abandoned himself to the complete enjoyment of its peculiar mixture of chitchat and silence. The men lazily

lounging in the streets, the watermelon rind scattered everywhere, the garrulous, gesticulating, beslippered women, the
humble dwellings through whose open doors one glimpsed prints
of saints lighted by little lamps, Mt. Vesuvius in the distance
with its spirals of smoke curling skyward—it was all fascinating
and exhilarating. As for Via Toledo, it was more Spanish than
the name implied, with its noises and picturesque confusion
created by hand organs, petty quarrels, hawkers, balcony-to-
balcony whispers and dialogues, prattling hackmen with their
cracking whips everywhere, and quacks offering cure-alls to the
public.

The climb to the sublime Vesuvius was another thrilling experience. The journey was made by carriage and funicular train,
and lasted from sunrise to sundown. Most of the tourists were
English, armed with Baedekers, wearing heavy-soled shoes, and
uniformly dressed. They peered inside the crater and beheld a
horrible sight. The heat was stifling and the smell of sulphur
asphyxiating, but two intrepid English girls kept on returning
and exclaiming: "Oooh! Wonderful!" So enthusiastic were they
over the horrendous spectacle that they planned to visit Palermo
the next day for a glimpse of Mt. Etna. Would not Señor Galdós
join them? Mustering his best English, he haltingly declined.
One active crater was enough to last Señor Galdós a lifetime.

The Italian trip of 1888 was the last of Galdós' Continental
travels except for his continued excursions to England and
France. Paris he visited frequently and always with fresh enthusiasm. As his contacts with French literary circles widened,
especially during the years of his dramatic career, he made many
trips to the French capital for business reasons. But it was the
human charms of Paris which attracted him most. Of his literary
journeys to Paris there are a few records, but the purely human
joys he experienced there were of such an intimate nature that
they must remain shrouded in secrecy.

Galdós greatly treasured his travel impressions and gladly
shared them with the young admirers who, in the declining years
of his life, frequently came to his house to cheer him with their
warm devotion. They reveal a restless soul, ever seeking new

sensations, ever youthful in its vigorous refusal to be hemmed in. From his vantage point in Madrid Galdós saw all Spain, and from his lookout in Spain he observed the limitless spaces of the world. This far-reaching vision he owed to the rich experience of his travels. He came to understand more deeply the common denominator of humanity and to scan the entire stretch of time from the past to the present. In his early travels he may have sought to introduce himself to the world, but he ended by discovering for himself an ever-wider world. It followed naturally that his works, too, had an ever-widening horizon. Gradually and unconsciously he abandoned the limited spaces of immediate realities and rose to the eternal sphere of the ideal. Concern with Spanish problems yielded to an ever-growing interest in the essence of humanity.

X

"Cradle" Politics

MORE THAN A DECADE HAD passed since the restoration of the Bourbon dynasty. The political convulsions of the late sixties and early seventies were forgotten by all except the incurable theorists who argued that national bliss depended upon the form of government, and the incorrigible revolutionaries whose opposition to the monarchy was dictated by personal ambition rather than by principles or doctrines. Republicanism continued to exist in Spain, but no longer did it have popular support or influence the conduct of public affairs. Of its former leaders, some joined the liberals, others deserted politics, and still others conspired against the regime from places of safety in self-imposed exile. The masses found little cause for complaint in either the personal or the official behavior of Alfonso XII; if no startling progress was to be expected during his reign, he had at least achieved a measure of national unity and tranquillity.

Only the professional politicians took an interest in the oratorical contests in Cortes or in the ministerial conferences in the palace. Conservatives and liberals maintained a semblance of energetic rivalry, but the differences between them had little to do with political philosophy. Even in Spain it was no longer easy to kindle passions over questions of doctrine. Parliamentarism and constitutionalism mattered much less than did the economic and social problems confronting the nation. The whole concept of government had undergone a radical change, and there were few Spaniards who could honestly deny that, with respect to basic rights and freedoms, the Restoration government practised a generous liberalism not frequently surpassed even in

196

England or France. In the fundamental sense of the term, Spain was governed democratically.

Galdós, who early in the Restoration had rushed to rescue the national soul in his so-called transcendental novels, gradually developed an attitude of forbearance toward the dynastic monarchy, and with the advent of Queen María Cristina he even defended it sincerely. Although Galdós had exulted in the revolution of the sixties, he was never really an advocate of violent change. He still believed in progress, but he had become convinced that lasting reform could not be achieved by precipitous action. His study of history and human nature convinced him that the lives of nations, like those of individuals, were regulated by laws whose tempo could not be altered at will. "Time respects nothing which is done without regard for it" [1] was the thought that shaped his reflections on Spanish politics. Without denying that the Revolution of 1868 has been justified by the several basic human freedoms that had been won, he emphasized the failure of the republic to secure national unity and tranquillity. The success of the Restoration in this respect convinced him that for the time being a liberal constitutional monarchy was the most suitable form of government for Spain. He admitted that the national political instrumentalities were not functioning satisfactorily, but he doubted whether the pure dialectics—he called it "political theology" [2]—of the reform advocates would effect the necessary improvements.

* * * *

When Galdós entered politics in 1886, he aroused considerable speculation as to his motives. His friends insisted that he merely wished to observe the Spanish political game at close range for literary purposes. Less friendly souls accused him of aspiring to prominence in national affairs. Neither explanation is borne out by the facts—the second much less than the first. In 1886 Galdós was as fully aware as he had ever been of his incapacity for politics, and his record reveals that his interest in the deliberations of Cortes was little more than that of a spectator.

In later years he often told with delightful irony the story of how he had been "made" a deputy by the Sagasta political machine. He was the product of *cunerismo*—a "cradle" deputy who never deviated from the party line during his five-year term. He attended all the Cortes sessions punctiliously and paid closer attention to the debates than did most of his colleagues. The speeches of Castelar, Cánovas, Pidal, and Sagasta compensated him vicariously for his own oratorical deficiency. As a writer he was more interested in the speakers' literary style than in their political acumen or dialectic skill, yet he listened intently to their arguments so that he might vote as intelligently and honestly as party discipline permitted. Only once during the five years did he participate in a debate. His good friend, the young poet Manuel Reina, had introduced a bill to protect children from traffic accidents in the streets of Madrid. Galdós rose to thank Reina and to commend his humanitarian motives. He spoke in a voice so nearly inaudible that his colleagues had to wait until the close of the session to learn the import of his remarks.

The story of Galdós' political career is as simple as his motives were probably mixed. In the summer of 1885 patriotic fervor ran high in Spain. Germany, in her search for a colonial wedge in the Pacific, seized the Caroline Islands, a remnant of the Spanish empire. The incident created a flutter of activity in the European chancelleries. The Spanish masses and the press, though aware of Germany's strength and their own weakness, clamored for the prompt vindication of national sovereignty and honor, but the conservative Cánovas government handled the affair so ineptly that it was loudly accused of being pro-German. Sagasta's liberal party, seeing the opportunity to promote its political stock, promptly organized its forces for a test of power. Even the republicans saw a ray of hope. On the fourth of September mobs rioted in the streets of Madrid and staged a menacing demonstration before the German embassy. The crisis became so grave as to jeopardize the existence of the regime. A political revolution was brewing, and this alone persuaded the Germans to settle the dispute diplomatically. Europe could not afford an upheaval on the Iberian Peninsula.

Galdós had contributed to these exhibitions of patriotic ardor. In his frequent reports to *La Prensa* he momentarily relived the passion-kindling days of 1868. Gone were his restrained tone and deliberative reflections. He was sufficiently realistic to sense the danger of a settlement by arms, but his anti-German sentiments got the better of any attempt at objectivity. And although he decried the haste with which the politicians appropriated the international conflict for their selfish gain, he joined the liberals in demanding the resignation of the Cánovas cabinet.

The fall of the conservative government was inevitable. Sagasta assumed power on the day after the death of Alfonso XII. The new cabinet received Galdós' hearty approval, and he praised its individual members freely. With the liberals in the saddle, the destiny of the nation was in competent hands. Still under the spell of the Caroline Islands incident, he echoed loudly the popular demand for a better and larger navy to defend Spain's colonial interests. He applauded the nation-wide interest in naval armament, smiling at the same time over the naïveté of the provinces, cities, and individuals that pledged the cost of new cruisers, not realizing that the expense would greatly exceed the financial resources of the entire nation.

Galdós was completely unaware that his patriotic ardor was attracting attention in political circles. Nor did he realize that his defense of liberal constitutional monarchism was taken as an endorsement of the machinations of the dynastic liberal party. He was therefore surprised when his good friend José Ferreras— the man who had sponsored him early in his journalistic career and was still giving him loyal support in *El Correo*—began hinting that the liberal cause needed a man of his prestige. Had the overture come from someone else, Galdós would have responded with a polite, ironical smile, but Ferreras could not be thus dismissed. He was intelligent, honest, devoted, and politically sagacious, and he was Sagasta's right-hand man. Galdós was attracted to Ferreras because his temperament and intellect were similar to his own. He had no reason to doubt the sincerity of the suggestion that he join the liberal party. At the *tertulias* which he, Ferreras, and Urzáiz—the "three Anabaptists," as they were known in Madrid—held around the fireplace in the office of *El Correo* and on friendly strolls, the matter came up again and again.

It is quite likely that Ferreras approached Galdós at Sagasta's request. The liberal leader, anxious to infuse young blood into his party, was looking for men of intellectual stamina and he did not balk even at ex-republicans and revolutionaries. The *progresista* stuffing of his Constitutional Party needed renovation, and he was shrewd enough to realize Galdós' window-dressing value in any attempt to attract the so-called advanced intellectual element—conceivably even the remnants of the parlor revolutionaries of the 1868 vintage.

When Ferreras first offered a seat to Galdós in Sagasta's majority bloc in Cortes, he was politely but firmly turned down. Galdós' dislike of *cunerismo* was profound, and he abhorred the idea of becoming one of those deputies created out of nothing, as it were, by the minister of the interior. Moreover, he argued that Spain did not enjoy national representation, for the members of Cortes reflected only the opinions of their political leaders. National sovereignty was not controlled by the deputies, but by the Crown with its camarilla and the rural *caciques* (political bosses). True, he had accepted the principle of constitutional monarchy, but that did not oblige him to approve the political system within the regime. Under no circumstances would he have a part in a game played for the promotion of personal ambitions.

But Ferreras pleaded persistently. Finally Galdós yielded and promised to confer with Sagasta, whom he had already met, though not privately. One morning in March, 1886, he called on the politician at his home at 22 Calle Alcalá. Sagasta, naturally genial, and also clever, welcomed Galdós like an old, steady acquaintance in whom he had always been interested. He reviewed the significant events in the novelist's career, and even referred to his youthful pranks—the paper birds and other figures that had once attracted so much attention in the Madrid cafés. On this friendly and personal basis Sagasta tried to convince Galdós that in reality they were quite similar in character and

ideas and in their ultimate aim to secure happiness for their
country. The bright future in store for Spain under a liberal
constitutional monarchy required the direct cooperation of all
high-minded citizens.

Galdós' reply to all this was merely polite acquiescence. When
Sagasta steered the conversation to the subject of his Constitutional Party, Galdós balked. Hoping to forestall an outright offer
of a seat in Cortes, he dwelt on his utter incapacity for public
life as it was then lived in Spain. He criticized Spanish politics on
the ground that it did not rest on moral principles or philosophic
concepts, but was merely a set of consecrated practices indulged in
by conservatives and liberals alike.

Sagasta's reaction was half festive, half serious. He said he
knew that reflection had made Galdós metaphysical and that
disillusionment had destroyed his optimism. But that was nonsense which it behooved him to forget, for it would lead him
nowhere. Perhaps Spaniards were living in a fictitious political
world, and real representation was impossible so long as deputies
were all created in the same image, but these were evils which
only the Constitutional Party—the happy link between royal
power and popular sovereignty—could eradicate. The party had
a great future, as even Galdós would be convinced in time. In
any event, Sagasta was determined to regenerate the country, and
if he should fail it would always be on the side of freedom.

The interview ended inconclusively. Galdós reached no immediate decision, and the shrewd Sagasta pressed him for none.
That task was reserved for Ferreras. The "three Anabaptists"
had several long discussions which gradually weakened Galdós'
resistance.

Reflecting on his conversation with the liberal leader, Galdós
began to wonder whether he was justified in refusing to support
a principle merely because he disapproved of the means available
for its implementation. Before reaching a decision, however, he
scrutinized his own reactions to the national political scene.
Republicanism still attracted him, but only as a phenomenon to
be studied, certainly not as a philosophy of government to be
supported. In reality there was no single, unified republican

movement in Spain; the divergencies among the republican factions were sometimes greater than those between conservative
monarchists and liberals. The group to which he was still occasionally drawn was Castelar's *posibilistas*. This was a sort of
aristocratic and intelligent group, without adherents among the
masses, which derived its limited prestige from its highly respected leader. In substance, however, its program differed little
from that of the liberal monarchists. Within the form of government it advocated the various functional agencies would operate
just as they did under Sagasta's leadership, and the influence of
"functionarism," the army, and the clergy would probably survive. A republic such as Castelar envisioned could become a
reality in the event of a total disintegration of the monarchists,
but it could probably continue to exist only under the aegis of
Castelar. Without his spellbinding personality the return of
Carlism and absolutism would be almost a certainty.

Of the other brands of republicanism, Pi y Margall's federal-
ism impressed Galdós as sheer Utopia championed mainly by
impulsive men. There was little likelihood that pure theory and
unconsidered action could establish a federal socialist republic in
Spain, granted that Pi y Margall was an estimable man. Zorrilla's
progressive republican party must be viewed with apprehension.
Galdós regarded its leader as a man of limited intellectual power
but very astute and strong-willed. A person of few scruples and
principles, Ruiz Zorrilla was determined to establish a republican regime at any cost and by any means. From his self-imposed
exile in Paris he constantly conspired, with the aid of army officers, to effect a pronunciamento. A republic headed by this
unscrupulous conspirator would inevitably degenerate into a
dictatorship maintained by force. Its existence would be brief and
it would be followed by a period of grave national convulsions.

After careful consideration of the republican offerings, Galdós
decided he preferred the status quo to an uncertain future. In his
fervent desire for prolonged peace—even with its concomitant
insipid normalcy and national somnolence—he differed from the
rank and file Restoration bourgeoisie only in his abhorrence of
Carlist disturbances. Rather than risk a revival of the dynastic

quarrel that had ensued upon the death of Alfonso XII, he was willing to support the Bourbon dynasty. To some extent Galdós' thinking was probably influenced by the universally chivalrous attitude toward the regent queen. At any rate, he shared the prevalent opinion that Spain had finally acquired a realistic political sense. Henceforth the nation's destiny would be determined by hard-learned lessons and tempering experience, not by romantic passion, hollow rhetoric, and vain promises.

Galdós was forced to conclude that he could not consistently endorse the Restoration ideal of peace and tranquillity without accepting the available political agencies for its attainment. Added to this was perhaps the consideration that his participation in politics might redound to his literary prestige. Conceivably his collaboration with the dominant party would lend him some respectability in the eyes of those who tended to identify his works with the disruptive forces of the nation. Besides, there was Sagasta's apparently sincere declaration that the Constitutional Party stood for national regeneration and freedom. Was not that precisely what had animated him, Galdós, in his thinking and writing? Indeed, he could cooperate with Sagasta without bruising his conscience. The recent death of the monarch imposed on all enlightened citizens the duty to preserve the modest gains of the Restoration. Galdós' resistance to Ferreras' pleas broke down completely.

The election campaign got under way in March, 1886, and Galdós followed it with approval. He did not have to participate in it actively, since he and other candidates were designated by Sagasta to represent Spain's possessions in the Antilles. As the electoral machine functioned in the traditional manner, public interest did not run particularly high. Everyone knew that in keeping with established practice the liberals would parcel out some representation to Cánovas' conservative party in order to give the regime a semblance of political free play and parliamentary check and balance. Laying aside his former scruples, Galdós fairly condoned the picturesque election comedy. He argued speciously that in view of the Spanish tendency toward political fragmentation any election conducted with meticulous non-intervention by the dominant party would result in a *ciempiés* (a centipede)—a legislature in which any sort of rule would be impossible. His newly discovered tolerance led him to believe that Sagasta would use with the utmost honesty a system inherently devoid of it.

The regency elections were held on April 4, 1886, and literally overnight Galdós became Cortes deputy for the district of Guayama in Porto Rico. He was elected by the ridiculous number of seventeen votes, and he ironically regarded his success as a personal triumph. That year the voters of Cuba and Porto Rico did not choose to approve all the candidates dictated to them on the eve of the elections. In later years he often recalled with mock glee that Eugenio Sellés, the famous dramatist, was rejected by the Spanish-American electors in 1886.

Now that he was officially a *Sagastino* or *cunero*, Galdós served the party with unswerving loyalty. With no personal ambitions to further, he easily mastered the rules and tricks of the political game. His duties were few and simple: whatever his personal views on a measure, he always voted with the party. Fortunately for his newly born political conscience he was never obliged to censure Sagasta's policies during the so-called "long parliament," which lasted almost five years. The first liberal cabinet, formed the day after the death of Alfonso XII, he had already endorsed wholeheartedly in the columns of *La Prensa*. His conscience suffered no qualms, for he really had faith in the intelligence, sagacity, and personal integrity of Sagasta and his ministers. He even hoped, though with strong misgivings, that the liberal government might eventually unify the nation. Unfortunately his misgivings were borne out more than once during the "long parliament" by defections from the Constitutional Party—the first only a few months after Sagasta's advent to power. Galdós accepted the incident with philosophic resignation. Long before he had concluded that Spain was a country of many excellent musicians but scarcely a single orchestra that was even tolerably good. As he phrased it, every Spaniard sounds well as an individual, but there is no way of concerting him with other players.[3]

Galdós' marriage to politics was a happy one. Sagasta greatly appreciated the political value of the novice deputy and conferred special distinctions upon him. Galdós' first service to the liberal cause was purely literary. He was named to the commission that composed the government's reply to the Crown's message. He enjoyed the assignment immensely, particularly the collaboration of his colleague Antonio Maura. He followed the debate on the message—such debates often constituted the *pièce de résistance* of Spanish parliamentary sessions—with rapt attention, mainly because of his interest in the oratory.

The Cortes of 1886 was distinguished by such famous orators as Castelar, Salmerón, and Cánovas. Always conscious of his own inadequacy as a speaker, Galdós experienced vicariously the thrills and triumphs of this oratorical galaxy as it parried and lunged in prolonged debates over issues that had little bearing on vital national interests. Only one circumstance interfered with his pure enjoyment of the verbal gladiators. As a writer he was primarily interested in the artistic aspect of their performance, so he had to make a conscious effort to dissociate form from doctrine, and style from ideas, in order not to be influenced in his voting. But since he rarely voted independently, the occasions for conflict between the artist and the conscientious party man were few. The speaker who influenced him most readily was Castelar, but the political distance between the *posibilista* republican and the liberal *cunero* deputy was short indeed.

Galdós always extolled the ex-president of the ill-fated republic—his idealism, his philosophy, his character, and his superb platform style. Salmerón, on the other hand, elicited severe criticism from him more often than praise, probably because of his association with the opportunistically militant republican Ruiz Zorrilla. As for Cánovas, leader of the opposition and prime promoter of the Restoration, he admired his political skill and unadorned eloquence. Disapproving though he was of Cánovas' extreme conservatism, he nevertheless recognized his statesmanship and even hoped that his party—which he regarded as the only relatively permanent cohesive force of Restoration politics —would never disintegrate.

The assignment that made the deepest impression on Galdós was the witnessing of the birth of Alfonso XIII. He who was one day to be the titular head of the Republican-Socialist Coalition regarded it as a high privilege in 1886 to be a member of the official commission to receive for the nation the only Spanish ruler who was born a king. The ceremony of the "presentation" of the royal infant had the same reassuring effect upon him as upon the other dignitaries who attended it—some three hundred in all. He welcomed the birth of Alfonso XIII because, among other reasons, he thought it was destined to strengthen the monarchial principle and weaken the cause of the perennially trouble-making Carlists. He was convinced that neither reactionaries nor revolutionaries would henceforth threaten the nation with turmoil and chaos. A revolution was impossible so long as the public conscience was kept tranquil by the benevolent and liberal course of the Restoration.

Feeling keenly his responsibility to deputy Galdós, Ferreras resolved to make his political career a profitable one. It was Ferreras who advised Sagasta to favor the novelist-politician with assignments that would lead to valuable acquaintanceships and new experiences. Those who attribute Galdós' preponderant interest in the lower middle class of Spain to his lack of direct knowledge of the upper social strata overlook the extensive contacts he made during the "long parliament." True, his persistent awkwardness and timidity prevented him from participating regularly in the activities of Madrid's distinguished society, but he never shunned on that account an opportunity for an unusually interesting social experience—and more often than not he enjoyed it immensely.

Of the friends Galdós made in Cortes, the Marqués de Castroserna was the most congenial. A staunch supporter of the Sagasta government and owner of a priceless collection of paintings, he won Galdós' respect and admiration. One of the marquis' charming traits was his generosity with his seemingly unlimited supply of excellent Havana cigars. Galdós never refused his invitations for lunch at the Casino, for the titled gentleman was a gracious, refined, and interesting host. In the spring of 1886

Galdós was persuaded to join a delegation of deputies on an official visit to the International Exposition at Barcelona. His initial hesitation vanished when the Marqués de Castroserna and Ferreras suggested that the three could go as an independent unit within the larger group.

The visit to Barcelona proved to be a memorable event. The schedule of festivities was heavy, including a daily courtesy call on Sagasta at his headquarters in Hotel Arnús. The three friends paid their respects to the queen at her improvised residence in the City Hall, and in due time they were favored with an invitation to dine with her and King Oscar II of Sweden, who had arrived unexpectedly in his yacht. What mortal could fail to be elated to banquet in the company of two crowned heads! Galdós was so overwhelmed by the elaborate etiquette at the table that he dared not talk above a whisper. At first his self-consciousness interfered with his enjoyment of the occasion, but the democratic bearing of the Swedish king soon put him and his companions at their ease. In his naïveté Galdós was surprised that the monarch behaved very much like any mortal, pleasantly chatting, exchanging stories, joking and laughing. If he was still in need of justification of his support of the Spanish monarchy, his Barcelona experience furnished it. He felt more than ever that no reasonable person could have hostile designs on a government headed by an intelligent queen, widowed mother of a tender child whose birth invalidated the claim of the anti-dynastic trouble-makers. Galdós was temporarily living in the best of possible worlds.

* * * *

Whatever may be said of Galdós' contribution to his country's government, there can be no question that, so far as he himself was concerned, his experience as a liberal deputy was far from sterile. His friends were wrong when they complained that his assiduous attendance at Cortes merely consumed time that might have been more profitably spent in writing, for it did much to sharpen his perception of Spanish life and character. Moreover, his insight into Spanish politics was never dimmed by the incidents of political history, its immediate actualities. Although a member of a disciplined party, he never became partisan, and he learned to distinguish sharply between political philosophy and the practices of the politicians.

⌊Galdós' own political philosophy might be described as a mixture of enlightened patriotism and liberal nationalism.⌉Viewing Spain in its historical continuity, he was deeply proud of its strength and tolerant of its weakness. Both attitudes were restrained, rooted in reason and reflection. For some of his countrymen, indeed, his historical novels lacked patriotic ardor. Confusing patriotism and literature, they criticized him for being too impersonal, too devoid of lyrical warmth and exuberance. Oddly enough, Galdós' very objective patriotism prompted some of his French critics to accuse him indignantly of chauvinism.

In answer to his countrymen Galdós asserted that patriotism was not a matter of eloquence and hyperbole, and to the French critics he replied that he regarded chauvinism as a form of dementia of which he hoped never to be a victim. National pride was not vanity, nor did criticism of another country imply scorn. His evaluation of the treatment Spain had received from other nations was prompted not by arrogance but by a consciousness of Spanish dignity. Indeed, all his nationalism rested on his conviction that dignity and self-respect had helped Spain to survive many a grave crisis in the past and would do so again. Coupled with this was his innate Spanish sense of justice, which he would assert if necessary—especially in the case of international conflict—by resorting to arms, regardless of the odds.

Such, for instance, was Galdós' point of view in the disagreement between Spain and Germany over the Caroline Islands in 1885. It seemed to him, both then and later, that the particular position of a nation was the cumulative result of its historical destiny, and that justice dictated resistance to any attempt to alter it. Thus the preservation of the Spanish empire was for him a sacred trust, and he bewailed the failure of Spanish statesmen to provide adequate strength, material and economic, for its execution. His historical studies had taught him that in international relations force ruled over reason. The weak nations that wished to preserve their historical role should develop England's source of power: unity and vigor of national spirit, love of work, and avoidance of sterile internal struggles.

Obviously Galdós' meditations on nationalism and patriotism did not lead him into uncharted zones of abstract speculation. His opinions were, by and large, neither independent nor advanced. They coincided with the views of the average Spanish middle-class citizen of his time. Even in his appraisal of Spanish political practice he did not surpass his fellow countrymen in wisdom and understanding; he merely substituted criticism for apathy.

As a silent but interested deputy Galdós observed that Spanish parliamentarism was characterized by incessant irritation and strife, violent disagreement, and interminable oratory. Ironically he attributed this to the poor physical conditions of the Cortes building. The vitiated air and the faint overhead lights produced an atmosphere of annoyance and tended to make the legislators gloomy and pessimistic. Even he, a naturally composed individual, would enter a session with a feeling of boredom that soon changed into an urge to argue and quarrel with someone. Of course he always contrived to behave correctly, but often he would sit impatiently waiting for some individual or group to precipitate a general wrangle. Paradoxically, the anticipation of such a row would ultimately calm his jangled nerves in that heavy atmosphere and under those irritating overhead lights.

The hoped-for excitement rarely failed to materialize and it always took the form of a devastating verbal crossfire. It was mainly these parliamentary clashes that attracted Galdós to the sessions. He watched them with a mixture of ironical tolerance and sincere admiration for the ability of the lawmakers to maintain a debate on a purely conceptual plane indefinitely, and with so little regard for the facts of the issue under discussion. Absorbing as all this was to a literary person, he nevertheless thought it a pity that so much valuable time should be wasted in attempting to define abstract concepts with which Spanish parliamentarians had been vainly struggling ever since the Constitution of 1812. How futile to debate over the basis of public authority or the principle of sovereignty when only concrete events could

reveal their real meaning. What had abstruse theories and subjective opinions accomplished during all these years of oratorical
pugilism?

There were times when Galdós' conscience rebelled against the
farce in which he was a participant, but he reasoned that it would
be utterly useless to criticize the national vice of excessive
loquacity. Without the gift of oratory his criticism would be only
a naïve and futile gesture. In Spanish politics only the glib-
tongued were masters of the arena; all others were merely "aides
or footmen paying court to the loquacious victors." [4] If national
happiness depended upon nothing more than the volume of parliamentary eloquence, Spain would be the happiest country in the
world.

The boisterous and confused sessions of Cortes led Galdós
to inspired reflections on political democracy in general. A profound admirer of English self-government, he observed regretfully that its Spanish adaptation was reduced to meaningless
formulas. British and Spanish democracy were, to be sure, different in organization, but even where the procedures were almost
identical the results in England were invariably good, in Spain
consistently bad. This phenomenon was of course not peculiar to
Spain. Conceivably English self-government also failed in other
countries because of the belief that political progress could be
achieved through the reform of laws. Galdós believed that it was
the character of the people that must first be reformed, that
radical changes in the laws would not in themselves improve the
situation in Spain, would not correct such inherent weaknesses of
democratic government as excessive debate, lack of initiative,
and an ineffectual system of popular representation. Nevertheless, even at the risk of being condemned as a reactionary, he
opposed the vociferous critics of constitutional democracy; he
was convinced that their sole aim was its complete destruction,
and that, he feared, might result in a return to some form of
absolutism. For all its inefficiency, parliament did serve as a
check on governmental activities, and politics could not be
healthy unless conducted in the open. Modern government with
its emphasis on social and economic problems was unthinkable

without free discussion, even if that entailed inefficiency and a disproportionate expenditure of energy.

The tolerance with which Galdós viewed the inherent weaknesses of democracy in general vanished when he contemplated its specifically Spanish abuses. As a liberal deputy he regarded with apprehension the tendency toward strife and disagreement within the ranks of his own party. He drew little comfort from the fact that it was traditional for the liberals to be united in opposition and divided in power. It surprised him that even shrewd politicians failed to understand that no group could be successful under multiple leadership, and it shamed him to see that political rivalry was almost invariably begotten by petty personal ambition. The bickering of the little politicians was a sordid spectacle which was largely responsible for the instability of Spanish democracy. Unfortunately there was no cure for this national pathology so long as Spaniards were lacking in solid judgment, patience, tolerance toward an enemy, and respect for others.

Nor was there a remedy in sight for another Spanish trait: the belief of every individual that he can do things better than anyone else, with the result that all do everything worse than others. Spaniards would have to learn that the essence of political art, like the essence of the art of life, consists in preferring an average that is attainable to a risky and elusive perfection. In Galdós' opinion, many of Spain's political ills could be traced to a passionate struggle for the best—an attitude which precluded enjoyment of the good. It was likewise due to a craving for frequent changes and embellishments in the existing structure of principles and statutes. There was something nomadic in Spanish political life. It was lived in flimsy portable tents, ever going from adventure to adventure, never knowing where it would find itself the next day.

There were as yet no signs that Spanish politicians were willing or able to give real meaning to democratic government. The necessary improvements would have to come from the intelligent intervention of the individual citizen. But thus far Galdós found that the masses, disillusioned because the liberties they had won had not improved their condition, were as apathetic toward political problems as toward philosophic doctrines. Mass apathy was responsible for the flourishing of *caciquismo,* a deep-rooted political evil that could not be eradicated by legislation from above. It could be destroyed—and very slowly—only after the individual Spaniard had developed a strong moral sense in public affairs. Governments having lofty purposes could accomplish much, but only if their acts received the support of the common citizen, the source of all good and evil in national life. For Galdós public and private morals were intimately related; the source of all human behavior was the individual conscience. Once again, as in his earlier novels, he considered it his duty to call the attention of the Spaniards to this obvious truth.

Having discovered the mainspring of political conduct, both individual and collective, in moral strength and integrity of conscience and not in theories and doctrines, Galdós naturally considered governmental form of minor importance. Certainly in the late eighties he was in no mood to countenance another republican experiment. He was, of course, at some pains to reconcile his presumable spiritual radicalism with his avowed political conservatism, but he contended that as a realist he was interested in expediency more than in philosophic speculation.

Under the pressure of concrete realities Galdós supported the existing monarchy energetically. As correspondent for *La Prensa* he praised the queen lavishly and missed no opportunity to denounce the machinations of the Zorrillistas to restore the republic by violence. He denied that his concept of liberalism was incompatible with monarchical rule, and quietly urged his fellow Sagastinos to demonstrate that liberalism could be effective within the existing governmental institutions. That was the course Castelar was taking; the ex-president of the first republic endorsed the monarchy with dignity and courtesy, but without abandoning his lifelong conviction as to the ideal form of government. His idealism was not in the least weakened by his realistic political conduct. How different he was from others who insisted on change by fire and blood, who would establish a dictatorship many times more oppressive than the worst tyrannies of the past!

Galdós as a Young Man

Youthful Cartoons by Galdós

(See pages 56–58)

Strongly as he condemned political revolution, Galdós conceded that there might be justification for a radical social movement. Yet even here he feared that in Spain the issues were confused. Admitting the existence of economic distress, he maintained that the workers who were periodically aroused against the government were in reality confusing hunger and politics. Their agitation for improvement under the banner of a political party was only a device, ignorantly adopted at the exhortation of demagogues, to attract attention to their grievances.

Galdós appreciated the increasing gravity of the social problem and foresaw that it would develop into the great battle of the twentieth century. He failed to see, however, that its solution did depend upon the political structure of the country. He frowned upon republican agitators who exploited for their revolutionary ends any dissatisfaction in the ranks of labor. The socialists' solution impressed him as impractical. Reducing socialism to the simple concept of class equality, he characterized it as visionary. He was aware of the constant slow shifting of classes, but he refused to believe that any social theory or philosophic program could reduce society to a single level. At any rate, Galdós was firmly convinced that Spain lacked the elements for an effective social revolution.

* * *

[When the Bourbon dynasty was restored, Galdós received its promises with apathy and envisaged its influence with considerable apprehension. The specter of reinstated traditionalism and obscurantism haunted him constantly.] The threat to the spiritual welfare of Spain was great, and he sought to revitalize the national conscience by dealing in his novels with the transcendental religious theme. So absorbed was he in his self-imposed task that the ephemeral incidents of the Restoration impinged upon his consciousness only like the annoying drone of a bee. A few years earlier he too had believed that national destiny was inseparable from government. [In the late eighties he thought otherwise. Now he made national self-realization dependent not upon political formulas and parliamentary patterns, but upon a clear understanding of racial character in the light of historical

continuity and upon an unbiased appraisal of contemporary
realities.

To this concept Galdós adhered even after he became a
"cradle" deputy. His affiliation with an organized group pledged
to support the monarchy did not imply the abandonment of his
basic ideas. It certainly did not mean a suddenly conceived
respect for Spanish politics or faith in its immediate efficacy.
In point of fact, even before he joined Sagasta's Constitutional
Party he had reached the conclusion that the Restoration provided the political stability without which a nation could not
devote itself to deliberate searching of the conscience and to a
realistic fulfilment of its historic mission. The knowledge and
wisdom he gained in his extensive travels tended to confirm his
belief that Spain needed to cultivate patience and perseverance—
virtues which enabled other nations to evolve ideas and to apply
them practically in slow, progressive movements. While Spain
was supreme in her ability to accomplish things by impulse and
improvisation, it lived more dangerously for that very reason,
always suspended between sudden ruin and quick salvation.

Galdós harbored no illusions about the power of parliament
or the ability of writers and philosophers to effect radical modifications in the Spanish character, but he apparently believed
that knowledge of one's own virtues and vices is its own reward
and, in the case of nations, a guarantee of indefinite survival.
He made no impression on his political colleagues and occupied
negligible space in the official records of Cortes, but as a "cradle"
deputy he was able to glimpse the complex nature of the
Spaniards from a new vantage point. Sagasta may have used
Galdós for his political ends; Galdós in turn used Sagasta for
his literary ends. The novelist unquestionably profited more
than did the liberal Constitutional Party.

XI

Trial and Immortality

THE BANQUET OF 1883 WAS only a temporary apotheosis. Opposition to Galdós, variously motivated, soon manifested itself again. In some quarters it was loudly hinted that the national recognition so noisily accorded him had made him haughty, conceited, overconfident; that with an exaggerated opinion of his own wisdom he was resolved to impose upon the public his new fictional style of long, diffuse novels of fatiguingly minute observation. Elsewhere it was maintained that Galdós was now commercializing his reputation by producing bulky works in rapid succession and selling them at higher prices than Spaniards were accustomed to pay for fiction. Added to this there was always Galdós' alleged conversion to Zola's naturalism. In Spain this literary doctrine had become a convenient bone of contention for critics and reviewers and café preceptists to wrangle over whenever an author departed from his customary vein. The hostility of the anti-naturalists did not often derive from esthetic precept or philosophic doctrine; what they objected to was the absence of conventional plot in Galdós' novels, his practice of interrelating the characters in his works, and his failure to give his stories conclusive endings or to solve the problems he posed.

Clarín's esthetic acrobatics convinced no one that Galdós' new phase was the result of a recondite artistic process, independently conceived by a superior talent and implemented by a perpetually youthful and vigorous imagination. Just as in the seventies Manuel de la Revilla had led the chorus of the literary preceptists, so now Luis Alfonso, writing in *La Epoca*, set the tune to which the lesser critics danced. When *Tormento* appeared in

1884, no one found fault with the theme or the scrupulous honesty of Galdós' observation and interpretation, but concerning its form there were numerous reservations. The principal objection was that it lacked an outstanding central figure—a weakness which presumably robbed the story of interest and beauty. It was also pointed out that the naturalistic analysis of this particular slice of Spanish life violated the principle of classical unity. Luis Alfonso argued analogically that oneness or unity was a universal law; hence a novel must have one central character for the same reason that humanity believes in one God, an army has one leader, a country obeys one ruler, and so *ad infinitum.*

The next work, *La de Bringas* (1884), was all but inexorably condemned on the ground that Galdós continued to stumble along the path he had chosen in *La desheredada.* This time it was contended that since Señora de Bringas had already been fully drawn in *Tormento,* the novel really had no justification. In cafés, bookshops, and private homes—everywhere—the work was reportedly branded as boring and abominable. All conceded that Galdós was a genius by any standard, but unfortunately he had lately erred in the type of characters he depicted and their uncouth language, in the interpolation of contemporary political events, in references to well-known living personages, and in the practice of interlinking his novels to give them the semblance of a series. The blame, it was suggested, lay squarely upon the shoulders of certain critics who encouraged Galdós in his error and inspired him to stretch his themes beyond the point of exhaustion and to accumulate confusing details of observation that taxed the reader's patience. Was the novelist perhaps indulging in voluminosity in order to justify the higher prices of his recent works?

Galdós' new motives frankly puzzled some critics, and they piously hoped that he would mend his ways and return to the molds of his earlier novels. There was little likelihood of his immediate reform, however, especially since French critics who commented on *Tormento* and *La de Bringas* generously granted him the right to aspire to the title of Balzac of Spain—and it was common knowledge that Galdós professed inordinate admiration for the author of the *Comédie Humaine* and had an almost pathological craving for recognition in France.

Barring Clarín, Galdós' defenders raised their voices only faintly and intermittently. Without warmth of conviction they asserted that his new procedure was in consonance with his aim of recreating the dull, gray realities of Spanish life. Reality, they argued, is fluid and continuous; life is not arranged in patterns. For the readers who seek in literature merely a means of beguiling their tedium there was an abundance of novelistic novels, but Galdós was obviously determined to teach the public that fiction can have a significance beyond mere entertainment. In this respect his success was noteworthy if not widely recognized.

But those who reasoned thus found slight confirmation of their position in the reception of Galdós' next novel, *Lo prohibido* (1884–85). A treatise on pessimism in two volumes, one critic called it. The author's premises about human behavior were traitorous and his conclusions indefensible. Even José Ortega y Munilla, one of Galdós' staunchest supporters, wondered whether this time he was not guilty of consciously imitating Balzac's practice of seeing through the social microscope things that really did not exist. It was hard to accept the author's conclusion that happiness is not of this world. Unacceptable, too, was the autobiographic form of *Lo prohibido* with its excessively slow exposition and the painfully retarded appearance of the protagonist.

Less guarded than Ortega y Munilla's was the opinion that in this instance Galdós had produced an interesting socio-philosophic study and not a novel. The purely imaginative element, it was noted, actually amounted to a repetition of situations, scenes, characters, and customs to be found in his other novels, introduced here as an excuse for a depressingly frank analysis of heredity. Lacking interest, beauty, extraordinary situations, and stirring passions, but abounding in abnormal characters and experiences, this work furnished regrettable evidence of Galdós' resolve to adhere to his preconceived notions about fiction. Once again the critics, who were wandering in what seemed to them a naturalistic desert, longed for the fleshpots of Galdós' first phase.

Galdós paid little heed to the advice of the critics, explicit or implicit, but he did not fail to take cognizance of something else. Some of his readers apparently shared Luis Alfonso's views and ignored the sledgehammer blows with which Clarín was pounding the opposition. In statistical terms Galdós was still the pre-eminent Spanish novelist, but he noticed that the circulation of his works dropped in proportion to the realistic minutiae they contained. The decrease, he was convinced, was due not to the effectiveness of critical opinion in Spain but to the scant interest that the rank-and-file readers took in his contemporary series.

It was a real problem: he had to choose between popular favor and his artistic conscience. But he did not hesitate. Belying the accusation that he was commercially minded, and with little regard for his mounting needs, occasioned by the irregularities of his passional life, he was resolved to pursue the end of fiction as he then conceived it. Privately he laughed at the critics who, after his forthright disavowal of naturalism in 1882, could no longer accuse him of imitating Zola and thus often resorted to the subterfuge of rejecting the structural features of his latest novels. He reacted with ironical silence to the manifest shallowness of their criteria. He was determined to study Restoration life at close range, to probe the meaning of the humblest manifestations of external reality, to grasp the subtle interrelationship of the psychic, spiritual, and physical forces of life. In short, he was set on reconstructing the Spanish *Comédie Humaine,* and neither the disapproval of critics nor the apathy of readers could induce him to alter his course. Never swayed by any esthetic sectarianism, he might some day modify his aims and procedures, but it would be in response to the promptings of his own artistic conscience, not to the verdict of his contemporaries.

One point raised by the critics Galdós was apparently impelled to comment on formally, though indirectly—the recurring insinuation that artistically his novels of the first epoch were superior to those published since 1881. It may well be that, wishing to make clear that his new procedure was determined by artistic considerations, he put the following observations in the mouth of the protagonist of *Lo prohibido:*

> I wish it were possible for me to offer in these memoirs curious and interesting material for those who seek entertainment and strong emotions from their reading. But I have been unwilling to transgress the law which I imposed upon myself at the very beginning, namely, to relate in plain fashion my adventures in Madrid from the fall of '80 to the summer of '84. They are incidents that do not differ in the least from those that fill and constitute the lives of other men. I did not aspire to produce any effects other than those that derive from the simple and sincere expression of the truth. I had no intention of moving the spirit of the reader with contrived frights, surprises and mental or verbal deceptions, causing things to seem one way and to turn out another way. And it would not have been difficult for me, especially counting on the expert hand of my intelligent scribe, to alter the truth, within the bounds of verisimilitude, for the sake of interest. . . . I wish it were possible to raise in this field of fresh truth all the kinds of grass that are the forage on which fools graze, but it could not be, and what has been written down must stay.[1]

A slight reaction in Galdós' favor can be detected in the comment, however limited, inspired by the four-volume *For-tunata y Jacinta* (1886–87), indisputably his masterpiece. It may be that the sheer magnitude of the work inspired respect for the author. Ortega y Munilla probably voiced the prevailing opinion when he stated that this novel should be considered in the nature of a national event, and that all ordinary criteria must be suspended in the presence of so great an artistic achievement. What mattered, he asked, such criticisms as faulty expressions, lack of verisimilitude, and insufficient dramatic interest in the case of a novelist who matched wits with life itself?

So profound was the impression produced by *Fortunata y Jacinta* that for the first time in Galdós' career a critic was

inspired to study one of his works painstakingly before formulating an opinion. Pedro Muñoz Peña published a series of
four extensive articles on the novel in *La Libertad* of Valladolid.
Clarín promised a full analysis, but for the moment satisfied his
conscience with a diffuse review in the form of a letter to the
author, published in *El Globo*. As was to be expected, he heaped
indiscriminate praise on Galdós and bewailed the failure of
Spain's most competent pens to occupy themselves with this
unusual novel. Nevertheless he was frankly worried about the
general reception of *Fortunata y Jacinta* because of its excessive
dimensions. With mock seriousness he suggested that if Galdós
expected Spaniards to read four-volume novels he would have to
import the English climate, for so long as the sun shone bright
and the skies stood high and clear over Spain, one could not
expect its people to exchange political riots and bullfights for
indoor reading of literature, however superior.

Clarín's misgivings about the popular success of *Fortunata y
Jacinta* were shared by Galdós. He did not anticipate that the
novel would be widely read and he thought that the first volume
with its elaborate setting of the Restoration social scene was
least likely to please. In fact, he was aware even as he was
writing this work that he labored under a compulsion to include
all observed reality without regard to the demands of artistic
selection and the need for heightened intensity. He could not
write otherwise, for he was in love with reality as never before.
There is more than a hint of the depth of Galdós' interest in
full and rich realism in the following confession, which he is
said to have made to a friend:

> At last I found a book which captivated and fascinated
> me completely and which absorbed all my attention.
> What do you suppose it was, Señor X? Well, it was a
> rather extensive treatise on physics. I am reading it
> with delight. This, too, can be explained as a transitory
> state of mind. But aside from this I must confess to
> you that for some time now I have been attached to
> and fascinated by truth, by the phenomena of nature,
> and even more so by social phenomena. Right now,

instead of reading, I like to draw close to a group of friends, to hear what they are saying, or speak to a woman, or witness a quarrel, or enter a popular tenement house, or watch the shoeing of a horse, or hear the cries of the street vendors or the speech of deputy X, son-in-law of Z.[2]

It was undoubtedly this fascination of truth and social phenomena that produced the exuberant novel. One is tempted to assume that Galdós anticipated that both critics and readers would be stupefied by the 1761 pages of solid fiction which he laconically characterized in the subtitle as "Two Stories of Married Women." Perhaps he meant to justify his procedure in the comments he put into the mouths of two characters as they were accompanying Fortunata's remains to the cemetery. One of them, "a very eminent sentencer of literary works," remarks that in the story of that stupendous woman there is ample material for a drama or a novel, but the artistic fabric would not be attractive without the introduction of certain warps essential to the conversion of ordinary life into esthetic substance. He thinks that life cannot be translated into art without proper dressing and seasoning and without baking it on the right kind of fire. His friend does not share his views, and a reasoned dispute ensues, which ends in a stalemate. The upshot of the discussion is merely this: that ripe, raw fruit is a very good thing, but so, too, are preserves—provided the cook knows his business.[3]

It would appear that at this stage Galdós was beginning to feel the urge of serving his readers less ripe, raw fruit and more preserves—if by the former he meant external, observable reality and by the latter transcendental spiritual forces. In a certain sense he had already yielded to that urge in *Fortunata y Jacinta*. There is more than the ravings of a distraught mind in the sublime magnanimity with which Maxi forgives his unfaithful wife and in the depth of his belief that, once freed from what he calls "the filthiness of reality," he will abandon himself with his idol to the full enjoyment of freedom and light somewhere among the stars where only his own ideas and thoughts can delimit his behavior. In Maxi's dream of bliss achieved with one's own spiritual energy there is evidence that Galdós' perception of life was beginning to shift. He had apparently decided to concentrate more on the higher realities as they affect the individual conscience. This decision did not result from the counsel of critics and reviewers, but from his own meditations on the meaning of life and the best means of self-realization. Galdós was as restless spiritually as he was venturesome philosophically and esthetically. He clung tenaciously to beliefs once crystallized, but not indefinitely. In point of fact—as he himself admitted in his Academy speech welcoming Pereda—his beliefs were only provisional, always darkened by shadows of doubt. The cause of his spiritual restlessness and philosophic doubts was the search for truth with its ever-beckoning but elusive beauty.

But the definitive shift of philosophic orientation and the consequent modification of artistic procedure were not to be effected for two years. In the meantime, in 1887, Galdós wrote the three short works *Celín, Tropiquillos,* and *Theros,* fantasies illustrating and commenting upon the divisions of the solar year. In the words of the author's preface published in 1890, they were the result of artistic caprice and—what is more to the point—of a feeling of spiritual weariness induced by years of uninterrupted contact with the visible things of life. Possibly they were also a self-imposed assignment in the exercise of free imagination preparatory to the new stage upon which Galdós was about to enter.

If Galdós hoped to rise to the realm of the stars on the wings of fantasy, he was disappointed. The very effort of the flight convinced him that after many years of contact with reality he could not detach himself from it all at once. He had not yet exhausted the social phenomena to which he had been so strongly drawn. In his next novel, *Miau* (1888), he returned to concrete social realities and dealt with the theme of Spanish bureaucracy. For some reason this work provoked more extensive comment than had most of his recent writings. Galdós himself did not regard it as anything noteworthy, merely as a sort of light course between two entrees with which he hoped to keep the public satisfied while he was preparing to serve them something more substantial.

* * * *

A purely fortuitous event occurred to give added point to Galdós' search for a new direction. From about the middle of 1888 to the following May, the city of Madrid—in fact, most of Spain—was agog over the famous Fuencarral murder case. A miserly old lady, Doña Luciana, had been found dead in her apartment, her body badly charred. Suspicion fell on her servant, Higinia Balaguer, and her worthless son, José Varela, serving a sentence in the Madrid prison. What slight mystery attached to the murder might have been quickly solved had not the press, politicians, and the meddlesome public interfered with normal judicial procedures.

Galdós followed the case with profound interest. He watched the unfolding of the investigation in its minutest details, obtained permission to interview some of the suspects, assiduously attended all sessions of the trial, and reported his observations fully and frequently in a series of articles in *La Prensa*. For the moment he was so engrossed in the Fuencarral murder that all else seemed to him of secondary interest. He had promised the Buenos Aires newspaper an eye-witness account of the protocol visits between Queen Victoria of England and Regent Queen María Cristina of Spain in Biarritz and San Sebastián, but since the opening date of the trial coincided with the day the court left Madrid, he remained in the capital. For Galdós this was indeed a sacrifice, fond as he was of the pageantry of royal ceremonies.

It was neither idle curiosity nor love of scandal that held Galdós enthralled during the long months of the trial. Nor was it simply that as a phenomenon of external reality it might some day prove useful to him. What attracted him chiefly was that it presented the opportunity to learn how vast can be the difference between absolute truth and what is ordinarily regarded as truth. As Galdós phrased it: "The slow appearance of truth, in the midst of so much contradictory testimony and behind the frauds proffered by the criminals, produces in the spirit of the listener a wholesome pleasure which compensates him for the suffering caused by the parade of so many horrors."[4]

The trial convinced Galdós that in Spain more than elsewhere, because of the innate tendency of the people to appraise a specific phenomenon without reference to logic or common sense, it was essential to purge reality of all the alloys introduced by the imagination. Only thus might one hope to discover the mainsprings of life—the subtle and elusive spiritual forces which impel action. He reached the conclusion that far more important than the ability to record human behavior directly is the ability to discern its motives. For these cannot be explained in terms of physical or social influences, but must be understood in relation to the conscience—the principal source of ideas, dreams, imaginings, ideals, ambitions, and aspirations. In short, the Fuencarral trial inclined Galdós more than ever to view life as an intimately bound combination of cause—mysterious and complicated—and effect—external and visible phenomena.

These convictions found expression in the next two novels: *La incógnita* and *Realidad*. The first was written during the Fuencarral trial, and the second appeared shortly after its conclusion. Both works marked a decided departure in technique. *La incógnita* combines observation with action, the latter dexterously arranged in a conventional plot design. Perhaps Galdós thus intended to silence those critics who for almost a decade had deprecated his utter disregard of traditional novelistic architecture. It is an epistolary novel dealing with the relative truth that a given phenomenon conveys to those who view it externally and with detachment. The absolute truth of the same phenomenon constitutes the subject matter of *Realidad,* a novel in dialogue, essentially dramatic although not intended for the stage. In it the true reality is revealed by the characters as they search their consciences and lay bare impulses and convictions which are at variance with apparent motives and obvious causes. The two novels have not only the social documentary value inherent in all Galdós' works, but the added quality of superior analysis of conscience, spirit, and soul. In them he very definitely opened a new phase of philosophic and artistic exploration.

La incógnita and *Realidad* inevitably derailed some critics and confounded others. Few were sufficiently discerning to grasp the author's purpose with respect to content as well as form. To superficial reviewers the novel techniques offered a pretext for admonishing sermons and pontifical pronouncements. Once again Galdós was warned that the reader's patience was limited; that it was altogether unwarranted to write so long an epilogue as *Realidad* to a theme that had been fairly exhausted in *La incógnita*. What was the author's excuse for the lack of unity in the treatment of the two works? Why the epistolary style of the first novel and the dramatic but obviously non-theatrical form of its sequel? Even sagacious Clarín was hard-pressed to discover artistic virtue in the dialogue novel—from a purely formalistic standpoint.

All the advance warnings in the press that the ever-resourceful Galdós was charting a new course had apparently failed to prepare the critics for the proper appraisal of the new philosophic and esthetic material. They could do no more than hide their confusion behind authoritative pronouncements on the inviolability of sacred artistic precepts. The flashes of new morality in *Realidad* blinded the reviewers, and stumblingly they speculated whether, having exhausted his creative vein, Galdós was perhaps seeking to be startling when he could no longer be convincing. The new strain of reason balanced by imagination—matter seeking to lift itself on the wings of spirit—was accepted as conclusive evidence of decadence. It was even suggested that the very confusing innovations in his recent works bespoke a conscious effort to discover new ways of retaining his hold on the public. How far were even the shrewd and perspicacious critics from suspecting that the dramatic form of *Realidad* was a forecast of the next stage in Galdós' literary career! None apparently remembered the zeal with which the reformer had entered the artistic arena when he became aware of his incapacity for struggle on other battlefields.

* * * *

When *Miau* appeared in 1888, Fray Candil was able to say: "The Madrid press, with few exceptions, almost attaches more

importance to a dog than to a novel by Galdós." [5] Fray Candil
was then among the supporters of Galdós whose cause suffered
an occasional defection because of his alleged espousal of naturalism. There were others who, like Fray Candil, were frankly
concerned over the injury inflicted on the novelist's reputation
by Luis Alfonso's sugar-coated barbs and the poison-dipped darts
shot from ambush in the popular cafés. José Ortega y Munilla
and Clarín did not quite succeed in convincing the public that
every new work by Galdós not only raised his own literary
stature but also elevated Spain's cultural and artistic level. They
argued in vain that Galdós' development followed a normal
course dictated by the inner laws of artistic creation and the
demands of the age. In time Clarín began to worry seriously
about the growing complaints against certain features of Galdós'
style and technique. Hoping to induce his good friend to mend
his ways in details of minor esthetic significance, he too criticized
Galdós for indulging in prolixity which sometimes obscured the
central theme. Whereas formerly Clarín had invariably converted into a virtue whatever others called a vice, now he occasionally made bold to suggest that Galdós was perhaps a victim
of excessive methodicalness—that his literal adherence to the
motto of *nulla dies sine linea* necessarily resulted from time to
time in quantity rather than quality.

If Clarín's observations were intended as advice, they probably
fell on deaf ears. Although Galdós was not insensitive to the
march of his artistic—and financial—fortunes, he had the fortitude to pursue his set course. He realized that in view of the
average Spaniard's penchant for chatter, gossip, polemics, and
independent criteria, he would be naïve to aspire to a unanimously sustained reputation. He compared the course of personal fame in Spanish morals, literature, and politics to the
growth of rickety, wart-covered, and worm-eaten trees: wherever
one goes one hears the incessant noise of the industrious insect
boring and wasting away the most robust trunk. So there was
really nothing he could do to retain his appeal and to bolster his
reputation. Even if he had chosen to satisfy the demands of the
critics and readers he could not have maintained his privileged

position indefinitely. As matters stood, he at least had the satisfaction of being loyal to his concept of art.

But Galdós' friends rested less easy in their consciences, and quietly they launched a movement to have him elected to the Royal Academy of Languages in order to re-enforce the high pedestal on which he had been placed in 1883. The origin of the movement remains rather obscure, but it is fairly certain that it was enthusiastically sponsored by Marcelino Menéndez y Pelayo, Spain's most distinguished scholar. The banquet of 1883 had in a sense been tendered Galdós as a consolation prize for his failure to secure a place among the academic immortals. Now, it was felt, the promise of success was greater. True, everyone anticipated that his candidacy would be opposed by those who persisted in regarding his novels as a malicious distortion of the traditional values of Spanish life, but it was hoped that Don Marcelino's endorsement would swing enough votes to elect Galdós. Only a few years earlier the erudite scholar had taken Galdós severely to task for encouraging Spanish heterodoxy, so his support now should convince everyone that the honor was being sought on grounds of literary merit alone. The campaigners felt they had ground for optimism when even the critics who had been chastising the novelist for his naturalistic sins conceded that his talent and achievement deserved the highest reward. Nevertheless, a battle was in the offing.

The year 1889 had hardly opened when Galdós found himself in the center of a mild but discomforting storm. The press discussed the forthcoming meeting of the Royal Academy as if it were a national event of supreme importance, and in the popular cafés it was the main topic of conversation. The discussions did not always move on a purely academic plane. The battle line was sharply drawn between liberalism and traditionalism—still a hotly contested issue in Spain—and the fighting took place behind a screen of esthetic doctrines and literary principles.

Galdós' partisans, assuming that his right to the seat vacated by the death of the Duque de Villahermosa required little defense, concentrated their fire on the rumored rival, Francisco Andrés Commelerán, an obscure professor of Latin in the

Instituto del Cardenal Cisneros and author of a classical ety-
mological Latin-Spanish dictionary. A similar strategy was
adopted by the enemy, whose confidence of victory rested on
their conviction that the predominantly conservative majority
in the Royal Academy would vote for its candidate. In Galdós'
camp this point was converted into powerful ammunition, and
in the closing days of the conflict the battle was locked over the
extent to which party politics was influencing the immortal
electors.

Unfortunately the political cannon proved to be a boom-
erang. Once the issue had been injected, the outcome could not
be seriously in doubt. Galdós was still a liberal Cortes deputy,
and in the Academy the conservative Cánovas del Castillo
wielded a powerful influence. It was recalled that in 1883 there
had been much speculation whether Cánovas would attend the
Galdós banquet, but that he had finally joined in the impressive
homage. Would the shrewd politician be equally magnanimous
now? Galdós' most optimistic champions hoped that he would
be guided by public sentiment, which, gauged by the accounts in
the liberal press, seemed definitely unfavorable to Commelerán
because of his obscure and insignificant contribution to the promotion of the Spanish language. But the outcome was not to be
known until January 17, 1889.

In the days immediately preceding the elections, speculation
was greatest over the probable alignment of the electors. Where
advance tabulations failed to show a majority for Galdós, there
was consolation in the belief that the most distinguished writers
and intellectuals would surely vote for him. Few questioned
that Menéndez y Pelayo, Núñez de Arce, Castelar, Valera, Zorrilla, and Balaguer would cast their ballot for the novelist. As
for Commelerán, he could count definitely on the support of
only four celebrities: Cañete, Tamayo y Baus, Cánovas, and
Alejandro Pidal—all arch-conservatives. Yet it was generally
felt that the Latin professor had hidden support among the
obscure members of the Academy, and that he would snatch the
victory from Galdós by a vote of twelve to nine. Somehow, the

number of the electorate was fixed at twenty-one out of the normal membership of forty.

On January 17, 1889, twenty-four immortals assembled in the Royal Academy for a furious battle. The opposing sides were led by Menéndez y Pelayo and Cañete. The odds against Menéndez y Pelayo were great, but the stakes were high. He fought gamely, and his eloquence netted him one deserter from the conservative camp. When the ballots were counted, it was revealed that Galdós had received ten votes against fourteen for Commelerán, who had been helped by the attendance of several habitual absentees.

Galdós profited by the episode, however. No cabinet crisis resulted from the conservative victory in the Academy, but old political feuds were revived and fresh literary debates precipitated. Many a café *tertulia* buzzed with gossip about politicians, statesmen, and immortals. Galdós, it would seem, regarded his defeat as another of the numerous manifestations of the ironies of life. Perhaps he construed it as retribution for the many playful sins he had committed against the Academy in his writings. The reaction of his admirers began with violent indignation and ended in unalloyed sarcasm. Somehow scornful public opinion turned the painful defeat into a moral victory. Galdós was loudly proclaimed superior to any official honor. In fact, some asserted that it would have been a deadly insult to elect him. Numerous letters from the "anonymous masses" reached the defeated candidate, congratulating him on the outcome. The students of the University of Madrid—including many youths who subsequently distinguished themselves in cultural and literary pursuits—added to the post-election tumult by presenting to Galdós a testimonial of admiration and loyalty which the liberal press publicized.

The irony of the situation was intensified by the public's attitude toward his defeat. To a letter of condolence from his Las Palmas friend, Dr. Gregorio Chil, he replied on February 28, 1889: "My distinguished friend: I am infinitely grateful to you for your kind letter prompted by the ill-fated academic question.

What has happened is very strange. I have been defeated and they are the ones who are swallowing the gall of rout."

But Galdós was apparently fated to earn immortality after all. Approximately six months later, on June 13, 1889, he was unanimously elected to membership in the Royal Academy. Most of his friends were elated, but there were some who urged him to decline the honor in view of what had happened in January. What Galdós' own reaction was is not known. It would appear, however, that he was much interested in the spring meeting of the Academy, for he regretfully declined the invitation tendered him as a writer of "recognized merit" to represent his profession at the national coronation of Zorrilla in Granada on June 8. His position was perhaps stated accurately by his friend, José Lázaro, who wrote as follows:

> We understand that in view of the explanations that have been made and the apologies that have been offered by those who formerly stood in the forefront of opposition to him—apologies in the sense that Galdós' nomination was signed by the very same academicians who proposed Commelerán—a nomination which was a literal copy of the one that the defenders of Galdós presented on the other occasion—he could only forget the past or else appear to be overcome by a pride which is at marked variance with the benevolent nature of the illustrious author of the *Episodios Nacionales*. [6]

Two worries now beset Galdós, and unfortunately the regulations of the Royal Academy of Language imposed no limit on their duration. For the initiation ceremony, formal dress and an elevated discourse were absolute requirements. It was to be a solemn event, with Menéndez y Pelayo as Galdós' sponsor. For several years the academician-elect worried about the requirements without doing anything to meet them. Late in 1891, however, his friends resolved to end his procrastination. The most impatient among them was Dr. Tolosa Latour, to whose will Galdós bent almost as readily as to that of the feminine members of his own family. In 1894 Galdós promised to summon up the courage needed for a visit to a fashionable tailor and to prepare his discourse. That pleased the doctor. "I suppose," he wrote in a letter dated June 29, "that within a month or so you will be going up and down the streets, trying out your new 'formals' and getting ready to join the Royal—to use the language of academic amateurs and aspirants."

But many other preoccupations prevented Galdós from carrying out his honest intentions before 1897—eight years after his election—not the least serious of which was the writing of the discourse. It took much moral courage, more will power, and still more stylistic and rhetorical effort. Moreover, in some hidden recess of Galdós' mind was the ever-present fear of facing a crowd. And so he postponed the task as long as possible, writing by slow and easy stages, but finding even this procedure extremely irksome. He might have been tempted to renounce earthly immortality forever had it not been for an incident that increased his responsibility in the matter.

For years his good friend Pereda had craved immortality. As a resident of Santander, however, he had been frustrated by the statutory requirement of legal residence in Madrid until the combined juridical acumen of several friendly academicians, headed by Menéndez y Pelayo, contrived a scheme that enabled him to clear the hurdle in the spring of 1896. Galdós and Menéndez y Pelayo contended for the privilege of being Pereda's official initiator into the Academy, and Galdós won through sheer determination and obstinacy. Then the trouble began: instead of one discourse, he now had two to prepare. He was mindful of his new commitment, but did nothing about it for some time. Pereda, on the other hand, was consumed with impatience to put the ordeal behind him. He implored Menéndez y Pelayo to goad Galdós into activity. The following letter of Pereda's, dated October 11, 1896, illuminates the awkward situation of the three men:

> Dear Marcelino: Your father delivered the message you left with him for me, and I thanked him for the courtesy. The worst of it is that we are not making any progress this way, because to date Galdós has not

picked up his pen to fulfill his commitment, nor do I
see in him the slightest inclination to do so. I was
afraid that it would turn out thus. And so it would
be best if you advised him that your speech is completed and the two of you went ahead with the selection of a date for his initiation. Even so, the winter
will be over before I am initiated. Goodness knows
that I haven't much courage left for the ordeal.

Since Galdós could not serve as Pereda's sponsor until he
himself had been initiated, he was compelled to act promptly.
His most serious difficulty was the writing of that part of the
discourse known as the "salutation of modesty." Convincing
himself that his stylistic powers were inadequate to the task, he
entered into a secret arrangement with Menéndez y Pelayo
whereby the latter would write this section for him and severely
criticize the rest of his discourse. The following letter from
Galdós to Don Marcelino exposes the "deal":

My dear Marcelino: Tomorrow I will read this thing
to you. I will come to your house between 12 and 1.
If you cannot be there at that time, please leave word
for me at what hour you will expect me in the afternoon, and where.

And in the name of whatever you hold dearest in the
world, please have ready for me by tomorrow, in a
couple of pages, the "salutation *of modesty*" and the
brief eulogy of my predecessor (i.e., León Galindo
de Vera). The part I have done is not complete yet,
but it is passable, although it will require some corrections and additions.

The momentous day of February 6, 1897, came, and Galdós
could no longer evade the ordeal of getting into his formal
clothes—and the Royal Academy. An unusually large crowd
filled the reception hall. Madrid's élite was present in impressive
numbers. And never before had a similar function attracted so
many ladies! Among the famous authors who attended were
Núñez de Arce, Valera, Tamayo y Baus, Sellés, Castelar,

Echegaray, and others. Commelerán was also present. The occasion was one of greatest significance and was invested with great solemnity. The press had whipped up considerable curiosity about Galdós' discourse on "Contemporary Society as Fictional Material," and anticipation ran high. What would the greatest Spanish fiction writer say about the novel in theory? The reporter of *El Liberal* rightly said the following morning: "Few academic functions have been celebrated with the solemnity of the one held yesterday afternoon on the occasion of the initiation of the illustrious author of the *Episodios Nacionales*."

Galdós contributed a note of somberness to the ceremony. His timidity and the consciousness of his oratorical ineptitude made him very ill at ease. His muffled voice did not carry very far, and the words tumbled out of his mouth only partly articulated. The crowd, which filled all the seats and some of the standing room, listened with rapt attention, but to those who came to hear and not merely to applaud Galdós, his speech was a keen disappointment. Obviously it was not a labor of love, and it was very brief, perhaps to shorten the ordeal.

Unlike his other writings, Galdós' academic discourse is distinguished more by form—manifestly labored and artificial—than by substance. Aware that gallantry and courtesy were *de rigueur* on such an occasion, he employed a solemn tone and took pains to express himself with elevated correctness and commendable brevity. In print the speech occupies eleven pages, including the three and one-half pages devoted to the "salutation of modesty." Thus it is not an adequate treatment of his subject but a mere outline indicating the ideas the author might have developed had he seen fit to do so. In the final analysis it is only an eloquent recapitulation of Galdós' theory of 1870 concerning the relation between the rising middle class and the modern novel. It might, however, be taken as a bit of veiled self-defense, for by inference he attempted to justify the several stages of his career, arguing that art cannot remain static while shifting forces are constantly changing the complexion of society. Moreover, he suggested in polite but unequivocal terms, critical criteria must be flexible, since they are no more infallible than the creative artists themselves. And as if to insure that there would henceforth be no more misunderstanding of the new direction in which he had turned, he laid particular stress on the idea that the primary concern of modern art is with human rather than social values.

Listening to the speech was as much an ordeal for the audience as its delivery was for the speaker. It was obvious that the dark, slender, tallish, and rather loose-jointed man with a hard-working air felt very uncomfortable in formal dress and that he was frightened by the countless eyes fixed upon him. The entire assemblage shared the new immortal's visible relief when, after a thunderous ovation, he resumed his customary attitude of serious meditation. He sat down awkwardly and, shrinking in his chair, settled down to listen to the eloquent phrases of his sponsor.

Don Marcelino's oratory was ample compensation for the discomfort Galdós had caused everyone. His discourse—almost three times as long as the novelist's—by its elevated tone, rhetorical richness, and skillful display of erudition, restored everyone's faith in the constancy of the Royal Academy's traditions. There was a murmur of amazement when the orator reduced to five the eight years that had actually elapsed since Galdós' election, but this was soon dispelled by the widely undulating lines with which he traced the history of fiction and the evolution of the modern novel in Spain before the appearance of Galdós. When he came to discuss the novelist's treatment of religion, some listened with visible apprehension, fearing a renewal of Don Marcelino's attack on Galdós' heterodoxy. But the eminent scholar remained laudably objective and even retracted some of his former harsh judgments. In the remainder of the speech he eulogized the new academician in a number of epigrammatic observations that have become axioms in Galdosian *materia critica*.

Two weeks after his initiation, on February 21, 1897, Galdós made another public appearance at the Academy to welcome Pereda. This time he spoke much better, and his discourse was more carefully thought out. After that day he occupied chair N—

the one assigned to him—on only a few occasions. Unlike other members of the learned society, he had no honors or titles to accompany his name when it was added to the list printed at the head of the Academy dictionary. He rarely referred to his academic distinction, and privately he evaluated it in terms of the modest honorarium he received for attending sessions. During the years that he lived with his sister Carmen and her family he surrendered his academic earnings to her as ceremoniously as he was wont to bring to her the bag of caramels that was the traditional daily emolument of congressional deputies. He did, however, use his new position to promote the candidacy of those who sought his support. Galdós was academically helpful to Ramón Menéndez Pidal, Andrenio, the Conde de las Navas, and others. But his influence was insufficient to obtain immortality for Emilia Pardo Bazán.

About fifteen years after his reception Galdós had occasion to wonder whether the unanimous vote he had received in 1889 reflected the immortals' sincere opinion of his worth. The Royal Academy of Language—with a slightly different membership, to be sure—refused to endorse officially his candidacy for the Nobel Prize on the ground that it would be an insult to Catholic and patriotic Spain to grant the award to the half-blind, indigent patriarch of Spanish letters. In this instance his immortality obviously brought him no earthly joy. However, official pomp was not permanently denied him. In 1916 he was guest of honor at the annual festival of the "El Sitio Society" of Bilbao in commemoration of the famous siege of that city during the Carlist War. He insisted on wearing the same formal attire in which he had twice appeared before the Royal Academy. The physical discomfort was even greater in 1916 than in 1897, his girth being larger, but the renewed sensation of immortality in this life was an ineffable joy. For Galdós entertained the ironical notion that a set of garments that had survived so long must be immortal, and that whoever wore them necessarily partook of the essence of immortality.

XII

Dramatic Début

IN THE LATE EIGHTIES Galdós viewed with misgivings the progressive decline of the national drama. The taste of the public had seemingly undergone a radical change which tended to discourage dramatists. Whereas in the sixties and seventies even an average play held the boards for at least two weeks, now the best was unlikely to run longer than six days. Consequently the theater failed to lure the literary novice very strongly. Young men who a decade or so before had courted glory with a volume of poetry or an original theatrical piece in verse now sought fame with a first novel. Provincials who streamed into the capital, instead of camping on the doorsteps of impresarios and famous actors, besieged publishers and reviewers. The established dramatists and their numerable followers were still being applauded, but were hardly attracting new disciples. The revival of the romantic drama by Echegaray represented only a temporary halt in the general decline. His genius for moving audiences with dramaturgic devices was indisputable, but his imitators inherited only his penchant for frightful situations, which in time proved unpalatable to the public. There was growing evidence of a marked preference for the forthright artistic presentation of everyday life and of a definite aversion to tumultuous passions and emotions.

This change in taste may be partly attributed to the simple and natural performances which visiting French and Italian companies were giving in the largest Spanish theaters. Certainly the foreign artists contributed at least to the simplification of the native histrionic style. Solemn declamation, heavy gesticulation, and marked affectation were becoming increasingly intolerable, as were sonorous and dazzling verse plays. Audiences applauded less and less the formally attired artists who, in the manner of grandiloquent tenors, recited long lyrical speeches to the accompaniment of stereotyped gestures.

But the symptoms of this change in taste and in the externalities of dramatic art went unnoticed by the dramatists, who continued to write verse plays dealing with adultery and insoluble problems. Aided by the press and their friends, they enjoyed a period of impressive success, but it was short-lived. The moment was propitious for a courageous dramatist fired with the reformer's zeal to lay the foundation of a new dramatic style characterized by simplicity and naturalness. Echegaray might have been that reformer had he recognized that it is not terrifying situations derived from physical accidents and a host of circumstances unrelated to the play of passions that produce the most lasting impression on the spectator, but those resulting from the affections themselves, those whose mechanism is supplied not by the coincidence of time and person but by the very mesh of characters. Echegaray would also have had to recognize that the historical drama of passion in ancient garb and romantic phrasing must inevitably disappear, as well as the contemporary drama which was modern only by virtue of the *levita* (Prince Albert coat) worn by the actors and which was basically alien to the spirt of the times in speech, sentiment, and human behavior. But Echegaray was clearly unware of his great opportunity; he persisted in the use of dazzling scenic effects and gorgeous imagery, thus depriving his plays of even an illusion of truth and reality. It was obvious that the neo-romantic group could not be counted on to save the Spanish drama.

There was even less hope of salvation in the exchange of national tradition for a French trademark. Virtually all the dramatic species in vogue in France—including the political comedy *à la* Scribe—were being tried out on the Spanish public. Scribe's parodists were lamentably ignorant of the essential differences between Spanish and French politics, and their plays showed greater understanding of the model than of their own

society. Their appeal was as limited and brief as that of the
Spanish version of the French sentimental comedy of moral-
izing tendency. With little discretion and intelligence the Spanish stage was converted into a pulpit for sermonizing on the
sacredness of family ties, the need for compromise in family
quarrels, and the calming effect of honestly contracted matri-
mony upon infantile passions. All this commonplace wisdom
emanated from conflicts involving wicked fathers and penitent
mothers, stupid Don Juanesque heroes and silly weakling maid-
ens, meddlesome servants and tender-hearted spinsters. Always,
too, there was in such plays a copious stream of tears. In fact,
they incorporated everything there was in the foreign models
but little of national character and customs.

The magnificent structure that was once the Spanish drama
was rapidly crumbling into a heap of ruins inhabited by crawl-
ing imitators and translators. The few remaining authors of
repute ceased writing for lack of themes, and this in turn made
the public indifferent. The level of acting and stagecraft was not
much higher. Talented artists were constantly quarreling among
themselves, rendering impossible the organization of an impressive company. The best of them were touring in South America.
The national Teatro Español, which had lost much of its prestige, often tolerated actors whose talent measured up only to the
standards of second-rate neighborhood theaters. In February,
1886, the Duque de Rivas' *Don Alvaro* attracted only a score of
spectators, the majority of whom were admitted on complimentary tickets. And if it had not been for the occasional eruption
of the *halberdiers* the performance would have taken place amidst
sepulchral silence and languid yawns.

The only prospering theaters were those that offered programs
of one-act skits of the vaudeville variety. Their nearest com-
petitors were the so-called coliseums, which produced translations of Dumas *fils* and Sardou. The most famous works by
these authors enjoyed long runs, but in time they too began to
pall on the public, and the translators had to fall back on
second-rate dramatists like Ohnet, Gondinet, and Pailleron,
and even on plays dealing with Parisian boulevard adventures

such as constituted the regular bill of fare in theaters like the Gymnase and Variétés. Occasionally translators tried to adapt the French original to Spanish life and customs, but the results were absurd and incongruous. The outright translations were not much better, since they were made without adequate knowledge of the French language. Their gibberish was not easily intelligible to Spaniards—even the French would not have understood it readily.

Such was the state of the Spanish drama as Galdós himself observed it and recorded it in *La Prensa*. Since he was at the height of his novelistic fever, it is likely that his interest in the drama was only one aspect of his general curiosity about the literary panorama of Spain. It is significant, nevertheless, that he interspersed his impressions with personal interpretations and concepts. Perhaps in rejecting Echegaray as the needed dramatic reformer he dimly visualized himself as the person best qualified for the task. He had already formulated a broad point of departure. Without discounting the attitude of the public and the abstention of the good dramatists, he insisted that the decadence of the drama was an inevitable phenomenon of literary and esthetic evolution.

For Galdós did not regard the experience of Spain as unique. He believed that in England and in Germany, too, the drama was declining in conformance to an historico-literary law. Neither the solicitude of critics nor the talent of traditional dramatists could restore dramaturgic art to its former plane. The situation in France seemed to him somewhat brighter, but even there he saw signs of an impending crisis. Everywhere the most venerable traditions of art were powerless to halt the degeneration of the drama into sheer spectacle and the displacement of comedy by pantomime. One must face the fact that for the moment the public eschewed the deeper emotions and patronized only laughter-provoking performances. With changing conditions of material existence even serious and sensible people had little taste for plays depicting the misery and agony of their own daily lives.

Did this mean that legitimate drama was doomed? Did theatrical spectacles move a people only during their adolescence?

Did society, like the individual, acquire sense at the expense of sensibility? Galdós' answers to these questions can only be inferred from his further analysis of the decadence of the drama. He believed that its waning appeal was partly due to its inability to reproduce life effectively with its outmoded artificial technique. Its time-honored devices and sure-fire tricks no longer surprised the public, and its stereotyped characters, utterly unrepresentative of living men and women of the period, were wearisome. The remedy was at hand—a new drama stressing character and moral and ethical values involved in the new problems of life.

Galdós' keen interest in the drama between 1885 and 1887 transcended purely esthetic speculation. A new idea was germinating in his mind, a new ambition was challenging him. His old urge to revolutionize the Spanish drama was gradually becoming a compelling force. He drew encouragement from Echegaray's spectacular triumphs, which often came to disturb him in his isolation. He knew that the end of his struggle as a novelist was not yet in sight, but he was prepared to plunge into a new conflict. Despite his placid exterior and mild manner, Galdós loved the excitement of struggle, and his resolute will and inflexible character thrived on obstacles. Fighting against odds sharpened his sense of the joy of living and stirred bold ambitions in him. The hostility of some critics toward him in the late eighties, far from undermining his self-confidence as a novelist, fired him with zeal to include the drama in his efforts to regenerate the national literature. The mission he had conceived in his youth was only partly accomplished.

But Galdós was not given to precipitate action. Before embarking upon his novelistic career he had gone through a period of careful deliberation and preparation, and now he did the same. He confided his intentions to several friends, who encouraged him wholeheartedly. They had all discerned a strong dramatic vein in his novels and often wondered whether he was not destined to revitalize the Spanish drama as he had the national novel. Several years before, Palacio Valdés, whose critical acumen Galdós respected highly, had said to him in a letter dated July 14, 1883:

Although you have a genius for observation, it seems to me that you excel even more in inventiveness, in dramatic power, in inspiration. I believe that there is latent in you a powerful dramatic author who, because of the special conditions of the contemporary drama, that is, because of its narrowness and poorness, has had to seek a wider field with greater space for his genius. If the drama had today the freedom it enjoyed in Shakespeare's time, I firmly believe that you would have become only a dramatist. If you live long enough you will see how future generations will appraise you in this sense.

Others shared Palacio Valdés' confidence. Eusebio Blasco, who in 1870 had almost succeeded in launching Galdós on a dramatic career, still had faith in his talent and seriously considered the dramatization of all the *Episodios nacionales*. It would have been a grandiose enterprise, perhaps too grandiose ever to have materialized. Most persistently encouraging was Tolosa Latour. When *Realidad* appeared in 1889—its dialogue form was perhaps as much the result of premeditation as of the inner logic of its theme—his pressure became fairly irresistible. Here was a work, he argued, which with a little pruning and a few internal changes could become the herald of a new dramatic era.

Galdós graciously accepted the suggestions and advice of his friends. Tolosa Latour's choice for his dramatic début was a happy one; he too regarded *Realidad* as a significant work. But he was not yet ready to take the serious step. Not only did he want to write an original work for his initial dramatic trial, but he needed to summon additional courage for the venture. Actually he was no less afraid than eager to take the plunge. Before setting out on the journey of whose perils he had heard so much, he wished to sound out public opinion. So he permitted rumors of his impending artistic conversion to be circulated, and watched with keen interest the furore the announcement created in literary *tertulias*. Once again Galdós became the topic of animated conversation and furious debate.

A combination of circumstances soon began to press Galdós for a decision. Foremost was the growing need for sustaining his popularity, which hostile criticism and an occasional outcropping of envy among the younger writers had begun to impair. His income had inevitably been affected, and with the passing years his financial condition seemed to worsen. The illustrated edition of the *episodios* yielded more worry than wealth; while the venture taxed the resources of his sister-in-law more than his own, the burden on his conscience was heavy. When his mother died in 1887, his hopes of a substantial inheritance were dashed. The family estate, consisting mostly of volcanic land which his brother Ignacio had struggled to convert into vineyards, was barely sufficient to support his spinster sisters.

But most serious was Galdós' inability to adjust his disbursements to his income. He was not wasteful nor extravagant as regards the ordinary necessities of life, but he was unable to divorce his own mode of living, which might have been simple, from that of his fictional creations. In the management of his private affairs his realistic perception of life completely failed him. Something akin to the moral and spiritual disability of some of his characters forced him into passional indulgences which only his own reserve, the inordinate respect of his admirers, and the zealous watchfulness of those close to him prevented from becoming a scandal. His family knew how great a strain his conduct imposed upon his resources, and to all who inquired they explained that his financial straits were attributable to his extensive travels. Galdós paid a heavy price for the privilege of living unconventionally like some of his characters. In the humble zones of Madrid, where he met many a prototype for his characters, he was frequently victimized by persons who knew how naïve and childlike he was in all that pertained to the simple realities of his own life. He was often also the prey of colleagues whose relations with him were none too close and whose position in the literary profession was precarious. To many such Galdós was a prompt and generous reply to their prayer for daily bread.

Early in the nineties Galdós found himself heading for an economic crisis. No matter how often he cast up his accounts in the margins of his manuscripts and however closely he scrutinized the ledgers of his half-partner and publisher, Miguel H. de Cámara, it was painfully clear that he was virtually bankrupt. To aggravate the situation, he was heavily involved in the construction of a rather elaborate home in Santander. Eventually Madrina had to come to the rescue, but the proud and conscientious Galdós struggled hard to finance the enterprise independently. Madrid and Santander money-lenders pressed him for occasional payments on the principal despite their exorbitant rates of interest. Cámara extended credit more and more grudgingly, especially when he perceived that his partner was growing suspicious of his honesty. When Galdós pressed him to explain why he was a poor man in spite of his high income, Cámara remained discreetly silent. He would not be the first one to pierce the silence in which Don Benito's intimate life was enveloped!

Casting about for a solution of his problem, Galdós began to reflect more seriously on the low state of the Spanish drama. He was convinced that reform was urgent, and he was fairly confident of his ability to effect it. But still he hesitated. Could he succeed where such figures as Zola, Flaubert, Daudet, and the Goncourts had failed? He might have delayed his decision longer had he not believed that a successful dramatic career would yield at least moderate wealth. That such monetary considerations did ultimately influence his decision is revealed by his correspondence with Cámara. In a letter dated May 6, 1893, by which time Galdós had produced three plays, his publisher attributed his continued financial difficulties to his diminished novelistic output. Testily he wrote:

> In short, you probably know all this, because you undoubtedly kept it in mind when you thought of opening new roads that would lead you out of poverty. The first was the theater—the thousands of duros your staged works were going to earn have apparently materialized only in your imagination....

But the factor that weighed most in his decision was a purely psychological one. Despite his outward humility, Galdós accepted his widely proclaimed supremacy as novelist with a pride that was not entirely untouched by vanity. He sincerely believed that he merited the praise heaped upon him. Privately he may have realized that the regenerative power of his novels was limited, but this only served as a further inducement to essay the drama, which he regarded as a superior vehicle for the conveyance of a message. Indeed, Galdós took himself rather seriously as the forger of a new national soul, the apostle of a new gospel, a popular leader of sorts. In the nineties he even began to crave some of the external glamor which usually accompanies popular leadership. He was seeking some means of heightening his consciousness of his position and achievement, and he finally concluded that he would find it in contact with his public in the theater.

Galdós confessed something of this to Blasco Ibáñez shortly after the turn of the century as he undertook to answer Blasco's question concerning the motives behind his new artistic orientation:

> "It is the mania of all great novelists," he told me. "Zola once got the same inspiration. They suffer the pangs of hunger for popular acclaim. If they were politicians and orators, accustomed to ovations or protests from the masses, they would not feel that craving for popularity, that longing to see the public at close range, to submit themselves to their capricious judgments. But isolated in their workrooms they feel as if fallen from grace and abandoned, even though their works may sell well. The praise of the press does not move them; they become accustomed to it, and applause in cold print strikes them as insipid. What matters it to them to know that there are many readers who laugh or weep as they read their works so long as the silent applause does not reach their ears and so long as they are not face to face with those who admire their genius?" [1]

San Quintín, Galdós' Chalet at Santander

Galdós in Middle Age

Late in the spring of 1891 Galdós made the decision to seek fresh laurels as a dramatist after almost twenty years of impressive success as a novelist. For his début he selected *Realidad*, and zealously set out to prepare the stage version, not without some misgivings. Most of his fears and doubts he kept to himself, but some he shared with his good friend Atilano Lamera in Santander. Among his problems was the title. He feared that it might be too abstract to be attractive, but he was reluctant to change it because of its symbolic implication with regard to the theme and his broad aims with respect to the new national drama. The more serious problem of getting the play accepted was solved in part by a fortuitous circumstance.

The two leading Madrid theaters were the Princesa and the Comedia. The latter became Galdós' favorite after his great decision. After an almost total abstinence of twenty years, he now attended an occasional afternoon performance. Gradually he became acquainted with the theatrical world, to which rumors came floating of his new ambition to make his dramatic début with *Realidad*.

The Princesa rejected the play, but the Comedia was more than mildly interested. Its director, Emilio Mario, though not given to encouraging novices, had a good reason for treating the dramatically untried Galdós with more than his customary deference to the great. The Comedia, like other Madrid theaters, had been facing great difficulty in maintaining its company. Just before the opening of the 1891 season Señor Mario was deserted by his principals, Antonio Vico and Carmen Cobeña. These were replaced by Miguel Cepillo and María Guerrero, actors of only fair reputation, and young Emilio Thuillier, who had still to win his spurs. The new company promised to be only moderately successful, but with Galdós' début it could well become the sensation of the season. This thought was really Echegaray's, but director Mario was finally persuaded to adopt it.

When the season of 1891 opened, Galdós became one of the assiduous afternoon patrons of the Comedia and was even invited to some of the rehearsals. He was anxious to observe the new members of the company for his guidance in the scenification of *Realidad,* which was proceeding slowly and painfully. Before long he had made up his mind about the distribution of the roles, although he knew that the artists themselves might not agree with him. And, indeed, some slight difficulties did arise. Once again Echegaray intervened, this time to persuade Miguel Cepillo to take the leading male part. Mario, too, balked for a while at participating in the drama, but finally agreed to take the rather minor role of Joaquín Viera. María Guerrero would, of course, be the leading lady. This delighted Galdós. He had first seen her in a translation of a French play—*Le Maître des Forges* by Philippe Derblay—and she impressed him as both an actress and the embodiment of feminine grace and winsomeness.

Rehearsals began toward the middle of February, 1892, and lasted four long weeks. Galdós broke his rigid daily routine and attended them all, more as spectator than participant. Being inexperienced, he was painfully modest and readily assented to all excisions and changes. But he followed the shaping of his first-born drama in all its details, even to the minutiae of stage-craft. Aside from the mechanisms required for the appearance of the ghost of Federico Viera, everyone was satisfied that in general things were progressing satisfactorily. Anticipation was great, but so were also occasional apprehensions.

The most composed person, outwardly at least, was the novice dramatist. To reassure himself, probably, he repeatedly asserted that the stories about foot-stamping audiences were merely stage folklore. How could his first play fail to be at least a moderate success—not a *succès d'estime,* mind you—in view of the constant reassurances of the most expert Spanish dramatist, José Echegaray, who in a sense supervised all the rehearsals? Doña Emilia Pardo Bazán, whose friendship for Galdós was said to transcend mere colleagueship, also dropped in occasionally, and her enthusiasm could only augur well.

*   *   *   *

The official announcement that Galdós was paying court to Thalia produced universal stupefaction. Even his friends, though admiring his courage, feared he might be jeopardizing his reputation. No one was able to recall another instance of a man of fifty, with an enviable record as a novelist, tempting fate so recklessly. But after the initial shock Galdós' infectious heroism inspired his supporters, who at once made the success of the play their personal responsibility.

Mariano de Cavia, a recent recruit to the company of guardians of Galdós' reputation, furnished the keynote for the ensuing campaign by reviving in the press the story of the banquet of 1883. It was a shrewd and effective move. The main strategy, it would seem, was to pose the question whether an experienced novelist can successfully turn dramatist and to answer in the affirmative with overwhelming logical and esthetic evidence. None was so sanguine as to predict immediate triumph; the struggle would be long and arduous, but Galdós' indisputable genius spelled ultimate victory. Had he not fought successfully against stubborn convention in the novel? Indeed, even if it were true that he was violating the esthetic laws of the drama, and that he was foredoomed to failure, he still deserved support for his daring and zeal and his high artistic ideals. Spain, proclaimed his ardent admirers, was fortunate to have such a man as Galdós to preach the gospel of vigorous progress in all aspects of national life. As Julio Burell voiced it,

> Galdós' attempt will leave a deep trace, and whosoever has the power will follow it without fear. That is what our drama will gain, and that gust of fresh air will introduce a bit of cheer into our bored republic of letters. And whether Pérez Galdós wins or loses— the public is not in doubt about it—the night when *Realidad* is produced, the spirit of Shakespeare will hover over the theater. . . .[2]

But it was no field day for the Galdós enthusiasts. His opponents, not satisfied to limit their campaign to slogans admonishing novelists not to poach on the preserves of the dramatists in the name of pseudo-esthetic principles, resorted to slander and rumor-mongering. To counteract the spreading interest in *Realidad* stimulated by the liberal press, they tried to intimidate the public by charging that the drama was naturalistic, morally subversive, and dangerous. Even worse, it was extremely boring and so long that the performance was certain to last until three in the morning. Leaning on the wisdom of the Spanish proverb —"Al ruin dadle un palmo y se tomará cuatro" ("Give him an inch and he will take an ell")—critics and first-night reviewers, who presumably feared that Galdós' new success might harm their own careers, warned that with a little encouragement from the public he might be inspired to dramatize all his numerous novels. Were he to monopolize the drama also, it would gravely menace the development of the national theater. Was not the only explanation of Galdós' latest ambition his unappeasable desire for money? Let those who doubted it consider the exorbitant admission prices—fifteen pesetas for an orchestra seat, and one hundred for a loge!

Galdós' apparent composure began to show signs of strain as the date of the first public performance neared. During the last rehearsals he constantly sought the solace of tobacco; his friend Federico Balart remarked that already *Realidad* was a stupendous success—for the national tobacco monopoly! In his immediate family everyone noticed that Galdós behaved like a person suffering from dizziness or seasickness. Little did they realize that this was only the beginning of a long *via dolorosa* for all of them. To aggravate matters, the original date of Saturday, March 12, was advanced because it conflicted with a benefit performance at the Royal Opera which might compete for the attendance of society folk. *Realidad* was re-scheduled for Tuesday, March 15. Three additional days of anxiety, mitigated only by evidence that the upper reaches of Spanish society were interested.

The night before the momentous event Galdós was at home to numerous friends and well-wishers. It had been rumored that he would not attend the première. This he neither confirmed nor denied, but he frankly admitted that he was worried and nervous. Someone present recalled his escapade the day before the banquet of 1883, when he was brought back to Madrid by force. Would he again attempt to run away? In his tribulation

Benito Pérez Galdós drew heavily upon the reserve of fortitude which all the Galdoses possessed and resolved to keep his rendezvous with destiny. But he forbade the members of his household to accompany him.

About an hour before curtain time on the long-awaited night the reformer of the Spanish drama was dining with Tolosa Latour in a popular restaurant (La Viña P.) on the Plaza de Santa Ana. M. Martínez Barrionuevo came upon them unexpectedly. Galdós looked outwardly calm, his face expressionless, but he had no appetite and smoked countless cigarettes.

As they left the restaurant Galdós and his companion headed in the opposite direction from the Comedia. They went to salute the statue of Calderón and to invoke his patronage for the night. As they approached the theater, Galdós confessed that he was frightened. Struggling to appear serene, he entered the wings of the stage, greeted the leading members of the cast, collided with the bustling stage hands, stumbled over everything in his way, paced distractedly in all directions, smoked incessantly, and mumbled to himself, "God's will be done." At one moment he was on the verge of drawing placidity from resignation when María Guerrero, the leading lady, upset him anew by candidly announcing that she was terribly nervous and afraid.

When the curtain was about to go up, Galdós felt the need of something to sustain him. He straddled a gilded chair behind the backdrop and glued his right eye to a hole in the canvas. All he could see was the stage set for the first act, but he knew that beyond it was the public, about to serve as the severest tribunal he had ever faced. What would be its verdict?

Not a seat in the house was vacant. Interest, curiosity, friendship, and hostility had brought together a brilliant audience in the Comedia, including an unusual number of feminine spectators. Present were Menéndez y Pelayo, who had come at the insistence of the author; cosmopolitan, aristocratic, meticulous Don Juan Valera, who was intrigued by the innovations that had been heralded; and Doña Emilia Pardo Bazán, who felt she had a proprietary interest in the work. As the curtain went up a deep hush fell over the audience.

The first act was received with profound interest, but without enthusiasm. The subtlety of its artistic qualities and the poor acting tended to weary the audience. There was applause, of course, but it was either perfunctory or motivated only by respect for the author's other literary achievements. At the end of the second act the response was spontaneous and prolonged, but scarcely an ovation despite the ebullient enthusiasm in certain sections of the house. The third act brought about the hoped-for demand for the appearance of the author.

For the vast majority of the spectators this was their first opportunity to see Galdós in person. He was a somewhat painful sight. Literally shoved out from behind the scenes, he came to an awkwardly rigid halt in front of the footlights, the personification of fright and terror! That sea of heads, those countless eyes, that deafening applause, the delirious shouting in the galleries, the excited waving of dainty feminine handkerchiefs— did all that mean that *Realidad* was a success? Like a hysterical child that has suddenly discovered itself parted from its mother, Galdós signaled the stage hands with a pathetic expression to lower the curtain. His agony seemed endless. It certainly was not a moment of complete spiritual tranquillity, as he reminiscently asserted in 1916 with childish vanity and boastfulness.

In statistical terms the success of *Realidad* was impressive— fourteen or fifteen curtain calls for the author, and as many onslaughts of terror. For Galdós' friends the thunderous ovations spelled complete triumph, which in turn augured well for the future of the novice dramatist. In their enthusiasm they overlooked the fact that most of the applause was meant for Galdós the novelist and that his new artistic venture was viewed with considerable reserve in certain quarters.

The Quinteros, who attended the première of *Realidad* at the risk of losing their jobs in a government office—they had been ordered to work overtime that night—retained a lasting impression of Galdós' dramatic début. In 1904 they recalled the reaction of the audience:

> The night of the première of *Realidad* people talked
> volubly between the acts. There were discussions and

disputes. The theater, from the lobby to the highest
gallery, was literally seething. You could hear round,
categorical opinions either extolling Galdós or mercilessly condemning him. You could hear contradictory judgments, hesitant, sometimes absurd, as if coming from people who were dazed and disconcerted
in the presence of something revolutionary and
strange. You could hear, too—and of this there was
the greatest abundance—strangely nonsensical remarks
and veritable outbursts. One of us, the one who first
told the chief that we would not come to work that
night, was on the verge of having a physical tilt,
since he had already had a verbal one, with a very
stupid chap, whose face was the color of a counterfeit
copper coin and who grated on our nerves all night
with the banal cliché, "Shoemaker, stick to the last."
"There goes the shoemaker's last," we said to him
every time there was an outburst of applause.[3]

While the Quinteros kept their finger on the pulse of the
lowly masses in the higher altitudes of the Comedia, Pardo
Bazán observed the more exalted spectators in the lower section.
She reported that Menéndez y Pelayo applauded without
thought of his academic dignity and hailed the new dramatist
as the Spanish Ibsen. Don Juan Valera, who privately envied
Galdós his ability to sell popular novels of literary merit, was
profoundly impressed with the intrinsic innovations of *Realidad*,
particularly its dialogue. He probably wondered how Don Benito
had managed to give each character individuality of dialogue.
And Federico Balart, who had accepted the popular prediction
that the fifth act would be a failure, was not only pleased over
its favorable reception but was even surprised by its essentially
dramatic intensity.

On the whole *Realidad* was surprisingly effective despite its
violations of conventional dramaturgy. There were scattered
objections to the hero's non-Spanish attitude toward conjugal
honor and to the use of a ghost for the revelation of truth. In
aristocratic groups the scene in the boudoir of the *demi-mondaine*

La Peri aroused moral indignation. The most blatant criticism came from envious literary tyros who summed up their esthetic concepts in the slogan, "Shoemaker, stick to the last." But none of this made much headway against the spontaneous enthusiasm of the audience as a whole. There was, for example, the student who after the performance proudly showed Pardo Bazán the palms of his hands red from furious applause. And there was the aristocratic lady, all out of breath, who remarked in a deep, hoarse voice: "I don't know if there is anything left of my throat. I'll wager that this drama is going to make me sick." [4]

Arrayed against those for whom the success of *Realidad* was complete were the *reventadores* (hired hissers), who scrupulously discharged their duty in the lobby during the intermissions. They circulated among the spectators disseminating unfavorable judgments—cautiously lest they create suspicion, now and then expressing a favorable opinion in highly equivocal terms. The similarity between their critical tidbits and those that appeared in the reviews the next day was striking.

Summed up, the gratuitous observations of the *reventadores* amounted to this: *Realidad* was an admirable summary of the two novels upon which it was based, but could hardly be regarded as a dramatic work. Its philosophy was perhaps profound, but it went over the heads of the audience. Some of the characters were a bit hazy, individually logical but not so in relation to one another. Aside from the second act, which was decidedly naturalistic, the play was largely conventional—even romantic. Its chief weakness, which robbed it of all value as a commentary on human behavior, was its socially inhuman solution of the problem of adultery. From a purely technical standpoint it had many flaws, doubtless because it was a mere condensation of two novels. Considering the inherent difficulties of such a procedure, the author had achieved something really noteworthy, however deficient it was as drama.

In evaluating *Realidad* the Spanish critics, who as a class are not conspicuously objective, cast detachment to the winds almost to a man. Most of them, even the most reflective, crystallized in elegant language the crude critical oddities which like miasma had charged the air of the Comedia on the opening night. It could not be otherwise in view of the fact that the strong and weak points of the drama had been so passionately discussed for weeks before its presentation, and that the author was one toward whom an attitude of impartiality seemed impossible. Galdós and *Realidad* had been converted into an issue, and as such they were treated for some time. The spell of the play was slow in wearing off.

The critics who were prepared to hand Galdós the dramatist's palm did so with unwonted effusiveness. The mantles of Shakespeare and Ibsen were gracefully placed on his shoulders, and his achievement was hailed as the birth of the realistic philosophic drama, the destruction of conventional molds, the fusion of the analytic technique of the novelist with the synthetic procedure of the dramatist, and a lasting influence on dramaturgic art in all its forms. Conceivably *Realidad,* for all its revolutionary tendencies, did not yet reveal the whole formula of the modern drama, but it certainly pointed out unexplored highways and byways. No one had hitherto attempted to fuse in a single dramatic work artistic sincerity, realism of observation, transcendental thought, and originality of character. In short, predicted the reflective critics, the decadence of the Spanish drama was at an end, and happier days were not far off.

For Galdós' blind enthusiasts the question whether a novelist could become a successful dramatist was now a purely academic one. Admitting a few technical flaws in *Realidad,* they argued that they were not serious in a work having so many commendable qualities. Only a pedant or a malicious person could search for technical imperfections in a drama of such philosophic grandeur. Technique, in the last analysis, was merely a set of devices for arousing interest, and Galdós had demonstrated that there were more artistic ways of doing that. Barring an occasional lag in attention caused by the length of the drama, there were few dull moments. The lofty idealism of the subtly conceived figure of Orozco gripped the spectators more than any complicated plot of trumped-up conflicts could have done. Orozco was indeed a daring creation in his purely Christian attitude toward his erring wife. In demanding of her only a clear conscience he is not a *Juan Lanas*—a pitiful "easy mark." He is an idealistic egotist, a person lacking a social sense and missionary ardor. He neither forgives his wife nor tries to lift her to his level of morality. He rejects her, and in so doing has the satisfaction of expressing himself in accordance with his own ideas. Orozco is of course the antithesis of the stereotyped Spanish husband who avenges his outraged honor, but there—the critics sought to disentangle themselves from their own dialectic mesh—there is precisely where Galdós' daring, originality, and idealism lay. And so long as he could create characters of such magnitude, characters in no way inferior to those in his novels, one need not bewail the loss to Spanish letters which might result from his decision to revivify the national drama.

With the same vehemence that Galdós' defenders insisted that *Realidad* had been applauded for its promise of dramatic reform, his detractors maintained that the ovations were in recognition of his achievements as a novelist. If the public had not known that the endless succession of scenes was written by the author of *Gloria* and the *Episodios nacionales*, it would have condemned the so-called drama. For the impressively unanimous opposition the play was a long and languid travesty on the two novels *La incógnita* and *Realidad*. Its purely literary qualities were undeniable, but these argued little if any dramatic talent in the author. Galdós utterly lacked a sense of struggle or conflict, so fundamental in good drama. As for innovations, only those with second sight were able to discern them. The most that could honestly be said on this score was that the author rejected the old procedures; he certainly failed to compound a sadly needed recipe for a new modernized drama.

What hope, asked Galdós' detractors, could one draw for the regeneration of the Spanish stage from a play whose sole claim to novelty rested on lamentable naturalistic touches? If the crude scene between Federico Viera and his *demi-mondaine* paramour, La Peri, was truth, realism, and profound philosophy dramatically presented, then it was far better to perpetuate conventionalism, romanticism—in fact anything, if scrupulous people were not to be diverted from honest and licit entertainment. Granted that some spectators were callous to the slice-of-life scenes, few indeed contemplated that queer creation, Quaker-like Orozco, without feeling profoundly offended. Let no one accept Orozco as a person of high moral caliber and lofty idealism. In the last analysis he was a scornful, callous cynic, not the embodiment of a noble soul. Did not Galdós realize that the public would not tolerate a character who forgives an injury to his honor and the destruction of his personal happiness? In the novel Orozco was comprehensible as a rational entity, but in the play he was transformed into an abstraction—the power of will over instinct. What an incredibly naïve conception! No red-blooded Spaniard could accept so anti-national a solution of adultery.

Realidad was subject to attack from still another direction, which must have made Galdós feel poignantly how utterly fool-hardy had been his political sally under Sagasta's banner of monarchical liberalism. In the opinion of the anonymous and indoctrinated reviewer of the rabidly republican *El País*, the play was a complete failure, a fact which should not sadden Galdós unduly, for the drama was an inferior genre anyway. But even assuming that the cultivation of dramatic art was not reprehensible in a first-rate novelist, Galdós had obviously failed to realize that whereas it was possible to novelize a drama, to dramatize a novel successfully was a vain dream. In any event, argued the republican critic, *Realidad* revealed a Galdós woefully deficient in a sense of comedy and tragedy and every other dramatic sense. If he had to turn to the drama, why did he not, in the face of his inexperience, ask someone to do the job for him? He had a respectable precedent in Zola. Evidently Galdós had the destructive national trait of craving for universality.

What, asked the uninhibited reviewer, had Galdós accomplished? The first act of *Realidad* was cold, languid, and philosophical, filled with science and disquisitions. A beer-drinking German audience might have found it delightful, but not Spaniards. The theme of adultery was brutal, unmotivated, and, in its slow, monotonous unfolding, worthy of the talent of a cricket. Augusta, the adulterous heroine, was of the most repugnant stuff imaginable. Her lover's suicide was unmotivated. Viewed psychologically, adultery could lead to suicide, but there was nothing dramatic in that sort of motivation. If Federico had killed himself because he had been challenged by the wronged husband, it would have been all right. But to take his life merely because of gossip about his adulterous relations with Augusta, that was neither truth nor artistic realism. Only once did Galdós hit the mark—in the famous boudoir scene—but the enthusiasm of the audience in this instance only proved its inordinate interest in anything *flamenco*. It was really unfortunate that Emilio Mario had confidence in the dramatic ability of a first-rate novelist.

In the Catholic press bias of a different sort masqueraded as criticism. For the most part the reviewers had followed their own exhortations to all good people and did not attend the performance. Thus they had to rely on the press for their information and opinions. The little they said about the play was in reality an excuse for a round condemnation of Galdós and his allegedly disruptive ideas and subversive tendencies. *Realidad* marked the beginning in the Catholic press of a violent offensive calculated to lower, if not to demolish, the pedestal on which Galdós had been placed by popular favor and liberal opinion.

Almost without exception the ultra-conservative reviewers of *Realidad* followed a set pattern. After a few perfunctory tributes to Galdós' achievements in the *Episodios nacionales* and the expression of a pious hope that he might some day see the light as his friend Pereda saw it, the writers congratulated themselves on their foresight in absenting themselves from a dramatic event that was doomed to failure. In truth, they gloated, no more could have been expected from an author who constantly fluctuated between the gross and the fantastic. In his numerous so-called novels of manners there was not a single convincing character of the kind that Pereda, for example, created in such masterly fashion. As had been anticipated, Galdós' first drama revealed the very defects of his novels—inexplicable filth and mawkishness, adultery, and prostitution, which turned one's stomach and clamored for the arrival of the garbage truck. Little wonder that many ladies were obliged to leave the theater.

It served them right—they had been warned not to attend. If heavenly mercy spared Galdós some common sense, he would do well not to heed his adulators. By now he should be convinced that this was not the path of glory chosen for him by the Lord. Should he persist, nothing but disillusionment awaited him at the end of the journey. An empty house, Galdós was warned, would greet him on the night of the second performance.

But that was a false prophecy. Though *Realidad* was not an unqualified success, possibly only a *succès d'estime,* it continued to attract substantial crowds. The reviewers were unable to prolong indefinitely their philosophic-esthetic-technical lucubrations, and they shifted their emphasis to the interpretation of the play by Mario's company. They asserted that the actors had obviously been unable to discover the histrionic style that the work demanded. María Guerrero failed to come up to everyone's high expectations, though she was not devoid of charm in her role. As one critic expressed it, "María Guerrero did not satisfy me as the leading lady, but as a woman she was seductive. What an elegant outfit she wore in the first act! And, goodness, what a low neck!" [5]

But the show went on, and the twentieth consecutive night was designated as the author's benefit performance. It was the last one in Madrid, and its success was impressive. Galdós answered numerous curtain calls with as little alacrity as he had during the première. There were many gifts for him, which he received amidst the applause of the entire audience. At the end of the third act, which by now had become a signal for ritualistic ovations, a wreath of laurel and creeping double-flowered crowfoot came flying down from the upper galleries. This anonymous tribute was greeted more thunderously than the very artistic wreath tendered by Mario. Galdós went home early that morning happy and laden with portable evidence of success and glory —and *Realidad* took to the road.

The reports of its success in Barcelona confounded the critics who had contended that the repeated ovations in the Comedia had been inspired by Galdós' presence in the theater. He did not accompany his play to Barcelona, and yet his triumph there was as impressive as it had been in Madrid. Did not the Catalans know that Galdós was hostile to the doctrine of autonomy and separatism? But the score was evened for the anti-Galdós faction by his experience in Valencia. There the company was inhibited in its interpretation of *Realidad* by the patent prudishness of the audience. Word had gone out that the play was not suitable entertainment for proper people, and parents were urged not to let their daughters attend. The limited public that ignored the warning was cool and apathetic; *Realidad* was decidedly not a success in Valencia. The provincial journalists were flippant in their derogatory reviews, which did not go beyond an expression of disapproval along the broadest lines. For the vagueness of their observations they blamed the lateness of the hour when they were written; *Realidad,* they complained, was so long that when it was finally over they were too tired to think clearly.

*   *   *   *

On the opening night of the play, immediately after the performance, a small group of intimate friends had gathered around Galdós in tense and respectful silence. He looked calm and composed, likewise firm and resolved. As if divining the big question in the minds of his friends, he announced that he was determined to continue the experiment of which *Realidad* was only a trial balloon. Despite appearances, he thought the play was only a *succès d'estime.* The enthusiasm of the audience, the curtain calls, the hyperbolical comments in the lobby during intermissions, the bits of ingenious esthetic dialectics, the emphatic tone of his defenders, the flattering praise of this or that distinguished personage—these influenced him little in his analysis of this first dramatic experiment. He had been prepared from the first to discount the pontifical pronouncements of critical officialdom. Only the public mattered—the mass of spectators who served under the banner of neither friend nor foe—and the public had, on the whole, received his first dramatic offering with sincere and forthright benevolence. The sporadic manifestations of genuine enthusiasm did not suffice to make the drama a complete success, but he was not disappointed, certainly not discouraged. His immediate task was to create a public for his plays, and he was confident he could do this without abandoning his carefully evolved concept of the new dramatic art.

The next day Galdós scanned the reviews with a lack of concern that bordered on scorn. Neither the excessive generosity of his admirers nor the cautiously carping censure of the *reventadores* elicited from him the slightest respect for any of the critics. None of them had penetrated beneath the surface of either the theme or the characters of his drama; nor had the audience of the première. But he was ironically tolerant toward the reviewers. Theoretically they might be expected to show superior maturity and deliberateness of judgment, but he made allowance for them in view of the haste with which they had recorded their impressions in the early morning hours and the inevitable bias that must result from their obligations to the newspapers or theatrical magazines they served. By virtue of these connections the first-night reviewers constituted a sort of rigid dictatorship sustained by dogmatism and arbitrariness. In his younger days he too had worn the toga of a literary judge, and he knew that the facile rules and glib pronouncements of critics were based on improvisation and presumptuousness. Accordingly he was determined to disregard all that the press said in favor of or against *Realidad*. It was, to be sure, a drama without a suitable public, but he felt certain that the future would provide that. *Realidad*, mused Galdós arrogantly, would live long after the reviewers' criticisms had been forgotten.

The verdict of posterity did not quite bear out Galdós' confidence. The test came in February, 1904. Galdós was by that time the author of twelve dramas, of which two had been total failures, three only *succès d'estime*, two impressively successful, four gratifyingly so, and one scandalously sensational. *El abuelo*, his most recent production, staged on February 14, was so unqualified a success that it brought Galdós warm tributes from his colleagues, old and young. Ten days later Rosario Pino, leading lady of the Comedia, chose *Realidad* for her benefit performance, and her choice was highly approved. Success was freely predicted in view of Galdós' regained prestige. The widespread attention which the revival of the drama received in the press was no doubt prompted by the author's momentary popularity, but many were also interested to learn how far the public of 1904 had progressed beyond that of 1892.

But time had apparently failed to cultivate the taste of the Spanish theatergoers for preponderantly philosophical and psychological drama. Orozco, the man of advanced ideas—the Spanish husband of tomorrow—was appreciated more than he had been in 1892, but he was by no means generally accepted. Reaction to him was in the nature of respect for an imported product; he was recognized by his resemblance to characters in the foreign dramas that occasionally came to the Spanish stage. Against the other innovations of the play the deep-rooted traditionalism and conventional taste of the public asserted themselves unmistakably. The audience, bourgeois for the most part, was as shocked as the spectators of 1892 by the few highly realistic scenes, and in general received the drama with dignified coolness. In only one respect had Spanish dramatic art progressed since the première—the reviewers seemed more intelligent. Or had the opposition spent itself against Galdós' obdurate resistance for twelve years? At any rate, in 1904 the critics ruefully bewailed the esthetic provincialism of Spanish spectators and no longer questioned the wisdom or soundness of Galdós' innovations.

In 1904 Galdós also had the support of a few of his former enemies, deserters from the republican fortress whose batteries had been silenced by his attack on clericalism in *Electra*, in 1901. Accordingly *El País*, with its literary criteria still variously grounded, reprimanded the good Spanish bourgeoisie with obvious sarcasm. After pointing out that Spanish prudery was as loathsome in 1904 as it had been in 1892, it said:

> Very well, last night an odd phenomenon happened in the Comedia. After so many years, after having applauded Benavente's plays and after having attended the "Green Fridays" [*when risqué programs were offered*], our public, the good old public of Madrid, was shocked by *Realidad*, murmured its protest, which was silenced by the indignant hisses of some,

against the beautiful scene between Federico Viera and La Peri, blushed because García Ortega [*the actor*] embraced the *cocotte*, perhaps believing that he should have kissed her hand as they do at Palace receptions.[6]

Other critics, too, wondered whether tight hugs on the stage were the prerogative of Italian and French actors. Spanish audiences enthusiastically patronized the so-called daring plays by foreign authors—daring not in the philosophic or moral sense, but in their defiance of priggishness. Why, then, the frowning attitude toward Galdós? To a few critics in 1892 and many more in 1904 it appeared that the author of *Realidad* was a leader whose stride was too long for the public taste; his concept of the drama was beyond the reach of the average intelligence. They could only hope that, for the good of progress in general and literature in particular, the Spanish public would some day soon catch up with Galdós.

*   *   *   *

On the night of March 15, 1892, when Galdós had revealed to his friends his resolve to embark on the perilous journey to dramatic success, none doubted his courage and his ability to persevere. There was in the man a stubbornness that brooked no opposition, and an irresistible desire for independence and individual procedure. Galdós may well have incarnated a part of his own character in his heroine, Augusta. Conceivably she repeated Galdós' personal creed when she said of herself: "I reject all that is presented to me according to a fixed pattern, all that we are accustomed to call *reasonable* in order to hide its inherent simplicity. Alas! Those who insist upon stereotyping life cannot possibly succeed." [7]

XIII

Backstage with Galdós

THE FORTUNES OF *Realidad* provided the general pattern for
Galdós' career from 1892 to 1918. It was clear to him at the
very outset that blocking the road to success stood the doctrinal
inflexibility of certain of the critics, the provincial traditionalism
of public taste, and, oddly enough, the blind devotion of his
admirers. These were formidable obstacles destined to threaten
more than once the steadiness of his course. If he did not stray
far from it, it was largely because of his esthetic independence
and his almost arrogant resolve to effect a radical change in the
Spaniard's dramatic taste. It would be hazardous to assert to
what extent his independence and resolve brought success or
failure. Galdós enjoyed triumph and tasted defeat, but neither
was born of the intrinsic qualities of his dramas.

A superficial survey of Galdós' dramatic career might lead to
the conclusion that after an initial five-year period of trial and
error his progress was steady and rapid. One might gather this
from the sensational success of *Electra* (1901), the universally
conceded artistic triumph of *El abuelo* (1904), the noisy reception of *Casandra* (1910), the long run of *Celia en los infiernos*
(1913), and the admiration that *Santa Juana de Castilla* (1918)
inspired in public and critics alike. It is an attractive record by
any standard, but it cannot serve as an index of Galdós' progress
toward the realization of his principal objectives. The extraneous
circumstances attending the production of his plays often made
it well-nigh impossible to evaluate them objectively. His solid
reputation in another field, his participation in national politics,
his blindness after 1912, his resolute character—all these factors

262

tended to complicate his position as a dramatist. Perhaps the only assertion that is safe to make is that from first to last Galdós' dramatic career was a struggle against forces hostile to his concept of drama, which aimed to induct the public into the limitless spaces of spiritual speculation and psychological analysis, in quest of that inner wisdom which alone gives meaning and direction to human behavior. His concrete accomplishment? Artistically, the creation of an atmosphere propitious to further experimentation by the rising generation of dramatists; philosophically, dissemination of the gospel that however baffling life may seem, one can discover its meaning if he will only carry out the dictates of his conscience with sincerity and tolerance.

* * * *

The fronts on which the battle of *Realidad* had been fought were reopened for the struggle over Galdós' second play. *La loca de la casa* (January 16, 1893), which had been cut down for the stage from a dialogue novel of the same title, published in October, 1892, was pronounced a fair success by some and more or less a failure by others. Not even the author's surreptitious though minor concessions to conventional dramaturgy were sufficient to insure unqualified approval.

The final stage version was substantially shorter than Galdós' original text. The abridgment was made during the rehearsals, which were essentially a series of pruning operations performed with the unhesitating permission of the author. Echegaray was present throughout as consultant. Possibly because too many cooks had a hand in it, *La loca de la casa* turned out to be a work of uneven merit, as the audience was prompt to recognize. The first two acts aroused spontaneous enthusiasm and reassuring ovations to the author. The last two acts, however, were somewhat anticlimactic, and at least one scene provoked determined hissing. The heroine lost much of her stature in the latter part of the play, and for all except the most perspicacious spectators Pepet, the central figure, was a crude and repulsive character. Nevertheless the performance ended amidst vigorous applause and numerous curtain calls.

The reactions of reviewers were widely divergent. Some invoked the name of Shakespeare in evaluating Galdós' second achievement, citing Pepet as a creation worthy of the English dramatist. Jubilation was so great in Galdós' camp that it attracted new recruits. José Ortega y Munilla, who in the case of *Realidad* had virtually accused Galdós of selling his artistic soul for a mess of dramatic pottage, now hailed him as a courageous reformer and the new drama as a revolutionary milestone. At last, shouted the zealous convert, an intelligent public was born in Spain. But the panegyrists did not have the airwaves all to themselves. The opposition, too, was active once more. If *La loca de la casa*, they taunted, was the best model of the new drama of psychological and philosophic emphasis, it were better to abandon hope of reform and revolution. Let us not invent a play without action, pleaded one conservative critic, for then stage performances will paradoxically become stimulating narcotics.

While the critics wrangled thus, Galdós was busily engaged elsewhere. Within less than a month his third play was scheduled for production in the venerable Teatro Español. This was a historical drama based on his popular *episodio* of *Gerona*. To dramatize a widely read novel was a daring venture, but he embarked upon it with confidence, relying on the appeal of the story and lured by the challenge to fashion a new mold for the historical drama. He suffered only minor qualms when he found it necessary to resort here and there to traditional dramatic devices. Despite these, he reasoned, *Gerona* was still an innovation in that historical accuracy was not subordinated to imagination. Altogether he figured that the play had a fair chance to succeed.

On the night of February 3, 1893, Galdós had his first taste of unmitigated defeat. *Gerona* was a dismal, humiliating failure, and was withdrawn after a single performance. The audience was manifestly disposed to express its disapproval riotously, but out of respect for the author limited itself to several mild protests. Everything seemed to conspire against the play. The actors, inhibited by the attitude of the public, interpreted their roles with neither skill nor inspiration, and frequently showed signs of physical and spiritual weariness. One young inexperienced actress of very limited histrionic talent provided the only light moment in an otherwise depressing performance. By an unfortunate coincidence, at the precise moment when the content of her lines and her delivery were most displeasing, she exclaimed, "Everything is turning out just fine for me tonight!"[1] The theater rocked with laughter, which neither the sadness of the plot nor the mortal embarrassment of the artist could silence for a time. The incident had a catastrophic effect.

During the next few days there was much excitement in Madrid. In vain did Galdós' cohorts hurl recrimination, defiance, and threats at those who rejoiced over his failure. All their missiles were so many duds loosed upon a cruelly vengeful enemy who fired deadly bullets pointblank and with withering effect. Even after the defenders had withdrawn one by one, the attackers continued the assault with demoniacal gusto, determined to consume all the ammunition they had been storing up since the days of *Realidad*. Sarcastically they referred to the author as *ese pobrecito Galdós* ("that poor chap Galdós") and maliciously chorused the proverb *A la tercera va la vencida* ("Three strikes and out"). That poor chap Galdós, they gloated, should realize now that not even he could escape the doom implied in this wise saying. To give the celebration of its triumph a broader base, the opposition mobilized reserves of unattached journalists, café critics, boulevard "lizards" (*paseístas*) and others to chant a mournful dirge over the dead dramatic ambitions of Benito Pérez Galdós.

But not all Spaniards delight in cruel treatment of the fallen. A gleam of magnanimity came from republican *El País* to pierce the heavy cloud of sorrow in which Galdós was enveloped. Its reviewer stated frankly his impression of Galdós' third dramatic failure: "When the curtain went down slowly on all that heap of colorless figures, scenes poorly sewn together, and a varied assortment of artifacts, the hushed public filed out of the theater. It was visibly moved, not by the tragic effect of the caricaturesque finale, but by deep sorrow over the mortal calamity."[2] Even at the risk of incurring the wrath of the author's idolators, he besought Galdós to pay no heed to his impassioned friends who were leading him to ruin. By pushing him along the road to Thalia's temple, they were knocking out one by one the blocks from his pedestal of glory.

It had probably occurred to Galdós himself that his wobbly pedestal was badly in need of re-enforcement. If *Gerona* had failed partly because the representation of the Spanish defeat by the French offended the average spectator, would he not heal his wounded pride with a play that flattered the vanity of the masses? Some such reflection must have influenced him during the composition of his fourth drama, *La de San Quintín,* which was produced in the Comedia on January 27, 1894. There can be little doubt that in the writing of this play Galdós' desire for success outweighed any urge for artistic experimentation or even philosophic speculation. *La de San Quintín* was his first original play, so in writing it he was unhampered by the novelist's procedure. Indeed, he was consciously guided by the demands of conventional dramatic technique. The theme may well have been suggested by his reflections on the possibility of fusing the aristocracy and the proletariat into a new social species, but the naïve plasticity and diaphanous symbolism of the work must have been calculated to appeal to the callous-handed spectators.

The stigma of the failure of *Gerona* was wiped out by the instant and sensational success of *La de San Quintín.* The friendly press, as eager as the author himself to retrieve his reputation, spared neither space nor superlatives in its advertising campaign. A full house was assured for the première, since for many this was to be Galdós' crucial test as a dramatist. Would the new play finally furnish proof of his talent, or would it be merely the fourth manifestation of stubborn self-deception? A representative audience filled the Comedia—aristocrats, titled personages, middle-class citizens, and an impressive contingent of the masses. Many of Madrid's social élite attended in spite of a performance at the Royal Opera that night and an elaborate reception in the home of a prominent family. To the

Galdós enthusiasts this was evidence of a praiseworthy evolution in the dramatic taste of Spanish society.

It had been years since a Spanish audience had clamored for the appearance of an author in the middle of the first act, but Galdós experienced that thrill on the night of January 27, 1894. In fact, throughout the performance the repeated ovations and curtain calls taxed his courage and composure. At the point in the play where the Duchess of San Quintín, the heroine, called Victor, the putative plebian hero, "my poor dear"—thus naïvely symbolizing the impending *rapprochement* between the two extremes of society—pandemonium broke loose in the crowded galleries. The boundless enthusiasm of the proletarian spectators was almost matched by that of the occupants of the orchestra and loges. These rose in their seats, men and women alike, and, frantically waving dainty, monogrammed handkerchiefs, shouted a lusty approval of the symbolism of *La de San Quintín*. As someone remarked after the performance—when the graceful Duchess shook Victor's none too rough hand at the end of the second act, everyone in the theater, regardless of class, indulged in a spiritual handshake, thus eloquently demonstrating that in a single night Galdós came nearer a solution of the social problem than a score of books and treatises on the subject.[3]

Something resembling frenzy seized the spectators when the curtain went down. They fought their way to the wings to congratulate Galdós and staged demonstrations in the lobby and corridors. As the crowd overflowed into the street it surrounded the author in a riotous parade to his home, ignoring his pleas for less tumult and for a carriage to rescue him from all this embarrassing adoration. When, by a skillful maneuver, he eventually escaped into the Café Inglés, the crowd followed him and continued the celebration with increased vigor, despite his physical exhaustion. Lusty, thunderous *Vivas* rocked the crowded café as the roll was called of all the characters in the play and the titles of Galdós' novels. Well may the author have regretted then his literary fecundity. When the ingenuity of the clamorous celebrants seemed at an end, an uncouth looking young fellow shouted at the top of his lungs, "Let the 'guy' go on writing!" [4] The exhortation had its effect, and Galdós resumed his journey homeward to spend the rest of the night in fitful sleep.

Ever since the beginning of the controversy over Galdós' turn to the drama, his opponents had been accusing his supporters of being the victims of a strange new malady which they called *galdosismo* ("Galdositis"). The day after the première of *La de San Quintín* the press revealed that the malady was of epidemic proportions. Few were the reviewers not affected by *galdosismo,* and the few who were immune refrained from challenging their stricken colleagues to battle, presumably from a sense of chivalry. The field thus remained virtually free for frisky critical capers.

Ignoring the obvious lack of technical novelty in the play, the reviewers went through the ritual of laudation, characterizing it as the most profound, daring, original, skillful, revolutionary, and modern of all Spanish dramas. Said one critic who seldom burned incense at Galdós' altar: "Henceforth we have in Galdós a true dramatic author and a first-rate theatrical architect whose triumph last night gives us just hope of new and beautiful creations in the future." [5] And for the first time *El Socialista,* a newspaper serving a well-defined cause, took serious notice of Galdós' efforts in behalf of a better world via the drama. After categorically asserting that the theme of *La de San Quintín* is the clash between the bourgeoisie and the proletariat, the Marxian critic indulged in the following bit of party dialectics:

> But even if this grandiose and most happy synthesis were not sufficiently expressive, the very title is exceedingly significant: "La de San Quintín" and not "La Duquesa de San Quintín," as the author might have phrased it if he had not wished to express the idea which that phrase carries within itself in ordinary current language, namely, "the furious battle has been started" or "the furious battle is about to break out"

—when reference is made to a bloody and disastrous event. Thus, if we keep in mind the generating idea of the play, is not "La de San Quintín" a title which, without the euphemism imposed by circumstances, might easily be changed to "The Social Revolution?" [6]

But thoughtful critics with no ideological axe to grind missed in *La de San Quintín* the dawn of a new day on the Spanish dramatic horizon. They even ventured to question the soundness of its social theme. But, the odds being against them, they did not speak above a loud whisper. Fifty consecutive performances in Madrid and a number of happy parodies constituted indeed an impregnable fortress of popularity. With unprecedented confidence in his future, Galdós garnered in his hard-earned glory even as he worked feverishly on the next production. By a curious quip of human psychology, his latest triumph affected him sentimentally. As a perpetual reminder of the extraordinary event, he rechristened his newly constructed chalet in Santander and named it San Quintín. Its original outlandish name of Pohao-Pohao (a town in South Africa), bestowed in capricious commemoration of the Anglo-Boer War, fell into well deserved oblivion, to the great relief of the other members of the household.

Being a keen student of human nature, Galdós doubtless realized that the delirious reception of *La de San Quintín* was the result of an intricate combination of subtle impulses and reactions not directly related to artistic sensibility or philosophic perception. Nevertheless he could not help feeling that at long last public and critics had come to understand and appreciate the new type of drama he was struggling to create, that he was amply justified in continuing in the drama the quest for the eternal spiritual verities which he had recently set out upon in the novel. He felt too that he could safely take the next step without compromises or concessions.

The theme of his next play had been germinating in his mind for some time—the essence of individual salvation and the precise conditions and means for its attainment. Because of the universality of the idea, it had occurred to him that the valley of Ansó in upper Aragon, with its medieval ambient, would be an appropriate setting for its dramatization. He paid an extended visit to that picturesque region and gathered the necessary human and physical documentation for his next drama, *Los condenados*. From Ansó he returned to Santander via Madrid and at once began to write with blind enthusiasm. He had rarely worked with such genuine inspiration and with such unwavering anticipation of success. Never before had he written with so much artistic conscientiousness. He brought to bear upon *Los condenados* all the energy of his creative genius, as if anxious to reassure the public that its confidence in his dramatic skill was not misplaced. And as he watched the actors whip his play into shape during the long rehearsals, he was satisfied that he had produced a noteworthy drama. He awaited the première with confidence and serenity.

An eager audience filled the Comedia Theater the night of December 11, 1894. Advance press notices had described *Los condenados* as a work reflecting the spiritual reaction recently discerned in literature and in life. Considerable interest had also been aroused by the desertion of María Guerrero from Mario's company and her replacement with the famous Carmen Cobeña, who was appearing for the first time in a Galdosian play. The author sat in his customary place backstage. As the performance began, he fell into deep reverie, transporting himself in his imagination to the valley of Ansó and reliving his recent delightful excursion.

There was the picturesque square of the village of Ansó, an authentic relic of the fourteenth century, with its green-skirted *chesas*—graceful native women of airy movements—and its robust athletic men filling the air with their peals of laughter as they watched a puppet show. The entire cast of *Los condenados* was assembled in that quaint square of Ansó! They followed him as he roamed the somber-looking streets and the trim strips of farm land. They lingered with him in the tall stone houses of the natives and entertained him with their archaic speech and their pleasingly odd manners. They even accompanied him on the return journey from Jaca to Pamplona.

Throughout the many long miles, four of them—Salomé, Santamona, José León, and Paternoy—kept him amused with an account of their lives and personalities. They spoke softly, and the rhythm of their voices blended with the rhythm of the *rondalla* which the driver sang clearly and with perfect intonation. It was impossible to separate the music of the *rondalla* from the cadence of the drama.

Strange sounds soon awakened Galdós rudely from his reverie. He could hear shouts of protest. Insults couched in vulgar terms intercepted the speeches of the actors. Feet stamped with nervous impatience. Thuillier, the leading man, sounded frightened. The prompter faltered in his box. Something flashed through Galdós' mind. He recalled that during some of the rehearsals his attention had been called to the presence of suspicious individuals who indulged in much nudging of elbows and mysterious whispering. In his naïve honesty he had dismissed all that as unimportant. Now he realized its full meaning. His enemies had formed a conspiracy against him! They were resolved to avenge a wrong he had never committed against them. They had decided to condemn *Los condenados*. That they were succeeding was now painfully evident.

The scenes behind the stage after the catastrophic performance were like the aftermath of a major disaster. Galdós was stunned. His customary expression of outward serenity had given way to one of congealed immobility. The confused words of encouragement of his dazed friends fell on his ears like a hail of pebbles pelting a non-resonant surface. From Thuillier's room came the sound of panicky voices—the terror of the performance had caused a hemorrhage in his throat. Federico Urrecha, dramatic critic for *El Imparcial*, and another reviewer were heatedly arguing in the near-by corridor. Urrecha approached Galdós and counselled him to withdraw the drama. Emilio Mario was called into consultation. The deliberations were long and painful, but without recriminations. The artists had acted splendidly, the vehicle was sturdy, but evidently the public refused to rise to the sphere of symbolic ethics and spiritual salvation. Under the circumstances, wisdom seemed the better part of valor. Galdós agreed to retire with his drama and his grief into the sanctum of his conscience.

The next day it was maliciously rumored that the bereaved author had been "tyrannized" into withdrawing *Los condenados*. The management of the Comedia regarded this as a slur on its independence of judgment and as an affront to the author's freedom of action. Consequently, despite the announcement in *El Imparcial* that the play had been withdrawn, Mario's company braved it again that night and the next. This Galdós opposed, but Mario overruled him by invoking an alleged law which empowered the company to stage the play three times. It was an ill-advised move. The two additional performances only served to underscore the original verdict of the audience and emboldened the reviewers who were skirmishing over the corpse of *Los condenados*.

This time it was the turn of Galdós' friends to lie crouching in their dugouts while the enemy's mortiferous missiles whizzed about them. Now and then a fighter with a suicidal complex crawled out and like a voice in the desert clamored that Galdós' greatness should be respected. Granted that *Los condenados* was a bad play, ran the faintly challenging argument, it was still superior to the best works of other dramatists. But such heroic gestures were not numerous. Most of Galdós' valiant troops were ready to retreat without even rear-guard action. They had assembled in the Comedia the night of December 11 for another victory rally, but their respect for the author, whom they continued to regard as a national glory, dictated absolute silence. And silent they remained, even though Galdós, distraught and agonized, mistook their attitude for treason and roundly denounced them.

To the "enemy" Galdós' rout was only fair redress for the wrong they had suffered in the triumph of *La de San Quintín*, and they were bent on making the most of it. The less vengeful among them taunted the author with what they termed his gross artistic error and the painful miscarriage of an honestly conceived intention. They pointed up his latest defeat by conceding that he had displayed a modicum of talent in his previous dramatic works. It was laudable in Galdós, ran the comment, to attempt to transplant Ibsen to the Spanish stage, but he should first have taken stock of his qualifications for the task. His use of symbolism was objectionable not in principle but in application. Calderón's *La vida es sueño,* it was pointed out, was packed with symbolism, but it was all transparent. What did it avail him to present a problem of conscience—in itself a commendable purpose—when he lacked the skill to convince the public of its significance? From whatever angle one judged *Los condenados* one was regretfully constrained to reject it in its entirety.

Even more severe was the chastisement dealt Galdós by less pious reviewers. Typical of the insolence with which he was lashed was the dictum of one commentator: "Theme, characters, situations, incidents—everything that enters into the composition of that drama is far removed from what is rational and human, and on other scores one could say that *Los condenados* is nothing more than the ravings of an overheated imagination."[7] Critical venom like this was often the product of intellectual impotence. In other cases it stemmed from ill-concealed envy masquerading as benevolent interest in the author's good name. Thus sputtered another critic:

No dramatic author succeeds these days in arousing public expectation as does Galdós. Covered with laurel wreaths, glorified at a banquet table, with the unanimous applause of the most brilliant Spanish geniuses, elected by the Academy of Language, lifted to the highest pinnacle of public esteem and singled out by the critics as the first among our contemporary novelists, he must have heard that mysterious voice of the character in the work by the Duque de Rivas, which said to him: "Lisardo, there is much more in the world! . . ." I do not think that this drama was a lamentable mistake; it is not an isolated mistake; it springs from the arrogant ambition of destroying molds that were still being used to good advantage by men like Ayala, Tamayo, and Echegaray and in

times not at all removed from our own. Within these
molds, Señor Galdós, whom the Lord has endowed
with unusual talent, could have triumphed all along
the line and he might have brought to the stage the
beautiful dramas he unfolded in his admirable novels.[8]

All the grievance and resentment against Spanish critics which
had been gathering in Galdós' heart were touched off by the
scorn with which he and his drama were treated. For days the
explosion rocked the literary world. On the advice of Tolosa
Latour, and in his very home, Galdós penned a prologue which
he published forthwith together with his routed play. Dipping
his pen in vitriol, he plunged it deep into the flesh of his
calumniators. He sneered and scoffed, snarled and growled,
roared and thundered. His modesty and humility, his reserve
and reticence, yielded to pride and arrogance, disdain and contempt. The literary Samson of Spain, with his locks still un-
shorn, stood between the pillars of his fame and hurled defiance
at the jeering Philistines all around him. Woe befall the pigmies
who dare to tease the giant again!

Naturally Galdós' wrath did not inspire soft-spoken answers.
The public, which received some of his lashes, perforce remained inarticulate, but the critics who felt the full brunt of
his fury did not retire to lick their wounds. If the dismal failure of *Los condenados*, they shouted, was solely the handiwork
of the "youngsters of the press," then his previous triumphs
must also have been their accomplishment. What had become
of Galdós' reputation for modesty and humility? His ranting
was only the yelp of hurt pride, wholly beneath the dignity
of a man of his stature. He was quite wrong in ascribing the
impoverished state of Spanish art to the ignorant and malicious
critics. His plays had no artistic merit, and had he been sincere
he would not have persevered so stubbornly in a literary genre
for which he patently had no calling. Why did he not emulate
Chateaubriand, Lamartine, and Balzac, who quietly withdrew
from the dramatic arena the moment they realized their mis-
takes? Apparently Galdós was more interested in positive results—in fat profits—than in the promotion of national art. No

one begrudged him his earnings, but these would be more abundant if he resumed writing novels. The critics would be happy to work for his success as they had done when he wrote *Doña Perfecta, Gloria,* and the *Episodios nacionales.* These works and no others were the pillars of his immense reputation. If it was gold that he wanted, let him continue exploiting the rich vein he had discovered in those novels. Gratitude, moaned the critics, was a rare virtue indeed. Was it to be scolded and insulted by him that the Spanish public once tendered Galdós a sumptuous banquet, elected him to the Academy, and applauded his dramas undeservedly?

When after the publication of the prologue Galdós resumed his normal serenity, he realized that in part he had spoken with the voice of rage rather than courage. He was frankly worried about its effect and impatiently awaited the reaction of his closest friends, to whom he had sent copies of his homily. Echegaray, as ever, proved a friend in need. "Thousands of thanks for your drama," he wrote. "What a 'dandy' little prologue! You want to know if you 'put your foot in it'; I would say you put your paw in it. We'll talk about it later. Courage and keep up the good work." [9]

Clarín, from his provincial retreat in Oviedo, pounced upon the penny-a-liners in an article for *La Publicidad* (Barcelona), which Salvador Canals featured in his *Diario del Teatro.* In the same paper Eusebio Blasco, who regarded himself as Galdós' dramatic godfather, published an open letter in which he congratulated him on his stand against the disrespectful Spanish public and press. Salvador Canals reported that he was receiving numerous letters and articles from readers who were neither writers nor journalists, endorsing Galdós' rebuke to the "youngsters of the press." In short, *Los condenados* was a failure, but its prologue was apparently relatively successful.

One is tempted to read a personal symbolism into the title of Galdós' next play—*Voluntad*—and its theme of salvation through will, energy, and works. Undaunted by his recent experience, yet resolved to proceed cautiously, he braved public and critics with this new drama in the Teatro Español on the night of December 20, 1895. It ran for six nights, not without some unpleasant incidents.

Twelve months had apparently been insufficient to heal the wounds inflicted by the prologue. The audience was divided into two distinct camps: the author's foes crowded the galleries, and his friends occupied the orchestra and the loges. Among the enemy there was a sizable contingent of mercenaries. The penny-a-liners were resolved to avenge themselves on the author by "burying the play that very night in the pantheon of oblivion." [10] It became clear after the first act that the clashing reactions of the two camps were not necessarily motivated by divergent artistic standards. At the end of the second act the conflict came out in the open: the orchestra clamored for the author, while the galleries protested insidiously. Galdós responded to the orchestra and bowed disconcertedly amidst hisses and applause. The applauders routed the hissers by sheer superiority of numbers and perseverance. When the curtain went down on the last act, the mercenaries in the galleries were again routed, but the author's triumph remained very much in doubt.

Despite its negligible contribution to Galdós' dramatic reputation, *Voluntad* was well worth the effort it involved. The uniformly moderate tone of the reviewers demonstrated that the prologue to *Los condenados* had had a salutary effect. Although no one praised the new play—save to commend its dramatization of the national problem of *abulia* and the remedy for it—the opinions expressed had a sincere ring. Some suggested that *Voluntad* deserved a much better reception than it got, but that the spectators had reacted lukewarmly in protest against the harsh treatment the author had dealt them the year before. In any event, after *Voluntad* the skies cleared over the Spanish theater, and on both sides there was an inclination—but nothing more than that—to forgive and forget. In the Comedia rehearsals of Galdós' next drama were progressing rapidly.

One may safely assume that in choosing to dramatize his popular novel *Doña Perfecta,* in 1896, Galdós was moved chiefly by a desire to rehabilitate his waning dramatic fortune. At that, the choice was a daring one. Aside from the potentially explosive theme, there was the uncertainty of the public's reaction to what it would be likely to regard as tampering with its property. For, whether accepted or rejected, this novel had succeeded in weaving itself into the spiritual texture of Spain. Moreover, by offering another dramatized novel—conceivably to reaffirm his doctrine of the fusion of the two techniques—Galdós once more defied the critics who insisted that it was this doctrine that was the root of his dramatic weakness. In any event, *Doña Perfecta,* scheduled for the night of January 28, 1896, promised to be the outstanding theatrical event of the season.

And so it proved to be. It was received less noisily than *La de San Quintín* had been, but the reaction of the audience was more intelligently critical. Attention was focused on the three main elements in the work: the fusion of the symbolism with the human interest of the love plot, the stature of Perfecta, and the role of the priest, Don Inocencio. Those who anticipated demonstrations protesting the anticlerical challenge of the theme were disappointed, and on this score the author was highly pleased. The quiet reception of the play was reflected in the dignified, subdued, and cautious tone of the lengthy reviews that appeared the following day.

For the first time in Galdós' dramatic career there was at least a semblance of harmony between public and critics. Both groups were naturally tempted to draw comparisons between the novel and the drama, preference for the former being preponderant. Some reviewers who were only on a truce basis with Galdós emphasized what many others suspected—that the ovations were intended for the novelist, not the dramatist. A few even revived the controversy of novelistic technique versus dramatic procedure. Still others invoked naïve and pseudo-professional precepts about conflict, emotion, suspense, and the like. On the whole, however, Galdós had good reason to include *Doña Perfecta* among his noteworthy successes. It revived the general feeling that he was still a vital force in the reform of the Spanish drama, and—what was more important—it stimulated an intelligent reappraisal of the conflict between progress and conservatism in Spain on the eve of the twentieth century. Curiously enough, old conservatives were at one with ultra-advanced youth in asserting that the theme of *Doña Perfecta* had lost its reality in modern Spain, except, perhaps, in the backward provincial zones. The more reasoned opinion, however, was that the central national problem had remained unmodified, and that the only evidence of progress made in a score of years lay in the intelligence and objectivity with which the play was received. Most of the credit for this advance, it was alleged, belonged to the author.

It would seem that the revival of *Doña Perfecta* took Galdós back, artistically and philosophically, to the decade of the seventies, the days of his intense historical interest and symbolic realism. This required no effort on his part, since even in his novels he had been gradually veering away from the realism of direct and minute observation toward the spiritual realities which were then the essence of Continental thought. One could hardly say that any of his dramas thus far had dealt with ephemeral actualities. As a thinker he was slowly ascending the heights of idealistic contemplation and serene judgment. In 1876, when *Doña Perfecta* was published, he had identified fanaticism with conservatism and reaction, and tolerance with liberalism and progress, and these he had in a sense interpreted as forces released by human institutions; now, in 1896, he was inclined to view fanaticism and tolerance as the result of one and the same spiritual pathology—tyranny.

Thus in his next dramatic work Galdós was quite naturally led to treat speculatively what was in a sense the reverse of the theme of *Doña Perfecta*. His eighth drama, *La fiera*, was a plea for tolerance on the part of both liberals and conservatives. For the time of the action he went back to the early years of the nineteenth century, the fruitful period of his *Episodios nacionales*. In this he was guided not only by a sense of artistic propriety, but possibly also by a vague desire to make amends for the dismal failure of his earlier historical drama, *Gerona*. Perhaps, too, he was counting for success on the spectator's familiarity with the language and the characters. But to make doubly sure that his audience would be properly conditioned for his latest play, he had several newspapers carry in advance lengthy analyses of the historical background, the significance of the leading characters, and the real meaning of the theme. They even outlined the main threads of the plot.

These precautions bore little fruit. *La fiera*, produced in the Comedia on December 23, 1896, impressed the spectators only superficially. They failed to discern its meaning, were apathetic toward the social medium and passions of the early nineteenth century, and were depressed by the sadness and gloom that pervaded the work. And, oddly enough, they resented its conventional technique. Led to expect a breath of novelty—the much-heralded Galdosian "new molds"—they were disappointed by the naïve and awkward attempts at theatrical effects. After the second act Galdós received four or five curtain calls, and there was some vigorous applause at the end of the performance, but in both instances the source and sincerity of the response were open to question. Galdós' eighth play was a semi-success and a semi-failure.

The homiletical effects of the famous prologue had not yet worn off, and as in the case of *Doña Perfecta* most reviewers discussed *La fiera* with fair earnestness and sincerity. Hyperbolism and panegyrics were much less frequent than in former years, but a new stylistic quirk cropped up among those for whom praise of Galdós was almost a badge of professional identity—profuse apology for the expression of any opinion short of unconditional approval. In some instances the quivering voice of the critic suggests that the indifferent fortune of the play had grieved him more than Galdós himself.

But if the rank-and-file reviewers lived in a world much improved by Galdós' castigation, the recalcitrant ones displayed a growing tendency to champ the bit. Indeed, the neutral reception of *La fiera* emboldened these to vent their pent-up grievance against Galdós with disarming sincerity. Their complaint ran something like this. Theatrical directors were making a mistake in always turning to distinguished authors for vehicles, to the complete exclusion of the fledgling dramatists. The practice was not without precedent, to be sure, but neither was the protest of critics against it. Years back, Manuel de la Revilla had severely censured the impresarios for encouraging Campoamor, the fireside poet of Spain, in his vain dramatic ambitions. The practice of soliciting the works, good or bad, of famous authors and of rejecting even without a reading the plays of obscure writers was an iniquitous and incorrigible abuse. Incorrigible? Not altogether. In self-defense the young untried dramatists who were temporarily wearing the toga of the literary critic were determined to train the public to introduce into the theater the salutary tradition of the bull ring—to hiss off the stage any play that displeased it. Let Galdós take this as a threat or as a warning, but let him beware!

Those who were resolved to evict Galdós from the temple of Thalia could not have renewed their efforts at a more opportune time. For he himself had already considered the advisability of interrupting his struggle for dramatic reform and recognition. Not that the five years of trial and tribulations had discouraged him; on the contrary, they had steeled his will to continue the battle against all odds. As a matter of fact, in his own conscience he never admitted complete failure in a single instance. The adverse judgments of the critics impressed him no more than a gadfly on the back of an elephant. He was much more seriously concerned over the reaction of the spectators, whom he regarded as the dramatist's collaborators; it was they who determined the success or failure of his work. During the five years of his dramatic career Galdós never despaired of training a public for his dramas. What really caused him to hesitate at this time was disappointment over his meager stage royalties and his increasingly pressing financial needs. These considerations made the temporary interruption of his dramatic career virtually inevitable.

Strictly speaking, Galdós the dramatist did not spend the years between 1897 and 1901 in continuous idleness. Recalling how his prestige had risen in Spain when the outside world began to take notice of him, he conceived a grandiose scheme. He would introduce himself to the Continent as a dramatist; if he succeeded, he would perforce rise in the esteem of his countrymen. Could he honestly aspire to Continental recognition? Indeed he could. It was precisely the broadly European spirit of his dramas that was at variance with the provincial Spanish taste. Had not some critics repeatedly mentioned him in the same breath with Ibsen, Hauptmann, Maeterlinck, and others? He had a suitable work with which to make his Continental début. His dialogue novel, *El abuelo*, reduced to stage dimensions, could not fail to appeal to an intelligent, critical audience. Its theme—the superiority of character to distinction of blood—had grandeur and universal significance, and the protagonist, the Count of Albrit, was of Shakespearean stature.

Galdós became obsessed with a desire for greater conquests. He sent out feelers to Germany, France, and Italy. His friends in those countries—mostly translators and literary free-lancers— made his cause their own. *El abuelo* wandered from land to land, lingering longest in Italy. It was Galdós' cherished ambition to have it produced by the famous Italian actor Novelli. Without neglecting opportunities elsewhere, he concentrated his best effort on the theater in Rome. Negotiations eventually reached the awkward stage somewhere between acceptance and rejection. But Novelli continued to be interested, and Galdós remained optimistic. Pending a final decision, he refused to produce the drama in Spain, much to the disappointment of his closest advisers, who were confident of a startling success there.

Time passed, and friends and counsellors increased their pressure on Galdós to return to the Spanish stage. José de Cubas, who acted as his theatrical scout in the capital during the seasons he spent in Santander, reported signs of favorable changes in the theatrical world. Most persistent were Tolosa Latour and his wife, Elisa Mendoza—once a leading Madrid actress—whose influence Galdós was not always able to escape. Tolosa Latour repeatedly urged him not to forget his duty to the theater, reminding him that he had not yet accomplished his mission of dramatic reform. "It is important that you do not forget the theater," he wrote on July 4, 1899. "I am convinced that you are destined to give new direction to the form and the content of our drama. And I base my conviction on your indisputable authority and the successes you have already achieved, in addition to a certain change you may have been able to observe in our public."

Tolosa Latour was certain that Spanish audiences were ready for the psychological drama. Were they not hissing Feuillet, Augier, Goldoni, and Ohnet, and applauding Ibsen, Hauptmann, Maeterlinck, and others? He felt sure that the time was propitious for a Galdosian dramatic resurrection.

Galdós was almost persuaded. The Continental fame upon which he had been counting for his dramatic resurgence proved increasingly elusive. But it was necessary to prepare the public effectively for his return. For almost two years now the resumed publication of the *Episodios nacionales* had been reviving interest in the historical novel. He was regaining prestige and public favor. Had he rallied a sufficient following to risk a return to the drama? He did not know, but he was anxious to find out. The failure of *Gerona*, the dramatized *episodio*, had been on his conscience like an unexpiated sin. Would a revival of this drama initiate his reconciliation with Madrid theatergoers? He believed it would, and he sought the aid of his theatrical friends to effect a "rectification" of *Gerona*.

Stage folk did not think that the tableau-like scenes of *Gerona* represented the road to absolution. Donato Jiménez, an actor who enjoyed Galdós' absolute confidence, spoke for his colleagues in a letter dated December 3, 1899:

> I have read *Gerona* and I think it is beautiful, as is everything else that comes from your pen, but it is devoid of dramatic form. This is doubtless why the anguish of Don Pablo does not move, and the love affair between Josefina and Monteagut is not interesting. I believe that for a "rectification" you would have to write another drama. What kind of a drama? I do not know, but it has to be another drama. And so, my dear Don Benito, it seems to me that we had better not open old wounds, for your sake, and, above all, for my sake . . .

These were oracular words, ominous and foreboding. They suggested patience and resignation. Galdós continued with the *Episodios nacionales*. The canvas of Spanish history looked more attractive to him than did the curtain of the Madrid stage—and it was more profitable. His triumphant return to the drama had to bide its time.

*   *   *   *

Benito Pérez Galdós, reformer of the Spanish stage, artificer of new dramatic molds, trainer of the public taste, and castigator of critics, gathered much of his outward strength from a consciousness of inner weakness. In the earlier days of his theatrical career he naïvely believed that technique was not necessarily dictated by unalterable laws of the genre, and that its successful manipulation was largely a matter of acquired skill rather than innate ability. With increasing experience he began to question this conviction, and his moments of doubt were reflected in occasional concessions to conventional dramaturgy. Unwavering as was his concept of dramatic content, he was hesitant and uncertain about form. These conflicting attitudes robbed the creative process of much of its spontaneity and joy. By his own admission he never quite succeeded in unlocking the arcanum of dramatic literature.

Galdós preferred to work at drama during the summer months in his Santander retreat. He made very careful preparations, even to minute details. Settings, costumes, coiffures absorbed a great deal of his attention, and he spared no effort to insure their authenticity. Here he was aided by the skills and procedures which he had evolved during twenty years of novel-writing. The stage of gestation was pleasant enough, but the hours of travail were filled with anxiety.

To the end of his days Galdós puzzled over the physical distribution of characters on the stage. He was never able to visualize where they stood or sat with respect to one another. And even more troublesome was the problem of the relative length of scenes, which he came to regard as his particular nemesis, implacable despite his extreme humility and modesty. *La loca de la casa* required two days for its reading, and painful excisions had to be made during the rehearsals. Having no special sense to guide him in this matter, he placed himself at the mercy of friends and actors. These also came to his rescue when he became entangled in the mesh of his own plots and could not see the end of the road. Sometimes his confusion was so discouraging that he would drop the play at hand and begin work on another. *Bárbara*, a tragicomedy staged in 1905, was conceived and begun before *Electra* (1901), was resumed after *Mariucha* (1903), and was dropped again in favor of *El abuelo* (1904). *Santa Juana de Castilla*, produced in 1918, was written more intermittently than any other Galdosian play with the possible exception of the dramatization of *Marianela*. In this case the Quinteros were ultimately invited to do the job after many other young writers, including Valle-Inclán, had promised but failed to do it.

The confidence with which Galdós viewed his ultimate position as a dramatist he rarely felt during the composition of a given play. Even in his old age, when applause of his efforts had become *de rigueur*, he leaned heavily on the advice of actors. Thus, after finishing the second act of *Alceste* (1914), he humbly left it to Fernando Díaz de Mendoza to decide whether it would be worth while to continue the drama. Don Fernando praised the first act, but found the second "dangerous because of its difficult mixture of the comic and the sentimental, which might throw the public off the track." [11] He believed, however, that a strong third act might save the tragicomedy.

In a sense Galdós wrote his plays with the collaboration of the actors. After several years of experience he unconsciously adopted the playwright's practice of creating roles for specific stars. This form of collaboration did not always further the cause of dramatic art, but it sometimes served as an instrument of peace within the theatrical company. Where certain actresses were involved it even afforded Galdós a form of gratification wholly unrelated to art. When he saw these made-to-measure roles on the stage, they were often a distortion of his intentions, though he usually found it politic not to betray his disappointment to the models. But he did not always succeed in repressing his displeasure. During rehearsals or at the first performance, those around him could infer his emotions from his puzzled air and faraway look. He seemed to be groping for an explanation of the discrepancy between his conception and the artist's interpretation.

The trials of the creative process were trivial by comparison with the emotional strain of the premières. It availed Galdós nothing to spend an hour or two immediately before curtain time in a modest restaurant with a few intimate friends or members of his household, eating, smoking, chatting and, in general, behaving as if he had spent a quiet day that he was topping off with a good dinner. For his earlier premières he preferred to remain inconspicuously behind the scenes, relying principally for comfort on Tolosa Latour and on the soothing effect of countless cigarettes. But he soon discovered that this observation post gave him a rather distorted impression of the performance; his work seemed disjointed, artificial, incoherent. He moved his station to the *saloncillo* (director's office), but the change neither eased his mind nor calmed his nerves. Fitful sleep, or even protracted wakefulness the night before was obviously not calculated to steel him for the ordeal. In the *saloncillo* the constant arrival and departure of friends before the first curtain made him restless and impatient. Then there were those nerve-racking bells calling the orchestra, the actors, and the stage hands!

At last everything was quiet, and Galdós would settle down in his chair in impressive solitude. But not for long. He would pace the corridor, smoking incessantly, waiting for the first report on the progress of the play. Whatever the news, his self-control usually collapsed after the first half hour, and he would go down the few steps leading to the stage in order to listen. The first round of applause invariably drew from him the comment, addressed to anyone who happened to be near him: "It seems to be going well. It's going well." To enthusiastic admirers who called to congratulate him between acts he would remark: "You like it, do you? I am awfully glad. Awfully glad." [12]

But Galdós' real nemesis were the curtain calls. Those that forced him out of his hiding in the first half of the performance he took in his stride. An actress would rush in and pull him to the front of the stage before he had time to become too frightened. But the repeated curtain calls after the last act wearied him physically and emotionally. At the end of *La loca de la casa* he found it difficult to maintain his graciousness in the face of the insistent enthusiasm of the audience, and he threw himself on a couch with stubborn determination not to come out on the stage again. Eluding the cast, he sought asylum in a corner of the Café Inglés. Later he explained: "I was frightened by the sight of so many eyes staring at me at the same time. It is a terrible sensation! Terrible!" [13]

How relieved he used to feel at the sound of the gradually dying applause! Now he could abandon himself to the enjoyment of his triumph. Over a cup of chocolate in Doña Mariquita's fashionable tearoom, or a glass of coffee in the *saloncillo*, Galdós would join friends and actors in post-mortem conversation. His tone was festive, the atmosphere exhilarating. Everyone was joyous, including the waiter from the nearby café, who would refuse to charge for the coffee. The actresses would pat him on the back, asking if he was as happy as they. In the early years he was likely to answer equivocally, but in time he was willing to concede that the enthusiasm was largely spontaneous and general, and he would remark: "If I had staged this ten years ago, they would have pelted me with chairs on the stage." [14] Naturally he was happy, but also tired. It was time to go home—provided no crowds were waiting to escort him.

In later years, with gradually developing blindness and senility, the anguish of the creative process was mitigated for Galdós by his anticipation of the excitement of the première. In those years he rarely gave thought to the source of the applause or its volume. What mattered was the fact that the public applauded; the sound of clapping hands excited him and filled him with childish joy. He no longer tried to listen to the actors on the stage, and he did not speculate about the reaction of the audience. He would sit dozing in the *saloncillo*, waking up periodically with a start to inquire whether it was time for a curtain call. It was all reduced to the routine so characteristic of senility. The performances were no longer followed by celebrations in the *saloncillo* or anywhere else. The post-mortem comments were usually made at the author's bedside on the following night. Galdós would distribute complimentary tickets among his younger literary friends with the stipulation that they were to report to him all they saw and heard during the performance. This they invariably did with the solemnity of a ritual, and their flattering accounts would soothe the aged master into a sound sleep. Someone would remove the cold cigarette stub from the corner of his mouth, and the callers would tiptoe out of the monastically austere and simple bedroom.

Earlier in his career, however, the première was always an occasion for deep anxiety. One of his chief aims was to modify the taste of the theatergoer, but he was never in a position to measure his success. Convinced that dramatic art obeyed no immutable laws, he regarded public taste as something readily molded by the compelling beauty of the vehicle. But as his career fluctuated between failure and success, his pronouncements on theatrical audiences became correspondingly contradictory. In the main, however, he attributed to the Spanish theatergoers an evolving sensibility away from convention, which was not borne out by impartial observation. Clearly the wish was father to the thought.

The wish came to him early. After the dismal failure of *Los condenados* a group of intimate friends honored him with what might be termed a consolation luncheon. The conversation naturally revolved around his recent experience, and the audience was censured for its share in the fiasco. At first Galdós remained silent, partly enveloped in the smoke of the cheap cigar on which he was drawing energetically and distractedly. During a brief lull in the discussion he remarked in a slow, deliberate voice: "We shall have to get accustomed to one another—the public to my works, and I to the verdict to the public. But . . . we'll come to some understanding." [15] And he fell into deep meditation. Presently he mystified his hosts with the following anecdote. In San Quintín, his newly constructed chalet, he had several domesticated, glossy-furred rabbits from the West Indies. One day it occurred to him to introduce among them a few mountain rabbits, gray and fierce, accustomed to freedom and the open spaces. There were furious fights between the two breeds. It was an interesting experiment the results of which he was following with immense curiosity.

Ten years later came the indisputable success of *El abuelo*. Behind the scenes after the performance, Galdós was overcome with joy. One of the hosts of the luncheon of 1894 inquired about the results of the *lepus cuniculus* experiment. As if resuming an interrupted thought, Galdós replied: "Well, the experiment was most successful; the grays and the whites learned to tolerate each other, got accustomed to living together, and even came to understand each other." He paused and added thoughtfully: "You see, we've got used to each other. You may remember that I announced that the public and I would get to understand one another." [16]

There is not much evidence to support this assertion, and he himself had occasion to modify his opinion shortly afterward. His very next play, *Bárbara* (1905), was coolly received, so coolly as to make him skeptical whether the work he was preparing for the following season would be a success. In a letter to his daughter María, under date of August 13, 1905, he expressed his doubts about *Amor y ciencia*, a work vaguely inspired by the life of Spain's renowned histologist, Santiago Ramón y Cajal: "I am continuing with my new work. I believe it will be one of the first to be put on in the Comedia. I imagine that it will not go well and will not be liked, because the public is becoming daily more wretched."

Amor y ciencia was not well received. As a matter of fact, after the riotous première of *Electra* in 1901 Galdós' difficulties were no longer limited to the conservative taste of the public and the dogmatism of certain recalcitrant critics. The priggish elements in Spanish society virtually put his dramatic works on the Index, and this influenced other classes of spectators. Some theaters, fearing the boycott of season subscribers, refused to stage his works. Galdós himself hinted at this with an air of sad recrimination in the preface of *Alma y vida* (1902). Significant in this connection is the fact that the première of *Mariucha* (1903) was held in Barcelona, a city much more susceptible to artistic innovation than Madrid. Even *El abuelo* was not the unqualified success it was claimed to be by reviewers and by Galdós' young admirers among the so-called Generation of 1898. At its twenty-seventh performance in honor of the author, an occasion that was graced by the presence of the royal family, the better social elements were not widely represented.

Perhaps chiefly because he was discouraged, Galdós produced only one play, *Pedro Minio* (1908), between 1905 and 1910. Its reception was lukewarm, and this inspired the more serious critics to ask whether public taste had in recent years undergone a change for the better. They were forced to conclude that it had not, pointing to the prevailing preference for diaphanous ideas, clear and transparent plots, innocent entertainment, surprises, and violent emotions. Plays of intellectual and sentimental appeal were still doomed to failure. As for symbolistic dramas, they only made the audience nervous and impatient. And the professional reviewers, complained the same critics, had made as little progress as their public, notwithstanding Galdós' two blistering sermons of 1894 and 1902. Forgetting that in the latter year he had laid the blame squarely upon them, they reasserted that Galdós was not a dramatist, as was proved by the audience's rejection of *Pedro Minio*.

Benavente made a futile attempt to silence the noisemakers by suggesting that the Spanish vice of envy was the only reason that Galdós was begrudged the palm of dramatist in addition to that of novelist. Other writers of the new generation also strove to shame the "respectable" public into acknowledging Galdós' dramatic talent. Their failure was in some measure due to the general decline of Galdós' reputation in the wake of his participation in republican-socialist politics. And the noisy demonstrations during the first performance of *Casandra* (1910) did little to raise the value of his stock. In certain quarters this drama was denounced—not without some justification—as an outright anticlerical manifesto. It was even maliciously rumored that Galdós had instructed his servant, Victoriano, whom he had immortalized the year before in his novel *El caballero encantado,* to instigate the radical demonstrators the night of the première. As for the remaining five plays, produced during the last eight years of Galdós' life, their fortunes were too intimately interrelated with his personal vicissitudes to offer conclusive or even corroborative evidence of the extent to which he had eventually succeeded in accustoming the public to his new-type drama.

＊　　＊　　＊　　＊

Galdós was conceivably right when he insisted that the dramatic reviewers seriously hampered his efforts to educate and refine the public taste. Although he exaggerated the peculiarly Spanish nature of what he called the "literary service" supplied by the press, it is undeniable that the zeal of his friends and the animosity of his foes tended to confuse and inhibit his audiences. No Spanish dramatist ever received as much publicity and precipitated as much discussion as did Galdós. On this score he could have had no cause for complaint. The first announcement that another Galdosian play was in the offing inspired speculation and even advance criticism—based, of course, on sheer hearsay—by journalists, dramatic colleagues, theatrical people in general, and a host of literary camp followers. This was a step calculated to create a proper atmosphere for the première, an atmosphere in which the public at large found itself enveloped before very long.

The Madrid theatergoer struggled in vain to remain unprejudiced. By some he was told that Galdós was the pride of Spanish letters and possibly the most positive artistic personality in all Europe. Others argued that the author of the *Episodios nacionales*—and this form of identification was maliciously intentional—should never have ventured outside the spacious field of the novel, in which he had unquestionably distinguished himself. Galdós' promoters denounced the opposition as parasites of theater lobbies, café spongers, and literary leeches; only the deplorable Spanish tendency to pigeonhole talent, the envy which amounted to a national trait, and the frugality with which merited praise was meted out could prevent the forthcoming play from being a resounding success. Galdós' detractors, on the other hand, appealed to the courage, independence, and self-respect of the public. Only faint hearts and timid souls would permit themselves to be browbeaten by those who worshipped in the new church of the Galdosian faith with more passion than piety. The Spanish public had always exercised the sacrosanct right of iconoclasm with respect to the greatest national geniuses, and it should not hesitate to demolish the new idol too, even at the risk of being called sacrilegious idiots by the idolators. It was high time to defeat the diabolical strategy of coercion and intimidation pursued by the roving Galdosian bands.

The plight of the distraught spectator who watched a play by Galdós was indeed distressing. With the din of the noisy advance harangues in his ears, he could not avoid being inhibited; he probably suspected that his reactions and opinions were prefabricated, as it were. The dramatic reviews of the following day only added to his confusion. If he had applauded the night before, he discovered that his applause probably expressed his admiration for the author rather than his play—a gesture he must not be ashamed of, since it showed that he was capable of respecting a great figure despite his sad equivocations of the moment. Nor were the spectator's doubts removed by the reviewers who prefaced their observations with professions of humility, reserve, and timidity, and with declarations of misgivings and hesitations. How could he, a simple spectator, formulate a sincere opinion when the critics, schooled in the subtleties of dramatic art, repeatedly proclaimed their incompetence to evaluate the latest Galdosian production?

In these circumstances the bewildered spectator probably wished that Galdós had not attempted a revolution in the drama. Perhaps he accepted with resignation the verdict of the critic who mournfully asserted that neither the laborer in the gallery nor the pampered, pretty-faced lady in the loge nor the middle-class moneybag in the orchestra was prepared to understand and hence to enjoy Galdós' dramas.[17] Or he may have considered himself a part of the limited public which Galdós liked to regard as supporting his determined effort to regenerate the national drama and which, he believed, would have grown gratifyingly had not the critics intervened with their dogmatic clamor and their erroneous, improvised, contradictory opinions, pronounced like an irrevocable sentence on the day following the première. The dilemma of the spectator was very real. Galdós' success as a dramatist could not then, and cannot even now, be determined.

XIV

The Return of the Native

A GREAT MAN HAS RESPONSIBILITIES which the average mortal escapes. Among other things, he owes allegiance to his birthplace much as a person owes devotion to his immediate family. If he makes no show of his attachment to his native heath, he invites censure. He may also put his compatriots in the position of parents whose favorite child has become estranged.

The story of Galdós' relations with the Canary Islands is a case in point. During his lifetime no one raised the question of his attitude toward Las Palmas and its implications for his art. Although his insular origin was common knowledge, there was a tendency to regard him as a genuine Madrilenian because of his magnificently intimate canvas of Madrid. After his death, however, it was noted that his birthplace was virtually missing from his vast panorama of Spanish life, an omission that was considered remarkable in a country where fiction tended to be strongly regionalistic.

The first to point this out were Luis and Agustín Millares Cubas, Galdós' fellow islanders. For them it explained his alleged lack of popularity with his countrymen, who naturally found the world he painted strange and uninteresting. However, without concealing their feeling of hurt pride, the brothers Millares Cubas magnanimously assumed that Galdós neglected the native scene because it was perhaps incapable of inspiring a great author. In his earlier works he occasionally did recall Las Palmas. The prototypes of Juan Tafetán and the Troya girls in *Doña Perfecta* were easily recognized by the natives, as were also the severe, tedious atmosphere of Ficóbriga and the description of the storm in *Gloria*. For these and other scattered reminiscences the "Fortunate Islands" were grateful, but on the whole they felt foresaken by their famous son.

The sentimental local pride of the islanders was converted by Miguel de Unamuno into an argument, which others repeated with greater or lesser conviction, against Galdós' claim to artistic distinction. At the Galdós memorial meeting in March, 1920, sponsored by the Atheneum of Salamanca—a bare two months after his death—Unamuno censured the departed novelist with characteristic tactlessness for his failure to include his native land in his spacious fictional world. For Don Miguel this was conclusive evidence of a lack of lyricism and sensitiveness—of a prosaic soul completely run dry. Galdós was not a poet. The absence of the varied Las Palmas landscape from his novels betokened a lack of feeling for nature. Far from being an effective artist, the universally mourned novelist was in Unamuno's opinion only a literary artisan.

The Salamantine philosopher probably did not suspect that his improvised comments would acquire a vogue unwarranted by their validity or propriety. They were avidly seized upon by two strikingly dissimilar groups. Catholic critics used them as additional ammunition with which to demolish Galdós' reputation, thus shielding themselves against the charge of viewing Galdós with religious bias. The youthful soldiers of the literary vanguard, on the other hand, appropriated Don Miguel's opinion because it was Don Miguel's and because it fortified their hope of personal aggrandizement at the expense of demolished idols. How much permanent harm was thus done to Galdós' fame it is hard to estimate—probably none.

* * * *

Superficially viewed, Galdós' attitude toward the Canary Islands could be aptly summed up with the Spanish saying *Si te he visto no me acuerdo* ("I may have seen you, but I cannot recall"). After his last brief visit in 1869 he went back home only once, for reasons not altogether clear. He had planned to make the voyage shortly after his excursion to Ansó in the summer of 1894, but his preoccupation with *Los condenados* forced him to

postpone it until the following fall. In previous years not even
the death of his parents and two brothers had induced him to
return home. In 1894 the only surviving members of his immediate family in Las Palmas were three spinster sisters and one
brother. His contact with them had been intermittent and usually
indirect. It devolved largely upon Carmen and Concha, the two
sisters with whom he lived in Madrid and in Santander, to maintain the precarious family ties.

To his friends Galdós was wont to attribute his seeming estrangement from his kin in the Canary Islands to his horror of
seasickness. In view of his enthusiasm for sea travel to England
and other countries, his apology is obviously false. Actually he
was kept away from home by the strange influence of his
mother and sister-in-law. Mama Dolores had never encouraged
him to visit her during his student days lest he be unduly distracted from his academic duties. And even when she had come to
realize that Benitín would never become a distinguished jurist,
she still felt that it would be wrong for him to interrupt his ill-
chosen work for a pleasure trip to the Canaries. Throughout her
life the severe, strong-minded lady insisted that her son's place
was in Madrid. It is not known that Galdós ever challenged his
mother, since on this score she was fully supported by her
daughter-in-law, although for different reasons.

Magdalena's hatred of Las Palmas, born of her tragic experiences there, in time became a mania so intense that her whole
existence seemed to be identified with it. The strange satisfaction
she derived from keeping Benito away from the Canary Islands
may be inferred from her willingness to agree with Mama
Dolores on this score. And to Galdós Magdalena's wish was
command, and her word law. Timid and unassertive with his
sisters, he was for various reasons submissive to his sister-in-law,
so much soft clay in her hands. He pitied her for her personal
misfortunes; he felt drawn toward her because of her kinship
with pathetic little Sisita; and he was grateful for her continuous
material and moral support.

In the fall of 1894 Magdalena knew that the end of her life
was near. Either out of contrition or, more likely, because her

personal affairs required immediate attention, she permitted Benito to visit Las Palmas. He welcomed the opportunity for several reasons. For one thing, he could investigate the family fortune at close range. His interest in his share of the estate became more and more pronounced as the proceeds from his plays failed to solve his pressing economic problem. Besides, his visit would at last gratify his countrymen, who had been yearning for a glimpse of their distinguished compatriot. That would reassure them that their pride in him was not entirely one-sided.

The islanders' faith that Galdós had not cut every tie with them was not altogether a delusion. During his student days he had maintained contact with the Canary colony in Madrid by joining its *tertulia* at the Café Universal, and his Madrilenian friends associated him intimately with this boisterous provincial group. As his literary fame grew, his home attracted all sorts of islanders visiting in the capital, and he always received them with unaffected courtesy. And when he established his own publishing house on Calle Hortaleza in the late nineties, his office and studio served literally as the headquarters of the Canary colony in Madrid; in fact, it was popularly referred to as the *canariera*— the canary cage.

In the privacy of his home Galdós had frequent occasion to recall his birthplace. His sisters and nephews often foregathered to chat nostalgically about Las Palmas, its peculiar life, its interesting persons and picturesque characters. Galdós participated in these family conclaves with an eagerness one would not expect of so innately reticent a person. He entered with particular enthusiasm into discussions on the insular accent—which not even he had completely lost—, on the cuisine of the region, and on its local vocabulary. His general interest in picturesque speech led him to compile a dictionary of words and idioms peculiar to Las Palmas.

In his last years Galdós dwelt on his fondness for his native land with the persistence that characterizes senility. His fading memory and intermittently confused mind were often crowded with sharp childhood reminiscences. He insisted that the projected statue of him in Madrid's *rosaleda* should bear the insular coat-of-arms. To his admirers this obsession served as a sad reminder that the disintegration of a great mind had set in. Equally depressing was the monotonous regularity with which he urged that a special appeal be made to his countrymen to contribute funds for the monument. He argued that they were just as eager to give as he was to receive. And when his death was a matter of days, his agonized mind was filled with delirious memories of Las Palmas, especially his childhood games and the native popular songs. He grieved that the book he had been promising himself to write with a Canary Islands background had to remain among his numerous unrealized projects. With pathetic sincerity he explained repeatedly that his many duties and bad health had prevented him from returning home to refresh his memory.

But Galdós' failure to give artistic expression to his affection for the Canary Islands did not lessen his countrymen's steadfast loyalty to him. Indeed, there is something pathetic about the pomp and ceremony with which they solemnized the repeated triumphs of their famous son, who obviously remained indifferent toward them. It must have humiliated his compatriots that he rarely took cognizance of the pride they felt in his growing glory, yet they always strove to show a cheerful face.

The most zealous watchers of Galdós' success were the local newspapers. Hearts fluttered and pens quivered as the native writers dealt with his books and plays and the comments of the Madrid critics upon them. The latter were often reproduced prominently. For the outstanding events in Galdós' career special correspondents were dispatched to Madrid, whose reporting was obviously not unbiased. But their bias need not be held against them; reflected glory is often highly intoxicating.

At the time Madrid was honoring Galdós at the magnificent banquet of 1883, the thirteen "Fortunate Islands" celebrated the occasion in a series of literary-musical programs which filled theaters, casinos, and other places of assembly. The most elaborate homage was rendered by Las Palmas, where the leading cultural organizations cooperated so splendidly that the inhabitants of the archipelago were confirmed in their belief that psychologically they differed from the Spaniards of the main-land.

On the night of June 2, the Cairasco Theatre—the "aquatic theater" which had been immortalized in labored verse by the youthful Pérez Galdós—was filled to overflowing. Only one distinguished Las Palmas family was absent—Mama Dolores and her children. In that household the injunction against cele-brating Benitín's triumphs as a "writer of stories" was still being strictly enforced. On June 14 the leading local paper, *La Co-rrespondencia de Canarias,* devoted almost half of its four-page issue to eloquent verse, altisonant prose, and original musical compositions reviewing the stirring tributes Galdos had received. The event was described as a phenomenal spectacle of a com-munity honoring one of its citizens during his lifetime, and many islanders filed away a copy of the paper as a memento of the great occasion. Galdós was formally notified that back home they were glorying in his achievements.

The success of *La de San Quintín* in 1894, which temporarily assured Galdós a place of honor among Spain's dramatists, was an occasion for great rejoicing in Las Palmas. His compatriots had been following his struggle on the stage with evident dis-appointment, and those among them with a penchant for literary criticism had been expostulating against the stubborn Madrid reviewers. But now their own Benito Pérez was conquering all along the literary battle line! This dramatic triumph deserved a celebration even more impressive than the one of 1883.

The first to convert this thought into a reality were the stu-dents from the Canary Islands at the University of Seville. They held a sumptuous banquet and sent Galdós a long message of congratulation to the effect that he was the greatest Canarian of the century. The city of Las Palmas gave a gala performance of *La de San Quintín,* which was played by a second-rate Madrid company. The theater was decorated with flags, banners, and streamers bearing the titles of Galdós' works; municipal bands furnished music; and local societies, newspapers, and prominent citizens sent a profusion of floral offerings. On the stage a portrait of Galdós, executed by a local artist, was immersed in a sea of native flowers. There was, of course, the usual round of eulogistic speeches, and amateur poets recited special compositions. The celebration definitely surpassed that of 1883.

But nothing in the history of insular cultural activities rivaled the welcome Galdós received upon his return to Las Palmas a short time later, in October, 1894. Only he himself might have described adequately the heart flutters, the pent-up emotion, the feverish preparations, the elaborate plans. For weeks before his arrival the entire city seemed to live in and for Galdós. The press relegated its normal content to a secondary position. The bookshops sold nothing but the works of Galdós, which were widely reread and discussed in cafés and in private gatherings. One would have thought that the literate population of Las Palmas was preparing for a rigorous examination on the novels and plays of Benito Pérez.

Some features of the festivities planned by the city council had to be canceled almost at the last moment out of respect for Galdós' grief. Word had reached him in Cádiz that Magdalena had died, and he continued the journey only after consulting the family in Madrid. Yet for nothing in the world would the city forego the gala reception at the pier. For two days the population had been priming itself emotionally in response to the proclamation that Mayor Felipe Massieu had issued on October 16:

RESIDENTS OF LAS PALMAS

After a prolonged absence of more than twenty years, we shall very shortly experience the intense joy of seeing on our beloved native soil our illustrious fellow citizen, Don Benito Pérez Galdós.

I feel confident that, without any urging on my part, all the corporate bodies and societies, and all the social classes of this noble and loyal city, which yields to none in enthusiasm when it is a matter of rendering a tribute of praise and admiration to its celebrated compatriots, will come with demonstrable affection to welcome at Puerto de la Luz the illustrious son of

Las Palmas, who yesterday morning sailed from Cádiz
on the steamship "Pío IX."
But, even though I harbor such an intimate conviction,
because I know the civic ardor of these inhabitants,
I deem it my duty to beseech the City to receive effu-
sively the pre-eminent Canarian, prince of our national
literature and glory of Spain.

The inhabitants of Las Palmas were equal to the occasion.
On the morning of the eighteenth the Puerto de la Luz was
dressed in bunting and flags; music and whistling filled the air;
the harbor was crowded with craft of every description; and
the atmosphere was heavy with smoke from bursting flares and
skyrockets. An official boat met Galdós at the steamer, and
from the pier he was led in an immense parade to the family
winter home in Santa Catalina. Installed in his room after the
cheering crowd had been dispersed, he quickly drew up plans
for a restful private visit.

The honored guest spent almost three pleasant weeks in his
native city. He rose at dawn every day and by six o'clock was
ready to take the first streetcar to town—more specifically to
the public market. There he passed the morning hours in minute
observation, precisely as he had so frequently done during his
student days in the Colegio de San Agustín. In the afternoons
he roamed through the principal streets of the city and the
picturesque outlying districts. He visited old friends and exchanged pleasant reminiscences with them. He reconstructed the
old city in his mind, went to childhood haunts, took frequent
excursions to the smaller settlements near Las Palmas, jotted
down notes, contemplated the mountains and the ocean, stood in
ecstasy before the overpowering landscape of the Canaries—and
found time to work.

Galdós' companions on these trips were impressed by the notes
he was assiduously taking. What were they for? The press hoped
that his refreshed impressions were to be embodied in his next
novel. Perhaps they did find their way into his works, but obviously not in a form to make them readily identifiable. In the
opinion of Miguel Sarmiento, an old-time friend of Galdós,

there is a native residue in all his works. Critics may consider him an essentially Madrilenian novelist, he says, "but there is in all his books, in the grace with which he bestows nicknames on people and in the sluggish gossip of the children of his sublime mind, a tinge and something like the concentrated essence of the peculiar charm with which the Canarians are wont to paint and comment upon their local types and their special customs. Sporadic turns of speech, fleeting traits, graphic terms redolent of a life quite different from that one [i.e., of Madrid] and only intelligible and rightly appreciated by those of us who were born here."[1]

One cannot know whether Galdós was emotionally affected by his stay in Las Palmas, but it is certain that he revived his childhood interests. As a boy he had frequently visited the San Telmo church, where he was fascinated by the miniature galleys carved from precious woods. It had always been his ambition to possess one of these as a memento of a rapidly vanishing art. Accordingly one of his first visits—perhaps the first one—was to the little church. He felt sure that now he would at least be permitted to view again what he had so longed to possess in his childhood. The president of the seamen's society that supported San Telmo had been told that the visitor was *chiflado con los barcos* ("cracked on the subject of boats"), and so he invited him to choose one of the galleys. The visit to Las Palmas was fully justified! Manuel Miranda, custodian of the church mementos, renovated the miniature boat selected by Galdós and shipped it to him in December. It reached Spain in excellent condition and was installed in a conspicuous place in the San Quintín study.

But Galdós soon discovered that there is no unmitigated happiness on this earth. The insular museum at Las Palmas housed a fine collection of miniature boats, ex-votos donated by the San Telmo Brotherhood, and Galdós went there to feast his eyes again. But instead he found himself officially inspecting the institution, escorted by a committee consisting of his good friends Dr. Gregorio Chil, Juan Padilla, and Julián Cirilo Moreno. Trailed by the trio, he traversed the main hall without stopping, only looking perfunctorily to right and left. He passed through the next room in similar fashion until he discovered the large collection of miniature old caravels, brigs, schooners, and pilots' boats. He stared at these so avidly that Juan Padilla violated the rules of the museum and offered him a few of the miniatures. But before Galdós could make his selection Dr. Chil ushered him into the *ossarium*—the anthropological section—and disappeared.

Galdós was delighted to be left with Juan Padilla, who was a more humane escort than the local naturalist. Insisting that the air in the *ossarium* was giving him a headache, he prevailed on Don Juan to return to the collection of boats. But his delight was shortlived. Dr. Chil, reappearing with a guest book in his hands, interrupted Galdós' rapturous contemplation and marched him into the director's room. There, amid a goodly number of people, all solemnly expectant, he was seated before a table with a writing set on it.

Was this a conspiracy, and was he being victimized? Galdós looked up and saw Don Juan standing beside him with the guest book in his hands like an acolyte presenting the missal to an officiating priest. He wore an expression of determination, and behind him stood Dr. Chil looking equally resolved. "Your signature with an appropriate remark to commemorate your visit to this institution," Galdós thought he heard someone say. Someone had, in fact, said that. He turned beseechingly to Julián Cirilo Moreno and whispered that his mind had gone blank, that he was awkward at that sort of thing anyway. Don Julián suggested that under the circumstances his signature might suffice. But Don Juan, his humaneness all gone, announced imperiously: "Everybody puts down something; it is the custom!" A moment of mortifying silence ensued. Galdós looked agonizingly at Don Julián for aid. Finally he picked up the pen and scribbled: "How beautiful is the Canary Museum! Benito Pérez Galdós."[2]

Galdós almost forgot his ordeal in the Canary Museum when he discovered that one of his cronies, Maestro Joaquín Gutiérrez, a man considerably older than himself, was still living. Gutiérrez was a carpenter, tinsmith, talker, and drinker. The talking and drinking he carried on simultaneously; one drink sufficed to unloose an incessant flow of hendecasyllables the burden of which was that he was Benito's peer in novelistic power, albeit only of local fame and *inédita* because of his impecuniousness. In proof of his parity with Benito, poor Joaquín contrived to walk, talk, and gesticulate very convincingly like him.

The two friends became inseparable walking companions. Together they visited mutual cronies and revived old memories. Daily, at sunset time, they would go to sit on the Poyos del Obispo (the Bishop's Benches), beyond the San José district on the Telde highway. The highway ran close by clusters of rustic dwellings splashed on the mountain slopes, past the undulating banana groves of San José, which stretched far out to the sea, and the smiling valleys where as a child Galdós had loved to wander aimlessly.

One afternoon, sitting on the Poyos del Obispo with Maestro Joaquín, Galdós was inspired to indulge in a childish prank. A group of *magas*—native women of the region—came down the highway with baskets of eggs on their heads. How about tripping one of them but without hurting her? The eggs would naturally break, but he would pay the damage. Joaquín was willing and skillful. The eggs spread out on the pavement like an uncooked omelette, and the women shrieked wrathful epithets at the pranksters. A settlement was immediately effected. On the way home Galdós jestingly grumbled that he had experienced his first disrespectful reception in his native land. His companion consoled him by stressing the pleasure it had been to hear the "natural" speech of the *magas*. Maestro Joaquín was a genius. His consoling words enlightened many who, in the days following, sought the wherefore of Benito Pérez's odd prank on the Telde highway.

Galdós' visit drew to a close. Las Palmas strained itself to show its genuine affection. The city council met and decided to commemorate his sojourn by placing a plaque on the façade of the house where he was born and by naming a street for him. The first decision was not carried out until 1901, but that oversight

was not typical. Local poets, some of whom held their inspiration
in check until long after his departure for the mainland, paid
homage in verse. A sample of such offerings is a sonnet entitled
"To Galdós" and humbly claimed by A.G.O., which was composed on October 19 and published two months later in *El
Defensor de la Patria:*

> I thought I would exalt your name, Don Benito,
> Without worrying for even a moment that in doing so
> I would be placing a millstone about my neck
> And burn my own fingers to a crisp.
>
> Now a thought comes to me, now I delete it,
> Seeking a better one, loftier and more beautiful,
> And writing and erasing I filled the paper with scrawls
> Until I could not read my own scribbling.
>
> But I thought of *Gloria* and *Gerona,*
> I looked at your figure and I looked at myself,
> And a reason which bespeaks my good sense
> Appeared to convince me simply
> That my laurel was too poor for your crown
> And that it was best for me to be silent.

On November 9 Galdós left Las Palmas on the *Hespérides.*
The official farewell—with a parade, music, flags, salvos, and
boats escorting the steamer—was even more elaborate than the
welcoming ceremony had been. Galdós, visibly moved, remained
on deck until he could no longer see the returning escort craft.
It may be that his reaction was not exclusively emotional, for the
Diario de Cádiz reported on November 4 that for the first time
in his life he had been seasick throughout the voyage. That was
regrettable news. In the same paper, however, the Canarians
read that Galdós had carried away so favorable an impression
of his native land that he would try to keep his promise to the
family to make a return visit in the spring.

But Galdós did not go back to Las Palmas in the spring, nor
ever again in the remaining twenty-six years of his life. Yet his
countrymen remained steadfastly loyal to him. His entrance

into the Royal Academy of Language was celebrated more elaborately in Las Palmas than in Madrid. He was the first islander to be thus honored and accordingly, on February 18, 1897, the city officially demonstrated its pride with a production of *La de San Quintín* and choice scenes from other Galdosian plays in the Tirso de Molina Theater (the old Cairasco Theater had gone up in flames some years before despite its location on the shore of the Atlantic). After the performance a badly painted portrait of Don Benito was unveiled on the stage in a bed of native flowers sent by different organizations. To the lusty cheers of the audience the actors read the accompanying messages, and more floral offerings were placed at the foot of the portrait. The program ended with the traditional series of musical numbers played by the municipal band. And all the while overflow crowds milled about the theater and in adjacent streets.

In the words of the local reporters, it was a genuinely universal celebration. The press heralded Galdós' academic honor with all the rhetorical wealth of the provincial Spanish editor. The burden of most of the eulogies was that Galdós, whatever Spaniards of the mainland might say, was first and last a Canarian. One feels, however, that this was asserted with only feeble conviction, that in the last analysis they strongly suspected Galdós of having shamefully neglected his native land. But it was comforting to assert that the man who symbolized the literary glory of Spain was primarily the greatest glory of the Canary Islands.

Only once did Galdós make a gesture of affection toward his countrymen. In 1900, after the Spanish-American War, malicious rumors persisted on the mainland that the Canaries were plotting to commit themselves into the clutches of the Yankee beast. The American navy was pictured as momentarily coming over to receive the archipelago from the hands of the traitorous natives. These rumors may have had a flimsy basis in the hidden thoughts of a negligible minority. There had always been—and there still is—a handful of advocates of home rule, but at no time had even the most rabid among them suggested the surrender of the islands to a foreign power. The slanderous rumors had to be silenced, and Don Benito, Spain's great patriot, was the man to do it. If he lifted his voice in protest, the entire Hispanic world would be convinced of the islanders' patriotic fervor.

Accordingly, in December, 1900, the Canary colony in Madrid assembled at a banquet at which Galdós was toastmaster. Its ostensible purpose was to celebrate the completion of the third series of his revived *Episodios nacionales,* but the guests knew better. The principal address—and the briefest—was Galdós', which was delivered for him by a vocally superior Canarian. The "toast"—as the Canarians modestly called the speech which soon became their badge of patriotic faith—deserves to be reproduced as a partial reflection of Galdós' spiritual attitude toward the so-called Spanish disaster.

> You have seen that the hour has come to revive in our souls the love of the little fatherland in order to kindle with it the inextinguishable flames, the love of the great fatherland; you have observed that the preference for the native soil must now widen its horizons, leading us to love and worship with greater enthusiasm the entire pattern of traditions, deeds, and traits, of glories and misfortunes, of joy and sadness which constitute the national home, so immense that its smoky-looking walls cannot be enclosed within the pages of history.
>
> And so, here, in the intimacy of regional patriotism —familiar and almost domestic—I take the liberty of affirming in the name of all who listen to me that in us lives and always shall live the soul of Spain, and that today more than ever is it necessary to state it as a comforting remedy for the pessimism and sickly sadness of the Spain of today. Let us expand our hearts here and there, let us have faith in our destiny, and let us state and affirm that we shall not be torn by force like a weak and fragile branch from the sturdy trunk to which we belong. Let us not believe even in the possibility that there can be a foreign hand strong enough to cut or tear us off and make our archipelago into a lance which is not Spanish.

It is both unwise and dangerous to speak so much of attacks by greedy foreigners. Spain is having nightmares in which she dreams that she is being despoiled, mutilated, and horribly amputated. That is absurd; it is puerile and reveals a spiritual decay and an impoverished vitality which, unless it is energetically corrected, may lead us to death.

Against this pessimism, which, if we examine it closely, has the appearance of laziness, we are duty bound to protest and to affirm our faith in right and justice, and to deny that violence is the only law of today and tomorrow, and to proclaim as accidental and transitory the examples of the rule of brute force in our world.

Now that our national faith seems cold and dark, now that some see us as the branch of the tree of the fatherland most exposed to the danger of being torn off—in this hour let us set an example of faith in the future. Let us not be boastful, but let us neither be sinister and fatalistic augurers.

Let us, the smallest, be the greatest in the firmness and vigor of our resolve; let us, the last in strength and in historical lineage, be the first in confidence just as we are the first in danger; let us, the most distant, be the closest in the heart of the fatherland.

In this way we shall make our contribution to what is so sorely needed—national faith. Each one in his own sphere, be it modest or exalted, must help to build it and to strengthen it, for without this great virtue there is no national salvation. Let us, then, be the first and most fervent believers, and let us proclaim that the Canary archipelago, Spain's forward sentinel in the ocean, knows well the responsibility of its post, and there it stands guard as it always will, vigilant, neither boastful nor afraid, fully confident in itself and in its right, feeling in its soul the flaming heat of the Spanish soul which was always the soul of great virtues, of those virtues which surpass heroism or which are its most spiritual form—patience and the strictest compliance with duty.[3]

A stupendous ovation punctuated the fervently patriotic words of the foremost Canarian, and all felt that the good name of their fair land had been vindicated. The banqueters departed aglow with faith in the future of Spain and with the desire to effect its immediate regeneration.

It is perhaps superfluous to record the immense joy with which Las Palmas greeted the sensational success of *Electra* in January, 1901. For several days after the première the press gave space to little else. It published detailed accounts of the play, the reaction of the public, the riots it precipitated, and the opinions of the critics. The thought sprang up spontaneously everywhere that now was the time to honor the author on a grander scale than ever before. Somehow a rumor circulated that in this hour of phenomenal glory Galdós recalled affectionately the city of his birth and promised to visit his family in the spring of that year. No, this was not a revived memory of the promise he had made in 1894. Every living soul in Las Palmas would join in a rousing welcome to Don Benito this time.

But there was nothing to indicate that the promised visit would ever materialize, and meantime Las Palmas was eager to commemorate Galdós' phenomenal triumph. A public-spirited citizen embarrassed the municipal council by recalling that it had not carried out the resolution of 1894 providing that a street be named for Galdós and that a plaque be placed on the oldest building in it and another on the house where he was born. A wave of shame swept the city, which presently became a storm of indignation. The council of 1901 hastily made amends for the negligence of its predecessors. On April 16, the day *Electra* was staged in Las Palmas, the Tirso de Molina Theater became the Pérez Galdós Theater, and twelve days later the two plaques were unveiled with impressive solemnity. The one placed on the unpretentious Galdós home is austerely simple and bears the following inscription: *In this house was born Don Benito Pérez Galdós on May 10, 1843. A tribute voted unanimously by the municipal government of this city.*

Las Palmas made plans to emulate the riotous reception that Madrilenians had given the anticlerical play. The audience, tutored in noisemaking by the press accounts of the première, gave vent to intermittent outbursts of unbridled enthusiasm, against which the actors struggled to make themselves heard. Apparently the spectators were determined that there should be no question where they stood in the conflict between progress and conservatism. In the city streets serpentine multitudes carrying a portrait of Galdós like a sacred image, hoarsely cheered the dramatist, Spain, and freedom. A great serenade that had been planned in honor of the Galdós family was forbidden by the authorities lest it produce an open clash with those few citizens who, though inordinately proud of Don Benito, disapproved of his harsh treatment of church and religion in *Electra*. In fact, to avoid violent incidents, the police ordered all restaurants, cafés, bars, and other public gathering places to close at midnight, immediately after the performance. Contrary to general expectation, the citizens of Las Palmas went to bed early on the night of April 16, 1901.

Thirteen years passed before Galdós had another direct contact with Las Palmas. It happened in 1914, the year of the miscarried national subscription launched to rescue him from poverty. Inspired by the king's inauguration of the campaign with a donation of ten thousand pesetas, the city council unanimously voted to match the royal contribution. Unfortunately for the aged and indigent author, the approved sum never left the municipal coffers. His disappointment was keen. Other pledges—in fact, many of them—had also gone unredeemed, but this one, he felt, should have been made good. It reflected a low state of culture in his native land as well as criminal irresponsibility in its governing body. How was he to interpret the numerous professions of love from his fellow countrymen? Were the Canary Islands in fact spiritually and culturally divorced from the rest of Spain despite the demonstration of patriotism which they gave at the memorable banquet of December, 1900?

Galdós let his indignation be known in Las Palmas. His nephew, Ambrosio Hurtado de Mendoza, was an influential political liberal, but the municipal purse strings were apparently held by others. The only redress he was able to offer Uncle Benito was a seat in Cortes, and he contrived to elect him on the Reformista ticket of Las Palmas. But the election did not, of course, reimburse Galdós for the loss of the ten thousand pesetas. Moreover, it cost him a much greater political honor— Count Romanones had been scheming to make him a life senator!

Las Palmas did not have to wait long for the next opportunity to demonstrate its affection for its favored son. When word of Galdós' death in 1920 reached the island, the entire community went into deep mourning. The newspapers broke all previous records in the space they devoted to the story of Galdós' illness and death, the funeral arrangements, and the loss sustained by the nation and the world. Many natives contributed reminiscences, some of them undoubtedly improvised. Those who had known Galdós personally regaled the public with stories about his childhood and the years of his greatest fame. Overnight, as it were, a body of Galdosian folklore sprang up in Las Palmas. And since the popular muse often prefers verse, local poets gave mournful utterance to the grief of the community. One of the dirges deserves to be known for its charming naïveté and engaging simplicity. Its author was an eleven-year old girl, Josefina de la Torre, sister of one of Galdós' nieces-in-law. It was published in *La Jornada* on January 12, 1920:

> TO DON BENITO ON THE DAY OF
> HIS DEATH
>
> I noticed when I arose
> that the day was gloomy,
> I felt a great sadness
> inside my heart.
>
> I knew something had happened,
> and my sister said to me:

Do you know, sister, do you know?
Don Benito is dead!
Don Benito! That old man
that poor blind man,
the one I liked so much,
because he was so kind.

Sister, sister, sister,
is Don Benito dead?
Everybody, everybody was crying,
everybody, all the family.
And even now my pen
as it writes quietly,
seems to be saying silently:
Yes, Don Benito is dead!

When the period of stentorian mourning was over, the Canary Islands lapsed into an attitude that might be best described by the Spanish proverb *A los muertos y a los idos no hay amigos* ("Out of sight, out of mind"). A few genuine devotees began to agitate for the erection of a Galdós monument, over which the city fathers deliberated for several years. Eventually the "Sociedad de Fomento del Turismo" commissioned Victorio Macho to do the job, and the monument was finally completed in 1926. But its placement was inexplicably delayed. Through shameful negligence it lay about for approximately four years, first in the attic and then in the courtyard of a former hotel building. The head and torso had been converted into a drying-place for family laundry. By accident a Madrid journalist touring the Canary Islands discovered the unexpected location of the Galdós monument and the strange use to which it had been put.

The discovery precipitated a scandal which, for recrimination and vituperation, surpassed anything in the history of the archipelago. After much dispute the city fathers ordered that the monument be placed on the very edge of the ocean, facing the center of the city in the distance—a kind of unpremeditated retribution for the ridicule Galdós had in his youth heaped upon the theater-by-the-sea? The unveiling ceremony in August, 1930, was a dismal failure. The masses refused to attend because it was presided over by conservative Leopoldo Matos, who, as minister of the interior in the semi-dictatorial government that followed the fall of Primo de Rivera, was distinctly *persona non grata* to the liberal islanders. For the mass of the population, especially the workers and tradesmen, the unveiling had really not taken place. That was arranged for the week of January 4, 1931, the eleventh anniversary of Galdós' death, the principal sponsors being the confederated trade unions of Las Palmas. It was a genuinely popular and delicately moving event. Galdós' daughter María was present as guest of honor.

XV

Spirituality and Solvency

ALTHOUGH THE STRUGGLE THAT marked the first years of his
dramatic career absorbed most of his artistic and spiritual ener-
gies, Galdós found time to carry forward his new vision of life
in a series of novels. From *Angel Guerra* (1890–91) to *El abuelo*
(1897) he endeavored to analyze Spanish life in terms of the
new spiritual preoccupations of the waning nineteenth century.
Whether this new orientation was the result of the impact of
prevailing Continental movements or the independent philosophic development of a sensitive thinker must forever remain
an academic question. The important fact is that Galdós, always
skeptical of rigid conviction as a guide to the understanding of
life, now tended more and more toward philosophic flexibility
in his interpretation of the human scene.

Galdós first sounded this speculative note in *Realidad* (1889).
In succeeding works it became increasingly dominant, but always
accompanied by a vigorous overtone of skepticism. Even in *Angel
Guerra* it was apparent that he had not yet gained a solid philosophic footing. Less sure than ever of the validity of material
reality, he turned to the realm of ideas, hoping that beyond the
immediate darkness he might find foci of concentrated light
leading to unsuspected and unexplored zones of spiritual reality.
These he was privileged to glimpse, and he found them fascinating, but he also discovered that the roads pointing to the
zones of mysticism, humility, meekness, self-abnegation, salvation, mercy, and honor were dotted with dangerous mirages that
might lure the unwary traveler through tortuous turns to areas
of mental confusion and spiritual discomfiture.

Spiritually viewed, *Angel Guerra* is one of Galdós' most personal novels, only a bit less inspired than his monumental *Fortunata y Jacinta*. In no other work had he revealed more of his own psychology, character, and ideas, and never before had he taken greater pains with a setting. The canvas of Toledo introduced in the second volume required extensive and minute study, but the weeks he spent in the city afforded him his richest esthetic and spiritual experience. In the disillusionment of his hero after the ill-fated Villacampa coup against Queen Isabel II on the night of September 19, 1868, and in his subsequent groping for a life formula in terms of the divine and the eternal, he reflected his own state of mind early in the last decade of the century. Like Angel Guerra, whose dream of a better social order was shattered by his contact with the ugly realities of Spanish politico-military uprisings, thus compelling him to seek other means of human redemption, so Galdós, after failing to discover the eternal verities in observable reality, attempted to scrutinize man's soul speculatively, untrammeled by social prejudices and philosophic preoccupations. He created Angel Guerra out of the substance of his own reveries, illusions, hopes, and disappointments. For the character of the nun Leré, and the subtle ways by which she became the incarnation of the protagonist's ideal, Galdós had a living model—a sister of mercy whom his rabidly anticlerical nephew José Hurtado de Mendoza loved in dead earnest.

The ultimate meaning of this novel escaped all except one or two of the critics. All detected its heavy psychological accent, but only a few perceived the author's effort to introduce the idealistic realism of the day into Spanish literature. Once again Galdós was censured for diffuseness and lack of concentration in his densely crowded canvas. His masterly evocation of what is peculiarly Toledan was duly praised, and some even commented on the Cervantine flavor of his style. All applauded his delineation of character, and one critic was so fascinated by Leré that he thought she deserved to have a novel written exclusively around her.[1] Yet the aggregate critical response to *Angel Guerra* suggests that even the intellectually advanced in Spain may not yet have been fully aware of the prevalent quest for a new spiritual dogma to replace the gospel of nineteenth-century materialism.

Galdós' next novel, *Tristana* (1892), might be figuratively termed the unfinished opus of his repertory. Its theme of feminine independence—a fairly new one in Spain—is suggested but not developed. Tristana, the heroine, like Augusta in *Realidad,* is irked by the rigid pattern of behavior which precludes the exercise of the imagination and the expression of one's temperament. When she becomes fully conscious of her particular nature, she yearns for a richer life than is implied in marriage and domesticity. She wants to rebel against a society that condemns her to permanent infamy for having committed a serious indiscretion long before she had even come to understand life's demands upon the individual. But Galdós does not permit her to come to grips with her problem. Tristana goes down in defeat without a fighting chance, and as a form of compensation for the human happiness denied her she sublimates her affection and emotion in religion. Ultimately she achieves a measure of spiritual tranquillity, but only because she believes that she has successfully transmuted human love into an emotion divine in essence.

It would be manifestly unwise to treat with philosophic seriousness a work upon which the author himself looked disdainfully. Whatever his initial intentions, he definitely lost sight of them in the process of composition. He may well have wished to point out, as in *Angel Guerra* but from a different angle, the dangerously tenuous line which often separates mysticism or spiritual exultation from conscious or unconscious self-deception. His quest for spirituality had not yet reached the stage at which reason and sense are submerged in reverie and ecstasy. He may have left the theme of *Tristana* unfinished because he wrote it at the height of his preoccupation with the staging of his first drama. The very brevity of the work is perhaps a reflection of his momentary concern with the problem of artistic compression. Oddly enough, in order to give the story a conclusion of a sort he was obliged to resort to the very trite patterns and devices which he aimed to destroy in the new national drama. Fortunately the critics were seemingly as much absorbed in the forth-coming theatrical event as Galdós himself, so that *Tristana* appeared unheralded and received little notice.

An even worse fate befell the dialogue novel *La loca de la casa* (1892). It was completely ignored, for the reviewers preferred to wait for the stage version, which was submitted to the impresario simultaneously with the appearance of the novel. But critical abstinence came to an end with *Torquemada en la Cruz* (1893), the second volume in the Torquemada series, launched amidst relative silence with *Torquemada en la hoguera* (1889). This work received a great deal of attention, no doubt because of the tremendous interest aroused by Galdós' appearance as a dramatist.

The critics who denied that Galdós had dramatic talent used this novel in two ways. Some pointed to the evolution of Torquemada into the protagonist of an extended series as evidence of the author's lack of the two skills most essential to a dramatist—synthesis and compression. Others evaluated it with strained generosity, as if to suggest that their disapproval of Galdós' dramas was due neither to hidebound conservatism nor to feeble comprehension. Friendly commentators, too, appraised *Torquemada en la Cruz*—and for that matter also the concluding volumes of the series (*Torquemada en el purgatorio*, 1894, and *Torquemada y San Pedro*, 1895)—with obvious regard for the controversy of which Galdós was then the center. Few refrained from using the occasion to emphasize his cumulative greatness as a veiled warning to his detractors that only fools enter where angels fear to tread.

Galdós' admirers argued that the note of universality in his latest works overshadowed his past achievements. To continue thinking of him as the genial critic of Spanish clericalism revealed literary provincialism and philosophic myopia. Only routinary critics, they sneered, could continue harping on such matters as insufficient action, loose plot, excessive characters, uniform dialogue, and the like in judging a transcendental work. Admittedly, the concentration on character delineation almost to the exclusion of action was bound to discourage the

average reader, but such a flaw—if indeed it was a flaw—
scarcely deserved mention in view of the grandeur of theme and
subtle embodiment of the spirit of the age, for which his creation must be regarded as the supreme achievement of an author
already unique in the history of Spanish literature.

Of all the national novelists, insisted Galdós' devotees, he
was the first and only one to discern the symptoms of the universal spiritual revival that was gradually penetrating even
Spain. The reaction against materialism and atheism evidenced
in the resurgence of the religious spirit was contemporary and
opportune, and by reflecting it Galdós was also preserving a
record of the times. Whoever may some day wish to learn what
were the most distinctive traits of nineteenth-century Spain will
only have to look at Pepe Rey, León Roch, Angel Guerra,
Pepet, Torquemada, and other Galdosian creations. Each one
symbolized a definite phase of the spiritual evolution of the
nation.

It is difficult not to suspect that some of the excessive good
will toward *Torquemada en la Cruz* emanated from a perhaps
subconscious desire to bolster Galdós' reputation after the disastrous failure of *Gerona* the previous year. And it might be
plausibly assumed that the spectacular success of *La de San
Quintín,* which had its première only a few days after the appearance of most of the reviews of the novel, was at least partly
due to the propitious atmosphere created by the friendly critics.
There must have been design in the stress they laid at this time
on the significance of Galdós' total literary accomplishment and
his rightful claim to Continental pre-eminence.

Whether Galdós intervened personally in what looked like
a campaign of rededication it is not safe to state. It is well to
recall, however, that his dramatic ambition far outweighed his
other aspirations. If in some sectors of the press the opposition
was premeditated and unyielding, the support in others was
equally calculated and stubborn—even fanatical. Ultimately his
dramatic fortunes were unaffected by the flurry of enthusiasm
over the Torquemada series, yet it did encourage him sufficiently
to contemplate a fifth volume, to be entitled *La herencia de*

Torquemada. When *Torquemada y San Pedro*, the last of the series, was received almost unanimously as the best of the four, Galdós actually promised a fifth and last installment. He was deterred by the statistical evidence that the public did not favor serially published novels. After all, critical commentaries, honey-sweet though they might be, would not silence usurers and female extortionists.

Rivaling *Angel Guerra* in its revelation of Galdós' quest for the meaning of the spiritual revival of the day is *Nazarín* (1895), a novel in which the juxtaposition of plastic realism and transparent as well as subtle symbolism baffled critics and readers alike. For this work Galdós had an affection with which only *Marianela* competed. It was flesh of his philosophy and blood of his spirit. When in his declining years he was asked by nephew José Hurtado de Mendoza for a personal memento, he presented him with the manuscript of *Nazarín*. Don José revered it as he might have revered a sacred relic. Throughout his life Uncle Benito continued to live for him in this precious manuscript.[2]

Literary Spain had barely recovered from the confusing ethical symbolism of *Los condenados*, staged some six months before, when it found itself mystified by this latest fictional creation of Galdós. Was Nazarín, the modern incarnation of the spirit of Christ, the author's answer to the contemporary quest for a new ideal, or was he merely the expression of his cynical and ironic reaction to the resurgence of religious preoccupations all over Europe? The cryptic comments concerning the protagonist which Galdós scattered throughout the novel did not help matters. The critics readily discovered the *españolismo*—the Spanishness—of the work in its Cervantine flavor and picaresque atmosphere; they naturally discerned its transcendental aim; but the essence of the theme eluded most of them.

Did Galdós really mean that just as the eighteenth century ended with the triumph of reason, so the nineteenth century must end with the triumph of the spirit? That seemed to contradict the gospel of realism he had preached and practised these many years. What was to become of his constant insistence that one must keep both feet on the ground even as he gazed heaven-ward? Socialistically minded critics escaped this perplexity by interpreting Nazarín as the Christ of a new social tendency, and as such they deemed him Galdós' sublimest and most grandiose character. On the other hand, a few religiously inclined re-viewers forgot the anathemas they had once hurled at the author and spoke sentimentally of the story as a sort of object lesson in Christian charity and faith. They applauded *Nazarín* as evidence that modern society, reacting against science, was returning to the Gospel, and they urged everyone interested in Christian love to read it both for profit and for pleasure.

The religious note of some of the reviews inevitably aroused the ire of those who contended that science and technology had created the best of all possible worlds, and they directly pre-dicted a cataclysmic upheaval if society were to guide itself by Nazarín's vagaries. Less hesitant than Galdós, the positivistic critics characterized Nazarín as an extravagant, almost demented simpleton. To them he was not a symbol of Christian virtues, and most assuredly not a martyr. His endeavor to cure society with antiquated remedies merely showed that he was a fool. Could he have found nothing more useful to do than wander out on the dusty highway? It was regrettable, ruefully con-cluded the materialists, that Galdós should have chosen to introduce a false mystic note in some of his recent writings and thus create the misleading impression that he was reflecting the dominant theme of the best contemporary Russian works.

The critics naturally did not know that, whatever the theme of *Nazarín,* it was to be fully developed in the next novel, *Halma* (1895). When they did discover this, their pride compelled them to apply to *Halma* the criteria and concepts they had established none too confidently for its predecessor. Due notice was taken of the shift of scene from the lowest to the upper reaches of society. Some were disappointed at Galdós' apparent conception of mysticism as a whim and not as the lyrical expression of the human desire for perfection. Whether he knew it or not, ran the argument, he was the best Spanish exponent of modern mysticism, although, lacking lyrical exuberance, he drew his inspiration from north-European influences. And neither was he original in preaching the gospel that spiritual happiness was to be found in the peaceful life of the country. The doctrine of the return to nature had been gaining vogue for some years on the Continent, and in Spain Pereda had anticipated Galdós by approximately a year in his *Peñas Arriba*.

It is not easy to explain why Galdós resented any hint of foreign influence. In his preface to Pereda's *El sabor de la Tierruca* (1882) he had blandly brushed aside the penetration of French naturalism into Spain with the observation that native traditional realism had nothing to learn from foreign theorists or practitioners. Again in 1894 he had speciously established different types of symbolism in an attempt to refute the charge that *Los condenados* aimed to transplant Ibsenism to the Spanish stage. Was Galdós addicted to the very brand of provincial patriotism he decried in his fellow Spaniards, or was he jealous of his reputation for philosophic as well as artistic originality? It was probably the latter, and this attitude, which at times bordered on vanity and arrogance, was no doubt encouraged by friends and critics who constantly spoke of his vision, wisdom, and talents as of something divine in origin.

In any event, he took offense at the discussion of possible Russian influence in *Nazarín*. It irked him to be coupled with Tolstoy, and the subtle distinctions made between Slavic and Spanish mysticism irritated him. He thought the matter was of sufficient importance to take cognizance of it. Moreover, he was strongly tempted to reprimand the critics of his recent novels as he had berated the reviewers of his dramas, but the unpleasant experience with the prologue of *Los condenados* the year before unquestionably deterred him. Yet he did not desist altogether.

In *Halma* Galdós converted Nazarín into a topic of universal discussion which divided people into *nazaristas* and anti-*nazaristas*. The ideal of this extraordinary character was creating with ominous rapidity a new spiritual movement—*nazarismo*—the Spanish offspring of *rusianismo*. When Nazarín was asked to reveal the source of his inspiration, he denied any first-hand

knowledge of Russian literature and expressed the conviction
that human sentiments and ideals recognized neither geographic
nor racial boundaries. In this he was supported by Manuel
Flórez, a conscientious cleric with aristocratic contacts. Regarding
the possible relationship between Nazarín and the Russian
mystics, Flórez, speaking for the author, replied with obvious
impatience to journalists who insisted on russifying Nazarín:

> Let each one think whatever he pleases about this un-
> fortunate Nazarín. But it could occur only to the
> devil to seek in Russia of all places the filiation of this
> man's ideas. You have asserted that he is a mystic.
> Very well. But why bring from so great a distance
> something native to our household, something we
> have in our soil, in the air and in our speech? Why,
> gentlemen, must we import from foreign lands abne-
> gation, love of poverty, patience, sacrifice, the urge
> to be no one—all natural fruits of this land as is shown
> in our history and literature, with which you must be
> acquainted? Import mysticism when we have enough
> of this commodity to supply the whole world! Do not
> be so light of judgment and learn to know the place
> where you live and inform yourselves about your lin-
> eage. It is as if we Castilians were to go to the banks of
> the Don for chickpeas, or the Andalusians to China
> for olives. Remember that you are in the land of
> mysticism, that we breathe it, eat it, that we carry it
> in every globule of our blood, and that we are mystics
> with all our energy, and that we comport ourselves
> as such without knowing it. Do not travel so far to
> investigate Nazarín's filiation, for very clearly it is
> here in our own midst, in the land of saintliness and
> chivalry, two things which are so similar and which
> perhaps are only one and the same thing, for here—
> don't laugh now—you might call a mystic the poli-
> tician who ventures out into the unknown, dreaming
> about the perfection of the laws; you might call a
> mystic the soldier whose only desire is to fight and

who fights without food; you might call a mystic the
priest who sacrifices everything for his spiritual
ministry; you might call a mystic the starving school-
master who instructs children; you might call mystics
and cavaliers the farmhand, the seaman, the me-
chanic, and even you who wander over the fields of
ideas, worshipping a Dulcinea who does not exist, or
looking for a beyond which you do not find because
you have fallen into the strange aberration of being
mystics without being religious.[3]

Galdós was not content to limit his reply to the all-important
issue raised by the critics. Seeing a splendid opportunity to ridicule the superficialities and inanities of most Spanish literary
criticism, he staged the following conversation between two
journalists who had interviewed Nazarín and a writer who had
not yet seen him:

"Do you know whether he has read a slender volume
that bears his name and is circulating hereabouts?"
"He has read it," replied one of those who came
with Flórez, "and he says that the author, moved
by the desire to fictionalize facts, ennobles him unduly, praising undeservedly ordinary actions that are
not in the category of heroism, not even of extraordinary virtue."
"I was assured by him that he does not recognize
himself in the humanitarian hero of Villamanta,
that he regards himself as a very ordinary man, certainly not as a poematic or novelistic personage."
"And he also says that in his tussle with the gangsters
in the Móstoles prison it was easier for him to curb
his wrath than the book says, that he curbed it at once
and with only a moderate effort."[4]

An aristocratic gentlemen who overhears this bit of critical
analysis advances the opinion that the novel about Nazarín is
a fabric of lies. A relative of Don Pedro de Belmonte—one of
the more important characters—he can guarantee that the author

has falsified him beyond recognition. The journalists admit
this damaging testimony, but in order to exhaust all possible
evidence they solicit the opinion of Andara, Nazarín's prosti-
tute-disciple. Asked whether she has read *Nazarín,* she expresses
her literary reaction thus:

> "They read it to me," replied the prisoner, "because
> black print and I don't get along very well. My, what
> whoppers! If I was you, I'd put it in the papers that
> the writer of this book is a liar, and I'd show him up
> so he'd beat it to some other place with his tall
> tales. The nerve of him to say that I set the house on
> fire!" [5]

Galdós' irony could not have escaped the pedestrian critics,
for the allusions to their unimaginative approach and lack of
pentration were not even delicately veiled. That they did not
choose to defend themselves with the same weapons with which
they had counterattacked on the occasion of the prologue to
Los condenados only testifies to the prevailing conviction that
the rift between Galdós and the "kids of the press" was too wide
to effect a literary *modus vivendi.* Nothing would have been
gained by prolonging a dispute in which one side was not likely
to listen to compromise. As in the drama but for different reasons,
Galdós was resolved to pursue in the novel esthetic and philosophic aims growing out of his artistic concepts and his particular
powers of perception. Neither censure nor praise could distract
him from his objective of portraying faithfully and sincerely
the ebb and flow of Spanish life. At the moment he was especially
interested in the eternal mainsprings of human action, the
spiritual forces that determine outward behavior, and with
these he would deal as long as his vision remained fixed in that
direction. Now as before he was imbued with the spirit of a
missionary and the zeal of a reformer. The road before him
stretched endless and was beset with obstacles, but he had the
will, the energy, and the self-confidence to travel it alone and
without any thought of reaching a specific goal at once.

That is not to say Galdós accepted the tenet of art for art's
sake, for he never ignored his right to adequate remuneration.

While it is manifestly unjust to say that money was his chief objective, he may have created that impression by his great concern over the sale of his books. Schemes for their circulation in Spain and in translation abroad consumed a good part of his energy. His friends shared his conviction that a nation owes recognition to its great men during their lifetime, and their frequent references to the niggardly Spanish appreciation were calculated to prod the public into buying his works. For the *Episodios nacionales* it was not necessary to resort to unusual pressure, since they enjoyed gratifying and steady sales, but the reduced clientele of the contemporary series needed a stimulus. Clarín in public and Palacio Valdés in private warned Galdós that the bulkiness of his novels, his addiction to a densely detailed canvas, granted it would eventually earn for them a place among the literary masters, did also limit his reading public.

But the gradual decline of Galdós' income certainly did not amount to the difference between poverty and affluence. It was only his growing need for funds that made the drop in his revenues seem so great. By the prevailing Spanish standards he should have been able to live without financial worry. It is ironical that the author who criticized the economic ineptitude of some of his characters should so often have resorted to their devious machinations to extricate himself from financial entanglements. Here is at least one respect in which Balzac and Galdós stand on common ground. The numerous business documents he saw fit to preserve suggest that Galdós derived from his personal experience ample knowledge for the treatment of intricate financial situations in his works. Whenever the problem loomed large in his thoughts, he was wont to cover the margins of his manuscript pages with patterns of figures representing the four basic arithmetical operations.

Advancing age did not simplify Galdós' budgetary difficulties. On the contrary, he found it increasingly costly to live a life which in some respects fell into fictional rather than practical patterns. His emergence as a dramatist aggravated his problem by disrupting his routine of work, and his newly won popularity multiplied the opportunities to indulge his temperament and raised the price correspondingly.

In 1896 Galdós' economic situation became sufficiently serious to require immediate action. He gave thought to the possibilities of a dramatic tour, despite the fact that his occasional visits to provincial cities with companies staging his plays had proved neither profitable nor inspiring. The relative success of *Doña Perfecta* encouraged him to believe that a tour of the principal provincial capitals might be worth his while.

He left Madrid in March and spent several months on the road. His itinerary included Valencia, Alicante, Zaragoza, Barcelona, Valladolid, Oviedo, Bilbao, and Santander, and his repertory consisted of all he had staged thus far, except *Gerona*. His ill-starred *Los condenados* was given at the Teatro Lírico in Barcelona. The Catalans received it more favorably than the Madrilenians had done in 1894—perhaps out of a desire to demonstrate their superior esthetic sensibility. A brilliant serenade tendered the author by the city council shortly before the performance undoubtedly created a propitious atmosphere. At Valencia *Doña Perfecta* was staged without untoward incidents, and the author was invited to return after his stop at Alicante for an appropriate welcome. The municipal government and the Atheneum organized a popular festival in his honor in the famous Albufera district.

The climax of the tour came in Oviedo, where *La loca de la casa* was played. Very fittingly the native city of Clarín—the critic with whom Galdós was a veritable passion—received the new Spanish dramatist with a great show of splendor and ceremony. Clarín exerted himself to make the event memorable. He himself had experienced the tribulations of a Spanish novelist turned dramatist; only a little more than a year earlier his dramatic début with *Teresa* had been an abysmal failure despite the staunch support of Galdós and Echegaray. Galdós' success, even though only partial, therefore merited the highest recognition. A great banquet in Galdós' honor was attended by the president of the local university, the civil governor of the province, and the rising liberal politician Melquiades Alvarez. The entire population joined enthusiastically in the provincial apotheosis of the national playwright.

The pleasant memories of the tour were soon dissipated by the realities which disturb the peace of an impecunious and impractical writer. The music, the speeches, and even the sumptuous Oviedo banquet were a sturdy prop for one's reputation, but they could not be offered as legal tender to creditors, usurers, and an assortment of clamoring extortionists. The Bank of Spain would not even admit such assets as collateral. Now that Madrina was dead, the burden of maintaining San Quintín, the Santander chalet, seemed excessively heavy. Why should he be in such a predicament, Galdós wondered. On his tour he had gathered the impression that his works enjoyed a gratifying vogue, especially the *episodios*, and that with better management they could sell in even greater quantities. In Latin America, too, he had numerous readers. The unsolicited letters from admirers in every walk of life across the Atlantic bespoke a following that was almost a new cult. Where, then, lay the cause of his virtual bankruptcy? Could it be that his publisher and manager, Miguel H. de la Cámara, was inefficient or dishonest, or both?

Miguel H. de la Cámara and Benito Pérez Galdós had been associated in something like a partnership ever since 1873. Don Miguel was then the publisher of *La Guirnalda*, a none too literary family journal. He and his magazine began to prosper after he had arranged with Galdós for the publication of his historical novels and any other works he should produce. They became partners, sharing the expense of the machinery and the maintenance of the plant. Don Miguel was industrious and efficient, Don Benito prolific and alert; the business flourished. The income was so regular that the profits could be figured in advance with fair accuracy.

Apprised of this, Galdós soon began to live on borrowed revenue. In due course Miguel H. de la Cámara became critical of his partner's practice, at first because it violated sound business principles and eventually because red began to predominate in the sections of the ledgers devoted to Don Benito's accounts. Galdós reacted in kind; he in turn became critical of Don Miguel's business acumen and managerial skill. He even became suspicious of his proficiency in arithmetic.

In the early nineties the strained relations between the partners were rapidly reaching the breaking point. But an exceedingly delicate matter which embarrassed Don Miguel more than it did Don Benito averted a rupture for a while. If only he could have a father-to-son talk with the novelist he could show him that it was a certain form of personal indulgence that was upsetting his budget and making him dissatisfied with the progress of his business enterprise! But Don Miguel was not one to intrude upon the private life of any person, much less Don Benito's. With the same pious respect as the writer's family and friends, he ignored Galdós' private pleasures, which were often the by-product of his inquiries into the life and nature of certain elements of the Madrid population.

Sensing the strength of his position, Galdós pressed his case with the publisher and quarreled long and loud with him. Apparently callous to Don Miguel's delicacy, he interpreted his opposition to a private settlement as a consciousness of guilt and began to take his friends into his confidence regarding the situation. Among these was Don Antonio Maura, the distinguished jurist and politician. Don Antonio advised that the litigation be taken to court. From the middle of 1896 to the spring of 1897 Galdós suffered a form of retribution for his satirical sins against the legal profession. The seemingly endless hearings, with their heaps of legal papers, lawyers, consultants, notaries, and judges constituted an endless nightmare.

Galdós' fellow litigant, ably defended by a Canarian, Miguel Villalba Hervás—republican deputy from the island of Tenerife—was not disposed to yield. He knew the evidence against him would be invalidated if he chose to explain the delicate reason for his seemingly suspicious bookkeeping. In fact, he refused to produce all the accounts, but when a decision favorable to Galdós was handed down, Don Miguel appealed the case to a higher court. He was willing to protect the private reputation of Spain's great public figure but not to be penalized for it. It soon became evident that the litigation was less clear-cut than it had first appeared. Galdós was not an innocent victim, nor was Don Miguel an unscrupulous exploiter.

Many trying days were ahead, with ever-mounting costs. The litigants began to weary of the proceedings and the legal fees. Don Antonio Maura counseled Galdós to offer arbitration, and his partner gladly accepted the offer. Don Gumersindo de Azcárate, famous professor and jurist, was named chairman of the board of arbitration, and Manuel Marañón was appointed legal administrator pending a final decision. The publishing business, of which Galdós was given exclusive control within certain stated limits, was established in new quarters on the ground floor of Hortaleza, 132. The arrangement promised to be favorable to the novelist.

In October, 1897, the arbitrators announced their decision. Both Galdós and Miguel H. de la Cámara heaved a heavy sigh of relief—probably for the same unutterable reason. Each felt that he had won a victory: Don Benito a legal one and Don Miguel a moral one. Galdós retained all the rights to his works, and this he considered a distinct triumph. Of the more than one hundred thousand volumes in stock each partner was adjudged one-half. The rights of reissue were exclusively the author's, but he could not reprint the titles awarded to his partner without first buying out his share at the market price minus the normal commercial discount. Against this, Don Miguel could not sell any of his stock to the trade. Thus far all the advantages were on Galdós' side. But he lost his share of the original investment, and was also directed to pay his partner eighty-two thousand pesetas in cash, the approximate amount he had drawn against his unearned revenue. The exact sum could not be clearly established on the basis of the records Don Miguel was willing to supply, but Galdós deemed it prudent not to press him for more exact documents.

When the litigation was over, Galdós felt the relief of a child who has barely escaped being denounced to his parents for a serious breach of domestic discipline. So sweet was his hollow victory that for a while he failed to realize that his new cash obligations aggravated the very cause which had produced

his legal involvement. Yet the prospect of financial comfort
filled him with courage and enthusiasm, and he took steps to
become his own publisher. He transferred his studio temporarily
to Hortaleza, 132, and this combination of business office, den,
and warehouse became a beehive of activity. Friends were exceedingly helpful, and fellow Canarians rejoiced that at last
their illustrious compatriot would be more easily accessible than
in his home with other members of the family.

While the slogan of the new undertaking was "Keep expenses down to a minimum," the initial disbursements were considerable. Some members of the staff were more intriguing than
efficient. The office boy was a youth who might have rightfully
called his employer father had he not been born under circumstances which had long been shrouded in the utmost secrecy.
Although few interested Madrilenians remained for long ignorant of Galdós' new headquarters, it was deemed fitting to exhibit
a sign, shield, or marker calling attention to the location of
one of the capital's most interesting cultural centers. Arturo
Mélida, who had collaborated on the illustrated edition of the
Episodios nacionales, designed an artistic sign—*"Obras de Pérez
Galdós"* in gold letters on a black background. A skilled carpenter made an exorbitant bid, which was promptly rejected.
Had Galdós been less busy he would have built the sign himself. But Don Galo Cuervo, the high-priced carpenter, admired
Galdós more than he craved his money, and he offered to do
the job as a token of his profound esteem. Galdós' bookkeeper
was thus spared the annoyance of charging one more item to
current expenses.

And it was well that the staff had as few distractions as possible. The essential details entailed in the launching of the
enterprise consumed the time and energy of everyone associated
with it. The volume of correspondence was large, although
Galdós personally attended to a good share of it. Now was the
time to turn to advantage the numerous contacts he had made in
his extensive travels. He solicited the patronage of friends in
the provinces and tempted bookstores with attractive terms.
There were many anonymous business-minded admirers who

volunteered to aid Galdós in his great cultural endeavor. For example, why could not a traveling commissioner handling the best native table water add to his line the works of the illustrious author of the *Episodios nacionales?* Next to economy, publisher Pérez Galdós adhered to the policy of wasting no opportunities. All offers of collaboration were duly investigated.

An occasional glance at the records revealed promise of success. The first year's sales were three times what they had been in the past. Nevertheless, because of the heavy cash obligations dictated by the settlement, the debit column still almost dwarfed the credit column. If *Obras de Pérez Galdós* could only take on another line of merchandise, like some of its salesmen! But the Department of Internal Revenue ruled that the house must limit its output to what the board of arbitration had prescribed. Publisher Pérez Galdós was beginning to question the wisdom of his litigation with Don Miguel H. de la Cámara. Had he not been better off during the partnership, when he had usually succeeded in persuading his associate to rescue him from embarrassment? Economic freedom seemed now more than ever a mirage created and sustained by moneylenders. His own Torquemada was a model of Christian charity as compared with his kin in real life. To a friend Galdós remarked in a tone of bewilderment: "The more books I sell the less money I earn. I am going down in history as the only publisher who ruined himself by selling many editions." [6]

It is one of the interesting facts of Galdós' career that he wrote two of his best works precisely when he was most distraught mentally and spiritually. It may be that his superior achievement is directly traceable to his very inquietude. There are personal notes in *Misericordia* and *El abuelo* which deserve comment.

In *Misericordia* Galdós not only continued his quest for human salvation in an age beset by skepticism and disillusionment, but he also injected his personal sentiments into the portrayal of poverty and destitution in Spain's capital. In the fantastic schemes invented by Benina to keep her mistress economically afloat there is a clear reflection of Don Benito's own peregrinations among usurers and his efforts to prevent the bankruptcy of his respectability. This is not to say that *Miseri-cordia* was planned as an autobiographical novel, but it does suggest that the theme and the characters—many of whom were drawn from life—gained in sharpness, vitality, and intimacy as a result of his own emotional disturbances during the creative process.

This is particularly the case with *El abuelo*. Its remote resemblance to *King Lear* was promptly noticed, and it is undeniable. For some time before its appearance the press had carried hints of Galdós' intention to write a Spanish adaptation of this work. It would thus be idle to deny the evidence of Shakespearean influence. But other characteristics are equally noteworthy. It can escape no one that there is more symbolism than in most of Galdós' works. It is clearly a novel of reflection rather than observation. Even the settings, despite their minuteness of detail, are more definitely a product of the imagination than the almost photographic descriptions that are characteristic of Galdós.

In *El abuelo* Galdós transmuted and fused into an artistic whole fragments of striking personalities in his own family, bits of moral preoccupations of long standing, shreds of recent emotions, and an assortment of crowding and persistent memories. No one has to be reminded that unconventional sex relations is a recurrent element in his works and that Don Juanism appears very frequently, although at times only ironically. These interests go deeper than the desire to portray a Spanish social phenomenon or to indulge in a venerable literary convention. For Galdós the problem of sex was woven into the fabric of his personality. It had begun very early in his childhood with symptoms which not even his mother took seriously. During his adolescence it settled in his subconscious and was fed by the disturbing arrival of Adriana Tate and her illegitimate daughter and by the collapse of the idolized character of his uncle José María after his reprehensible behavior in Cuba had become public knowledge. For several years Galdós witnessed and unconsciously participated in a stirring family drama whose principal actors were stern Mama Dolores, proud José María Galdós, generous José Hermenegildo Hurtado de Mendoza y Tate, scornful and domineering Madrina, and defiant Adriana Tate. Precipitating the conflict and herself drawn into it was pathetic little Sisita. The violent solution forced by Mama Dolores, which caused a rift in the family, wrought havoc with Benito's emotions—havoc which time did not soon repair.

It was a shattering experience, which profoundly influenced Galdós' affective processes and ultimately his treatment of love. In his personal life, and vicariously in that of his characters, he was always the prey of a relentless obsession, a persistent subconscious demand. His occasional mild disapproval of the illicit relations of his imaginary creatures is only a brave attempt at self-exculpation. The visit to Las Palmas in 1894 was naturally a grand opportunity to renew family associations and reconstruct earlier scenes and incidents. It is conceivable that the most stirring events of his early years—the drama revolving around Sisita— was at the center of his reminiscences. The episodes which in his youth were only a procession of more or less related details in the life of the family now arranged themselves in a clear pattern of spiritual significance. The members of his family came to symbolize a variety of attitudes toward an important human value— the essence of character and the nature of personal worth. For Mama Dolores human worth was determined by purity of blood, and her belief was indestructible because it had the intensity of an instinct. Everyone else, guided by compassion and generosity, placed nobility of character above all other considerations and certainly above the accident of birth.

Did it really matter that Sisita had come into the world without the sanction of law and religion? The question was more than a retrospective reflection. Not so very long before he had become the father of a baby girl. Her mother was an attractive, talented woman. Thus, though he had failed to emulate the legal career of his uncle, he had unwittingly been imitating him in other ways. But he had no intention of being responsible for another Sisita tragedy. Legitimacy was not necessarily a legal or social concept; it was rather a manifestation of the individual

conscience. On this particular score Benito Pérez Galdós was resolved not to go through life with an easy conscience.

The train of reflections these incidents set in motion was not
halted by his quarrel with Miguel H. de la Cámara. Galdós
must have been frequently reminded of the central cause of his
economic plight. In his office he observed that some of his closest
friends seemed embarrassed in the presence of Francisco
Menéndez, his handy clerk. What was there about this youth
that caused people to scrutinize his face so closely? Vague bits
of gossip about the boy's origin came floating toward him from
time to time. Somehow it did not occur to Galdós that the stares
and whispers were meant to remind him that Paco was more than
an office boy to him. He interpreted them as veiled hints at the
boy's illegitimate birth, a fact with which he was hazily
acquainted. But what did that matter? He was very fond of Paco
and he repeatedly remarked that the boy would not have been
more honest, discreet, intelligent, and industrious if his parents
had received the traditional approval of the law and religion.

This was approximately the background of the genesis of *El
abuelo*. It is relatively easy to identify its persons, places, and
incidents in the author's own experiences. The protagonist, the
Shakespearean Count Albrit, is in part a composite of Mama
Dolores and Uncle José María. The heroine, Lucrecia, is a
transmutation of Adriana Tate and Madrina; like Mama Tate
she is half American. The return of the old Count from Spanish
America in search of an answer to the great question—the identity
of his legitimate grandchild—may have been suggested by the
return of brother-in-law José Hermenegildo to Las Palmas
from Cuba. Much of Don José Hermenegildo's ethical refinement can be identified in the superbly pathetic Don Pío. And
Dolly, the illegitimate grandchild who reveals to the tormented
Count a more noble truth than he had looked for—the meaning of love—is obviously Galdós' newest incarnation of Sisita,
whose spirit hovered over him, sometimes clearly and sometimes hazily, more than once during the creation of young
feminine characters. The settings, despite the author's admonition not to seek their identity in reality, reproduce elements of

the landscape of the Canary Islands. Surely the Galdós survivors in Las Palmas realize that the Count's La Pardina was modeled on their own mountain estate of La Montaña de los Lirios.

El abuelo, cut down to stage proportions, was the play which Galdós hoped to produce abroad as a prelude to his return to the Spanish theater. No doubt the unstinted praise with which the novel was received in 1897 greatly influenced his decision, although his intimate attachment to the theme and principal characters must not be underestimated. Despite the fact that personally he never shared the protagonist's preoccupation with the identity of his grandchild, he rejoiced with him in his ultimate discovery that love is more precious than family honor. With the aged, half-blind Count Albrit he shared the joy of spiritual purification. Illegitimate Dolly taught her grandfather the lofty, universal, and eternal lesson. The tender, generous, thoughtful little girl deserved all the affection that could be bestowed upon her. As he turned the pages of *El abuelo* during the preparation of the stage version, Galdós recorded a delicately subjective commentary on his latest work. In the margin of one of its pages he jotted down his own daughter's name and the date of her birth.

*   *   *   *

Both *Misericordia* and *El abuelo* were literary successes, but neither contributed much to the author's solvency. It was no doubt exhilarating to hear his name coupled so frequently with Shakespeare, the Count of Albrit identified with King Lear, and Dolly related to Cordelia, but those who profited concretely from such pronouncements were the publishers of the *Biblioteca clásica.* Something like a run on the volume containing *King Lear* was created by readers who wished to make their own comparison of Shakespeare and Galdós. And even though the comparison resulted in added glory for the creator of *El abuelo,* there still remained the problem of converting *Obras de Pérez Galdós* into something more than gold letters artistically carved on a black shield. Where lay the solution?

A little more than twenty years back Galdós had solemnly promised his readers that he would never again take up his pen

to write historical novels. It was perhaps a rash promise, for the
episodios were a dependable source of income. How would the
public react now if he were to announce his intention to resume
historical fiction? At the time he had taken leave of his readers
he assigned two principal reasons for his step: first, that the persons and events connected with the period following the death
of Ferdinand VII were too contemporary to be treated with
proper objectivity; second, that he suspected the public of being
weary, having followed him through a series of twenty novels.

In 1897—and in the light of his pressing financial needs—it
seemed to Galdós that these objections might be dismissed. There
was still the difficulty of historical perspective, but he felt he
could surmount it. The second scruple had certainly lost its
validity. A new generation of readers had grown up, who needed
spiritual stimulus even more than their predecessors. The regeneration of the national conscience, which he had undertaken in
1873, was still incomplete. The spiritual restlessness of the
decade was very acute in Spain.

Galdós was genuinely disturbed by the wave of skepticism
and apathy that was converting Spaniards into devitalized pessi-
mists whose sole manifestation of energy was verbal. He saw
no real justification for the widespread despondency, eventually
accentuated by the country's defeat in the Spanish-American War.
The spirit of Spain was threatened with paralysis, and its soul
with asphyxiation. He was an optimist, and almost un-Spanish
in his refusal to exaggerate the horrors of defeat. The courage
and spiritual resiliency with which he had met his own personal
problems he meant to instill in his fellow men. Like Gracián he
lamented the Spanish tendency "to make trophies out of their
own misery." Deeply grieved though he was by the disaster of
the war, because he saw in it additional evidence of the nation's
incapacity to discover its own source of vitality, he had no
sympathy with those who were soon to constitute the ghost-
generation of 1898 and who acted as if Spain had lost an all-
important battle.

Just as many of the young generation merged their personal
frustration with the national failure, so Galdós saw a splendid

opportunity for combining his own solvency with the salvation of the nation. It would be difficult to state which consideration was uppermost. He consulted friends, and they all encouraged him enthusiastically. With his exceptional ability to reconstruct past events critically and analytically, he could so present the immediate past as to explain the present and offer a glimpse into the future. In recent years he had perhaps erred in using palpable reality only as a backdrop for an all-absorbing interest in the human conscience, but he could now make amends. Galdós was easily persuaded to shoulder the burden of a double mission— personal and national—and with his characteristic energy he began the preparation of the third series of *Episodios nacionales*.

Quite appropriately, the new series opened with a volume about the famous Carlist military leader, Tomás Zumalacárregui. To obtain documentation about this and other important actors in the first Carlist War Galdós made an extended tour of Guipúzcoa, Vizcaya, and Navarra. In Cegama he met Miguel Zumalacárregui, a priest nephew of the warrior, who aided him in his research. It was a pleasant and instructive meeting, although before departing Galdós was obliged by the custom of the land to drink a glass of white wine, in violation of his normal habits. His itinerary included Azpeitia, birthplace of his maternal grandfather. Unfortunately he arrived too late to make the acquaintance of several distant relatives who had either died a few years before or had left for Cuba and adjacent islands. The last Galdós, a Bernardine or Dominican nun, had been dead some eight years. On the testimony of one of her associates, Mother Ignacia Galdós was a real saint. And lest the proprietress of the Arteche Inn consider him unworthy of his lineage—he had not been seen at mass during his stay—he informed her on the second morning of his visit that he would that day make a pilgrimage on foot to the Loyola Sanctuary to fortify his soul. This he did, and thus brought to a close his tour of Azpeitia and Azcoitia. From the latter place he left for Madrid via Bilbao and Santander, and arrived home on Friday, March 18, 1898.

Galdós quickly recaptured his stride in the *Episodios nacionales*, and the motives behind their resumption stimulated him constantly. He revived his old technique, but with it returned some of his difficulties. Twenty years of unhampered wandering in pure fiction did not make it any easier for him now to maintain a proper balance between fact and fancy, or to fit dates and historical events into the purely imaginative portions of the novel. But the job had to be done, and Galdós was not one to be discouraged.

The series progressed with clocklike regularity. This was essential if he wished to recapture and hold his audience. Like its predecessors, the new series was in reality a dignified serial novel in ten lengthy installments, with even greater emphasis on the element of suspense than before. In the seventies Galdós had frowned upon the *novela por entregas* (serial story), but now he resorted to some of its proven devices with a fairly easy conscience. In little more than two years he completed the third series. Three volumes appeared in 1898, four the following year, and three in 1900. He was not to match this rate of productivity again. The fourth series opened in 1902 with *Las tormentas del 48* and was completed in 1907 with *La de los tristes destinos*. The banner year this time was 1904, when three volumes were published. The last series of six novels appeared between 1908 and 1912 and was written more intermittently than any of the others.

Galdós virtually ended his career as a novelist in 1912. To be sure, *La razón de la sinrazón* did not come out until 1915, but it is a work of an indeterminate literary category—the author called it a "theatrical fable." Nevertheless his creative days were not entirely over. In 1912 he was sixty-nine years old, infirm and virtually blind, yet he managed to produce five plays before his death, the last one in 1918.

*   *   *   *

Galdós' resurgence as an historical novelist rekindled a smoldering fire. His disappearance from the theater after the comparative failure of *La fiera* (1896) and his return to the contemporary novel had given his detractors hope that he had taken their advice and decided to stick to his last. Now the young writers would not have to compete so fiercely with the man who had virtually built up a national literary monopoly. There was not much to fear from any contemporary novels he might write, since, whatever their artistic merit, their concern with spirituality could not have wide popular appeal. But, reflected the apprehensive opposition, the reappearance of the *episodios* was cause for alarm. Their marketability was an established fact, and their continued wide circulation could therefore be taken for granted. In the interests of equal opportunity it behooved all concerned to defend their rights in a struggle which promised to be hard and uneven.

A veritable campaign of obstructionism was launched. A heavy smoke screen was thrown up to conceal the real motive behind it, which was envy. Since it was an era when Spaniards searched their souls for the reasons behind the visible national decline, it was easy enough to obscure personal ambitions with talk of the so-called mission of the Spain-to-come.

The organ of the vociferous new missionaries was *Germinal*, a journal of a decidedly socialist-revolutionary hue, edited by Joaquín Dicenta with the enthusiastic support of the *gente nueva*, self-anointed saviors of the nation. With the notorious talent of revolutionaries for dialectical simplification, the builders of the new Spain blamed their country's ills on the men of the Revolution of 1868—politicians and writers alike. In the new order they envisaged there was no room for literature unless it throbbed with revolution and breathed the spirit of internationalism. Men like Pereda and Galdós were held in more or less contempt for their bourgeois patriotism, and the critics who praised them were nebulously accused of complicity in a reactionary movement. Clarín was scornfully referred to as "His Majesty's Critic." The literature of the *gente vieja*—the men of the generation of 1868 —was derided as small-townish and savoring of the unappetizing national stew. Occasionally some deference was shown Galdós, with rather painful magnanimity, for the sparks he had sporadically drawn in his younger days with his sledge-hammer blows at Spanish clericalism. Yet even he, according to the *gente nueva*, had been tending of late to condone the errors of religion and the manifestations of traditionalism. Alongside Zola, concluded the young zealots, Galdós looked like a clericalist. It would therefore be idle to expect even a modicum of the current spiritual leaven in his new *Episodios nacionales*. The vein from which he had extracted the first two series was completely exhausted, and the resumption of the historical genre at this time was no doubt inspired by the desire to repeat a financial success.

Accustomed to being the center of periodic literary storms, Galdós faced the Vulcans of the new Spanish destiny with dignified silence. This was not the first time that envy or some other human failing had blustered at the gates of his artistic fortress. As far back as 1885 it had been loudly charged in certain quarters that he had entered upon a period of decline. At that time he had made it clear that he regarded his continued productivity in the nature of a mandate from the reading public. "When favor grows faint," he promised, "and when I detect in its immense face [i.e., the public's] signs of frowning or weariness, then I shall permit myself to incline slowly in the direction of obscurity and finally I shall get out of the way completely, always with due respect." [7]

But the time for such retirement had not yet come. Tolosa Latour, who served Galdós as literary scout and spy, observed in 1898 and thereafter that the opposition of the *gente nueva* sprang from sheer envy, and that they had no followers among the public at large. Impartial readers were delighted with the new *episodios* and were indifferent to the flaws in technique or content which the critics discovered. Enjoying the suspense, they rejected the reviewers' objection to the continuation of one or more central figures throughout all or most of the series. The great Echegaray, for example, had reportedly asked in the Fernando Fe bookstore for the second part of *Mendizábal*, so fascinated was he by the adventures of young Fernando Calpena! Wasn't that significant? Other friends also assured Galdós that public reaction was highly favorable, and his ledgers indeed confirmed their assertions.

The opposition did not go unchallenged. Clarín, who had a personal stake in the controversy, returned the enemy's fire point-blank. He replied caustically to those who denounced the lack of significance in the men and events Galdós had chosen for the

evocation of recent Spanish history, and who accused him of re-
tarding Spain's regeneration:

> The trouble is that certain whippersnappers who had
> not discovered Lafuente or *The Lives of Celebrated
> Men* by Quintana until we lost Cuba, now live and
> breathe in Otumba and Pavía, Lepanto and Bailén,
> and they want everything stewing in its own red hot
> blood, and they cannot bear to see that the sun sets
> on our possessions.[8]

Even placid Andrenio felt sufficiently ruffled to direct a pin-
prick or two against the pseudo-critics. "Here where so little is
read," he observed pointedly, "without the intervening stimulus
of scandal or noise, literary notoriety has often been sought by
picking a quarrel with the great writers, by rushing headlong
with iconoclastic fury into those who are at the top, as if the
arrow in its upward flight were calculated to raise high the
archer who shoots it."[9]

Not even Galdós' devotees, however, greeted the revived
episodios with unqualified approbation. For the most part they
found the third series inferior and less impressive than its predecessors. They cited evidences of hasty composition, improper
distribution of the historical and fictional elements, vague evocation of the period under treatment, and the excessive use of
narration rather than dramatization in the presentation of events.
The historical material lacked grandeur and at times even
significance, but this, it was remarked in a spirit of attenuation,
was naturally not the author's fault. Spanish history of recent
decades was unfortunately a drab affair.

Clarín was perhaps the only one who consistently saw white
where others saw black. But his insistence on Galdós' more highly
developed power of observation, his more profound psychological
insight into the structure of the novel, and his superior style did
not offset the impression others sought to convey that by resusci-
tating the *Episodios nacionales* Galdós had not disproved Cervantes' observation concerning the inferiority of second parts. They
pointed, among other things, to Galdós' apparent inability to
reconstruct history with due detachment. In the opinion of

Maeztu, Galdós was no longer the chronicler of liberty, exact
truth, and neo-mysticism, because his eyes were fixed on the
contemporary scene. Instead, he regretfully laid emphasis on material progress—the curse of the modern era.[10]

Some of the younger critics censured Galdós on less serious
scores. His practice of ending a novel in the middle of an important event was interpreted not as a literary exigency but as a
commercial device for arousing interest in the next volume.
There was even objection to the byline indicating the time consumed in the writing of the book. This, chorused the literary
tyros, had all the earmarks of senile vanity—as if taunting youth's
sterility by contrast with the fertility of old age.

In fact, it was Galdós' fertility that was the real thorn in the
side of the self-styled generators of the new literary and spiritual
dynamism, as some of his supporters well knew. In 1903 the
reissue of *Napoleón en Chamartín* (the fifth volume of the first
series) brought its total circulation up to 38,000—a tremendous
record for Spain. The event offered an opportunity to chastise the
opposition:

> They have placed on sale the thirty-eighth thousand
> of *Napoleón en Chamartín,* a famous novel by Galdós,
> that bore who is scorned by the esthetes who are going
> to hold forth, or rather to stretch their weary limbs
> before the public of the Atheneum.
>
> Well, well, gentlemen esthetes! When you get to
> put out 38,000 copies of any of your works, then we'll
> get together and talk about it. In the meantime, be
> content to appear modestly on the stalls of second-
> hand books with the well-known sign: "50 céntimos
> a volume." [11]

In 1903 Galdós' camp followers were still able to defy the
enemy unequivocally. His temporary apotheosis as a result of the
tremendous success of *Electra* in 1901 had made his position all
but impregnable. For a while even the youth of Spain recognized
that Galdós was destined to lead the nation along the vaguely
marked paths of regeneration. There was scattered dissent—in
conservative ranks it was unanimous—but prudence dictated that

it be not too loudly expressed. Momentarily Galdós was virtually the monarch of the spiritual domains of Spain, and in the minds of some he even had power to annex its political dominions. *El País,* organ of the die-hard antimonarchists, took Galdós into its bosom and smothered him with caresses. The author of the *Episodios nacionales* and of dramas dealing with human redemption was converted into a symbol of republicanism, anticlericalism, and progressivism. His mission was identified with the destiny of Spain—the establishment of a republic. But since the promised redemption was no nearer realization after *Electra* than before, disaffection began to spread, and desertions became frequent, especially as *galdosismo* acquired an increasingly republican tinge.

It may well be that these desertions were offset by the heavy republican replacements, so that the score remained unchanged so far as Galdós' popularity was concerned. This gave him fresh encouragement to pursue the new course he had set for himself in the novel in 1898 and in the drama in 1901. If he occasionally swerved, he did so because the winds were blowing ever stronger from the direction of the republican encampment. He found himself veering almost unconsciously toward a political planet of vague contours. And as he was nearing it, the intermittent murmurs of his conscience were barely audible amidst the ever-louder calls of the republican sirens. There were moments, however, when it occurred to him that he had better turn around and go back to the placid regions of literature.

In 1905 Galdós announced that with the publication of two more historical novels—*La vuelta al mundo en la Numancia* and *Prim*—he would abandon the genre forever. The strain of research and the haste of composition were beginning to tax his body and mind, and the joy of creation no longer possessed him. Besides, he had several contemporary novels in mind, on which he was anxious to begin work. But he was expressing a vaguely formulated desire rather than a stout resolution. By this time he had ceased to be a free agent, as it were. The air of Spain was heavy with pessimism, recrimination, and spiritual confusion. It was no time for philosophic retirement.

When 1906 came, Galdós broke his promise without serious qualms of conscience. In the *episodios* he had reached the period of the impending downfall of Isabel II and the significant events that ensued. There was so much in the national scene of those days that might serve to illuminate the dark horizons of the contemporary mind. He could not, in conscience clear, stop so abruptly. In 1901 and 1902 he had made frequent trips to Paris, where his boyhood friend, Ambassador Fernando León y Castillo, piloted him through the busy lanes of the commercial literary traffic and secured for him several delightful audiences with the exiled queen. There was so much he wished to say about the deposed monarch to dispel the erroneous notions about her character and personality that were current.

Three more historical novels appeared in 1906 and 1907. Galdós' rate of productivity was now considerably slower. His formal association with antimonarchical politics was absorbing much of his time and energy. He was a co-worker in a great cause, and the atmosphere of the political arena enveloped him and extended to his literary creations. Charges and accusations of bias swirled about his head. His own artistic conscience also dared raise its voice against a partisanship which was actually neither sincere nor deep-seated. What had tempted him into an activity that promised only disillusionment? Was he perhaps merging his personal ambitions with national aspirations? Was he propping up his literary reputation with political supports? In 1908 Galdós made another announcement—the third since 1879—that *España trágica*, the second volume of the fifth series, would be the last of the *episodios*.

And for a year and a half it did seem as though Galdós meant it. However, his freedom of action was now more restricted than ever. His cause had a firmer grip on him than he knew—and the cause, let it be understood, was not purely political. The country's salvation was somehow inextricably entangled in the solvency of the venerable debt-laden novelist-dramatist. The prospect of the discontinuance of the *Episodios nacionales* almost threw panic into the battling republican camp. Without them its banner would be deprived of an alluring emblem.

The "public" expressed its disappointment in shrewd but none too subtle terms. *España trágica* was the object of flattery which only the politically blind could have regarded as oblique. Once again Galdós was pronounced the only worthy continuator of the classical novel, and the artistic merit of this work so great as to secure the author's reputation forever. For the politically tinged critics Galdós had now arrived in two senses. Let no one question any longer, they admonished, the political stature of Galdós, and let no one cast doubt on his ability to make the reader feel and think—an achievement totally absent from the *marionette* works which filled the younger writers with enthusiasm.[12]

Tactfully silent on the third breach of promise, Galdós yielded to the insistent demands of the "public," whose ranks were swelled by the recent fusion of republicans and socialists. The politicians fused their doctrines and platforms for expediency; Galdós combined politics and his literary interests for the same reason. The press reviews of the last four historical novels could hardly be termed literary criticism. Galdós' art meant infinitely less to the critics than his ever-growing spirit of revolution and anti-clericalism. His concepts were described as daring and mature, and they were praised as the essence of the new gospel that was destined to rescue Spain from decadence.

As if to reward the author for his handsome contribution to the cause, politically minded reviewers frequently wandered tangentially into the field of drama to denounce the conservative and incompetent critics who stubbornly refused to place a dramatist's crown on Galdós' head. They paid slight attention to the artistic innovations in the last *episodios*. Only the genuine literary critics —if there really were any such where Galdós' works were concerned—pointed out his ever-diminishing interest in the human aspect of persons and events, and his increasing employment of fantasy and the marvelous—all of which gave evidence of his conscious attempt to keep abreast of new artistic modes and moods. To the republican-socialists Galdós' abandonment of artistic spontaneity for conscious artistry meant less than his illusively deepening political faith. But to his sincere admirers the disappearance of his real liberalism, progressivism, and equanimity was cause for grave concern. Even in the interpretation of politics he was preoccupied more with its external phenomena than with its ideas and ideals. Those who did not believe that the united radical front was the road to national regeneration looked upon Galdós' political faith as something puerile and archaic, the credo of a "national episode." [13]

But in the last decade of his life Galdós' personality was beginning to disintegrate. He was no longer the conscious master of his own self. Sickness, poverty, and senility made him a prey of conflicting impulses and aspirations. As the ravaging forces of old age cut deeper into his physical, mental, and spiritual well-being, two obsessions dominated him completely—a craving for money and hunger for applause. The two were very intimately interrelated. Always given to treating critical opinion with a measure of scorn—particularly if it was unfavorable—he tended to ignore it completely in his last years. He preferred to listen to the flattery of those who still spoke of him as the only trustworthy interpreter of Spanish life and as the spiritual guide to the bright horizons of the national future. When the last historical novel, *Cánovas*, appeared in 1912, Galdós regarded his work as far from ended. To complete the fifth series he planned four novels: *Sagasta, Las colonias perdidas, La reina regente,* and *Alfonso XIII*. For the first of these he had already accumulated much documentary material and sketched the outline. But blindness and rapidly failing health defeated his plan.

*   *   *   *

Reclining in his soft armchair, his long legs crossed and outstretched, his clasped hands resting in his lap, blind and introspective, Galdós spent the greater part of his last years in continued meditation and reflection. Past and present, reality and dream, fancy and imagination passed steadily before him. He might have entertained himself recording his own life—which would not have differed much from the books he had written about the lives of others—but he preferred to share his meditations and reflections with his young friends, who occasionally brought him the glow of life and the warmth of the palpitating present. In his intimate conversations with them he

spoke of the ponderable and imponderable values of life, sometimes with complete detachment and again in the spirit of personal revelation. He had neither saved Spain nor achieved
solvency for himself, but he made no apologies. Salvation and
solvency implied the attainment of a goal, the end of a definite
stage, whereas to Galdós life was a perpetual process of ebb and
flow. This philosophic conviction, with other more personal
considerations, he offered as an explanation of his thrice-broken
promise to discontinue the *Episodios nacionales*. In a conversation
with Gregorio Marañón he said:

> On three occasions I thought that I had finished my
> history of Spain. The last one, when my life no longer
> had anything to yield. Always believing that a stage of
> Spanish life had closed. And always compelled to take
> it up again. Because in history the flower of today is
> the root of tomorrow. Because today's life is the same
> that it was in the past and that it will always be. To
> live with a full consciousness of life is nothing more
> than to repeat the yesterday and to dream of the
> morrow.[14]

National salvation and personal solvency were two goals with
which Galdós was preoccupied simultaneously at one stage of his
life. Neither was ever completely attained. Yet Galdós was not
disappointed, for he had enjoyed a full awareness of life. Each
day he relived the many yesterdays and dreamed of the morrows
with their promise of complete salvation and solvency.

XVI

Apotheosis

AT THE TURN OF THE TWENTIETH century Spain was living days of spiritual disorientation. To many the loss of the last remnants of a once great empire was painful proof of national decadence. In the ensuing days of disillusionment there was loud recrimination and severe criticism of past error and folly. Fairly united by the desire for regeneration from within, Spain was nevertheless groping for practical guidance. The break with the immediate past was complete, but the road ahead was not clearly marked. Youth was eager to discover the new national destiny, but it lacked competent leadership. Neither the great intellectual ferment nor the deep spiritual agitation of the day seemed to bring the desired goal nearer. It was all like a wheel spinning in deep mire.

Although physically Galdós belonged to the generation blamed for the sorry state of the nation, spiritually he identified himself with the protesting youth, in whom he saw a reflection of his own spiritual position. What was all this perturbation if not the deep stirring of the new national conscience he had been patiently forging for years? He had not exerted himself in vain, but his work was not quite complete. He had helped to make Spain conscious of her power and eager to use it, but there still remained the task of harnessing the new spiritual energy to a specific objective.

Galdós was convinced that the regeneration of Spain was impossible without the utter destruction of clericalism. In this one force he saw the cause of all the nation's ills. And by clericalism he meant the powerful position of the monastic orders, particu-

346

larly the Jesuits. He held no grievance against religion as such nor the church, nor even the secular clergy, but his hatred of clericalism was an all-consuming passion. He was first appalled by its strength in the early days of the Bourbon restoration, and his fear of it had in part impelled him to write his so-called religious trilogy. During the regency of María Cristina he watched with dismay the growing influence of clericalism and consequent obscurantism, and he gave serious thought to the best means of combating them.

At the turn of the century, when the clerical problem was being discussed in the French parliament, Galdós was seized by the fear of an invasion of Spain by monks and friars expelled from France. Spanish clericalism thus re-enforced would be a greater national catastrophe than the so-called disaster of 1898. It was imperative to avert this danger, by violence if necessary. Here was an outlet for the new spiritual energy. The destruction of clericalism would unite all the forward-looking elements of Spain under a single banner.

As in 1873, and again in 1876, Galdós once more became imbued with a missionary spirit. Something of this sort had in part motivated the resumption of the *episodios,* but he now felt that this was not an effective way of serving the cause. He was eager for more immediate contact with the people, and for this there was nothing better than the drama. When he left the theater in 1896 he had not intended to abandon it forever. The time was now propitious for a return. The historical novels had restored some of his lost prestige, and the very controversial nature of their reception constituted an advantage for his new ambition.

Galdós knew that his reappearance as a dramatist would not pass unnoticed. The theme he had in mind was the conflict between clerical fanaticism and personal freedom. In a sense he had already prepared the public for it by his stress on liberalism in his recent *episodios.* He would thus give plastic expression to the widespread, though somewhat inarticulate, aspiration for a new progressive Spain. He would become the standard-bearer of the forward-looking legions of the nation. It was his duty to assume subtly the leadership of the rising generation, since it was to a measurable extent his spiritual progeny.

Electra was the drama that was to achieve the rebirth of Spain —and incidentally the author's dramatic rehabilitation. For some time Galdós had been slowly elaborating the theme and outlining the plot in his mind. He had even selected the artists for the two principal roles: Fernando Díaz de Mendoza for Máximo, and María Guerrero for Electra. But he had apparently counted without his hosts, for when he finally revealed his plans to these famous actors they merely promised respectfully to think the matter over. Could they risk staging such a daring play, especially in view of the precarious position of their company in the Teatro Español? After months of hesitation they informed the author that they had regretfully decided not to antagonize the respectable season subscribers. Galdós received the reply thoughtfully. He himself had often wondered whether the Spanish public was really ready for the revolutionary drama he was slowly whipping into shape.

Early in the summer of 1900 a fortuitous incident occurred to hasten Galdós' return to the theater. His good friend, the critic-poet Federico Balart, became the artistic director of the Teatro Español with a new company. Don Federico, who was not altogether ignorant of Don Benito's negotiations with Díaz de Mendoza and Guerrero, asked him to prepare something for the new season. Galdós was careful to say little about his projected play beyond asking if there would be any objection to a drama involving two apparitions. Balart assured him that there would be none, provided they were used as a device for revealing the conscience of a single person. Thus encouraged, Galdós began work on *Electra* with fresh enthusiasm. He finished it in Santander, dividing his attention between it and his latest historical novel, *Bodas reales*. Back in Madrid in late October, he spent a few days polishing off the drama, and the following month he submitted it to Balart.

Contrary to his past practice, Galdós did very little to secure advance publicity for *Electra*. And Balart did nothing at all, for as he read the play he had some misgivings about its success.

Director and author thought it advisable to proceed with as much secrecy as the press would permit, and they revised the work with extreme care before it was formally read by the entire company. The Español had several distinguished artists that season— Francisco Fuentes, Ricardo Valero, and Matilde Moreno—and on January 7, 1901, they met with their supporting associates to read the new drama and distribute the parts.

Galdós was not superstitious, but an incident which occurred that day gave him an unpleasant foreboding. As he entered the theater he met María Guerrero supervising the preparations for her departure from the Español. Winsome María remarked to Don Benito: "I am leaving the theater quite warm, Don Benito, and I hope you will not chill it off."[1] Galdós replied with a forced smile and proceeded to the *saloncillo* where *Electra* was to be tried out by Balart's company. The verdict was equivocal. The actors readily conceded the literary merit of the drama, but were apprehensive about the reaction of the audience. Privately they were almost certain of its failure. Neither Don Benito nor Don Federico challenged their opinions. The parts were distributed, and rehearsals began at once.

Never had Galdós played for such high stakes. He confessed that in *Electra* he had condensed the work of a lifetime—his love of truth, his constant struggle against superstition and fanaticism. In it he wished to reiterate how urgent it was for unhappy Spain to forget the routines, conventions, and falsehoods which dishonored and debased it in the eyes of the civilized world. The new Spain, resting on science and justice, would be in a position to resist brute force and the insidious, baneful influences upon its conscience.[2] He was not sure that he would deliver his message successfully, since public opinion about reaction and clericalism had not yet crystallized. If *Electra* could accomplish this, its triumph would be immense, and his own happiness boundless.

Laying aside all other tasks and preoccupations, Galdós dedicated himself exclusively to the staging of *Electra*. He assisted in the selection of costumes and supervised the designing and construction of scenery, five artistic sets being painted under his personal direction. He was present at all the rehearsals, where his old enemy—lack of compression—returned to plague him. With almost fiendish delight he repeatedly recommended excisions—and the play seemed to be an almost inexhaustible source of such delight. Federico Balart, having a premonition of failure, often cautioned restraint with ironic compassion. "Don't bother, Don Benito," he would say; "for the short time that it is going to last on the boards it is really not worth the trouble." [3] The actors shared his forebodings, and Galdós himself was none too confident of the artistic success of the new drama. But as the rehearsals progressed he began to foresee a triumph of another sort.

On January 29 a dress rehearsal of _Electra_ was held before a select audience of Madrid's intellectuals, writers, artists, and public figures in general. The favored guests were the youth of Spain, for whom the message of the play was to be a challenge and an inspiration. It was the first public dress rehearsal in the history of the Spanish theater, and an attempt was made to invest it with the solemnity of similar events in France. Galdós would have preferred to exclude the dramatic reviewers, whom he regarded as largely responsible for his past failures, but of course this could not be done. He did stipulate, however, that the drama was not to be written up in detail by either friend or foe, for he did not want the general public to be influenced beforehand. A broad interpretation of the theme, sufficient to arouse curiosity, was really all that was necessary.

But no stipulations could prevent the dress rehearsal from becoming a traditional Spanish première. There were few vacant seats in the Español, and the audience did not behave with the expected solemnity. The young writers came properly innoculated, as it were, and the injection took effect with amazing rapidity as the tendentious theme of _Electra_ began to unfold. They were literally electrified.

The tumultuous reception of _Electra_ was a Spanish version of the famous première of Victor Hugo's _Hernani_. The disillusioned Spanish realists of 1901 experienced something comparable to the frenzy of the French romanticists of 1830. Ramiro de Maeztu hurled the first thunderbolt with his outcry of "Down with the Jesuits!" During the third act the coldly intellectual and devastatingly nihilistic Pío Baroja shouted: "The entire meaning of the earth has been revealed here!" Azorín was sufficiently unnerved to exclaim: "Enormously beautiful!" Luis Bello voiced the thoughts of his youthful confrères when he announced: "Now we have a man in whom I believe!" And Valle-Inclán, sworn enemy of emotion in art, was seen crying behind his shell-rimmed glasses.

There was a deafening clamor for the author. For thirty minutes Galdós resisted. Finally an unidentified young man, followed by twenty others, leaped on the stage and pulled him out in front. Don Benito would have collapsed with emotion had not Maeztu rushed up to sustain him with a tight embrace. The success of *Electra* exceeded his expectations. Its message expressed in clear terms the vague yearnings that had kept the literary and intellectual youth restless and enervated for so long. At last the nation's spiritual energy had an outlet.

The press accounts of the following day respected Galdós' request that no full first-night reviews be published. They stated simply that *Electra* dealt with a profound social problem of the past century, which was now arousing fresh interest in Spain, and even more so in France. But the restraint of the press did not hinder the effective advertising of the play. The frenzy of the younger literati was slow in subsiding. In the afternoon before the première they gathered in a famous *cervecería* (beer emporium), where they gave vent to their emotion and exultation. Valle-Inclán set the pace with impassioned volubility. Pío Baroja broke the thread of his contemplative *Weltanschauung* and advocated dynamic action. Everyone revealed by word and gesture the hypnotic effect of *Electra*. Young Spain had discovered overnight a prophet. And to guarantee that none would remain ignorant of the discovery, an autographed postcard photograph of Galdós was widely distributed in Madrid. It bore the legend: "*Electra*, Teatro Español, Madrid, January 30, 1901."

With such advance publicity the première was assured of success. The "notables" filled the orchestra and the "people" crowded the galleries. Many who had attended the public dress rehearsal were present again in strategic seats. In front of the theater a large crowd of Galdós' anonymous admirers milled about impatiently. Unable to gain admission, they vehemently denounced those who, while they normally boycotted Don Benito's plays, had been attracted by the rumors about the radicalism of *Electra* and the loud denunciation in the clerical press. Everyone had the feeling of an impending epochal event.

When the curtain went up, a hushed silence fell on the excited audience. All listened with concentrated attention during the first two acts of detailed exposition. By the end of the third act the eager audience had grasped the full significance of the conflict and expressed its appreciation noisily. There was a determined clamor for the author, and the few who pleaded for silence were threatened with raised fists. The fourth act was repeatedly interrupted with delirious applause. The transparent symbolism of the theme, as it was grasped by the spectators, engendered alternately raging hatred and enthusiastic approval. When Máximo suggested in the last act the death of fanatical Pantoja as the best solution of Electra's problem, pandemonium broke loose. The performance was interrupted, and the author was literally dragged out on the stage by the actors.

The audience rose tumultuously. Above their heads was a sea of waving hats and fluttering handkerchiefs. Even in the orchestra and box seats decorum collapsed. Canalejas, famous leader of Spanish democracy and distinguished jurist, held his silk hat high in the air, shouting hyperbolical eulogies at Galdós. But this was only a soft prelude to the next demonstration. Máximo's suggestion that arson would free Electra from the convent in which Pantoja sought to imprison her by force was like tossing a flaming torch at the raucous-voiced and red-palmed "people" perched in the galleries. A box of matches came darting down toward the stage to the accompaniment of a throaty exhortation: "Do it now! What are we waiting for?" [4] For the galleries the illusion of the fifth act was complete. Actor Ricardo Valero, who played Pantoja, had to step out of character and plead that in life he was as good a liberal as those who threatened him with violence. A bourgeois family in the balcony, frightened by the riotous exhibition, moved to leave before the end of the last act. "The reactionaries are leaving!" shouted a contingent of hysterical liberals, and the good middle-class family thought it prudent to remain.[5]

The Teatro Español assumed the appearance of a political convention. Galdós had to answer fourteen curtain calls at the end of the performance. Exhortations to revolution and the suppression of the church, which had been expressed in mild tones between the last two acts, now rumbled through the air like loud thunder. The punitive-minded spectators demanded that corporal punishment be administered to those who had failed to applaud with sufficient fervor the new Spain which was presumably born that very night. Reporters dashed hither and thither interviewing "notables." Conservative Menéndez y Pelayo, who had been noticed applauding enthusiastically during the fourth act, was happy to state that *Electra* was the most beautiful thing in the Spanish language. Benavente, Azorín, Martínez Sierra, Angel Guerra, and other young writers hailed the artistic beauty and philosophic depth of the drama. All thought it augured a new and promising era in the evolution of modern Spain.

These impressions were communicated to Galdós, who was waiting in the *saloncillo* for the signal that it might be safe to leave the building. There he sat calmly, as if all that had happened that night did not concern him directly. With his customary benevolent smile and courtesy he received congratulations from friends and strangers. Now and then he rolled nervously the cheap cigar in his mouth. Among the callers he singled out for marked attention a young man named Ubao, brother of the girl who had recently found herself in a plight similar to Electra's and became the center of a public scandal. The amazing coincidence with the situation in his play intrigued Galdós, and he would have listened indefinitely to young Ubao's story had not someone whispered in his ear: "Don Benito, I think you have struck gold tonight." His half-closed little eyes flashed with cheerful expectancy. "Do you really think so?" he replied, and suggested that it was time to go home. He was very, very happy, but he was also extremely tired.[6]

In the office of the impresario of the Español the young writers were discussing plans for a vast celebration of Galdós' triumph at the Frontón Central. Presently shouts were heard coming from the Plaza de Santa Ana; the celebration had already begun. A crowd of some fifteen hundred persons was milling about in front of the theater, clamoring to escort the author to his home. Among them were elegant aristocrats, humble workers, students, artists, journalists, writers, and a sprinkling of noted liberal politicians. Canalejas and Segismundo Moret y Prendergast, their silk hats hoisted and lending respectability to the improvised parade, joined the front ranks of the celebrants.

When Galdós beheld the noisy scene he was overcome with fright. He could not go through with that riotous ceremony. Yet he felt that it would be neither politic nor polite to disappoint his public. One tactless move now might rob him forever of the fruits of his impressive victory. He invited Pío Baroja to get into a carriage with him. They were immediately surrounded by the shouting crowd in an improvised triumphal procession which began at Visitación and serpented through Lobo, San Jerónimo, Sevilla, Alcalá, Peligros, and Clavel and broke up in front of Hortaleza, 132. There was no band, but it was not a silent march. The air was rent with cries of "Long live Galdós!" and "Death to clericalism!" By way of variety some insistently demanded that churches and monastic buildings en route be burned. Fortunately wiser counsel prevailed and no public property was destroyed that night. Baroja asked Galdós what he intended to do about all that unleashed fury. Galdós was clearly annoyed and worried; he had anticipated nothing like that. If the public insisted on giving a political twist to a theme intended only as a study of certain aspects of the Spanish conscience, he might have to go abroad for a while. He did not wish to get burned as a result of playing philosophically with an idea to which he had not meant to add one speck of combustible stuff.

It was four o'clock in the morning when Galdós went to bed.
He slept little and fitfully, and when he got up he had one of
his violent headaches. All day his office swarmed with callers,
whom he was obliged to receive with his head wrapped in a wet
towel. A pitiful crown for the glorified leader of the new Spain!
Yet the pain he felt most keenly was remorse. Had he conceived
Electra in naïveté, or had he unwittingly yielded to motives
not entirely artistic or philosophic? He had always aimed to influence the thinking of the masses, but not to arouse violence. The
noisy demonstrations in the Español and in the streets had the appearance of a gathering storm. He must disavow his direct responsibility for it, but in doing so he would have to be careful
not to lose the ascendency he had obviously gained over the youth
of the nation. To an inquiring reporter he said:

> As for my impressions during and after the perform-
> ance, what do you want me to say? While the work
> was being acted, I experienced the emotion one feels
> upon reaching the end of a planned objective; when
> the drama was over and I came out on the stage, my
> joy was immense; I saw in those faces, in those ges-
> tures and in that enthusiasm of the public the hope
> of a new day for our adored fatherland. Afterward
> ... I detest ceremonious exhibitions; many friends
> and passionate partisans of the ideas that inspired
> *Electra* stubbornly insisted on accompanying me
> home; I could not prevent it without seeming dis-
> courteous or presumptuous through excessive mod-
> esty; the demonstration in the streets—I neither
> sought it nor did I have the right to reject it. I was
> only afraid of distorted interpretations of what was
> merely a tribute to ideas and proof of affection for
> myself. I hate farce and falsehood, paid-for enthusi-
> asm, discredited apotheosis, but I always esteem highly
> the spontaneous expression of sentiments which en-
> courage me in my work and inspire me with con-
> stancy in the pursuit of the path upon which I have
> entered.[7]

Galdós' public statement may have eased his own conscience, but it did not calm the turbulent spirits of his followers. Braving a heavy snow and extreme cold, an even more boisterous audience crowded into the Español for the second performance. By now the daring conception of *Electra* had seeped into the consciousness of the public, and the crowd came resolved to praise or to scoff. Even the innocuous first and second acts were received with explosive acclaim. Every happy phrase, every tense moment, was an occasion for demonstration. The theater shook with shouts of approbation and condemnation in accordance with the traditional Spanish formula. The audience was clearly divided into *electristas* and anti-*electristas*, the latter being hopelessly outnumbered and intimidated.

After the first performance the civil governor of Madrid had warned that he would be obliged to suspend the show if the subversive demonstration were repeated. This warning was met with a threat from the Association of Authors to close all the metropolitan and provincial theaters. Although the public was only vaguely aware that *Electra* had already become an issue of public order, it yielded to repeated caution against doing anything that might jeopardize the future of the play. But, needing an outlet for its revolutionary and anticlerical fervor, it clamored incessantly for the author at the end of the performance. The curtain-raisers worked so hard that night that *El Liberal* suggested in its next issue that their wages should be increased. The stage hands announced that they would graciously decline an advance in pay—they were only co-workers in a sublime cause.

But it was inevitable that *Electra* should precipitate a public clash of opinion, and the third performance furnished the occasion. Interest in the play had by now become so passionate that seats were sold out for seven consecutive nights, and the conservative press and government officials were manifestly uneasy. On the night of February 1, as a group of workers, members of the "Sociedad de Obreros el Porvenir del Trabajo," were waiting outside the theater to give Galdós an ovation, they suddenly heard in their midst shouts of "Death to Galdós!" and "Long live the Jesuits!" The agents-provocateurs were quickly identified, and a battle flared up. Sabers flashed, clubs found their objectives, and random missiles flew through the air. Order was restored by the police, who were present in impressive numbers, equipped for mortal combat; two workers were arrested. When all was over it was found that a police inspector and another officer had been wounded. There were other casualties, too, but they wisely refrained from publicizing their injuries.

The press was prompt to convert the riot into political stock. *El Imparcial* accused the police of conspiring with Galdós' enemies to suppress the play and called editorially for a fair interpretation of its philosophic message. Other liberal organs joined in, urging tolerance toward the religious elements criticized by Galdós and warning against treating *Electra* as an anti-religious drama. As for intervention by the authorities, it was to be averted at all cost. The conservative press was less fearful of consequences and may even have been seeking a test of power. *El Siglo Futuro,* mouthpiece of unyielding traditionalism, accused Galdós' friends of having instigated the riot in order to share the limelight with him. It asserted that the headquarters of "El Porvenir del Trabajo"—Horno de la Mata, 7—was the meeting place of all freethinkers and probably a notorious masonic lodge. If the authorities did not act promptly, it warned, grave results would follow.[8]

The civil governor of the capital was caught between two fires. Disavowing any intention to stop the play, he charged that Galdós' friends had been the first to resort to force on the night of the riot, and he reprimanded the liberal press for printing misleading accounts of it. The editor of *El Imparcial,* the first paper to report the clash with the police, was summoned for questioning by the district attorney. The paper reiterated its accusation against the police, defiantly denounced the Ministry of Interior for its partisan attitude, and hinted at political repercussions. The military had to intervene, and General Valeriano Weyler, Captain General of Madrid, warned Galdós one night that if he left the theater by the Calle Princesa exit he would have to arrest him in the interest of public order. Galdós obediently used the Calle Echegaray door, but the crowds met him there. *Electra* was fast becoming a national episode. There were reports of ominous echoes in provincial capitals, although the play was still in Madrid. Clouds were gathering on the political horizon. There was talk of a cabinet crisis.

While liberal Spain was dreaming pleasant political dreams, the conservatives fought desperately to check the spreading influence of *Electra*. An attempt to recruit the women of Spain and all other respectable social elements for a general boycott of the drama yielded no more than a puerile controversy in the press over the degree of its success. Presently an anonymous and violently patriotic citizen thought of a sinister solution. Shortly before ten o'clock on the night of February 9, 1901, a time bomb exploded under the window of Galdós' office. Luckily he was away at the time, and little damage was done to property. Since the incident did not disturb public order appreciably, the police conducted no investigation. In the press it was treated only as a current news item.

The conservatives were not the only ones to resort to coercion and violence. For the spectators Ricardo Valero became completely identified with Pantoja, whose role he played, and Pantoja came to signify fanaticism, obscurantism, clericalism, and Jesuitism. To this day Pantoja and Jesuit are synonymous in Spain. In the weeks of the *Electra* furore, Valero's publicly professed liberalism did not spare him occasional unpleasant encounters with the "people."

Shortly after the première he was unceremoniously accosted on the street by a sober Galdós enthusiast, who challenged him:

"Long live liberty!"

"Long may it live!" replied the actor in self-defense.

"Long live Don Práxedes Mateo Sagasta!" [rumored new liberal prime minister]

"Long may he live!"

"Long live Ferreras!" [editor of *El Correo* and staunch friend of Galdós]

"Long may he live!"

"You're the kind of a guy I like!" [9]

And the proselytizing champion of liberty and democratic politics went up the street, singing the revolutionary Riego hymn. Valero died suddenly about a week later without another humiliating challenge to his liberalism.

* * * *

The sensational course of *Electra* was obviously due less to its intrinsic merits than to the conditions that accompanied its presentation; wittingly or innocently, Galdós had chosen the opportune moment. Of the many external circumstances which insured attention for the tendentious, liberal drama, the foremost was the fact that a new social and political program was being sought after the Spanish-American War. Secondly, there was the much-publicized Ubao affair, which revolved around the interference of a monastic order in the intimate life of an obscure girl. Although *Electra* had been virtually finished months before the courts and the press had converted the episode into a public scandal, its presentation coincided with the wave of passion against the cloistered orders which seized certain elements of the population. In national affairs two things combined to favor Galdós. The masses were still expressing openly their displeasure over the marriage of the Princess of Asturias to the Infante Carlos and its threat of an absolute reaction. Then there were the failures, public and private, of conservative parties and conservative institutions, which renewed the hopes of the liberals and created a warm response to such a presentation of their views as was contained in *Electra*. A figure of Galdós' prestige with more pronounced qualities of leadership might have ushered in a new era. As it was, its only political effect was an eventual change of cabinet. Conservative prime minister Marcelo Azcárraga was succeeded by the liberal government of Sagasta. But frequent cabinet crises are merely evidence of the instability of modern Spanish politics.

Nevertheless the immediate reaction to *Electra* was political rather than literary. The very night of the première politicians already saw in it evidence that the storm of opposition against reactionaries and clerics was gathering fast. And throughout its phenomenal run—in the capital alone it enjoyed eighty consecutive performances in the Español, followed by more than a score in Novedades—it inspired more editorial comment than critical discussion, all inevitably tinged with the political bias of the particular paper in which it appeared. Nothing could have recorded the heartbeat of Spain more accurately than the non-literary interpretations of *Electra*.

According to the liberal press, the effect of *Electra* proved the public's receptivity to progressive ideas. Galdós merely expressed what everybody had been observing, thinking, and feeling for years. His outcry of indignation and alarm had echoed from one end of the land to the other because all Spain was a victim of outrages similar to Electra's and more than surfeited with such shameful servitude. In a single night Galdós had probably accomplished more for the cause of freedom and progress than an entire generation had done in a quarter of a century of vain effort. No other European author had ever succeeded in expressing so clearly the change in the moral climate of a people and the transformation of its soul.

Let the governing powers of Spain be warned, editorialized the liberals, that Galdós had uncovered the existence of an educated, independent public opinion. The influence of *Electra* was being closely watched in France. There it was expected that, as soon as the Cortes convened, Canalejas would oppose the establishment on Spanish soil of the religious associations destined to be legally expelled from France. The play was thus more than a literary creation of high merit; it was a hymn to life and to progress, a work of wholesome tendencies, most opportune. Incomparable was the service that its author had rendered his country. He heralded the birth of a new era, set liberty on the march, and paved the way for national resurrection. Beside this achievement the other merits of *Electra* were negligible. Its timely appearance at the climactic moment in a critical situation of long standing deserved to be described as a national episode.

But to the advocates of social revolution *Electra* held out no promise of a cataclysmic upheaval, and they scorned it accordingly. Republican *El País*, perhaps because of its desire for a gradual rapprochement with democratic liberalism, did discuss the play sympathetically and devoted to it almost the entire issue of January 31. But *El Progreso* and *El Socialista* refused to impair their doctrinal integrity and merely used the occasion to sneer again at the pitiful bourgeoisie. What inspired the liberals to talk so exultantly? In the opinion of the revolutionary-minded editors *Electra* was based on a sterile idea. Admittedly they had no business commenting on the drama at all—their reporters had saved time and the high admission price by boycotting the performance—but what information they had obtained indirectly convinced them that the Spanish proletariat would do well to use their enthusiasm sparingly. There was not a spark of the expected world conflagration in Galdós' latest work, and if the workers must be charitable, why do they not applaud his *La de San Quintín*—a play of infinitely greater social significance? Indeed, the aloofness of the radical press and its compassion for the philosophically benighted must have greatly humbled Galdós.

Middle-of-the-road opinion was naturally less contemptuous. Markedly conservative papers such as *El Nacional*, *La Epoca*, and *El Globo* wrote restrained editorials against what they termed melodramatic demonstrations of liberalism. They bewailed the conversion of *Electra* into a political shibboleth and fervently hoped that this would not harm Galdós' well-earned reputation in other spheres. With unwonted magnanimity they defended him against all imputations of impure motives. *La Epoca*, Catholic but not stridently militant, spoke tearfully of the many good Spaniards who were obliged to stay home when they discovered the dilemma that would confront them in the theater—if they applauded they would be classed with the demagogues, and if they remained silent they would be roundly denounced as Jesuits. Surely such reactions could not be mistaken for artistic appreciation. *El Globo*, master of political and spiritual tight-rope walking, ridiculed the sanguine predictions of the concrete political results that *Electra* would produce. Only daydreamers could speak of closing Spain to a possible influx of expelled French Jesuits. After all, argued one anonymous writer, Galdós had discovered no latent national forces nor had he indicated radical solutions for traditional problems. He had merely given utterance to what was in everyone's mind—vague aspirations for a more liberal state of things.

Searing blasts of sarcasm from the violently manipulated bellows of *El Siglo Futuro* betokened the unwarranted fear and terror which *Electra* had struck in the hearts of the spokesmen of Carlist Spain. What disconcerted the militant Catholics were the verified reports that Menéndez y Pelayo had apparently turned conservative liberal. Had he not applauded Galdós' drama? The sudden conversion of the scholar who in the eighties had rightly included Galdós among the enemies of Christianity and Catholicism had all the earmarks of apostasy and rank heresy. *Electra,* the crime of the age—as one infuriated writer called it— was the climax in a long series of liberal excesses, all designed to weaken the staying power of defenseless Catholics. The world was so topsy-turvy, moaned *El Siglo Futuro,* that it would surprise no one if Sagasta were permitted to mingle with the actors on the stage of the Español in order to interpolate a revolutionary speech. Why not? Was *Electra* anything more than a political pamphlet?

The fury of *El Siglo Futuro* mounted with the growing success of the drama, and its editors demanded official intervention to avert a national catastrophe. It was argued that Jesuits and other religious were entitled to protection from the violence of the liberals. The authorities were right to suppress the subversive *El País.* Why not muzzle the rest of the so-called liberal press? *Electra* was such a menace to national safety that it should be banned and its actors fined for complicity in a nefarious plot. As for the author, he deserved to be legally prosecuted.

Since the authorities dealt with *Electra* in the light of their own wisdom and particular interests, *El Siglo Futuro* sought compensation for its disappointment in cruel sarcasm. Inspired by a personal description of Galdós in *El País,* the Carlist paper published the following in the form of a charade:

"Whom do you think 'El País' is referring to in the following review?—'Small and shining eyes . . .'"

"To the pig."

"No.—'Big, wiggly ears . . .' "

"To the donkey."

"Neither.—'Big, wiggly and prehensile ears . . .'—
You can't guess?"

" 'Prehensile ears'?"

"Yes. Let's look at it again.—'Small and shining
eyes; big, wiggly and prehensile ears . . .'—You still
can't guess?"

"I guess it refers to a rationalist."

"You got it! None other than Don Benito. . . . In
truth, the hero would not have been less grateful to
'El País' if it had not photographed him so *au naturel*.
What wonderful friends you have, Benito! But in this
case they cannot be accused of unfaithfulness, not even
where 'El País' is involved." [10]

Little could be gained from a digest of the numerous more
directly critical comments on *Electra*. Calm judgment was obviously impossible in the case of a work so explosive in its effect.
The wonder is that some reviewers recovered sufficiently from
the shock to recall most of the stereotyped standards and pre-
ceptive clichés with which they had evaluated Galdós' other
dramas. Few of them were outspokenly unfavorable. The old
opposition was driven underground, where, with some violence
to its conscience, it collaborated with those who attacked *Electra*
with the weapons of political and religious bias. It was a sort of
sniper or guerrilla criticism. All other opinions, whether excessively favorable or passionately hostile, bordered closely on
the irrational. The most significant reactions were those of the
rising generation.

Galdós' proven admirers used extravagant language. José de
Laserna argued, without supporting evidence, that *Electra* was
Galdós' best drama and one of the very few supreme achievements of the contemporary theater anywhere. Its symbolism was
commendably transparent, and even its two acts of exposition
deserved only praise: first, because their unconventional length
was a technical innovation; second, because they were required by
the magnitude of the theme. As for the famous fourth act, which

sent the audience into an exhausting delirium, it was "grandiose, sublime, Shakespearean, exuberant with poetry and emotion, a perfect model of lofty thinking, deep feeling and plain speaking." [11]

According to Andrés Ovejero, *Electra* was one of the most universal dramas of all times. The heroine was of Shakespearean proportions—in the fourth act she reminded one of Ophelia— and Galdós equaled the stature of the English dramatist. Only ignorance or envy, or both, could henceforth prompt anyone to deny Don Benito the title of dramatist and reformer of the Spanish stage. He may not always have been a master of the art, but in *Electra* he revealed himself as "a portentous example of wisdom" in theatrical architecture. The characters were an enduring contribution to his already crowded and marvelous gallery. As for the theme, Señor Ovejero, himself a young man, seemed to speak for the youth of Spain when he said: "*Electra* is not only a dramatic work of highly singular merit, but also a beautiful, brilliant, magnificent manifesto of the aspirations of the intellectual youth of Spain, which in its recent preparations for the battle against clericalism has discovered in Pérez Galdós an indisputable leader." [12]

Other spokesmen for the so-called generation of 1898 made a few pertinent observations, whose specific import they later repudiated. Azorín dived into the profundities of *Electra* and came up with some philosophic reflections. It was disheartening, he complained, to see the unanimous enthusiasm over the small political talk in the play and the exaggeration of its tendentious element by the critics and the literary youth. Galdós himself probably had a good laugh at Spain's ignorance, lack of culture, and fanaticism, because of which one had to prostitute art with cheap anti-religious and political jabber in order to elicit the response of the public. The real theme of *Electra* was something profound and human—the eternal quest for truth and the meaning of life. Máximo (science) and Pantoja (religion) think that they know the goal of life, but Electra herself is only perplexed and confused by these two contenders for her guidance. Azorín saw *Electra* as the work of a great thinker, the plastic and picturesque expression of the conflict as he interpreted it. Of the two symbols he preferred Pantoja. Máximo drew the applause of the unlettered spectators with his liberal outbursts, but Pantoja made a more moving appeal by his serenity and detachment from worldly ends. Electra's decision to follow Máximo was perhaps not a definitive solution of the human problem. In the last analysis, said Azorín, both science and faith are only illusions with which to calm one's conscience.[13]

For Pío Baroja a changed Galdós was revealed in *Electra*. From a man of ideas and deeds, reflective, cautious, and reserved, he had become a man of aspirations, faith, enthusiasm, and fire—indeed, a seer. Spanish youth was looking for a common aim, for something concrete to do, for something to unite them. Their aspirations were in search of "spiritual flesh," of a way of being transformed into conscience. Paradoxically enough, mused Baroja, the spirit of Spanish youth had discovered a warm nest in the soul of the reputedly cold and indifferent dramatist who classified souls as a botanist might classify flowers. As for *Electra* itself, it was the greatest drama in the Spanish theater, a marvel as a creation of art and a "battering ram" as a social work. In it rebellion and dogma came to grips. Although dogma was defeated, it was not killed, for somewhere in the Spanish soul there is pure religion that must not be destroyed, since it can be used as a beneficial force in life. In short, speaking for his disillusioned generation, Baroja hailed Galdós as the prophet of a new era, a leader who had grave responsibilities, for "one cannot become with impunity the conscience of a multitude."[14]

The uncritical approach of the friendly commentators might conceivably be interpreted as the effect of the noisy première. But no such explanation can be offered for the froth and fury of most Catholic papers, since their writers usually boasted that they had not seen the play. They gnashed their teeth at the author, growled at the friendly critics, and barked at the liberal press. On the basis of hearsay they blandly refuted all favorable statements about the play, supporting their refutation with insulting and vituperative language. Typical is the following biased opinion:

Electra is an enraged attack upon truth, grammar, and
common sense, a real scarecr(ow) ... I mean a
bumpk(in) ... I mean ... How shall we put it without being discourteous and still say how bad it is?—
Ah, yes! *Electra* is a work by Pérez Galdós, as good in
form and content as the *Episodios nacionales* and the
other works by the same author.

... Don Benito's works can always be reduced to
one or more rabid Catholics who commit all knaveries
imaginable, and one or more rabid liberals who bite
them and assault them without leaving a single bone
unbroken.[15]

*   *   *   *

Galdós' low estimate of Spanish literary criticism made him
indifferent to both the praise and the condemnation of *Electra*. In
one or two instances he did resent unfavorable, even if honest,
opinions. Emilio Bobadilla lost his friendship because of some
harsh things he said in his review. Galdós would have been
superhuman had not the phenomenal success of the play blinded
him to its intrinsic merit, giving him a momentary consciousness
of unapproachable superiority. He was not permitted to forget
soon that he had suddenly become the standard bearer of the
nation's most vital cause. The day after the première more than
six hundred messages of felicitation reached his office. For some
time he could not appear on the streets without being surrounded
by admiring crowds. On February 1 law and medical students
paraded in front of his building, and a committee entered to
extend official congratulations. Two days later, when his presence was noticed in the Royal Opera, the audience interrupted
the program with a thunderous ovation for "the author of
Electra." This was singular recognition, coming from a social
element not ordinarily thought of as the "people." And it was
rumored that the literary youth were contemplating a journal
Electra, to perpetuate the spiritual significance of the drama, and
in time the journal did appear.

There were other less impressive but nevertheless flattering
devices of commemoration. Popular enthusiasm expressed itself

in song and sonnet. Madrilenians soon told time by Electra watches, ate Electra candy, and soothed their throats with Electra cough drops. Had Galdós anticipated this avalanche of popularity he might conceivably have taken steps to exploit it. With or without permission, merchants, manufacturers, brewers, distillers, and other business enterprises adopted Electra as their trademark. At one time Galdós' office took on the appearance of a display room of assorted merchandise. How he disposed of all these gratuities is not recorded, but he did take care to preserve the picturesque correspondence with his commercially minded admirers.

The Madrid literary circles were less efficient than the business world in converting their enthusiastic appreciation into something concrete. Barring the journal *Electra* and two immensely popular musical comedy parodies—*Alerta* and *Electroterapia*—other ideas, plans, and movements for the perpetuation of the unique dramatic and national event for the most part disintegrated amidst lengthy debates over the best way of promoting them. As a body, they bespeak the resourcefulness and generous impulses of Galdós' admirers.

The projected types of commemoration were gastronomic, literary, political, and architectural. The suggestion of a great popular banquet in Frontón Central met with the most enthusiastic response. The Frontón Central could accommodate two thousand guests, and the price was to be only five pesetas. All the organization details, including a parade through the heart of Madrid, were to be left to the young writers. Pío Baroja, enemy of *abulia*, was fittingly among the most energetic collaborators in this scheme, which vied with the plans of other groups for various celebrations and banquets of widely differing prices. Federico Alfonso, Astorga manufacturer of chocolates and cookies, offered a free case of his famous delicacies for any banquet in honor of Galdós, an offer he never had opportunity to make good. Neither did Galdós have occasion to exchange his modest home for the sumptuous "Villa Electra" that was to be erected for him in Madrid with funds raised by a national subscription. Among the less mundane proposals that did not materialize was that of Spanish liberals to organize the *acto público* to mobilize all Galdós' "co-religionists" at a mass meeting where distinguished political leaders would point the way to the eradication of reaction. The idea may have been abandoned because of the violent opposition of the republicans and socialists, whose organs denounced it as a scheme invented by the foxy Sagasta for his own political ends. Also abortive was the movement launched by the liberal press to publish a de luxe illustrated edition of *Electra*. The cost was to be defrayed by a public subscription—donations as low as ten céntimos being acceptable—and the edition was to be distributed free of charge throughout the provinces as a means of propagating the great beauties of the play.

What all these good intentions did achieve was to promote the success of *Electra*. After eighty consecutive nights in the Teatro Español the drama lost none of its popular appeal and revolutionary influence. When it reached the proletarian Novedades Theater on picturesque Calle de Toledo, the performances took on the atmosphere of political ritual, the singing of the Marseillaise and the Riego hymn being *de rigueur*. But even more gratifying was the eagerness with which Spaniards rushed to buy the text of *Electra*. The first issue of ten thousand was exhausted within two days after its publication on February 21. The Heraldo bookstore reported the sale of 980 copies in a few hours. A second printing of twenty thousand in the middle of March was sold out in two weeks.

But other expressions of appreciation were not altogether lacking. The Marqués de Santa María tendered him a banquet in his home on February 12, which was attended by writers, artists, military dignitaries, political notables of various hues, and other distinguished persons. In spirit and significance the occasion was reminiscent of the banquet of 1883. And the people did not entirely forget him either. In Santander a goodly crowd paraded solemnly to his modest villa and left an artistic floral offering. And similar expressions of esteem and joy in his triumph reached him in Madrid.

However, a sad note or two tempered Galdós' happiness.
From his lifelong friend Pereda came a letter—serene, sincere,
and affectionate, but firm—which conveyed disapproval of the
essence of *Electra:*

> Believe me that I am at a loss to discover the proper
> key for these brief lines ... You well know how cor-
> dially fond I am of you and how much I admire you,
> and you are aware, too, of how I think about certain
> questions which I regard with extreme delicacy, not
> through blind passion, but through rational and pro-
> found conviction. This is the source of my present
> embarrassment, for I should like to be among the
> first to applaud this new evidence of the talent and
> genius with which you were so prodigiously endowed
> by the Lord; but I should not like to add my applause
> to the frenzy of the people who hoisted the flag of
> death and extermination for certain things that have
> nothing to do with what takes place in the drama;
> more than that, I admit that Pantoja's *case* merits
> imprisonment and I should gladly vote in favor of
> shackles for him and—if I may be permitted to use
> small examples in a matter so great—on occasion I
> have even lashed out to the extent of my limited
> strength against *abductions* of this abominable kind;
> but I regard as even more so the nature of the other
> fanaticism which, aiming at the rotten branch, wishes
> to fell the healthy and sturdy tree. The one, I repeat,
> has nothing to do with the other, and I even believe
> that it was not your intention to confuse them in your
> work; I rather think that the exaggerated social sig-
> nificance it has taken on in *overheated* minds is due
> to circumstances, something that has been flying
> around for some time in the atmosphere of our mili-
> tant politics. Be that as it may, things have now been
> distorted, and this is why, as I have said at the begin-
> ning, I am at a loss to write you these lines, since on so

solemn an occasion for you, I, who am so truly fond of
you, must not and cannot remain suspiciously silent;
and as I am trying to say something I am afraid that
you will be annoyed at my reservations which I am
compelled to make out of loyalty and out of a sense of
the conscientious duty of a traditional Christian. . . .

On the provincial stage *Electra* was converted into a veritable
casus belli and a source of grief and even remorse for Galdós.
Its performances served mostly as a call to arms of both liberals
and conservatives—the box office invariably being the heaviest
casualty of the ensuing struggle. The play was not financially
profitable in the provinces, but Galdós persisted in producing it,
chiefly for the publicity it gave him.

The difficulties experienced by the traveling troupes or the
improvised local casts were innumerable, often resulting in the
cancellation of the performance. The stratagems of the opposition were varied and effective. In many towns the clergy offered
the companies bribes not to perform—twenty-five hundred
pesetas in Ecija. In some localities friar-teachers threatened to
suspend pupils whose families should go to see *Electra*. City
councils warned their employees of reprisals for participating in
Electra publicity. In Aranda de Duero the local actress who was
to take the leading role was summoned by the nuns, her former
teachers, and offered a handsome sum if she would agree not to
play. In the town of Toro the campaign of intimidation was
conducted so efficiently that not a single seat was sold. The
"Asociación de Autores, Compositores, y Propietarios de Obras
Teatrales" ruled in vain to deprive the community of all theatrical programs so long as *Electra* was kept off the boards.

In Ronda all the *Electra* posters were removed within a half
hour after they had been distributed, and all handbills were confiscated. A committee of ladies headed by the widow of a distinguished colonel and an intimate friend of the vicar made a
house-to-house canvass, urging women to boycott the performance. Their success surpassed their expectations. Even the gentlemen stayed home, thus reducing the audience to the members of
the "Círculo Obrero." The workers of Ronda spent the eve-

ning in one continuous ovation to Galdós, but they were restrained as compared with those in other communities. In Utiel, province of Valencia, the actors struggled in vain to control the spectators, who throughout the last three acts unceasingly demanded death for the hateful Pantoja. The indignation of the public was sometimes provoked by unjustifiable touches added by the actors to the conflict in the drama. In Salamanca, where *Electra* was staged by a vaudeville company, Pantoja not only martyrized the heroine spiritually but maltreated her physically —a histrionic license which the crowd approved roaringly.

In the provincial capitals *Electra* fared no better than in the less populous settlements. In Valencia a political campaign complicated matters, and for a time it seemed impossible to set a date for the production. Rodrigo Soriano and Blasco Ibáñez, candidates on the radical ticket, insisted that the play be staged before election day. The Jesuits—the term came to be applied indiscriminately to all who worked against the drama—fought in vain to postpone the performance until after the elections in the hope of defeating the radicals. A further complication was introduced by Valentín Gómez, politician and dramatist of undisputed inferiority, who tried to stage simultaneously his newly written farce, *El Galdós Neo,* as a means of combating the effects of *Electra.*

In Barcelona partisans of the church and monastic orders swarmed in the neighborhood of the El Dorado Theater for hours before the opening performance, intimidating ticket purchasers and lining up in front of the box office to discourage prospective spectators. They bought up blocks of seats in which a hostile claque was strategically distributed. So effectively did the hirelings perform their duty from the moment the curtain went up that fright rendered the artists almost speechless even in the early scenes. *Electra* was only a partial success in culturally superior Barcelona.

As was to be expected, the drama fared worst in the northern provinces, focus of Carlism and Spanish conservatism in general. Actor Antonio Perrín's letter of May 20, 1901, describing his experience in Pamplona, is typical and illuminating:

MY DEAR DON BENITO: Tomorrow is the day. *Electra* will appear like a banner of freedom over the trenches of Pamplona—and on a Friday, to boot!

You have no idea, dear Don Benito, what is happening here. Not even your pen could describe it in a new *Episodio* which you might write. You can infer from what I am saying what must be going on.

I and my handful of brave souls are going ahead, scorning threats, offer of money by the vicars, excommunication, wiles, baseness and, in short, inanities of all sorts, for that is what the weapons are which the scoundrels use, they who, pretending to serve God, are parodying the devil. Let me cite a few details.

On Calle de San Nicolás, numbers 16 and 18, the property of Señor (or whatever he is) Sanz, a member of the city council and brother of the recently elected congressman of the same name, there is a boarding house where four members of my company are staying. On their second day there, the lady who runs the boarding house is informed by the landlord that if she continues to give lodging to the "ham" actors, he will put her out. One more detail: The vicar of San Agustín addressed a letter to the owner of the Circo Theater, Señor Labarta, threatening him with eternal condemnation and telling him that, *no matter what the cost*, it was absolutely necessary to prevent the performance of *Electra*. Still another detail: Across the octaves which I posted on squares and street corners these words have appeared written in black pencil—it naturally had to be black—"Down with the company; Death to the 'ham' actors." Another detail: A delegation of *ladies* have worn out the soles and the morocco leather of their shoes, going around soliciting signatures from business houses and private homes to present them to our nice friend the governor, Señor Polanco, to suppress the performance of *Electra*. He received them with his customary courtesy and distinguished manner, but he pointed out to them very politely that the Lord created womankind for something greater and more dignified. Yet another detail: The workers are threatened with dismissal if they attend the show. And, finally, Don Benito—it's perfectly horrible!

These efforts to prevent the extension of the *Electra* conflagration often received the backing of church dignitaries. Bans were issued by the archbishop of Seville and the bishops of Badajoz, Córdoba, Vitoria, Lérida, Burgos, Santander, Cartagena, Cádiz, Vich, and other cities. None of these church heads had any direct knowledge of the work they banned, but their fertile imagination painted so garish and terrifying a picture that few could be expected to risk trading their eternal salvation for a few hours of politico-dramatic spectacle. However confident that the faith of its followers was deep-rooted, the church deemed it prudent to warn the public against the alluring power of Galdós' diabolically clever art. To quote the bishop of Córdoba, who condemned *Electra* as a play filled with passion, incitement to hatred and violence, and a perfect specimen of fashionable naturalism: "If to this are added the facts that *Electra* abounds in the author's masterly description, that its language is relatively correct, that the dialogues between the protagonists are sprightly and sparkling, and that there is a generous sprinkling of provocative and incendiary phrases, the public will readily understand the sort of idea Galdós had in mind when he wrote the play."

Not all the bans incorporated literary criticism. Most of them restricted their condemnation to reminders of the retribution that sinners must expect. The citizens of Pamplona, for example, were warned by the following proclamation, which received wide publicity in the press, from the pulpit, and on the walls of the city's buildings:

"ELECTRA": His Excellency and Reverence the bishop of this diocese has learned with profound displeasure that it is intended to put one of these days on the boards of the Circo Theater of this city the sadly famous drama of Pérez Galdós, entitled "Electra," condemned, as our readers know, by many prelates of Spain.

For the same reasons which induced these to take that decision, our venerable and most zealous bishop prohibits his faithful diocesans, under the pain of mortal sin, to attend the performance of "Electra"; so that, whoever witnesses this spectacle, even though only out of curiosity, by so doing lays himself open to the punishment of eternal damnation.

But laws and boycotts, sabotage and shouts, parades and posters, pleas and protests, bribes and bravado were powerless to stem the disrupting influence of *Electra*. For decades nothing had marked so deeply the line of cleavage between those who found security in tradition and those who sought salvation in innovation. The drama did not succeed in destroying institutions or in dislodging powers, but it did cause mild tremors which momentarily disturbed the smugness of the conservatives and shook the spiritual apathy of the liberals. Everywhere in Spain the wise and wary could hear the rumble of distant thunder. Impatient souls were eager to rush out to meet the approaching storm. They dreamed of a republic presided over by Benito Pérez Galdós. But Benito Pérez Galdós was not given to dreaming. For the time being he was content to remain a simple apostle of progress. The rumble of the distant thunder was only a signal to scan the skies and be on the alert.

*   *   *   *

Hero worship is not a salient trait of the individualistic Spaniard, but *Electra* momentarily modified even the national character. The first to rush to Galdós with their admiration were his friends, and the Madrid telegraph messengers kept up a steady procession to Hortaleza, 132. Not far behind came numerous cultural, political, and social organizations, including several official city councils. The messages, worded as altisonant resolutions, came from many parts of the land, often carrying long lists of signatures embellished with the traditional Spanish flourishes to the point of illegibility. Some offered Galdós honorary posts. Always methodical and courteous, he promptly thanked his hosts of well-wishers, particularly the simple anonymous people who now looked upon him not only as the supreme national hero but also as the man to whom they could bring their accumulated spiritual, social, economic, cultural, and even physical troubles. In tones pathetic, humorous, solemn, and frivolous they solicited his advice and aid, and pledged their support. Some offered him counsel, encouragement, and criticism; others condemned him; and not a few threatened him. Friendly correspondents identified themselves by name; the hostile ones often hid behind anonymity.

The popularity of *Electra* in Spanish America almost rivaled its vogue in Spain. It was performed repeatedly in Havana, Montevideo, Tucumán, Valparaíso, Santiago, Manila, Córdoba, Rosario, La Plata, Caracas. In Buenos Aires it was in the repertory of three companies simultaneously, and was even produced on Good Friday and the Thursday preceding. It was also staged in Portuguese in Rio de Janeiro, and a performance in São Paulo was followed by a riotous demonstration near the San Benito convents.

The Argentine capital may even have surpassed Madrid in *Electra* furore. Sensing the significance of this, Galdós appointed a certain Enrique García Velloso to represent his interests. Don Enrique discharged his duties conscientiously, but he had nothing to show for it. Had all the theaters paid Galdós the royalties due him, and had there existed a copyright convention between Spain and Argentina, the drama would have netted him two hundred thousand gold pesetas. But in lieu of wealth "agent" García Velloso had only interesting accounts to send. Before the première in Buenos Aires he reported: "In a few hours Buenos Aires will applaud *Electra*. Not a single seat is left in the box offices of the Argentino, Victoria, and Comedia, and likewise all *authentic* copies of the text were sold out in the bookstores. The very morning that the Magdalena docked, the books were snatched up. The next day, with characteristic American *dexterity*, they counterfeited your edition. Your own compatriots set the example, for the 'Correo Español' reprinted the first three acts in a single issue."

After the première Don Enrique was vibrant with jubilation: "You cannot imagine, my dear Don Benito," he wrote, "the enthusiasm your work has aroused. To date we must be satisfied with Electra cigarettes, Electra hats, Electra candies—in short, we are truly *electrified*. The *Camelots* on the Plaza de la Victoria are selling barometers with the mercury column in the shape of a priest's cassock. On the upper knob they wanted to imitate Pantoja's face, and so they used poor Ricardo Valero's. You would not believe it, but we even have smoking pipes with your bust for a bowl!"

The Continental reputation that Galdós had vainly sought to establish in the early eighties and late nineties came to him unsolicited after *Electra*. In Belgium M. Gaston Bergé, noted Hispanist, gave an illustrated lecture on the drama before a large audience at the University of Brussels. The Société des Étudiants Libéraux Gembloux of the Belgian State Agricultural Institute congratulated Galdós on his dramatic success and his heroic fight for freedom. Belgium did not soon forget the significance of *Electra*. In the last months of 1908 a certain Pizat announced the forthcoming production of his *Elèctre* in Brussels. The Belgian clerics confused it with Galdós' work and organized a vigorous campaign against it. Italy reacted to the epochal play with puzzling coolness. It had a brief and unsuccessful run in the Manzoni Theater in Rome during April and May of 1901. The translation was a wretched one, and even the important scenes failed to impress the public. In the opinion of Italian critics it was impossible to adapt the drama to the genius of their language. Portugal, too, though curious, was not enthusiastic. In Romalho Ortiago's translation *Electra* was put on four times in Lisbon from April 12 to 15, 1901. Several versions of the play appeared in Germany and Austria, but it saw the boards only in

Vienna, in May of 1901. And not long before Galdós' death, revolutionary Russia produced Spain's anticlerical drama in Moscow and Kief.

However flattering—but not always profitable—Galdós found the onward march of *Electra* on two continents, his overpowering ambition was to see it triumph on the French stage. He had many friends in France, whom he readily convinced that his drama had transcendental significance—at least for countries in which freedom of conscience was a vital issue. By March, 1901, Paul Milliet was authorized to translate it, and negotiations for its production in Paris got under way immediately. To whet the appetite of the Parisian impresarios, M. Milliet organized an advertising campaign. Early in April, 1901, newspapers and reviews suddenly turned their attention to Galdós and *Electra* with a simultaneity and emphasis that cast suspicion on the spontaneity of their inspiration. But the impresarios were not easily influenced by this stratagem, and toward the middle of the year M. Milliet regretfully suspended his negotiations with the Parisian theatrical world.

Once again Galdós refused to resign himself to defeat. For three years he continued to cherish the ambition of seeing his play on the French stage. In 1904 he thought that the propitious moment had arrived. Early that year relations between the Vatican and France had been severed, and the agitation against religious orders was intense. Surely *Electra* could lend tremendous aid to the anticlerical cause. Against the advice of his Spanish admirers, whose misgivings about the success of his second attempt he dismissed with a mixture of ironic impatience and overconfidence, Galdós appeared in Paris in person. Ignoring rebuffs and disappointments, he finally induced the none too scrupulous Théâtre de la Porte Saint-Martin to introduce a transformed and mutilated *Electra* to the Parisians. Since the French reactionaries had selected May for a huge demonstration in behalf of the religious orders, that was the month chosen for the dramatic event of the season. Galdós returned to Madrid, where he nervously awaited developments while his collaborator in Paris worked untiringly for a triumph about which both felt none too sure.

Paris almost matched Madrid in the riotous reception it accorded *Electra* the nights of the *répétition générale* and the première (May 19 and 20, 1904). The riot was for the most part, of course, instigated in the galleries, but other sections of the theater fell in with their malicious hilarity over aspects of the drama not even remotely related to anticlericalism. M. de Max, who interpreted the role of Pantoja, was frequently disconcerted by the audience as a whole, and at times he was so confused that even the conscientious claque was unable to restore his composure. When the last curtain went down, not a single spectator could have honestly asserted that he had not enjoyed himself, but many were puzzled to define the exact nature of the spectacle they had witnessed. Was it a performance of an allegedly transcendental drama or a boisterous pre-election rally?

But the dramatic critics who looked for something more than an evening's amusement received a very clear impression of *Electra*. Almost unanimously they concluded that the Pyrenees certainly separated the Spanish drama from the French. They found *Electra* artistically deficient and philosophically uninteresting. The reviewers who knew little or nothing about Galdós treated him almost flippantly. Paul Souday, for instance, defined *Electra* as a thesis play which maintained that girls who wished to get married should not be forced to enter a convent. In seventeenth-century France, he suggested, this might have been exceedingly interesting, but in 1904 there was such complete unanimity about the matter that M. Galdós had no right to bore an audience with painfully presented arguments in defense of his thesis.[16]

For a time Galdós' friends and "agents" in Paris endeavored to sustain his illusion that *Electra* was a transcendental work. But doubts began to assail him when they had to resort to explanations and apologies in their periodic reports and digests of press opinion. Yet the play continued on the boards with the aid of artificial respiration. From the Théâtre de la Porte Saint-Martin it went to playhouses in the workers' districts and from there to the suburbs of Paris. Altogether it had a run of 180 consecutive nights between May 19 and November 12, 1904. During the summer it also enjoyed a brief *tournée* in provincial theaters, especially in the Théâtre Gymnase at Marseille. But it did not earn for the author the distinction of driving a Spanish spoke into the literary hub of the world. Contrary to the popular adage, Galdós did not remain a hero for long except to his own valet.

*   *   *   *

⌊Galdós' dream of a Spain redeemed through the sorrow and suffering of the protagonist of *Electra* failed to come true during his lifetime, and it still awaits realization today. Thoughtful Spaniards like to regard this as evidence of the enduring reality of the conflict portrayed in this drama. In recent decades, whenever the challenge of political or spiritual reaction—the two are hopelessly intertwined in Spain—has been ominously loud, the forces of progress and enlightenment have frequently used *Electra* as their protective armor.⌉Other Galdosian plays, particularly *La loca de la casa* and *El abuelo*, have been revived more often, but none with so much faith in its imperishable spiritual significance as *Electra*.

Its first reappearance the night of January 30, 1913—twelve years after its première—was characterized by the liberal press as an artistic-political event. Although the date of the revival was probably related to the agitation for Galdós' economic rehabilitation, the play was nevertheless received with far more intelligent enthusiasm and sincerity than in 1901. Gone were the circumstances so largely responsible for its original noisy reception, and this time the reviewers were honest in their discovery of the abiding appeal of *Electra*. *El País* solemnized the anniversary with a reproduction of its special issue of January 31, 1901. Some of the articles must have brought blushes to the face of many a member of the generation of 1898, who in the intervening twelve years had been assiduously trying to demolish the literary and spiritual idols of the nineteenth century.

In the spiritual darkness of the dictatorship of Primo de

Rivera, Spanish intellectuals and literary men had frequent occasion to recall nostalgically the time when even in Spain one's mind and soul were relatively free to reveal themselves. Seeking relief from their agony, a group of writers in 1924 addressed a letter to Matilde Moreno, leading lady in the original *Electra,* asking her to revive the drama. The petitioners (Benavente, Pérez de Ayala, the Quinteros, Araquistain, Maeztu, Zamacois, and others) dismissed as intellectual superficiality the opinion that times had changed: "The genius of Pérez Galdós resists all possible dislodgment of time and place, and the production of one of his most popular works, interpreted by you who first put it on and who now live in the fulness of charm and talent, would be for all an event of art and literary exemplariness." [17] Matilde Moreno promised to revive *Electra* in the Teatro Cómico after the *Don Juan* season.[18] There is no record that she kept her promise. Conceivably the petition was intended only as a defiant gesture against the regime.

Nine years later, in 1933, the second Spanish republic was a little less than two years old. It had barely had time to consolidate itself when subtle influences sought to undermine its foundation. Inspired by the success of Eduardo Marquina's *Teresa de Jesús,* mercenary playwrights began to exploit the stage in what threatened to become a campaign against spiritual tolerance—one of the keystones of the new Spain. Once again Galdós' *Electra* was recalled. The revival of this now historic drama, it was argued, would disperse the menacing cloud of reaction.

The idea was first suggested by Núñez de Arenas in *La Voz* and was vigorously endorsed by Juan Chabás, dramatic critic of republican *Luz,* and others. Margarita Xirgu, skillful interpreter of Galdós' *Marianela,* and Enrique Borrás, unsurpassed in the role of Albrit in *El abuelo,* were urged to head the cast of *Electra,* which was to be revived, fittingly, in the Teatro Español. Galdós' drama, it was claimed, would afford some relief from the dead weight of contemporary dramatic inferiority. There was little fear that the effects might be the same as in 1901, but should this be the case it would only serve to demonstrate that nineteenth-century fanaticism was still alive in Spain of 1933. In any event, it was well worth trying; in the words of Chabás, "*Electra* was a work with literary dignity, full of fervor, and created in a moment of struggle, without any sectarianism or commercial eagerness to take advantage of protest or anger for the benefit of the box office." [19]

Núñez de Arena's idea did not bear fruit for almost a year, but the result was impressive. On the night of February 3, 1934, the thirty-third anniversary of *Electra* was observed with a special performance by Rivas Cherif's experimental Teatro Escuela de Arte in the Teatro de María Guerrero. To make the event a worthy tribute to the memory of Galdós, Luis Echaide, a professional actor of note, joined the cast as Pantoja, and the venerable Francisco Fuentes, who had played Máximo in 1901 under the author's personal guidance, directed the production.

The last performance of *Electra* gave renewed proof of its enduring significance for Spain. The atmosphere created by both actors and public testified to the vital reality and spiritual vigor of the theme. The years 1901 and 1934 fused to illuminate the contemporary moment. Pantoja came back to life and was at once recognized as a familiar figure. A challenging, warlike spirit again seized the spectators. They became painfully aware how little ground Spain had covered in thirty-three years. The freedom of the individual conscience for which their parents fought valiantly in 1901 still called for stout defense in 1934. The new Spain symbolized in *Electra* had not yet arrived. A false traditionalism still blocked the road to spiritual regeneration. Fanaticism was militant. The challenge of *Electra* was hardly less real.

* * * *

In 1901 Pío Baroja warned Galdós that one cannot with impunity become the conscience of a multitude. Galdós paid a high price for his new role. The crude apotheosis thrust upon him by the public, which he accepted in a moment of human weakness, made of him a clumsy popular hero, leaving an indelible mark on his character. It ill became him to regard—as he often did—his momentary exaltation as belated recognition of his enduring worth and position. This was a severe moral penalty of which he was perhaps unconscious. In retrospect, however, it is pleasant to reflect that Galdós incurred this penalty for having created a work which, though artistically not flawless, can still serve as an illuminated gospel of progress for Spain in her moments of spiritual dusk.

XVII

Republican Interlude

THE BOURBON RESTORATION IN THE early seventies had made
Galdós apprehensive about the spiritual health of his country.
Ominous symptoms portended the return of clerical influence,
which he felt called upon to combat vigorously. The purely
political issues and the social and economic problems confronting
the new regime caused him much less concern than the revived
strength of clericalism. His so-called religious trilogy was largely
an expression of this preoccupation, and five years of relatively
intimate contact with national politics as a "cradle" deputy
strengthened his conviction that the liberalization of Spain could
never be accomplished without the destruction of clerical power.
Parliamentarism with its vain personal rivalries and the pathetic
revolutionary gestures of the militant republicans seemed to him
so much fatuous folderol by comparison with the one vital
national problem.

When the disaster of 1898 threw Spaniards into mental and
spiritual confusion, Galdós was one of few who appraised the
situation clearly. He decried the prevailing pessimism, which he
feared might lead Spain to her death. It was no time for recrimination. It was more urgent to discover a common ideal for the
coordination of the scattered spiritual energy of the nation. As in
the seventies, he became imbued with a mission and felt a persistent craving for action. It was his duty to reassert himself as
the spokesman of liberal Spain. As if to acquaint his followers
with his new resolve, he made public in July, 1900, a letter he
had written to Fernando León y Castillo to congratulate him
upon his appointment as ambassador to France.[1] In this letter the

383

personal message served only as an excuse for a concise appraisal of the national situation.

The sensational success of *Electra* confirmed Galdós in his belief that clericalism was the paramount problem of Spain. Moreover, he interpreted the apparent willingness of the younger generation to rally around him, at least temporarily, as a mandate of leadership. And he was eager to assume it. Never before had he had a stronger urge to live dynamically, to be a man of action. Two courses were open to him: the political arena and the patriotic education of his fellow citizens. For the time being he wisely chose not to seek a seat in the congress of deputies. To an invitation to run for Cortes which he received during April, 1901, from the president of the Chamber of Commerce of Béjar, Galdós replied by telegram: "I regret exceedingly to be unable to accede to your desire. Please communicate this to your Chamber together with my most profound gratitude. A stranger to active politics, because it is a field ill adapted to the nature of my work, I shall decline as long as possible to join in any electoral struggle. As representative of the Chamber of Commerce, please accept my special appreciation."

There were other ways of serving the cause of progress. Even as *Electra* was still spreading his gospel through the land, Galdós spoke to foreign reporters in the name of Spanish liberalism and accepted invitations to write articles on the issues he had raised in his drama. For the *Neue freie Presse* of Vienna he wrote an extensive appraisal of the prevailing spiritual climate of Spain, in which he blamed the all-pervading clerical forces for many of his country's political, social, economic, and cultural ills. What in *Electra* had been merely insinuations against the Jesuits became forthright denunciations. In Spain itself the radical press was now less given to dismissing him lightly as the champion of outmoded bourgeois ideas and patriotic sentiments. From the rabble-rousing daily *El Motín* to the professional journal *Progreso Agrícola y Pecuario*, newspapers and reviews publicized his views on national issues, whether or not directly related to the spiritual welfare of the country.

At this time Galdós had only a creed, not a platform. He regarded existing parliamentary agencies as highly inadequate for the reforms he had in mind, and conditions were not yet ripe for revolutionary measures. While others harped on the causes of Spain's decadence, he aimed to inspire the nation with a will to survive and to forge ahead. The doctrine of will versus *abulia*, so widely discussed after the Spanish-American War, became his monotonous gospel. He cited himself as an illustration of what courage, determination, and an indomitable spirit could accomplish. With an optimism born of faith rather than reason he freely predicted a resurgence of national glory, provided misfortunes were accepted not as death blows but as warnings and lessons. Spain's regeneration, he emphasized, would not be achieved without sacrificing old attitudes, concepts, and institutions.

Galdós was infinitely happier in the pronouncement of principle than in the perfection of procedures. Thus, speaking before the Círculo Militar of Cartagena in December, 1903, he charged the army with the responsibility of injecting the scientific spirit of modern education into the soul of Spain. This was indeed a novel duty for the military, but he reasoned with his audience that it was the armed might that had built the great Spanish empire and had collaborated during the nineteenth century in the enforcement of the principles of liberty and human, civilizing laws. Why, he asked, could not the army effect the synthesis of an ideal Spain in the twentieth century by becoming the guardian of a new national education? Galdós was obviously carried away on this occasion by the natural desire to flatter his listeners and by the historian's habit of linking the past with the present. It did occur to him that the professional soldiers would need a skilled guide for the effective discharge of this new duty. Too humble to suggest himself, he urged the Spanish army and navy to emulate England in the task of educating their country in scientific living.[2]

If Galdós ever wondered whether the mandate of leadership given him by Spanish youth in the days of *Electra* was still valid, he received ample reassurance in 1904. The public tribute rendered him upon the success of *El abuelo* strengthened his faith in his mission. He began to take himself even more seri-

ously as the conscience of the masses. His position as artist had
never been stronger, and his personal relations with the "ninety-
eighters" had never been more cordial. Of all the great figures
of the nineteenth century he alone generally escaped youth's
iconoclastic axe.

The wisdom of following Galdós was seriously questioned by
Miguel de Unamuno, who did not consider him an altogether
satisfactory spiritual guide for the young generation. But before
very long Don Miguel modified his opinion, or temporarily
abandoned it for strategic reasons. For some time he had been
formulating a plan for collective action under a non-partisan,
liberal banner, with or without the monarchy. In July, 1905, he
openly solicited Galdós' cooperation. It would seem, however,
that Galdós found Unamuno's "possibilist radicalism" insuf-
ficiently dynamic. By now he was convinced that the solution of
the all-pervading religious problem required something more
concrete than Unamuno's gospel of a humble, suffering, personal
God. He saw no harm in dealing with religion philosophically
and speculatively—he himself had done so time and again in
literary works—but one could not offer the masses vague concepts in lieu of a program for collective action. And the time was
ripe for testing the effect of years of spiritual reorientation on the
national conscience.

Nevertheless Galdós was not disposed to indulge in precipitate
action. Late in 1905 he published the dialogue novel *Casandra*
as a sort of trial balloon. The reception of its frankly anticlerical
theme and forthright criticism of the stifling atmosphere of
dogmatism was deeply gratifying. It was hailed as his most revolutionary work, a faithful reflection of the social state of Spain.
From an artistic standpoint it might lack his customary balanced
tone, but virtually all agreed that his ringing passion and exultation were philosophically justified. Certainly none misread his
intention, and many spoke freely of him as a social reformer and
an apostle with a definite gospel. He was reminded of the obligation he had incurred in *Electra*. But *Casandra* was more than the
voice of the conscience of the masses; it was a final challenge.
Action was the next step.

How deeply *Casandra* stirred those who since the disaster of 1898 had been looking for a weapon against the national inertia may be inferred from the following comment:

> It is impossible to read this last book by Galdós, which sketches with strokes of fire our social state, without feeling that the shadows, the confused and nebulous germs of ideas which wander inchoately through the space of our mind, are taking on substance, are arranging themselves in patterns, are becoming strongly and clearly defined. *Casandra* is a guide that blazes a spiritual trail; it is a battering ram which is beginning to tear down a stout wall; it is a warrior leader who orders an attack; it is a banner that offers shelter; it is an oracle which consoles by predicting salvation through destruction.[3]

[Just as in the eighties Sagasta had discovered the value of Galdós' prestige to his monarchical liberal party, so now the left-wing politicians contrived to make political capital out of his spiritual ascendency.] Galdós, to be sure, had never openly espoused republicanism; indeed, as a "cradle" deputy he had frequently denounced Ruiz Zorrilla and other republican chieftains. But since the epoch-making *Electra* his liberalism had gradually taken on brighter hues, and he had been expressing himself in militant terms. To the professional politicians there seemed to be little difference between Galdós' repeated tactical moves against clericalism and their own frontal assaults on the monarchy. The ultimate objective was the same even if the procedures differed. Why not form an alliance with the distinguished writer? It should be an easy matter to convince him that a coordinated effort under a unified command would assure a quick victory.

*   *   *   *

By the close of 1906 the Madrid branch of the republican party badly needed an energizing agent. There was to be an election early the next year. The higher councils, sensing what tremendous support to the cause would be won if Galdós could be persuaded to become a candidate for Cortes, delegated

Demófilo (Don Fernando Lozano), littérateur-politician in the best Spanish tradition, to undertake the delicate mission of Galdós' conversion. Twice he bore the party's message to the author, and twice he received a negative reaction—although not a definite refusal. But the resourceful republicans were not easily discouraged. Headed by Luis Morote and Rodrigo Soriano, their Cortes representatives opened a drive for a national tribute to Galdós, to be sponsored by the lawmakers. These sensed quickly the real purpose of the project. They would have had to be quixotically magnanimous to support it. The sponsors of the drive were easily routed, though not without first engaging the opposition in several oratorical skirmishes which put Galdós very much in the news again.

By way of compensation there was talk of another huge banquet, like the one in 1883, with an even more broadly popular base. It was only an idea, but the journalists discussed it as a project already in the process of realization.

Here and there a naïve writer failed to grasp the real motives of the republican deputies and hailed the proposed tribute to Galdós as another tribute to a great artist. Abusing his poetic license, Eduardo Marquina dreamed in poetic prose about a veritable apotheosis for Don Benito. He would stage a popular celebration of unprecedented size in the Puerta del Sol, with the sun and light for the *mise en scène* and with shouts of triumph and hymns of solemn dedication for music. To give the music a touch of the soul of Spain, choruses singing regional songs would come from the four corners of the land. National banners and shields would flutter in the air. Myriads of eyes would be focused on the balcony of the Ministry of Interior, converted into a fitting dais for the man who had woven a new banner for the nation. Galdós would appear on the balcony to receive the plaudits of the vast concourse in the Puerta del Sol—the heart of Spain. No other form of tribute would be worthy of the nation's foremost figure.[4]

Galdós himself may have doubted the sincerity of the politicians' gesture, but he did not protest. Their overtures seemed to give form and substance to his recently reborn ambition to assume leadership and his craving for action. Apparently it did not offend his modesty to be described as the national champion in the following terms:

> The tribute to Pérez Galdós will provide an opportunity for a political manifestation of great repercussion and extreme usefulness in the face of the stratagems of ultramontanism, because around the exalted figure of the great Spaniard, of the fearless evocator of our struggles for liberty will rally all those of the left, all whose political ideas are rooted in democracy, to give absolute testimony of the inexpugnable strength born of their more or less accidental union and of their certainty of triumph against the battles of reaction.[5]

Demófilo's third visit sealed Galdós' conversion to republicanism. To make his decision appear deliberate, he discussed it with his friends. Their surprise was boundless, but he assured them that his political change was inevitable. Anyone familiar with the ideological substance of his works should have realized that he had always been pro-democracy, and since 1880 an almost-republican. His specious reasons did not satisfy his friends, but their remonstrances and warnings were futile. Before very long he announced his willingness to be a republican candidate for a seat in Cortes. His decision was accepted with unrestrained joy by the politicians, who agreed to his stipulations about his running mates in other districts. Galdós thus enlisted in the republican cause on his own terms, as it were.

Galdós' new comrades failed in their efforts to dramatize his conversion; the public announcement early in March, 1907, caused only a mild flurry of excitement in Spanish political circles. There was more interest in the convert's motives than in the conversion itself. On April 6 Galdós professed his new faith in an open letter to Alfredo Vicenti, director of *El Liberal* and a co-candidate on the republican ticket. To this document the liberal and radical press gave wide publicity.

Explaining his resolve to fight the monarchy, Galdós stated that, difficult as it was for him to exchange the quiet of his study for the tumult of the political arena, he could no longer evade his patriotic duty. There were those who looked upon patriotism as an old, rusty weapon. For him it was a noble sentiment which the masses fortunately still carried, and would always carry, in their hearts. He knew the road before him was rough, but he would rather travel it than live in a state of fatalistic indolence like many of the young generation. By his example he hoped to give new life to the sublime concepts of national faith, patriotic love, and public conscience. Despite his age—he was sixty-four— he felt younger and stronger than the anemic youngsters. He expected no reward other than the joy to be derived from discharging his civic duty.

Why did he choose to espouse the republican ideal? His waning monarchical sentiments had expired completely when the new law governing religious associations had been passed, for he was convinced that the government had abdicated so much of its sovereignty as to destroy all hope of national regeneration, of life free from clerical domination, and of culture. He refused "to be lulled to sleep in the laps of friars," to submit to the terrifying tyranny of ecclesiastical bossism. It was a critical moment in the history of Spain. The nation was threatened with asphixiation, and he for one was determined to break all spiritual confinement and seek a breath of fresh air. He felt deeply ashamed to continue being a European only "by virtue of geography, Italian opera, and the unrestrained use of the automobile."

As he entered the republican encampment, said Galdós, he was cheered by the sight of the numerous tents and the spirited, alert hosts. He was proud to be a comrade-in-arms and confident that many more would follow him to swell the ranks. Before very long the republican legions would be so numerous that national spiritual redemption would become inevitable. No revolution would be necessary to achieve the goal, for the monarchy by its continuous blunders would alienate so many of its adherents that it would necessarily collapse.

Galdós closed his manifesto with the solemn pledge to work for the complete realization of the republican program. For him the foremost objective was the eradication of "clerical barbarism."

Next came the erection of a scientific foundation for the education of future generations and the destruction of political bossism. And above all, he urged his new comrades to be united and firm in their resolve to keep alive their national conscience and pride.[6]

For some days the press made spirited comments on Galdós' declaration. The genuine liberals applauded him as vigorously as the conservatives condemned him. The plaudits and vituperation created a din which drowned out common sense. His friends regarded his move with frank apprehension. It was obvious, however, that neither advice nor pleas would induce him to turn back. He was absent from Madrid during the storm which he had precipitated, and when he returned he plunged into the strenuous political campaign.

It was a novel and stimulating experience. For the first time in his life Galdós took an active part in political meetings. The campaign managers knew the value of his personal appearance before the proletarian electorate. At none of the rallies did he speak extemporaneously; he read carefully prepared addresses or had them delivered by friends. But his lack of oratorical skill did not prove to be a political handicap. The campaign was bitterly fought, but victory was in sight. When the ballots were counted, it was at first believed that all the six republican candidates had been elected, but in the city hall a "deal" was made whereby only three were declared victorious, Galdós included. He did not quite understand the technique by which the other candidates had been eliminated, but he accepted the arrangement and prepared to embark upon the second stage of his political career.

Galdós the republican candidate of 1907 did not bear the slightest resemblance to Galdós the poised liberal of the eighties. His campaign utterances were so impassioned that they must have offended his own ears. The restrained thinker had seemingly turned demagogue overnight. As the official voice of anti-clerical Spain he presented clericalism as the paramount issue in terms and tones suggestive of a veteran street-corner orator. It is hard to believe that the following words were penned by humble, moderate, and reticent Benito Pérez Galdós:

Together we shall march to defeat recalcitrant clericalism. Our aspiration is the extinction of this locust that invades the land and the air and devours matter as well as spirit. Our aim is the total disinfection of our country by dissipating this sinister cloud of voraciously toothed and terrifyingly buzzing parasites. We seek the disappearance of the friar who blackens your life, who warily invades your home, who confounds your conscience and who sticks his hand into your plate, threatening you with the infamous *boycott* or with the suffering of *hell* if you dare call a halt to his brutal egoism. We must maintain that the real hell is the friar, and that this visible and tangible hell must be extinguished in Spain forever.[7]

It is quite possible that the sizzling passion of Galdós' campaign oratory was mostly verbal. In all his addresses there is evident a straining for literary effect—perhaps as compensation for his oratorical deficiencies. As their composition was not spontaneous, his customary stylistic simplicity yielded to extravagant rhetorical indulgences. He had always admired political oratory, and he may have been subconsciously under the spell of the famous speakers he had heard in his journalistic days. In any event, he carried on the nineteenth-century tradition of Spanish oratory—an odd mixture of baroque and rococo. How beautiful his constituents must have thought the following oratorical pyrotechnics to convey the idea that Spain had had a great awakening!

We thought that the hard flint would throw out light as soon as it was struck with the steel. But this flint of our fatherland has been even more efficacious. It has not needed to receive the blow: as soon as it saw the steel near, it began to sputter sparks in all directions. Strike energetically with your steeled wills and you will draw all the fire that you need for the generous conflagration of our generation.[8]

* * * *

[Galdós' usefulness to the republicans did not end with his election. His prestige was exploited for the organizational needs of the party, and his literary talent for the propagation of political ideology.] Among his early assignments in Cortes was the consolidation of the left-wing bloc of democrats, republicans, socialists, and liberals. He undertook this job willingly, since it entailed extensive travel in the company of outstanding radical leaders. It was a splendid opportunity for enhancing his literary popularity while making propaganda for the fusion of all the antimonarchical forces. His output, to be sure, was falling off appreciably—he published only one *episodio* in 1907—but the future would conceivably reveal the benefits of his personal appearances at mass meetings in Barcelona, Santander, San Sebastián, and Almería, and of direct contact with the progressive elements in those cities. He worked loyally for the "bloc." And when the left-wingers finally banded together in November, 1908, Galdós spoke with satisfaction of his generous contribution to republicanism.

[His new political faith and affiliations forced Galdós to modify radically his social convictions. Whereas formerly he had concentrated on the middle class, now he paid more attention to the proletariat and hailed its growing enlightenment, improved organization, and gathering strength. He was not yet prepared to advocate a social revolution, but he did urge the workers, and especially the peasants, to wrest leadership from the rich.] In the interests of a peaceful transfer of power he advised the representatives of wealth to rid themselves of the social parasites in their midst—the element that did nothing but consume the best that agriculure and industry yielded. He warned them that "rich, self-indulging, and *sportive* idleness," because it was indifferent to general suffering, was heading for serious trouble in the near future. He envisaged the redemption of the toiling masses at a fairly early date, which would naturally mean less affluence for the rich. Art and elegance would suffer, but he felt certain that the harm would be temporary. In any event, he reasoned, the welfare of the masses merited the sacrifice of refinements by the idle rich. [Eventually a new order would emerge in which the toiling masses as well as the wealthy industrial class would share justice based on art, capital, and work.⁹

Galdós' utterances on agrarian reform were more rhetorical than practical. He bewailed the tendency of peasants to abandon the land for scarce opportunities in the cities, and he pleaded abstractly for narrowing the gap between rural and urban life. Essentially a philosopher rather than a practical politician, he advocated mutual understanding, sympathy, and general rapprochement between rustics and city dwellers. Considering agriculture as the backbone of the nation, he urged amelioration of the lot of the farmer, but offered no more concrete solution than the suggestion that it would require something more than patience and sobriety—the virtues traditionally conceded to the Spanish peasant in lieu of governmental guidance and subsidies. It seemed unfair that the benefits of national agriculture should be enjoyed by the wealthy landowners who resided in the cities, while backwardness and barbarism prevailed in the rural regions. And having posited the problem in ethical terms, he indicated a similarly intangible solution—why not bring all the good things of civilization to the farm and put the city dweller occasionally in intimate contact with mother earth?[10]

In 1909 Galdós' political stature acquired a semblance of impressiveness. National life seemed threatened with internal convulsions. Public opinion everywhere, and particularly in Catalonia, was hostile toward the ill-advised military campaign in Morocco, and there were many anticlerical demonstrations, often accompanied by violence. In Barcelona bloody rioting led to severe repressive measures. The highlight of the nationwide disturbances was the military trial and execution of the famous Catalan radical, Francisco Ferrer. The incident assumed international significance, and in Spain it accentuated the cleavage between conservatives and liberals. The time had come for a showdown between the supporters of a blundering, reactionary monarchy and the militant champions of a truly democratic Spain.

The advocates of republicanism were quick to exploit the situation—and Galdós' views on it. In September he published a relatively mild protest against the unpopular African war and the government's violent measures against its opponents. The specific occasion was the censorship imposed exclusively upon the liberal press. Speaking as an individual republican, Galdós mixed sincere patriotism with party politics in unequal proportions. He protested less against the injustice of waging a war solely for the protection of private interests than against its administration by a conservative monarchical cabinet backed by the church and other elements whose patriotism was questionable. Conceivably he would not have raised his voice against such a military enterprise had it been sponsored by a republican regime. At this point it was the form of government that was his main preoccupation, and he did not quite succeed in squaring it with his otherwise bourgeois patriotism.

But official Spain was not easily moved by one who spoke in his own name. Accordingly, less than a month later Galdós issued something like a manifesto to the nation, which was widely publicized in the press and at public gatherings. With passionate eloquence he urged the Spanish people to meet the government's policies with something more than "amazement followed by fatalistic resignation." He denounced the passivity of the public, which lived in "a limbo of stupid somnolence" created by the Jesuits, who for years had been weighing down the Spanish soul with "lead of indifference, inhibition, and egoism." Although speaking ostensibly as an outraged Spaniard, he did not hesitate to suggest that the national disaster could be averted by a new governing body. In fact, in his closing words he reminded the Spaniards that the republicans were in the front line of action against what he described as the worst political barbarism since the days of Fernando VII.[11]

Even before the call to arms had died away, the republicans were preparing for the impending battle. They began negotiations for an official coalition with the socialists, Galdós and Gumersindo Azcárate being delegated to woo Pablo Iglesias, head of the Marxist party. It was the first meeting of the literary-political leader and the powerful organizer of the class-conscious Spanish proletariat. It was not easy to unite the socialists and the bourgeois-minded antimonarchists, but the fusion was ultimately effected, at least for election purposes, and Galdós became the titular head of a new organization known as "La Conjunción Republicano-socialista." It was a motley aggregation whose collaboration, superficial though it was, must have surprised even its constituents. Besides the two factions that gave the united front its promising name there were *progresistas*, *federales*, and representatives of the municipal republican minority of Madrid. Missing from the coalition were Lerroux' radical followers and the Republican Union Party.

Galdós' new political responsibilities made heavy demands upon his time. Both his Madrid residence and his Santander summer home became the frequent rendezvous of those who mapped the strategy of the antimonarchical forces. Galdós taxed his rhetorical power in the composition of harangues which were read at the branches of the coalition party in the principal cities. A manifesto he and his comrades drew up which included overthrow of the monarchy as a principal goal was refused circulation by the Ministry of Interior. This did not deter him from instigating a demand for the convening of Cortes. With public opinion divided over the execution of Ferrer on October 13, 1909, the republicans realized the value of maintaining the country in a state of continuous agitation. The conservatives' watchword of *Maura sí* was loudly challenged by the radicals' slogan of *Maura no*. Before very long the "nays" had it, and Antonio Maura, prime minister of the reactionary cabinet responsible for Ferrer's execution, was forced to resign. He was replaced by Segismundo Moret y Prendergast, whose government lasted from the end of October, 1909, to the beginning of February, 1910, when he in turn was succeeded by Canalejas. With the advent of a liberal cabinet Cortes met and announced a congressional election. Days of taxing political activity lay ahead for Galdós: he was a candidate for re-election on the republican-socialist ticket.

Perhaps no Spanish campaign was ever conducted more successfully and less orthodoxly than the one in which Galdós was now engaged. It was no mere coincidence that on the very eve of the campaign he staged the highly charged anticlerical play *Casandra*. Its political purpose escaped no one, and Galdós did not hesitate to state it subsequently in the preface of the printed text:

> It is not fair to demand of art that it limit itself exclusively to the lyricism of beautiful things. We cannot do this even if we should wish to, because out of the soil and the air of our fatherland there rises a mighty voice which says to us: "You who do not legislate nor have any part in the functions of the State; you writers and poets, professional idlers, relate and sing my cares so that they may reach the ears and the wills of those who can remedy them. Help me with your clamors to free myself from the death which waylays me and give me courage to control the life which I do not care to lose.[12]

Needless to say, Galdós' political comrades underwrote the success of *Casandra*, which carried still further the criticisms contained in *Electra*. They bent all their efforts toward converting the première into a memorable event. Rumors were circulated—and promptly denied by Manuel Domínguez, impresario of the Teatro Español—that the Madrid government was preparing to suppress the play. The liberal press forthwith fashioned a national issue out of the rumors and threw it into the lap of Prime Minister Canalejas. This was manifestly a part of the planned publicity, whose effectiveness must have exceeded the expectations of even its sponsors. For several days the demand for seats was so great that special ticket offices had to be opened under heavy police guard. Everyone was eager to see the drama advertised as the sequel of *Electra*. Its theme and its contemporary significance were widely publicized. The author was characterized as the altruistic defender of the aspirations of the revolutionary masses and the proponent of reform. Madrid waited impatiently for Galdós' bold words and revolutionary grimaces, for the slaying of old, hypocritical Catholic Spain—symbolized in Doña Juana—by the mighty weapon of the modern spirit, represented by Casandra. The première was somewhat delayed because the play had no suitable role for Enrique Borrás, and it was deemed advisable to wait until he should leave the company of the Español. It was maliciously rumored that the delay was premeditated in order to stimulate interest and, consequently, to raise the admission price.

Not since the days of *Electra* had Galdós received so many tumultuous ovations as on the night of *Casandra*. The strident tones of its liberal and even radical sallies were accentuated by the declaiming actors, who apparently counted more on vocal strength than on histrionic subtlety to impress the audience. The audience received the revolutionary gestures of Galdós with energetic applause. He had to respond to perhaps twenty curtain calls, some of them in the middle of the third act after a particularly impassioned speech. Few spectators failed to recall the première of *Electra* as they watched the play developing into a menacing demonstration, and a similarly disturbing recollection must have raced through the minds of the police guards posted near the theater. An official car was on hand to take Galdós home. This detail alone almost caused a clash between the police and the public, which was resolved to accompany the author in an improvised parade. A crowd of five hundred lustily cheered Galdós as president of the imminent republic. It was a noisy, disorganized procession, but no untoward incidents occurred. Evidently some of Canalejas' liberal spirit had descended upon the police force of the Spanish capital.

The political success of *Casandra* was even greater than its "triumph" on the stage. The reviewers of the liberal press very shrewdly emphasized Galdós' literary achievement and dwelt very lightly on the contemporary significance of his social ideology. Conservatives, on the other hand, raged against the play and its author, denounced him as the purveyor of poisonous ideas for financial gain and as the instigator of a revolution of atheists and freethinkers against God, Church, and Fatherland. He was pictured as a fanatic capable of deriving fiendish delight from the sight of friars dangling from lamp posts while convents and monasteries were going up in flames.

The fury of the anti-liberal critics only whetted the curiosity of the Madrid masses. For nearly two weeks long queues of ticket purchasers lined up in front of the Español. *Casandra* became the banner under which Spain's anticlerical hosts assembled. In republican headquarters the forthcoming elections were awaited with serene confidence. Campaigners with the oratorical genius of Demosthenes could not have accomplished for the republican-socialist coalition what Galdós had achieved with one theatrical work. As an expression of faith in his political acumen he was delegated to win the support of Alejandro Lerroux, wily leader of the Radical Party. This Galdós accomplished in Barcelona, where he went to witness the staging of his play. Although the victory was not won without disgusting political horse-trading, he was willing to overlook it for the sake of the cause. He accepted the cheers of the Madrid and Barcelona audiences not merely as approval of his views but also as a mandate for active leadership. When eventually the election returns revealed that his 42,000 votes topped the list of the six successful republican candidates, he was delighted. He even permitted himself to gloat a bit over the poor showing of the ministerial party, which elected only two deputies in Madrid. Dazzled by the admiration of the masses and beguiled by his crafty political associates, Galdós momentarily deluded himself with the vision of a national renaissance in which his share would not be the least conspicuous. He dreamed of a Spanish republic in a not too distant future.

In 1901 Galdós had frowned upon the suggestion that *Electra* was perhaps a call to arms. At that time he was convinced that any revolutionary movement in Spain would result only in a change of labels, that the really pressing needs were the destruction of political bossism, the elimination of the Jesuits, and the reform of educational institutions. By 1910, however, he had narrowed the problem down to the all-pervading power of clericalism, which he saw no way of destroying without revolutionary measures. He would have preferred gradual evolution, but nothing in the national scene offered hope for such a possibility. As for the nature of the revolutionary measures and the proper time to implement them, he vaguely suggested that either a general strike or military intervention might be the means of establishing a republic. For the time being it was urgent to win popular support for the republican movement. Galdós did not yet realize that his republicanism was actually no different from his abiding belief in a regenerated fatherland. He was soon to discover the futility of trying to define the essence of a thing by attaching a label to it.

*　　*　　*　　*

For the next two years Galdós discharged his duties earnestly and vigorously. Between 1910 and 1912 there were several moments of national tension and an occasional crisis in his political camp, all of which Galdós faced with a keen sense of responsibility to the nation and to his party. Twice in 1911 he protested fearlessly against the government's policies—once to denounce its unwarranted military adventures in Morocco, and again to demand the strict observance of constitutional guarantees. On both occasions his prestige won the support of the liberals. He always acted in his official political capacity, but he laid more stress on principles than on politics or party interests. The direct effect of his intervention in public life was probably negligible, but he had the satisfaction of performing his patriotic duty. He may also have hoped to stimulate the apathetic younger generation, whose contribution to the regeneration of the fatherland had been mainly vocal. Thoughtful Spaniards did not fail to admire the spiritual fortitude and youthful idealism of a man approaching seventy.

In Cortes Galdós was neither effective nor impressive. He attended all the sessions, but mostly as an observer. He still regarded Spanish parliamentary politics as a farce, but as a minority representative he now watched it with keener interest. When nothing of moment took place in the legislative chamber, he preferred to remain in the corridors, usually near the conference room, leaning on his cane and smoking incessantly. But when a new deputy delivered his maiden speech, or when a debate moved on a plane of ideas, he was among the most attentive listeners. His interest in oratory was still largely literary, but it had also a bit of the attitude of a semi-professional.

For in recent years he had made several political speeches and learned some of the finer points of the art. Although his friends spoke flatteringly of his limited oratorical skill, he was not encouraged to join in parliamentary debates even on matters of concern to his "bloc." He left that to his more talented colleagues, whom he knew to have superior histrionic talent if less power of expression.

On one occasion Galdós was obliged to make a speech. There was a vacancy in one of the congressional districts of Madrid, which the republicans were ambitious to fill. Galdós was largely instrumental in securing fifty thousand signatures to a petition for a special election. As a reward and in tribute to his prestige, it was arranged that he should present the petition to Cortes. When speaker Eduardo Dato announced that the chair recognized Señor Pérez Galdós, a wave of eager curiosity surged through the assembly. Señor Pérez Galdós spoke the few brief words which he had memorized and rehearsed the day before, and his colleagues listened in hushed silence. Galdós looked relieved when the ordeal was over. But his speech caused no ripple either of approval or disapprobation.

Galdós' enthusiasm for republicanism began to decline in 1911. His failing health may have been one reason. Possibly, too, he had become more keenly aware of the harmful effect his radical political activity was having upon his literary fortunes. But principally it was the realization that he and his republican associates were obviously inspired by widely divergent motives. His old skepticism of political labels and platforms returned. He still carried out his duties faithfully, but his heart was no longer in the work. His secretary, Pablo Nougués, began to notice that he was irritable whenever he had to attend political meetings or sessions of the executive committee of the "bloc." On one occasion, when he was reminded about an appointment with his comrades, he thundered: "Give them back my election certificate and ask them to leave me alone." [13] And when asked why he continued to serve as deputy, he remarked more in earnest than in jest that he wished to convince himself beyond doubt that the root of Spain's ills lay precisely in parliamentarism.

Years of intimate contact with republicanism and republicans had restored Galdós' conviction that personal ambition and not love of country inspired radicals and conservatives alike. He now realized that he had adopted republicanism only as a more striking symbol of his deep desire for a regenerated fatherland. At times he was inclined to regard the Spanish problem as merely a segment of the larger problem of all human society. Perhaps the only solution for this problem was socialism, which attracted him more and more because of its seeming sincerity. In comparison Spanish republicanism appeared petty to him, and the effectiveness of political action by a heterogeneous group like the "bloc" sheer daydreaming. He was quite ready to withdraw his support from an institution which he had mistaken for a cause.

*   *   *   *

Galdós' retirement from active politics was gradual and unheralded. He made no public renunciation of republican faith, nor did he intimate that he had experienced a new conversion. His friends were delighted that he would no longer be the tool of scheming politicians. It had been pathetic to see him, now almost totally blind, piloted from one public function to another by his servants Paco and Victoriano. It was hoped that he would rededicate himself exclusively to literature. True, there were signs that his power had declined, but few believed that his vein had run completely dry. Even during the five years of his most intense political activity he had managed to write eight novels and produce two dramas. In *El caballero encantado* (1910)— an odd combination of realism and fantasy floating in an atmosphere of subtle symbolism—he had demonstrated the enduring clarity of his vision of Spanish life and his ability to write a chastely classical style. He was an old man, but in mental vigor and spiritual suppleness he seemed more youthful than the rising generation of intellectuals and artists.

A seemingly spontaneous incident in the Teatro Español in December, 1913, gave the public the first intimation that Galdós had abandoned all hope of establishing a republic in Spain. The royal family was present at a performance of *Celia en los infiernos,* and Galdós was invited to its box during one of the intermissions. In all likelihood the meeting had been prearranged by the Conde de Romanones. The shrewd prime minister must have reasoned that an estrangement between the republicans and Benito Pérez Galdós would certainly not hurt the monarchy. But aside from any political consideration, he sincerely shared the prevalent conviction that Galdós' role as a public figure was awkward, pathetic, and harmful to his literary reputation. Galdós himself was by now not entirely averse to a reconciliation with the monarchy. The assassination of Canalejas, a solid liberal, by an anarchist in 1912 had already made him wonder whether there was any real connection between the welfare of a nation and its particular form of government. Moreover, in his harassing economic situation his thoughts had often turned to the advisability of securing a state pension or stipend. When King Alfonso officially inquired in the summer of 1912 about the outcome of the operation on his eye, Galdós felt that the first step had been taken toward a reconcilation.

Whatever the motive, the king's interest in his health encouraged Galdós to seek a rapprochement with the monarchy. When Romanones became prime minister and began to steer national politics on a promising course, Galdós wrote to congratulate him and, incidentally, to seek an audience with the king. Romanones' reply was frank:

> My dear Friend:
>
> Many thanks for your congratulations, which I cannot accept because I am not honestly entitled to them. I shall transmit them in their entirety to the one to whom they are due: to His Majesty the King, who alone is responsible for the new political orientation.
>
> If you wish to die a republican, do not come to the Palace; if you do come, my dear Don Benito, and speak with the King, I believe that you will have to experience a new conversion. You know that I am ever your fond friend and admirer,
>
> C. Romanones

Galdós did not care in what political aura he would die, nor would he have found a new conversion especially distasteful, but for some reason his audience with the king took place not in the palace but in the royal box of the Teatro Español.

The meeting with Alfonso caused more than a flutter in the audience, and the Madrid press publicized it with more irony than sincerity. But Galdós took it seriously, and he was extraordinarily voluble in describing it to inquiring reporters. His impression of the monarch was enthusiastically favorable. He stressed his wide range of interests and his grasp of the pressing national problems. It flattered him particularly that the king heartily approved the plea in *Celia en los infiernos* for the improvement of the lot of the workers and that he spoke confidentially of his intention to found an institute for modern and scientific training of youth. Galdós was now firmly convinced that the ruler of Spain was more genuinely interested in the welfare of the country than all the politicians, and that his differences with the regime had been rather nebulous after all. Altogether it was a memorable and enjoyable event, and he was looking forward to a similar meeting in Santander that summer. The suggestion came from Alfonso, who said: "When I go to Santander this summer, you will come to see me, won't you? . . . We are friends now." [14]

Pérez Galdós unquestionably had a friendly feeling for the king, but apparently it was not warm enough to melt the weak link that still bound him to the republicans. In the elections of the spring of 1914 he was a candidate from the congressional district of Las Palmas. Although his nomination was more in the nature of a local homage than a political gesture, it irritated Romanones, who had been sincerely trying to follow up the audience in the royal box with some official recognition for the aged writer. He expressed his displeasure in a letter to Galdós on March 2, 1914:

> MY DEAR FRIEND:
> I am told that you are going to present your candidacy in the Las Palmas district. This annoys me no end, because it endangers the election of Argente, who is so close to me that I consider him as if he were my own self.

Besides, you know that you are going to be made a
life senator and that to allow your name to be used
there amounts to lending aid to a political maneuver
without any practical value and whose sole object can
only be to harm me.

I am, as ever, your very fond friend,

C. ROMANONES

Galdós paid an exorbitant price for his success in the Las
Palmas election. The life senatorship never materialized, nor did
the audience with the king in Santander. Since he attached no
political importance to his seat in Cortes—and his constituents
did not take his attitude amiss—he saw no reason for discontinu-
ing his overtures to the monarch. Besides, had he not promised
to call on him in his summer palace? Accordingly, in August,
1914, he sought an opportunity to keep his promise. The royal
reply was a courteous refusal. Galdós' disappointment was keen.
The national subscription in his behalf was getting under way,
and a visit to the king would have been an invaluable asset.
Alfonso's excuse on the grounds of "the pressure of time" may
have been sincere; his attitude toward the indigent author probably remained unaffected by his latest political escapade. When
Galdós' sister Concha died in November of that year, the palace
sent him a personal message of condolence, and a little later the
king inaugurated the national subscription with a contribution of
ten thousand pesetas.

These friendly royal gestures added another to Galdós' senile
obsessions. Henceforth his interest in the king and his desire to
see him again was his most annoying preoccupation. During his
sojourns in Santander he never failed to wait on the terrace of
his home facing the principal boulevard to hear the king and his
escort pass by. Blind and tense, he would ask repeatedly whether
the royal car was in sight, and at the first sounds of the approaching escort would begin to bow deeply and reverently. It may
well be that in time Alfonso was apprised of the profound loyalty
of his distinguished subject, for in August, 1916, he invited him
to the Magdalena palace.

The king's cordial reception lingered for a long time in the

memory of the venerable author, and he wearied many a polite
listener with the details of the audience. Alfonso's manner was
charmingly simple and frank, and his cigars were superb. He was
genuinely interested in the artistic life of the nation, and his
appreciation of its literary production was profoundly intelligent.
Did any one wish proof? There was the king's statement that
he, Benito Pérez Galdós, was synonymous with the prestige of
contemporary Spanish literature. Someone would interrupt to
remind him that not so long before he had opposed the rule of
the Bourbons. With ill-repressed annoyance he would reply:
"That's dead and forgotten now. I a republican! I am a partisan
of Don Alfonso, who is the best Spaniard of the present generation." [15] No one doubted any more that the erstwhile president
of the republican-socialist coalition had regained his old belief
that political parties and parliamentarism alone could not effect
the regeneration of Spain.

*   *   *   *

When Galdós first appeared as a militant republican, his
admirers tried in vain to find a plausible explanation for his
move. Many believed that he had been caught in the storm he
himself had unleashed in *Electra*, and they predicted that because of his essentially timid nature he would be unable to wield
political influence. They deplored the way scheming politicans
exploited him without scruple, and were unable to square his
ardent patriotism with the lowly part he played in Cortes as
one of the seven in the obstructionist bloc. Was that the way to
a new, youthful, and vigorous Spain? Azorín must have spoken
the mind of his generation when he said:

> And this is where my perplexities and doubts begin.
> Galdós is one of our foremost literary figures; abroad
> his name is well known and respected; in Spain he is
> admired. His life has been a long life of work, a
> glorious life. How can one fail to be amazed at the
> sight of this illustrious man sitting every afternoon
> among the above-mentioned deputies, silent and with
> bowed head, waiting through the entire session to de-
> mand from time to time a roll call? Some are battling

polemicists in Parliament; some deliver many fiery speeches of opposition. But is it not rather sad to see this great figure serving silently as a complement in a task of obstruction carried on by the above-mentioned gentlemen? How explain that Galdós should have consented to play a role which other deputies declined?[16]

Galdós' enemies were less perplexed. They attributed his political partisanship to mercenary ambitions, maintaining that his republican activity was calculated to promote the sale of his books and to swell his theater audiences. And they clung to this explanation despite the fact that Galdós' popularity as a writer declined as his participation in politics increased. Even those readers who had once been willing to overlook the so-called radicalism of his contemporary novels—in consideration of his *episodios*—now resented the republican tone of his latest historical works. Obscure critics who before had not dared express their personal opinions about Galdós were now emboldened to characterize him as "the soporiferous Pérez," "the intolerable Señor Pérez." His enemies repeated the charge of personal gain even in the face of the evidence that his emergence as a republican figure increased the number of *sablistas*—incurable money-borrowers—who made successful attacks upon his charitable nature and dwindling income.

In the last analysis there is no single explanation for Galdós' republican interlude. His subconscious craving for action was certainly a factor. The mandate of spiritual leadership with which the youth of Spain had charged him in 1901, and which he had accepted with pardonable vanity, was another. His aggravated financial problems may also have influenced him; in his naïveté, which increased as he grew older, Galdós may have seen economic salvation in added popularity. But above all other considerations was his earnest desire to awaken in the younger generation a recognition of duty to country. It is quite likely that he had little or no faith in the ultimate success of the specific cause he espoused, but he sincerely believed in the virtue of devotion to a cause and he genuinely hoped—perhaps with a touch of vanity—that by his example he might instill that virtue in the apathetic, disillusioned, and pessimistic younger men of his day. Galdós had always attached great value to fantasy, imagination, dreams, and ideals—more in the last years of his life than in his youth—for he believed that only through the exercise of these could one avoid stagnation and ultimate decay. He doubtless had an inner conviction that the attainment of a republic in Spain was of the essence of chimera, but he was willing to reach out for it because of the strife and struggle it entailed. That was growth, that was life. Even though it apparently accomplished nothing concrete politically, Galdós' republican interlude may well have generated a spirit of vitality to which the Spain of the early twentieth century was subtly susceptible.

XVIII

A Nation to the Rescue

IN THE LAST WEEK OF 1907 Pablo Nougués became Galdós'
private secretary. They had met earlier in the year as co-workers
at republican gatherings. At first "Don Pablífero"—as Galdós
affectionately nicknamed him—only looked after the novelist's
correspondence, which was expanding with his political activity,
but soon he also took over the research work connected with
the *Episodios nacionales*. This he did cheerfully and competently,
the more so since the spirit of republicanism hovered over his
master's latest historical novels. He never complained of excessive work, not even when Galdós invited him to share the
drudgery of proofreading.

But as his duties multiplied Nougués began to wonder
whether it was not because of his employer's waning strength.
He knew that back in 1905 Galdós had suffered a stroke of
hemiplegia which had forced him to write thereafter with pencil,
but there was no evidence of a return of the paralysis. As he
observed his master closely he began to suspect that his sight
was failing. When he walked he often stumbled, and when he
wrote he did not always keep a straight line or maintain a uniform height in the letters of a word. Pablo Nougués was convinced that old age was not the only cause. Having once had a
serious ophthalmic disorder himself, he was familiar with the
symptoms. Galdós began to complain of a sharp pain in the
temples and of irritation in the corner of the left eye, but he
foreswore Don Pablífero to secrecy. He suggested that it might
be merely a recurrence of the splitting headaches from which he
had often suffered a few years before. And if it was a new

ailment, he would add jokingly, could he not rid himself of it by a rigid observance of Dr. Tolosa Latour's ban on potatoes in the interests of slenderness?

For almost two years Pablo Nougués kept the secret scrupulously. In Galdós' resolve to keep his trouble from his family there was something akin to a youngster's dread of having his misdemeanors reported to his parents. In time it became evident, however, that continued secrecy was no longer advisable. In the fall of 1910 Galdós was finishing his historical novel *Amadeo I*. By sheer will power he had managed to write the first 330 pages of the manuscript in his own hand. Gathering blindness obliged him to dictate the next four pages, but finding this procedure highly annoying, he resumed writing himself and reached page 346 in varying degrees of legibility. At this point Nougués intervened again and continued as far as page 370. With pathetically dogged determination Galdós struggled against surrendering to the inevitable but managed to complete only two more pages. The remainder of the novel he dictated. It was no longer sensible to hide the truth from the family.

Dr. Tolosa Latour immediately called into consultation Madrid's eminent ophthalmologist, Dr. Manuel Márquez, who diagnosed the case as a cataract that had progressed alarmingly and should have been removed a year before. He recommended an immediate operation, without guaranteeing its success. Galdós was then busily working on *La primera república*. By resorting to the psychological devices with which children are coaxed into doing something distasteful, Tolosa Latour prevailed on him to submit to the operation, which was performed in his study on May 25, 1911. When Dr. Márquez made the incision under the pupil, he discovered that the eyeball and the crystalline lens were abnormally large. As he was unable to remove the cataract whole, he extracted it piecemeal. When the pressure of the tissue was lifted, the nucleus of the cataract remained floating in the eye, so that it was impossible to get it into the necessary position for further incision. It was a rare case and beyond Dr. Márquez's skill. He held out the hope, however, that the blindness in the left eye would be only temporary, and that in any event the condition could be remedied through iridectomy.

The period of convalescence was trying for both the patient and his family. He was not told that he also had a cataract on the right eye, which would require another operation. In the presence of visitors he feigned optimism and spoke of his complete recovery, but when left alone he was sad and dejected. He spurned the solicitude of those who attended him, was querulous and resistant to the discipline of the cure. He rebelled against keeping the bandages on and lifted prematurely the doctor's ban on smoking. The interruption of his work routine and the suspension of his afternoon strolls and personal intimacies set his nerves on edge and made him irritable. To callers he complained about the dreary monotony of his confinement and spoke nostalgically of the last days before the operation, when, wearing dark glasses and piloted by his servant Paco, he had been making his rounds according to his customary schedule. Now the days merged with the nights, and time seemed indivisible. He spoke of his existence as a mere shadow which filled a spacious cavern. He felt a mysterious tension, an expansion of energy struggling to burst open the walls of the cavern and to release the shadow. Outside was freedom, form, shape, dimension—reality. Would he ever recover his real self?

On the recommendation of Dr. Márquez, Galdós went to Santander for the summer. His departure pleased the family, at the time busily preparing to move into the new home on Calle Hilarión Eslava which Carmen's son, José Hurtado de Mendoza, had built. In Santander Galdós divided his time between rest and work on his next historical novel. His convalescence progressed satisfactorily, and he returned to Madrid late in the fall visibly benefited by his vacation. He was optimistic, buoyant, and exhilarated, and a surprisingly cooperative patient. Although his blindness was progressing, he had profound faith in his ultimate recovery. Gone was the dull, muffled voice and the melancholy intonation with which he had spoken in the weeks immediately after the operation. Now he was jovial, and his voice cheerful and resonant. His visitors—politicians, journalists, and literary colleagues—were somewhat puzzled by his unusual talkativeness. The press commented with delight on his apparent good health. Reporters waxed sentimental in their accounts of their visits to the venerable master, underscoring the trivial but humanly delightful subjects they discussed with him. They stressed his modesty, humility, sincerity, irreproachable honesty, pure patriotism, and, above all, the monastic simplicity of his habits and the atmosphere of respectable poverty in which he lived. From all these accounts emerged a picture of an admirable yet pathetic patriarch of letters whom the fates were treating harshly in his last years.

*   *   *   *

The marked attention the press paid to Galdós' convalescence was more than an expression of sympathy for his condition. It was in reality the prelude to an extensive campaign, conceived and planned by Galdós himself during his stay in Santander, to counteract the mounting hostility to his political activities and to rehabilitate his literary and financial fortunes. The inspiration was furnished by the announcement that Maurice Maeterlinck had been awarded the Nobel prize. The award was not popular in Spain, and privately Galdós too disapproved the selection. He made no outright comparison between the Belgian dramatist-poet and himself, but he hinted that there were Spaniards fully deserving of the high literary honor. To be sure, it was a very indirect hint, but his admirers took it as a suggestion—even as a request—that they make a concerted effort to secure the next Nobel award for a Spanish author. If Don Benito was interested, they were willing.

The campaign began auspiciously shortly after Galdós' return to Madrid in November, 1911. Tomás Borrás unwittingly took the embarrassing initial step when he published in *España Nueva* his appeal that Jacinto Benavente be recommended for the Swedish prize. Republican *El País* promptly countered with a warm plea for the candidacy of Galdós. With two candidates in the field, the opposing camps mobilized for a clash, but the preliminary skirmishes were light and short. The militant literary youth backing Benavente capitulated when they failed to receive support from the candidate himself and from others of the generation of 1898. Of these Azorín was one of the first to enlist in the Galdós-for-Nobel-prize campaign. In an article published in *La Vanguardia* he warned against dragging out the red herring of Galdós' political activity and his religious ideas. He argued that the Czar of Russia never interfered with the bestowal of honors upon Tolstoy, nor did the queen of Italy withhold recognition from Carducci. Spain, he insisted, could not be less tolerant toward her great writer. Azorín's arguments probably did not convince Benavente's supporters that Galdós' literary accomplishment was worth forty thousand duros—all paid in one sum—but they withdrew in the face of the united liberal and radical front.

Lavish was the praise heaped on Galdós in feature stories and editorials. His partial blindness inspired extravagant sentimentality, and the publication of *De Cartago a Sagunto* the most eulogistic appraisals of both the man and the author. For nobility of character and beauty of soul he had few rivals, and he towered above all others as a genius of the Spanish race. In the constellations of the artistic firmament he shone as bright as Dickens, Balzac, Shakespeare, and Goethe, and among living authors of universal fame he was unique. It was idle to compare him with Maeterlinck in order to justify his claim to the Nobel prize. The Belgian, it was asserted, still had much arduous climbing to do before he would reach the height Galdós had attained. Unfortunate indeed were those who did not admire him, and the government was slighting its duty to the nation in failing to make the reading of his works obligatory in all secondary schools and universities. But the government now had an opportunity to make amends and to bring honor to itself and to the community of universal culture by helping Galdós secure the forty thousand Swedish duros.

As the campaign progressed, serious scruples assailed some of its sponsors. They argued that the Nobel prize, if awarded, would reflect credit only on the Stockholm committee. How would that satisfy the conscience of Spain? Was it not the duty

of the entire nation to express its gratitude to Galdós concretely
for his incomparable contribution to art and to the revival of
the Spanish soul? The pride of the nation thus challenged, Pedro
de Répide suggested several more enduring testimonials than
the perishable forty thousand Nobel duros. He urged that the
government publish a national edition of the *Episodios nacionales*
and distribute it widely. Or, the Bank of Spain might have an
issue of large denominations bearing the picture of Galdós and
present him with a handful of the attractive bills. Also, the
government could issue an appropriately engraved stamp.

Pedro de Répide's suggestions appealed to many, and the
idea of a nation-wide tribute rapidly gained currency. There were
those who proposed the erection of a beautiful villa on Madrid's
aristocratic Gran Vía in the heart of the city, where the impoverished literary patriarch could spend the rest of his life in
comfort. To enhance this tribute, others advocated that it be
supplemented by a national subscription for the publication of a
de luxe illustrated edition of Galdós' complete works. The proceeds were of course to go to the author.

Benavente, too, believed that Spain should do something more
than make the official recommendation to Stockholm. He feared
that if Galdós were to receive the award he would be assailed by
his political coreligionists and other *sablistas*. Something must
be devised to offset this probable loss, but Benavente's ingenuity
stopped short of a specific suggestion. More concrete and less
materialistic was the recommendation of a Spanish resident in
Paris. He was convinced that the conservatives opposed the
Nobel prize for Galdós largely because it was sponsored by the
very elements which in 1904 had labored in vain to prevent José
Echegaray from receiving it. But, reasoned the expatriate, not
even the conservatives should object to honoring Galdós in a
more becoming manner. Why not have a Galdós Gold Book
signed by all Spaniards genuinely proud of his literary
distinction?

Of the barrage of suggestions offered, one exploded with
especial violence. Writing in *El Imparcial*, Mariano de Cavia

argued that if the Stockholm committee were to be impressed with the Spanish candidate, the recommendation must be endorsed by the entire nation. He therefore proposed that the congress of the Federation of University Students, then in session in Madrid, improvise a series of band-led parades to Galdós' home. Such demonstrations, Cavia was convinced, could not fail to arouse nation-wide sympathy for the author. The student congress staged a noisy oratorical contest over the suggestion and adopted a resolution signed by three thousand young men declaring their unalterable opposition to granting Galdós the Nobel prize, because they neither respected his intellect nor regarded as holy dogma all that emanated from it.

The action of the students was warmly applauded by the conservative press. *El Debate* put the following words into the mouth of "A Reader"—probably the editor: "There is nothing surprising about it [*the student hostility*]. The *Frankfurter Zeitung*, which appears in cultured Germany, is also opposed to any and all tributes to Galdós. Indeed, it fails to see that Galdós' stature entitles him to the Nobel prize, or to any other recognition." [1]

Galdós' camp was stunned by the heretical stand of the students and the arrogant tone of *El Debate*. The issue was developing into an ugly international quarrel. Benavente, now pessimistic about Galdós' prospects, rebuked the students and sought to shame them by declaring that in his own day the university youth had believed in Galdós precisely because they did not regard him as the source of dogma. And Mariano de Cavia, after recovering from the shock, accused the congress of being the tool of anti-liberal and reactionary forces.

Instead of wincing under Cavia's accusation, the opposition fairly gloated over its easy preliminary victory. The leaders of the attack on Galdós were now convinced that they had been wise to concentrate their fire on his intervention in republican politics. This was a salient that not even his friends could defend stoutly, and the conservative newspapers pounded it incessantly. An editorial in *El Universo* reminded its readers that the recipients of the Nobel prize were expected to promote peace and civilization. On this score Galdós failed to qualify, given to violence and irascibility as he was, "in love with warrior exploits, an advocate of fire and sword for the settlement of affairs." [2] *La Epoca* contended vigorously that for the Spanish masses he was not a great literary figure but merely the president of the republican-socialist coalition. As such, he could only be characterized as "the leader of the revolutionary elements who have just covered with blood the soil of the fatherland and who persist in their subversive efforts." [3]

The fury of the assault increased when Galdós' candidacy was endorsed by the bishop of Jaca. Antolín López Peláez, the most liberal Spanish churchman of the day, pleaded for tolerance and generosity. Although he lamented works like *Electra* and *Casandra*, he maintained that Galdós was a great figure, worthy of the highest national or foreign honor. The kindly bishop called on the conservatives in the name of Christian charity and Spanish patriotism to check their wrath and violence. He too regretted that Galdós was walking a path leading away from God and the Church, but prayer and not hostile gestures would redeem him from grievous error. The bishop was roundly rebuked by the Catholic press, which sought to counteract his influence by putting forward Padre Luis Coloma and Marcelino Menéndez y Pelayo as the only Spanish men of letters who should be recommended for the Nobel prize.

As the time approached to pass from debate to action, Galdós' campaign managers began to fear that the discord in Spain would affect the Stockholm committee. To complicate the controversy, certain unfriendly literary youngsters pressed the Machiavellian suggestion that, in the event of success, Galdós should use the forty thousand duros for the establishment of literary prizes—precisely as Maeterlinck had done. Oddly enough, this recommendation marked the transition from words to deeds. Fray Candil (Emilio Bobadilla), who had lived in the Scandinavian countries, was delegated to probe the good will of his numerous friends there. He cheerfully accepted the assignment, but stipulated that his efforts be seconded by a continuous campaign at home. Moreover, he urged that Galdós himself should plead his case with his literary friends and admirers in Sweden, Norway, and Denmark.

Galdós' candidacy now really got under way. A petition was circulated among universities, academies, and literary, artistic, and scientific societies. The literature section of the Madrid Ateneo, under the presidency of Jacinto Benavente, obtained one hundred and fifty signatures within a few hours. Several days later the Spanish Press Association and the "Centro de Hijos de Madrid" joined the petitioners. The distinguished histologist Ramón y Cajal signed for the Royal Academy of Medicine, and José Echegaray for the Royal Academy of Language—the latter without committing the institution. Even before the petition was formally presented to the Swedish minister in Madrid, Count Romanones and a group of Cortes deputies endorsed Galdós in a telegram to Stockholm. The Count's magnanimity cheered the campaign managers, and they were even happier when *La Ciudad de Dios* and *España y América,* two Augustinian publications, supported Galdós in similar fashion. In the middle of February, 1912, the several petitions were solemnly presented to the Swedish minister in Madrid, with the emphatic assurance that the candidate was the choice of all the people of Spain. The Swedish diplomat, who had followed the controversy with extreme interest, received the petitions with a few brief and tactful remarks.

* * * *

Benito Pérez Galdós did not receive the Nobel prize for literature in 1912. There was keen disappointment everywhere, although the outcome was not unexpected. Only the official endorsement of the Royal Academy of Language could have dispelled the Swedish minister's impression that Galdós' candidacy had caused political and religious disputes—a situation in which the Nobel committee could ill afford to take sides. But Antonio Maura, president of the Spanish Academy, steadfastly refused to become involved. Galdós' supporters consoled themselves with the knowledge that their defeat was irrelevant to the merits of their cause, and they hastened to blame the immortal guardians of the purity of Castilian.

Not even his most intimate friends ever discovered how Galdós accepted his failure. When the decision of the Nobel committee became known, he was preoccupied with a graver matter. The vision in his right eye was rapidly deteriorating, and to prevent total blindness he underwent a second operation on April 5, 1912. This time the doctors all but guaranteed a perfect cure. But in the weeks preceding he had fallen into a melancholy and despondent mood from which he was slow to recover even after the operation. He was less communicative than ever, and his voice sounded monotonous and opaque. His callers were saddened at the sight of the semi-blind patriarch sitting silent, resigned, apathetic in his upholstered chair. At times he complained of neglect, and yet he evinced little interest in the visits of his friends. He seemed absorbed in intimate reflection; the immobile expression on his face screened his thoughts and lent his whole appearance a statuesque air.

A radical change came over Galdós in Santander, where he went early that summer. With the prospect of regaining his vision he cast off his gloom and apathy and became more animated. His voice became more resonant, and he greeted callers with his customary warmheartedness. As in 1911, the change was attributable largely to a new prospect of relief from financial burdens. Together with his closest friends—mostly young writers—he was evolving a new strategy for another assault on the Nobel committee. His chief aide was Ramón Pérez de Ayala, who was in communication with the leading person in charge of the award. It was rumored that this time the candidacy was receiving favorable consideration. At the proper time enough signatures would be secured to impress Stockholm with Galdós' popularity. He himself felt quite confident of success, either because there was not the noisy hostility there had been in 1912, or possibly because his expectations were nourished by his very acute financial needs.

So urgent was the solution of his economic problems that he

cast off his wonted reserve and talked freely about his personal plight. He was naturally careful not to reveal its true causes; instead, he referred in veiled terms to the dishonesty of those entrusted with his financial affairs and to the inroads which his political activity had made on his literary popularity. His sympathizers were willing to propagate these plausible explanations, although it was embarrassing to insist on the poverty of a writer who had for so long been the most widely read author in the country. The public, in turn, reverently abstained from probing into the real reasons for his growing needs—the exorbitant price he was obliged to pay for his continued surrender to abnormal urges and passions even in his old age.

This attitude of the public strengthened Galdós' delusion about the source of his impecuniousness and encouraged him to suspect of malfeasance everyone who had business dealings with him. There was an element of greed and avarice in his suspicions. He complained that his partial blindness made him an easy victim of unscrupulous money lenders, financial administrators, and lawyers. Even while his Nobel candidacy was being promoted, he publicly accused his business manager, Ernesto Pereda y Gandía, of serious irregularity in the handling of his many debts and other obligations. He charged that Pereda made him sign blank checks, presented claims of fictitious creditors, and extorted money from him in other ways. These dishonest practices, he claimed, had been going on for approximately six years and involved eighty thousand duros.

During October and November, 1912, Galdós was front-page news. The police deemed it advisable to arrest Pereda unostentatiously, so high did public indignation run against him. There was a trial, which in its early stages promised to uncover intriguing evidence. Since Don Ernesto was the secret keeper of Don Benito's intimate pecadillos, counsel very delicately advised both litigants to reach a private settlement. To this they wisely agreed with the equivocal announcement that while Don Ernesto was not wholly innocent, Don Benito was not entirely justified in his accusations. The public did not feel defrauded, because it was not altogether ignorant of the background of the controversy.

In a manner of speaking, Galdós won a victory. The list of usurers was slightly reduced and—what seemed even more important—Spain was made aware of the shameful poverty of her literary master.

This unfortunate incident should have convinced everyone that Galdós needed the Nobel prize even more than he deserved it, yet the second attempt in 1913 was no more successful than the first—and for the same reasons. Conservative Spain was resolved to make him expiate his sin of revolutionary politics and philosophic liberalism. In former years this would have aroused his fighting spirit, but his present plight called for immediate monetary relief rather than moral heroics. His real interest in the Nobel prize was material. As his needs were so pressing, he began to work on a scheme that promised an earlier solution. The idea of a national subscription, proposed two years before, appealed to him now as more practical and more appropriate. It was bound to yield some concrete results despite all opposition. His enemies could not prevent his admirers from expressing their devotion in something readily negotiable. Galdós thought he saw the road to solvency.

*　　*　　*　　*

The strategists took approximately a year to perfect plans for Galdós' economic redemption under the slogan that the nation owed a tribute to its favorite author. At first this obligation was vaguely defined as the desire of the masses to make a gesture of gratitude toward the writer. Since this naturally produced no results, a more practical procedure had to be adopted. The production of *Celia en los infiernos* in December, 1913, provided the occasion for a more vigorous approach. Friendly reviewers handled the play with unctious piety and in describing Galdós as he received the repeated ovations drew a picture of a weak, blind, and forlorn old man which was calculated to open the floodgates of charity. Editors vied with dramatic critics in demanding the immediate alleviation of his plight. The appeal seemed to be unanimous. The opposition, it was declared, was disarmed on the eve of the battle. On the night of the thirty-first and gala performance (January 7, 1914) Galdós was summoned to the royal box amidst thunderous applause. The incident had a political implication: it was taken to mean that Spain acclaimed the cessation of hostilities beween republicanism and the monarchy, at least so far as Galdós and the monarch were concerned.

Several days later José María Carretero (El Caballero Audaz) published in *La Esfera* a sentimental article picturing Galdós as old, infirm, melancholy, dejected, but still compelled to write his daily quota of pages in order to keep body and soul together and a roof over his head. The implication was that Galdós was heroically warding off the day when he might be forced to enter the poorhouse. The members of his household, who cared for him with disinterested tenderness, almost with piety, were deeply hurt by this public exhibition of Benito's avowed indigence, but in view of the delicate reasons behind his dire need, they could do nothing about it. As for Galdós himself, his seemingly callous attitude toward his family was due partly to the selfishness of progressive senility and partly to his complete enslavement by the pathological habits of his intimate life.

Editorial writers and reporters of the liberal press responded wholeheartedly to the appeal of El Caballero Audaz. Once again they attributed Galdós' anomalous poverty to his financial misfortunes and to the adverse results of his participation in politics. No one knew exactly whence the needed relief would come, but there was a veritable flood of suggestions. Several newspapers disputed their claims to priority in the launching of the campaign, but finally everyone settled down to the business of discussing procedures which would yield Galdós the necessary funds to satisfy usurers, hush up female extortionists, and remove the threat of foreclosure from his Santander villa.

First to offer a concrete suggestion was Joaquín Dicenta, who proposed a pension to be known as "Premio España," equal in amount and moral significance to the elusive Nobel prize. His colleagues on the staff of *El Liberal* and others endorsed the scheme enthusiastically, provided that Hispanic America be included in the enterprise. Dicenta having failed to indicate how the fund should be raised, *ABC*, already a rich and influential daily, appealed to every Spanish newspaper and review to publish a special edition devoted exclusively to Galdós and to turn all the proceeds over to him. To guarantee success *ABC* further proposed that every financially sound publication underwrite the project to the extent of five thousand pesetas.

But it must have occurred to the father of this plan that he had not yet defined its monetary goal, and so he presented a modified version. He recommended the publication of a composite, de luxe newspaper to be entitled *Galdós*, which should include literary contributions by the king and Spanish men of letters. There was to be only a single issue of some sixty thousand copies, which at five pesetas a copy would yield a substantial sum. Add to it one hundred thousand pesetas—box-office receipts from the performance of Galdós' plays throughout the land— and the total, soundly invested in insurance stock, would yield a thousand duros annually. These were practical proposals, stressed the *ABC* writer, and he intimated that he would admit none but very minor modifications.

Sound as were the *ABC* plans, other solutions of the Galdós problem were proposed. The Quintero brothers, who had always treated Galdós with filial devotion, offered to dramatize *Marianela*. This was by all odds his most popular novel, and for a long time he had been urging various younger writers to adapt it for the stage. Its strong emotional appeal and the blindness motif, it was reasoned, would surely arouse sympathy for its author as well as raise money for the national fund. The Quinteros' plan inspired a number of similar ones. *El Correo*, heroic champion of Galdós' dramatic ambitions, advocated the presentation of gala performances throughout Spain on a designated day. This would give an unmistakably national character to the Galdós tribute.

Andrenio, too, stressed the need for enlisting the interest of the masses, including their kin in Spanish America. Hence he was opposed to an official pension for Galdós, or any other form of state aid. The principle of popular participation appealed to others. Some of the cities immortalized in the *Episodios nacionales*—Zaragoza, Gerona, Cádiz—welcomed the suggestion that they publish de luxe editions of the novels bearing their names, but their enthusiasm was translated into no concrete action.

Even as Galdós' sympathizers were groping for a definite goal, the opposition began to harass them on both flanks. The conservative newspapers voiced their amazement that Galdós should be the neediest case in Spain. They described his Madrid and Santander homes as "palaces" redolent of wealth and luxury, cited statistics to prove that his income was more than comfortable, and hinted that there was sinister backstage play in this campaign. Whatever his personal difficulties, they argued, Galdós had no claim on public funds. He was not entitled to any sort of tribute, since he was a distinctly inferior artist.

The insinuations of the conservative journalists engendered skepticism in other quarters, and before long the very principle of aid to Galdós was seriously questioned. His supporters, sensing danger, paused to modify their strategy. The means of reaching the goal was a secondary consideration when the goal itself was threatened. The opposition was raising embarrassing questions: what had Galdós been doing with his income? Was there a precedent for rushing national succor to a writer in financial distress? Three authoritative voices spoke out in reply. Eduardo Dato, president of the Council of Ministers, endorsed the movement for a state pension on the ground that through Galdós the Spanish genius had become respected abroad. Conde Romanones, leader of the liberal party in Cortes, also gave his approval, both for himself as a private individual and for his *alter ego* the shrewd politician. Jacinto Benavente, unchallenged representative of the young literary generation, promised his wholehearted support and urged the government to make the first move to assure the success of the campaign. And to convince everyone that the matter had already passed the stage of discussion he announced a contribution of one hundred pesetas by an anonymous donor.

The day of Galdós' rehabilitation was now drawing near. All the grandiose and ingenious plans had been reduced to a simple national subscription. Benavente worked energetically and unostentatiously for the new objective. But progress was slow, for in a bureaucratic country the implementing machinery is necessarily cumbersome. By the middle of March a senatorial committee had been organized, designated the "Junta Nacional del Homenaje a Galdós," which included Romanones, Dato, Echegaray, Marqués de Estella, Melquiades Alvarez, Duque de Alba, Gustavo Bauer, Miguel Moya, Benavente, Cavia, and Tomás Romero. From the very start there was criticism of the secrecy in which the committee was formed, and fear lest it disregard all that had already been accomplished unofficially by individuals. Since it was in response to the personal solicitation of Galdós that most of its members had agreed to serve, the committee refrained from explaining its genesis. Instead, it charged Benavente with making a public announcement about the purpose of the national tribute.

The press did not wait for Benavente to speak in the name of the Junta. Editorials and feature stories mixed panegyrics with jeremiads in an effort to arouse the public before the official appeal was issued. Once again Galdós was described as the innocent victim of usurers and extortionists, and wealthy Spaniards were implored to respond promptly and generously, for time was of the essence. Forty thousand duros, it was alleged, were needed within three months; an even shorter time limit would have been set had it not been for the problem of reaching the public in Spanish America and other foreign countries.

The scene having been laid for the official appeal, on April 11, 1914, Benavente made a dignified and compelling speech on behalf of the Junta. To forestall argument about Galdós he cited his international fame, implying that Spain could not reject an author who would have received the highest foreign award had it not been for unwarranted opposition from certain quarters. It was the nation's duty to make amends for the two disappointments it had caused him in connection with the Nobel prize. It was the duty of the wealthy class to give concrete and adequate recognition to the standard-bearer of Spanish culture.

His call did not go unchallenged. Contrary-minded Spaniards enjoined all patriotic citizens to make no contributions to the national subscription. Certain Catholic papers which refused to publish the appeal reminded their readers what a threat Galdós' heterodoxy was to religion and repeatedly invoked the opinion of Menéndez y Pelayo. The Carlist *El Siglo Futuro* stripped Galdós of all merit. "Señor Galdós," observed one of its editors, "is neither novelist, nor dramatist, nor philosopher— good or bad—nor historian, nor anything at all." [4] Galdós' very poverty, the writer asserted, demonstrated that although many praised his works none bought them; fifty years after his death not a bookstore in Europe would sell his novels or dramas.

Undaunted, the Junta began to count the golden eggs before they were laid. Anticipating a great outpouring of the Spanish charitable instinct, it announced that the campaign would end on July 15 and funds collected would be allocated to several purposes. First, Galdós would be freed from all immediate obligations. That done, a fund would be established to yield him a comfortable income for life. After his death the Junta would continue to administer this fund, and with its earnings would establish literary prizes in his memory and erect a fitting monument to his honor in the heart of Madrid.

The national subscription got under way auspiciously. Indeed, several substantial contributions had come in even before the official appeal was issued. Heading the donors was Alfonso XIII with ten thousand pesetas, followed by Romanones with five thousand, Bauer with a like sum, and the Duque de Alba with one thousand. Within a week almost twenty-one thousand pesetas was raised, including one hundred from Pardo Bazán. More money—or, rather, more promises—kept coming in gradually. Among the early contributors was the National Cash Register Company and the *American Hebrew* of New York, which on May 20, 1914, addressed a letter to Galdós endorsing the national tribute and enclosing a "small gift" as a token of appreciation of *Gloria* and his other efforts in behalf of Jewry. Galdós instructed his secretary to reply that he had not consciously pleaded the Jewish cause in *Gloria,* but that he gratefully accepted the remittance. The list of contributors grew; included were the names of national figures, titled persons, city councils, and various labor, social, industrial, and cultural organizations. There was a scarcity of feminine subscribers and a preponderance of anonymous donors of sums ranging from twenty-five céntimos to two and three pesetas. It was largely the response of humble men and women—the masses of Spain— that accounted for the eventual total in cash and in pledges.

As the weeks wore on, it became apparent that the enterprise was not progressing satisfactorily. Although interest was keen and nation-wide, in terms of duros it fell considerably short of expectations. Two weeks before the deadline of July 15 only half of the urgently needed forty thousand duros had been subscribed, and even this sum was not immediately available in cash. And there was still to be deducted the allegedly heavy expense of raising even this disappointing total.

Obviously Galdós' admirers, though numerous and sincere, had little more to offer than appreciation. The Spaniards who had something to put in the collection plate apparently did not feel the urge to do so. This element blustered against Galdós in the conservative press and in aristocratic clubs and casinos. Catholic newspapers boycotted the subscription with sardonic sarcasm. They ridiculed Galdós as a starving blind beggar with green glasses, standing at church doors and making raids on the charitable parishioners. In town councils, regionalists and other sectarian groups discredited every suggestion for supporting the tribute. Apparently not even the participation of the king and other prominent personages of unquestionable orthodoxy sufficed to convince the conservative rich that Heaven would not punish them if they helped Galdós.

There was much of the ludicrous about the campaign. An article in *Le Journal* of Paris, which aroused the resentment of the Spanish press, described ironically the manner in which Spain went about honoring its towering literary figure. Recalling what lavish gifts had frequently been bestowed upon bullfighters, the writer asked whether Galdós did not deserve as much in exchange for the many neat works he had dedicated to the nation. From Spanish America came naïve endorsements. The city of Montevideo, for example, offered its wholehearted support in the form of an artistic testimonial signed by a great number of Spanish clubs. And though it would seem that the goal was explicit enough, there were nevertheless numerous letters requesting suggestions for effective cooperation. The Spaniard's lack of a practical sense, despite his great capacity for artistic realism, was never more evident.

So extensive, though pointless, did the correspondence become that the Junta could no longer function as a private volunteer organization. A cumbersome and expensive administration was set up in the offices of the Press Association. In a sense, bureaucratic Madrid saw its range of opportunities extended. The entire enterprise would have disheartened its promoters had it not been for the generosity of so many humble folk, among whom were Spanish residents of the United States and not a few native Americans. Workers and small shopkeepers in California, Arizona, and other parts of the Southwest made modest remittances to the Junta with sincere apologies.

By July, 1914, the total collected was still about one-third short of the minimum goal. The three-month limit was extended indefinitely, but the outbreak of the World War virtually disrupted the organization. Thereafter intermittent reminders appeared in the press that Spain had not redeemed its pledge to Galdós. The last statement on the progress of the subscription was made public on July 28, 1914. Less than two years later, on February 3, 1916, the Junta dissolved itself. Approximately 150,000 pesetas had been collected, but of this amount about one-third was still in unredeemed pledges.

Only pity for the aged man of letters had induced the Junta to continue functioning long after the futility of its efforts was apparent. After all, it was Galdós himself who had personally implored most of the members to serve. One of them had accepted the responsibility under the impression that Don Benito was a famous painter. But in time the Junta began to be annoyed by the frequent raids that its protégé was making on its assets. His demands often exceeded the available cash. He seemed unwilling or unable to abide by the agreements stipulating the size of his allowances.

The most irritating position was that of treasurer Tomás

Romero, editor of *El Liberal*. Several times he tendered his resignation, but each time his associates prevailed on him to continue in office. He found it distasteful to be regarded by Galdós as the niggardly trustee of a fat purse. Constantly harassed by the mounting cost of his intimate indulgences, Galdós repeatedly grumbled that he was being ill-treated by Romero. His financial burdens made him almost avaricious and often forced him into the ways of the miser. In his blind state he became suspicious of those with whom he had money transactions, and he freely expressed his mistrust without dignity or self-respect. The Junta found itself at times in the position of a parent called upon to arbitrate between two equally guilty, quarreling children, and it was genuinely weary of its assignment.

There was much unfinished business when Romero was obliged to continue single-handed the rescue of Galdós. The records of the dissolved organization were in a muddled condition, for they had not been kept according to orthodox methods. The cash in hand did not correspond to the recorded difference between receipts and disbursements. Galdós, who had always regarded arithmetic as something of an insoluble puzzle, found it more convenient to question the treasurer's honesty than to attempt a clarification. His troubled and weary mind failed to grasp the distinction between actual payments and pledges; with pathetic senile stubbornness he insisted that all recorded figures represented cash sums. His great needs made him greedy and disposed to exaggerate the generosity of his admirers. To him the national subscription became an inexhaustible source of financial relief. He was being robbed! He even accused Tomás Romero, whom he once included among his most intimate friends, of being the principal beneficiary of his countrymen's kindness. With little delicacy or graciousness he whispered his suspicions and accusations into the receptive ears of scandalmongering journalists. The national subscription became a favorite theme of gossip. Galdós was again front-page news.

At his insistence the Association of Writers and Artists intervened in the ugly situation. Legal aid was invoked to compel Romero to liquidate the business of the Junta in due form.

This was accomplished on April 27, 1916, in the office of Attorney Federico Plana Pellisa and in the presence of witnesses for both litigants. The liquidation did not satisfy Galdós. The neat, notarized columns of figures had an air of authenticity, but he regarded it all as so much legalized subterfuge. He asserted stubbornly that Romero could not have come out with clean hands from a transaction involving so many thousands of pesetas. He claimed to have evidence that more pledges had been redeemed and more cash payments had been made by cities and organizations than appeared on the treasurer's lists. The legal hocus-pocus, Galdós complained to sympathetic journalists, was only another device to defraud him. He was determined to have at least moral redress.

El Caballero Audaz, with his inordinate flair for sensational headlines, eventually appointed himself champion of Galdós' cause. In an article entitled "The Crumbs of a Subscription— Galdós Accuses," he reviewed the history of the whole affair.[5] Mixing sentimentality with indignation, and threats with accusations, and purporting to tell the story just as it had been related by Galdós, he charged Tomás Romero with deliberate dishonesty and vowed never to lay down his pen until justice had been done and the wrong righted. He called on all the contributors, from Alfonso XIII with his ten thousand pesetas to the humblest worker with his twice-counted coppers, to demand that their charity be not misapplied. He pledged that all rapacious creatures, beast or fowl, would be mercilessly exterminated.

In the enusing days the Madrid press offered its readers highly seasoned fare. Tomás Romero, a plucky fighter, answered the accusation in a stinging article entitled "The Ungrateful Master."[6] He partly lifted the veil which had hitherto covered Galdós' indiscretions, exposed his part in inspiring and implementing the national subscription, and revealed the Junta's difficulties in meeting his unreasonable demands for money. In short, Romero sought to exhibit Galdós naked. But he overshot his mark. Had he been more moderate in his revelations of Galdós' intimate life, he would probably have convinced the gen-

eral public that the pathetic patriarch of Spanish letters had not
always been an exemplar of virtuous conduct. But Romero revealed too much to be convincing. The public, by and large,
preferred to cling to the flattering picture it had always had of
Galdós. Nevertheless, it seemed for a while as if the quarrel
would end scandalously in the courts. Friends of Galdós, fore-
seeing the irreparable harm that litigation would do, urged him
to arbitrate. The quarrelers listened to reason, and thus ended
the most pitiful incident in the long life of Benito Pérez Galdós.

The rescue expedition had failed, but at least it kept Galdós
afloat for a while. When it became clear that the collective
generosity of Spain was not enough to tow him to permanent
safety, some of his admirers resorted to the one usually effective
Spanish maneuver—an assault on the national treasury, or the
"national manger," as Galdós himself called it. They had foreseen the failure of the subscription even before Galdós had
advertised it. Without apprising the nation, they laid siege to the
Ministry of Public Instruction. On January 2, 1916, Minister
Julio Burell had a royal decree issued appointing Galdós "Aux-
iliary Delegate" of the Ministry and charging him with the
arrangements for the Cervantes tercentenary at a monthly
stipend of one thousand pesetas. Though the plans for this
event were cancelled because of the World War, Galdós' appointment was never revoked, nor was he deprived of his emolument. In the years of his contact with Cortes he would have
spurned such state bounty, but now he accepted it as an overdue
settlement of an honorable debt.

Resentful of the patronage of the Ministry of Public Instruction, the Madrid Ateneo renewed that same year the agitation
to recommend Galdós for the Nobel prize. A committee labored
diligently to secure the official intervention of the Royal Academy of Language. President Antonio Maura again succeeded
in resisting on the ground that the statutes of the Academy
did not authorize him to make the request. He emphasized that
he was not actuated by the political differences between himself
and Galdós, offering as evidence his old friendship with the

literary patriarch and their common interest in water-color painting.

The failure of the Ateneo discouraged neither Galdós nor his sympathizers. Two honors that came to him unsolicited near the end of 1916 renewed his confidence in his international literary significance. On October 23, 1916, the Royal Society of Literature of Great Britain conferred on him the title of "Foreign Honorary Fellow of the Society" and awarded him a silver medal as the "most distinguished living representative of Spanish literature." At about the same time the Hispanic Society of America made him an honorary member and also presented him with a silver medal for "literary distinction." In the light of such solid recognition, Galdós felt certain that the Nobel committee would be constrained to ignore the opposition of his conservative compatriots. Accordingly, in 1917, he and Pérez de Ayala laid careful plans for the renewal of his candidacy. They were aided by H. J. Dahlander, an influential Swedish resident of Madrid with diplomatic connections in Sweden and in Spain, and by five hundred Ateneo petitioners. But apparently it was not written that the Spanish novelist should be the recipient of the coveted international award.

Thus ended Galdós' quest for material relief and universal recognition. But the conscience of his followers still did not rest easy. For a number of years after his death striking schemes were proposed for the righting of what many regarded as a great wrong. In 1928 a movement was launched informally to solicit a posthumous Nobel award for Galdós for the purpose of establishing a literary prize in his memory. Inopportune at the moment of its birth, the idea was doomed to a premature death. For those were days when Spain lay crushed under the heel of a floundering military dictatorship. How could a nation that was itself in need of moral rescue come to the aid of even the memory of its foremost modern champion of spiritual liberalism?

XIX

Melancholy Twilight

THE RATHER DISAPPOINTING figure of Galdós that emerges from the story of his resolute struggle for economic rehabilitation should be viewed largely in the light of his declining health, which first became noticeable after his operation in the spring of 1911. It was accompanied by symptoms of a weakened moral fiber and a disintegrating personality. Only his indomitable will remained unaffected, but this itself may have contributed to his rapid deterioration. In 1914, in defiance of all advice, he accompanied Margarita Xirgu on an extensive theatrical tour to promote the national subscription project then in progress. The emotional and physical strain was too much, and Galdós was confined to his bed for several days upon his return to Madrid. His recovery being slow, the Quinteros invited him to spend a month with them in their Utrera home. The rest was only temporarily beneficial.

More serious than the growing arteriosclerosis and uremia was the gradual loss of his sight, which was aggravated by a progressive softening of the medulla. In his near-blindness Galdós began to behave as if the moorings of his personality had been cut loose. He seemed to be little concerned with tangible reality and to live almost completely in the spheres of fancy and imagination. After his long struggle to grasp the essence of external reality, he foresook it and surrendered himself to introspection. In his unreal world, built from bits of his own past and fleeting glimpses into the future, and peopled with a confused crowd of real and fictitious figures, he reserved a pre-eminent place for himself. Like a child, he became self-centered, craving praise and attention, and extremely sensitive to purely physical comfort. In this new state he felt relaxed and completely freed of his former inhibitions—his timidity, humility, and outward modesty.

There were moments when Galdós fought desperately to return to the world he had abandoned and to recapture his identity. It was in such moments that he wrote four of his last works and finished the final one (four dramas: *Alceste*, 1914; *Sor Simona*, 1915; *El tacaño Salomón*, 1916; and *Santa Juana de Castilla*, 1918; and a novel in dialogue, *La razón de la sinrazón*, 1915). In varying degrees these works reflect the vision of the inner eye illumined by the spirit rather than the observations of the physical eye guided by the mind. They are all an eloquent tribute to Galdós' creative energy and philosophic vigor, but their slight concern with actuality testifies to his gradual absorption in a world of fancy.

Between 1914 and 1917 Galdós struggled hard not to lapse into the stagnant routine of a blind old man. Besides the four major works listed above, he wrote articles, took an active interest in the World War on the side of the Entente, dabbled occasionally in politics, and maintained contact with the literary world through the younger writers. These he frequently aided with flattering prologues to their books and persuasive recommendations to publishers. To the casual observer he seemed to be in full possession of all his faculties, especially since his robust appearance belied his impaired health. His persistent intimate indulgences, with even keener eagerness, was amazing.

Also amazing were Galdós' optimism, faith, and spiritual youthfulness. The blows and disappointments of recent years never forced him to admit defeat. He often rebuked his young friends when they seemed discouraged, calling them "old youngsters." Dream and illusion were for him the essence of intelligent living. When he was once told about a young woman with literary ambitions who was completely disillusioned about everything although she had suffered no great misfortune, had no physical disability, and was blessed with beauty and wealth, he raised himself in his chair, brandished his blindman's stick—

he called it his *garrote*—and shouted angrily: "Well, if this woman has no illusions, what is she doing in this world? What right has she to live? Tell me—what right?" [1]

But the last melancholy years could not be postponed indefinitely. Galdós settled down to a monotonous routine that was but a faint shadow of his normal life. He made only one radical departure from his usual schedule—he now visited his intimate haunts in the morning instead of in the afternoon. His daily program was simple. He rose at dawn, breakfasted, and attended to his correspondence. Since Pablo Nougués was now dead, faithful Paco, the handy clerk of Hortaleza, 132, acted as private secretary as well as guide and pilot. The next step invariably threw the household into mild confusion. Preparing Benito properly for his daily excursion required the skill of his valet Victoriano and the supervision of the entire family. A complete check was made to see that his clothes were free from cigar ash; that he did not forget pencil, paper, and cigar; that he had a clean handkerchief; that his hat and necktie were not awry; that he remembered to take along his *garrote*. His coat pockets were carefully searched by sister Carmen for the contents of the fruit bowl which he often attempted to smuggle out, allegedly for his very good friends, the neighborhood children. Since he always surrendered meekly, it was suspected that he was not quite truthful about their destination. This ordeal over, Galdós and Paco were free to enter the modest public cab waiting in front of the house.

Mysterious missions took Galdós and his guide through the Pozas district or toward the Puerta del Sol and southeast of it into the Barrios Bajos. Everywhere he went he had the illusion of riding in triumph to the cheers of the populace. Outwardly immobile, he nevertheless felt an inner glow as tavernkeepers, merchants, and plain citizens greeted him with respect and admiration. Because of his blindness, he could no longer conceal entirely the nature of his quests in certain streets, but the good Madrilenians delicately respected his secrets. The tribute Galdós prized most highly was the one he received from the hard-playing children in his immediate neighborhood. He smiled radiantly at their effusive greetings, and often stopped to converse familiarly with the fascinating creatures he had described in *Electra* as "man's children who make life cheerful." Not infrequently he rewarded his young admirers with something more substantial than a grandfatherly smile or amusing chatter. All this delayed his morning program, but he always managed to return home promptly at noon. After an ascetically frugal lunch with his family he retired to his soft chair, where with a shapeless, wrinkled cap on his head, a heavy Indian blanket wrapped around his awkwardly long legs, and a cigar that continually went out in his left hand, he fell into prolonged revery and introspection.

Musing, thinking, dreaming, and even scheming—with himself often as the nucleus of his inner world—Galdós would remain in his chair awaiting the arrival of callers. He craved company, and the presence of youth exhilarated him. If the first caller arrived well ahead of the others, he usually paid dearly for his indiscretion. It was an ordeal to carry on a sustained conversation with Galdós, who was distracted and subject to frequent lapses of memory. He would forget things told him a day or even a few hours before. When his own works were discussed—something he rarely permitted—he often forgot the names of his characters or confused them with his acquaintances. Political talk was strictly forbidden, and the solitary visitor rarely ventured to bring up the subject of literature lest he sound naïve or indiscreet. There was only one effective way of entertaining Galdós before the arrival of other callers—to compete with him in listing the most unusual and sonorous Spanish place names. He always won against light competition, and Madrigal de las Altas Torres carried off the prize every time.

Although Galdós sincerely appreciated individual callers—particularly Gregorio Marañón, Ramón Pérez de Ayala, Emilio Ramírez Angel, and Margarita Xirgu—he was especially delighted with the small groups that formed *tertulias* in his room. Those who attended most assiduously were Victorio Macho, Marciano Zurita, Emilio Ramírez Angel, the Quinteros, Andrés

González Blanco, José Francés, and Diego San José. Surrounded by this court of admirers, Galdós felt reunited with the outside world. In their praise, flattery, and courteous attention he relived his days of glory and thunderous applause. Far from hilarious, these *tertulias* were like meetings of master and disciples in an atmosphere of lightheartedness and occasional levity. Everyone sought to cheer the near-blind patriarch. The most successful was Ramírez Angel with his presentation of a cigar that lent a festive touch to the *tertulia*. This was virtually the only moment in the entire afternoon when Galdós was an active participant. Generally he sat as an attentive spectator, saying very little. If the conversation did not interest him, he changed its course with a pointed question on some other topic. This was his privilege as host, and the guests respected it.

Most pleasurable to Galdós were the infrequent feminine *tertulias*. In the words of one of its members:

> It delighted him to be in the company of young women who knew how to introduce laughter into the sadness of his eternal night. He possessed an exquisite gallantry, which was his pride and which he practised with the refinement of an eighteenth-century abbot. "My two Margaritas, my springtime!" was his salutation when Margarita Xirgu and I entered his room, and he took one of our hands and raised them to his mouth at the same time. He likewise exaggerated his ailments in our presence so that we would humor him more. With ingenuous cleverness he pretended not to be able to light his cigar. My sister would light it for him, and then he had no trouble at all grabbing her hand and kissing it to the accompaniment of a delicate conceit.[2]

But these refreshing visits had to end at a relatively early hour. At about half past four in the winter and half past six in the milder seasons, Galdós would struggle up to his bedroom on the second floor with the aid of Paco. After a frugal supper served in bed, he would go to sleep. Generally he slept well—because he had a clear conscience, he said. The occasional dreams he had differed little from the extravagant dreams of characters in his novels or from his afternoon reveries. Whenever he was slow to fall into a sound sleep, he summoned his second guide and pilot, Victoriano Moreno—nicknamed "the opulent cowboy" because he ran a modest dairy store to supplement his income. Galdós and Victoriano staged many delightful dialogues of the Don Quixote–Sancho Panza type. They undid the monarchy, founded a republic and, true to Spanish political practice, distributed lucrative jobs among their friends. With the country's problems solved, the drowsy republican would grin roguishly and, like a child soothed to sleep by its mother's song, would turn over and close his dimmed eyes.

On very special occasions Galdós permitted a bedside *tertulia* of his fellow Canarians. While they were reverently examining the monastic simplicity of his bedroom—its plain iron bed, the artistic crucifix fastened to a square of old church brocade, and the modest night table on which were scattered a few caramels, an old cigar case, an eye-dropper, and a bottle of medicine— Galdós strained to recall persons, places, and incidents of his homeland. During a lull in the conversation he would surprise his listeners by humming bits of popular folk songs and comic opera lyrics of his boyhood days. It was always a great emotional strain, which left Galdós exhausted. At the first indication that he was becoming drowsy, the callers tiptoed out of the room, one of them always lingering behind to extricate the cold cigar stub from his mouth.

Like most human beings, Galdós rebelled occasionally against the monotony of routine. In his immediate family it was known that somewhere in Madrid lived a cultured and refined old lady of moderate wealth whom he loved with youthful ardor and tenderness. Her name was Teodosia Gandarias. Their love was of many, many years' standing, during which they had rarely missed seeing each other daily. These meetings were betrayed by Doña Teodosia's pet rabbit, who loved to nibble on his shirt cuffs and trouser hems, and by phonograph records of popular lyrics which Don Benito bought with his lady's money—to the great amazement of the family, for he had once been a sworn enemy of that sort of music. Apparently he took pleasure in chatting with her to the accompaniment of a popular air and the rhythmic nibbling of the rabbit. When the operations on his eyes confined Galdós to the sickroom, nothing depressed him more than being parted from Doña Teodosia. The fond and effusive notes he wrote her only sharpened his yearning for her company.

Then followed those melancholy years when ebbing strength kept Don Benito away from his lady more and more frequently. These enforced separations were followed by touching reunions. On one such occasion the lovers enjoyed a carriage drive through the less frequented streets of Madrid with the utter abandon of youth. What a glorious sensation to break indiscreetly the deadly monotony of routine! After the drive Don Benito was seized by a spirit of rebellion. He was going to stay that night with Doña Teodosia, and he ordered Paco to fetch his personal effects.

Shades of Mama Dolores! When nephew Don José learned of Uncle Benito's whim, he flew into a fit of indignation. Not once in their forty-five years together had his uncle spent a night away from home. Never, never would he permit him to sleep in a strange house. It might set a dangerous precedent for the childlike patriarch. Paco pleaded that his master was determined to carry out his caprice. He was tired of being regimented—and by a younger nephew! Don José sent word to his uncle that he would invoke the aid of the police if he refused to behave sensibly. He didn't want to create a scandal, did he? Don Benito slept miserably in his own bed that night. Don José felt deeply remorseful ever after for having been the first in the family to gainsay a wish of Uncle Benito.

* * * *

The nearer Galdós approached the end, the more he reverted to childhood days and ways. He had always loved children—somewhat like Rousseau in some ways—and those of his fancy shared his fondness with those of flesh and blood. Of the youthful creatures in his works, one was vividly etched in his memory. Ugly, tattered, pathetic Marianela stood before him, radiating warmth and light in the dark, chilly space around him. She had always been his and the public's favorite. The fickle, ungrateful public had apparently forgotten him, but it could not possibly have forgotten Nela. Would he not retrieve some of his popularity if he dramatized the moral and spiritual graces of the pitiful orphan girl?

Galdós had always been conscious of his unique national role. Early in his career he had felt that he merited recognition, if only for his interest in cultural progress. With advancing age his desire for tribute became more personal. His participation in republican politics and the prominence he gained during the controversies over the Nobel prize and the national subscription engendered a touch of vanity which advancing senility accentuated. He began to think of himself as the nation's undisputed favorite. In a word, he craved applause. During the premières of his last plays his eagerness for ovations was little short of childish. He was no longer the man of resolute will who knew how to repress his emotions. He fairly trembled with impatience as the time approached for a curtain call, like a man bidding for his grandchildren's affection. Yet there was always something in his attitude which inspired respect. One sensed that he was saying farewell to glory, that he was out to enjoy the last direct contact with life. On such occasions Margarita Xirgu, the Quinteros, and others would observe with moist eyes the pathetic impatience of the man who had learned so well the lesson of patience and had taught it to others.

Galdós' hunger for applause spurred his old desire to see *Marianela* on the stage. In fact, he himself had already begun the dramatization back in 1897, but had never got beyond a preliminary, partial outline. In 1904 the job was taken over by Valle-Inclán, who abandoned it two years later, however, when it was almost finished. At Galdós' suggestion the Quinteros revived the idea in 1914 as their contribution to the national subscription. Only the failure of that project and Don Benito's incessant goading finally brought about the dramatization of the novel in 1916.

The time devoted to the work was a period of artistic, spiritual, and—one might say—even physical rejuvenation for the aged author. His exultation could scarcely have been greater had he discovered the fountain of youth. Again and again he repeated that no one was better qualified than the tenderly sentimental "Quinteritos" to test once more the strong lyrical appeal of Spain's most popular child figures, Nela and Celipín. There were several friendly disputes over Galdós' direct collaboration and the distribution of the royalties. Galdós insisted that the Quinteros should share the box-office receipts, and his opinion finally prevailed. The Quinteros, on the other hand, were determined that the author should cooperate in the dramatization of the novel, and their opinion prevailed too.

All the artistic and personal interest that Galdós may have had in the scenification of *Marianela* was swept away by the emotional wave that took possession of him as the dress rehearsal and the première drew near. In his household a light cosmic disturbance was in the making. He strictly forbade all talk about the drama. During the period of rehearsals he advised everyone that it was no matter for excitement even as he himself fairly trembled with impatience, like a parent about to be reunited with his favorite child after a long separation. More than an emotional reunion it was to be a spiritual resurrection. In vain did Galdós feign calmness in the presence of the Quinteros. They gauged his feelings more truthfully: "The première of the stage adaptation of *Marianela* will fuse two dates in the spirit of the illustrious novelist and dramatist—his bright dawn and melancholy twilight. Yesterday, during the rehearsal, the master's deep emotion and flowing tears spoke to us with the ringing eloquence of all that was going on in his heart and mind." [3]

The night of the dress rehearsal, October 16, 1916, Galdós sat between the Quinteros near the footlights on the stage of the Teatro Princesa. The entire play was given without interruption, but those present were more interested in watching Galdós' reaction. As the actors began their lines, tears came to his eyes, and he sobbed loudly as Nela appeared. When the Quinteros, somewhat worried, inquired how he felt, he could not speak. His trembling hands clasped theirs and held them throughout the first act; with every important scene he sighed, and his body shook. The first emotional crisis came with the appearance of Celipín. At the sound of the plucky ragamuffin, Galdós shivered with nervousness, stretched out his arms, and exclaimed: "Celipín! Celipín!"

During the brief intermission after the first act Galdós became somewhat calmer. He asked the Quinteros whether they had enough for two more acts. He could not recall what followed. Nela and Celipín crowded everything else out of his mind; he was impatient to see them again. Perhaps they reminded him of the Nelas and Celipíns in some of the novelistic episodes in his own life. In his younger days he would have been able to resolve the confusion, but now in his blindness, under the strain of emotion and possibly contrition, Nela and Celipín may have seemed like his own children pointing accusingly at him.

When the rehearsal was over, someone asked Galdós if he would attend the première. As if coming out of a daze, he replied: "No. I have been powerfully impressed—one of the most lasting impressions of my life. I had not seen those children in so long! I shall have to rest, calm myself, before I come back. I am no longer strong enough for such emotions. What a long time ago. . . . What a long time ago. . . ."

Feeling his way cautiously toward the door, he remarked to Xirgu that her interpretation of Nela surpassed the original. She replied that it was a pity he could not see the actors. Galdós muttered: "But I do see you, my dear children. I do see you. Believe me that I do see you." [4] And calling trusty Paco, he took his arm and disappeared slowly in the corridor off the stage, noisily dragging his feet and drying his tears.

No one was surprised when Galdós broke his promise and returned for the première of *Marianela* on the night of October 18. From the standpoint of sincere, spontaneous response it was his greatest triumph since *Electra*. The Princesa was filled to capacity, the more distinguished spectators in the orchestra and loges and the "people" in the galleries. The atmosphere was charged with pity, respect, and admiration for the blind author who had become conspicuous in recent years as the most pathetic Spaniard living. The audience seemed determined to demonstrate its esteem and affection for Don Benito.

Galdós settled down in a chair in the wings of the stage, resolved to stay until the end of the performance. He was restless, nervous, impatient. Every few minutes he asked the stage hands how much longer the first act would last. He got tired sitting so far from the stage. He wanted to get closer—"to hear," as he put it. To hear what? Not what the actors were saying. He wanted "to hear" the outburst of applause that would soon rend the air.

The Quinteros had managed to get only three acts out of the novel, but Galdós furnished a fourth one spontaneously. Hardly had the last words been spoken when he advanced haltingly to the center of the stage and stumbled into the outstretched arms of Margarita Xirgu, who had not yet come out of character. The Quinteros, who had tenderly guided Galdós, vanished like specters when they beheld the pathetic tableau of Don Benito in the arms of Nela. After a brief moment of hushed silence there followed an outburst of frenzied applause. And there the tableau remained for a long while. Blind, hieratical Galdós bending under the weight of his seventy-three years, leaning on frail and emaciated Marianela, looking like a living statue. When he recovered from the ecstasy of the consecration, his still eyes searched for the Quinteros. They came forward hesitatingly, and he embraced them. A thunderous ovation rocked the theater.

On the way out—precisely as he had done two nights before—Galdós muttered: "I am not coming back, I am not coming back. Those emotions are too strong for me." [5]

*   *   *   *

During the winter months that followed Galdós was confined to his home. The gray, chilly Madrid afternoons were spent in his chair dreaming of contact with warm life, of the radiant appreciation of his audiences. The applause on the night of

October 18 kept ringing in his ears, and he talked ceaselessly of the triumph of *Marianela*. Ignoring his infirmities, he conceived the ambition of touring the country with the company in the spring. He schemed, plotted, pleaded, and finally persuaded the Quinteros to accompany him. He wanted them with him, re-calling how comforted he felt in the arms of the "Quinteritos" after the frenzied ovation when he was frightened, as in former days, by the consciousness of thousands of eyes upon him.

Once again every city of importance on the itinerary acclaimed Galdós. In Utrera, home of the Quinteros, he delivered a speech over a glass of wine which he did not drink. In Valla-dolid he silenced the audience clamoring for a few remarks by bringing his forefinger to his mouth without uttering a word. He was experiencing a veritable rejuvenation. All his childish whims and caprices were satisfied, and he was elated beyond words to feel that he was still the nation's literary favorite. The play that was furnishing him so many thrills no longer meant anything to him as a product of his dramatic talent; it was only the excuse for a repeated ritual whose incense gave him a strong taste of glory.

The performance in Barcelona demonstrated clearly that it was all merely another ceremony of consecration. The curtain went up, and Galdós settled down in a chair to smoke and doze intermittently. His cheap cigar went out continually, to the annoyance of the stage hands. Every now and then he bobbed up and down in his chair with outstretched arms and called for help to stand up. He was assured that it was too early—he would be called in time for the next ovation. At the end of each act he was helped out of his chair; leaping with the peculiar awkwardness of a blind person, he reached the stage to receive the applause with obvious self-consciousness. The ceremony over, he returned to his chair to doze until the next call.

The triumphant tour was followed by a period of rest in Santander, where Galdós went to spend the summer of 1917—his last one there. It was then that the final disintegration of his personality set in. To strangers he was an object of pity mixed with reverence; to his family he was a source of grief and irritation. His memory was failing fast, and fact and fancy blended effortlessly in his thoughts and in his deeds. The present meant increasingly less to him, save in the demands of his physical existence. Out of the past came crowding around him his hundreds of characters, who became real people to him. Only his callers and the newspapers read to him by Paco gave him a precarious contact with the world. It was often necessary to identify for him well-known political figures in the news. In the absence of newspapers on Mondays, he had selections from the *Quijote* read to him.

Possibly under the influence of the Knight of La Mancha, Galdós seemed determined to demonstrate the superiority of mind over matter. His imagination was still forging vistas and shaping creatures. He talked of writing several more historical novels to carry his series through the reign of Alfonso XIII; of making research expeditions to Cuba and South America, where he also hoped to gather material for a group of novels about the conquistadores; and of writing a social novel about the wretched life of the Río Tinto miners. But it was too late to realize these dreams. Yet he apparently retained some of his creative energy, for a year and a half before his death he finished and produced *Santa Juana de Castilla*.

Perhaps because he felt that his life work was not complete, Galdós' spiritual disintegration lagged behind his physical decline. He continued to regard himself as a vital national force and watched with interest the impact of the World War upon Spanish life. In this he was humored and encouraged by the many admirers he still had. His name continued to be one to conjure with, and promoters of political and social movements sought his endorsement. Naturally he was not averse to this flattery. On rare occasions he even put in an appearance at a public function, with consequent harm to his health. As late as October, 1918, he graced the speakers' table together with Unamuno and Cavia at a rally of protest against new unconstitutional practices by the government. The press featured Galdós' presence almost as much as the speeches, dwelling especially on his appearance. Most of the reporters saw him as

> tall, thin, hieratical, strangely and impressively rigid. The years weigh lightly upon his shoulders. They have resigned themselves to rendering his feet clumsy. He takes short little steps, scarcely lifting his feet off the ground. Only then does he produce an impression of senile, physiological decadence. But the moment he is quiescent he assumes the appearance of a hard, dry statue, carved in Spanish fashion out of a block of oak. His immovable and serene face seems absorbed in the contemplation of the eternal, which only he can penetrate. Behind his stilled pupils there is the dazzling vision of a future Spain, and farther back and deeper still there is the evoked image of the heroic and tumultuous Spain of the nineteenth century.[6]

* * * *

In 1918 Galdós was perhaps a bit more preoccupied with a personal matter than with the problems of Spain or the international catastrophe. Early in the year the members of his home *tertulia*, wishing to brighten his last days, conceived a plan for the erection of a monument by popular subscription. He welcomed the idea with childish hilarity, as a child might receive a toy he had long hoped for. He played with it in his solitude and in the presence of callers.

In March a committee was formed of the Quinteros, José Francés, Andrés González Blanco, Emiliano Ramírez Angel, Marciano Zurita, and Victorio Macho the sculptor. It was decided that the monument should be a distinctly popular tribute and accordingly, on May 15, an appeal was issued for funds to cover the cost of material and labor only. Contributions might be as small as twenty-five céntimos. The appeal aroused wide interest, but the donations came in slowly and the committee had many anxious moments. Yet everyone was confident of ultimate success. The press cooperated unstintingly to insure that Madrid should have a statue of its distinguished citizen, whom Valle-

Inclán described as "blind like Homer and poor like Belisarius." [7]

Days of nerve-wracking suspense were in store for Galdós. He was impatient to receive the results of the subscription and to "see" the progress of Macho's gratuitous work. The price of the stone was estimated at about twelve thousand pesetas. Contributions of one thousand pesetas each came from the Fine Arts Club, the Madrid Casino, the Royal Academy of Language, and the city council. The goal was still distant, and Galdós made extravagant suggestions for its attainment. If the committee would only approach a certain ambassador, a good friend of his, or a certain Casino whose treasury was affluent, all the troubles would be over. And why not appeal to municipal governments, especially in the Canary Islands, where he was esteemed and loved? The committee solemnly promised to act on all these suggestions, which he repeated almost daily. The nervous strain fairly wrecked Galdós' memory, and it required patience and indulgence to take good-naturedly his tiresome repetitions of the same questions. It was pathetic to hear him urge ardently, as his own, ideas that had been offered by others a day or two before. His most persistent obsession was that King Alfonso was to unveil the monument, as someone had speculatively suggested. For days he greeted all callers with the news: "Listen, my dear friend, did you know that apparently the king, Don Alfonso, is going to unveil 'our' statue?"

When reminded about his republican affiliations, he invariably replied angrily:

> "Don't mention republican to me! I am a great admirer of Alfonso. He is a very spirited young man, very courageous and, above all, every inch a Spaniard."
>
> "But you were once a republican deputy."
>
> "Nonsense! I was also a Sagasta deputy in the first Cortes of the Regency—and I could not stand Sagasta." [8]

The periodic reports which Paco and Ramírez Angel made to Galdós on the progress of the statue did not satisfy him; he insisted that he must "see" it with his own eyes. And so, one sunny morning in January, 1919, a few days before the official unveiling, the entire committee escorted him to the site on the Paseo de los Pinos. It was an exquisitely moving scene. Don Benito, dragging his feet in short, hesitant steps, was led to the enclosure above which rose the statue. At the entrance, and before anyone could have seen anything, he exclaimed with tumultuous joy as he embraced Macho: "Colossal, Machito, colossal! What talent you have, my dear boy! It is a marvelous statue! Go ahead! Keep on working!" [9]

The official unveiling took place on Sunday, January 19, a day of agony for Galdós. The fervor with which he had followed the progress of the statue had seemingly exhausted him, and when the day of days came, he was spiritless and dejected. He permitted no one of the family to accompany him or attend the ceremony.

It was a popular ceremony. The crowd was small but congenial, enthusiastic and sincerely moved. Many simple folk were there—men and women who looked like characters out of Galdós' novels. The mayor of Madrid and the municipal band represented official Spain. Galdós was brought to the Paseo de los Pinos by the Quinteros, who carried him to the chair reserved for him in front of the monument. He looked overwhelmed, crushed, as he sat at the base of this stone replica of himself. He assumed his characteristic quiescent, almost reclining position of recent years, which Macho had reproduced so faithfully.

The program was a simple one. As soon as Galdós arrived, the crowd broke through the police cordon and surged to kiss his hand. The mayor, before accepting the monument on behalf of the city, planted a kiss on Galdós' right hand, and the crowd applauded and cheered madly. Galdós remained rigid and silent, his face paler than ever, tears streaming from his half-closed eyes. A little blind girl, representing the Colegio de Ciegas, tendered him a floral offering, which he kissed with visible emotion. The band played selections from the operatic versions of

Zaragoza, Gerona, and *Cádiz.* Serafín Quintero unveiled the statue and delivered the only speech on the program. The crowd listened spellbound:

> Sturdy old oaks form a canopy over his throne, and behind these is a vast background of diverse trees for its natural protection, straining the leaves of their branches far and near to offer shade to the venerable brow of the artist. A eucalyptus, sentinel-like, stands guard and speaks to him of perennial health. . . . A tender almond tree will bring him every spring an offering of the first blossoms of the year, a symbol of the cordial homage which the youth of all times will render unto him.[10]

After the ceremony Galdós was escorted to his home in a triumphal procession. The afternoon was gray, and it was promenade time. The streets were filled with strollers, many of whom joined the compact crowd of students, workers, modistes, and small shopkeepers behind the carriage. Cheers and applause reverberated through the air. Another crowd had already assembled in front of the Galdós home. When he arrived there, a thunderous ovation broke the silence of the ordinarily solitary Calle Hilarión Eslava. For a moment Galdós seemed on the verge of collapse. Tears sparkled in his dim eyes. Making a supreme effort, he beamed a smile of ineffable joy at the cheering crowd and waved his black hat high in the air. And as gathering dusk began to cast shadows over the trim little garden in front of the house, Don Benito stumbled wearily up to his room. His last apotheosis confined him to bed for several weeks.

Galdós' recuperation was aided by his amusement over the press comments on the artistic merit of the statue. Because Macho's technique was new in Spanish sculpture, his work was both attacked and defended. Some critics sweepingly condemned everyone and everything connected with this last public tribute to Galdós. They regretted that what they called "a poor imitation of a statue" would have to exist for the Lord only knew how long. It was a painful effigy of an old, dying man— "a poor mausoleum of a provincial cemetery."[11] José Francés, on the other hand, praised Macho for the genial way in which he had expressed the cardinal virtues of Galdós' art: sobriety, realism, equilibrium, serenity, simplicity. The plain citizen was likely to feel that the statue was lacking in monumental grandeur. As one Madrilenian put it: "Is this all there is to the statue—an old gentleman sitting down?"[12]

Galdós had his own opinion. In general it corresponded to Juan de la Encina's:

> The master with his serene and somewhat feline face has a certain sphinx-like air. He has already accomplished his formidable task and, with neither passion nor fear, seems to be looking on the world and recalling his own work which is confused with it. There is in his face—not in the features but in the expression—a certain vague resemblance to the classic bust of Homer, and it produces on us the same mysterious impression as the Hermes.[13]

Indeed, the statue in the Rosaleda was a faithful image of the silently musing and introspective old man who was reclining rigidly in his red, heavily upholstered chair. As the twilight of his life was rapidly receding into the gathering shadows of eternal night, he often wondered whether the world he had observed and the world he had imagined were not both part of the same inscrutable eternity.

XX

Into Eternity

ON THE MORNING OF AUGUST 23, 1919, Galdós sat sulking in his chair. He was dressed to go out, and his carriage was waiting in front of the house. But Don José and Paco argued that it was no longer safe for him to venture out. In recent weeks it had required almost acrobatic skill to maneuver him in and out of the carriage and up to his room. The day before he had been practically carried up to the second story, and this morning they had had even greater difficulty bringing him down.

Galdós admitted all this, but habit was stronger than reason. He was suspicious of the motives behind the family's solicitude. Had not everyone been plotting of late to deprive him of personal freedom? Even Paco seemed hesitant to carry out his instructions. Why should he forego his simple pleasures merely because his gait was becoming a bit awkward? With the aid of Paco he raised himself out of the chair and remained standing for a while. He tried to take a step forward, but his shoes seemed glued to the floor. And, somehow, he was unable to balance himself. Perhaps he was too weak to go out that morning, but he would resume his routine the next day.

Three weeks later Galdós was confined to his bedroom. On October 13 he suffered a severe attack of uremia, and thereafter he was rarely able to leave his bed.

At about this time he had a devastating emotional experience. One afternoon a shy, pleasant young woman called and timidly introduced herself as María Galdós. She asked permission to be with her father, Don Benito, whom she had not seen since he was last out in August. She had hesitated to call before for fear of an unpleasant reception. Don José graciously ushered María Galdós into her father's room.

At first Galdós received the news of his daughter's presence with a stony expression. There was a moment of agonizing silence. Don José felt as if a sharp knife were cutting downward inside him. He stared into space. María broke the silence. With tears in her voice she reproached her father: why had he never permitted her to enter his home? An expression of ill-concealed guilt spread over Galdós' face. For the first time one of his most intimate secrets was shamefully bared before a member of his family. He fidgeted in his chair, twitched his lips, but said nothing. María continued reproving him. Why had he always said that her appearance in his home would amount to a cataclysm?

The word "cataclysm" jolted Don José. Had Uncle Benito ever used it outside his books? He looked at Galdós as if requesting an answer. None came. The pathetic old man was wincing in his chair, muttering something in an opaque voice. Was he explaining, apologizing, or begging to be left alone? Don José assured María that she could stay with her father as often and as long as she pleased.

Galdós entered upon his final period of agony. The combined care of his family, his daughter, and Dr. Gregorio Marañón could not delay the end much longer. He had very few lucid moments. Most of the time his mind was obsessed with his boyhood days—his birthplace, his brothers and sisters, his mother. He muttered incoherently about Mama Dolores, but rarely mentioned his father. He wearied his listeners with explanations of his boyhood games, and repeatedly begged them to listen to his humming of his native island songs. But his confused loquacity was less annoying than his complaints. In his wakeful hours and often in his dreams, he complained bitterly of being a virtual prisoner in his bed, forced to neglect the work that was accumulating so alarmingly. Why could he not go to Río Tinto to gather data about the miners? And why did not someone rescue the library of the burning Escorial? He had to consult some important documents there, and the valuable collection must be saved. Don José tried desperately to distract his uncle with promises and bribes. Galdós' obsessions were endless, and he often defended them with logical arguments. Somewhere in the neighborhood a new apartment building was under construction. Galdós was exasperated by the whistles and bells calling the men to work. He wanted the noise stopped. It should not be necessary to call workers in this fashion, he argued. Did he ever wait for bells or whistles to summon him to work?

During his last week Galdós alternated between semi-consciousness and delirium. One afternoon a veritable "cataclysm" was averted by one of his delirious dreams. The coadjutor of the Paloma church—confessor of his sisters Concha and Carmen—was sent by the bishop of the diocese to prepare the patient for the impending end. The cleric found Galdós sound asleep and offered to wait at his bedside, but Don José was violently opposed even to his presence in the house. An unpleasant argument ensued, in the course of which Don José suggested that the final decision be left to María Galdós. She permitted the priest to see her father. Both stood at some distance from his bed. Galdós began to stir. His breath was heavy, and he groaned. Suddenly he raised his head with a jerk, stared at the cleric in the doorway, and exclaimed irascibly: *"Ni Santo Cristo, ni Dios Bendito!"* ("neither Holy Christ nor the Blessed Lord"). María and the priest were disconcerted. Did Galdós bluntly reject spiritual comfort? The coadjutor left the house, promising to return the next day.

It occurred to Galdós' daughter that she might have made an ill-advised decision. What if her father really refused the ministration of the Church? And just what did he mean by that puzzling exclamation? Don José explained that the phrase was a colloquialism of the Canary Islands, which Galdós often used to impress everyone that he was too busy to receive callers. Conceivably Uncle Benito may have just come out of a delirious dream about his neglected work when he beheld the priest; if so, no special significance could be attached to his exclamation. On the other hand, suggested Don José, the phrase could be interpreted literally—that Uncle Benito desired no spiritual solace from a cleric. Her cousin's equivocal explanation did not set

María's mind at ease. She had promised to let the priest return the next day; what was she to do? Don José offered to rescue her from her embarrassment. The next morning Paco carried a message to the priest that Don Benito was considerably improved and would not need his aid until further notice.

That notice was never sent. On December 29 Galdós' condition became hopeless. He had an intestinal hemorrhage which was temporarily arrested but was followed by a violent delirium, during which he stormily demanded to be taken down to his study and cried out repeatedly: "I have a lot of work to do . . . an awful lot!" Presently he seemingly took a turn for the better. He rested and took some food less protestingly than on previous days. The family was mildly pleased but not encouraged. All realized that uremia, arteriosclerosis, and intestinal hemorrhages were not a curable combination. In fact, back in October the doctors, expressing amazement at Galdós' vitality, had expected the end momentarily.

The end came early Sunday morning, January 4, 1920. Galdós had required attention at midnight, and then had fallen into a sound sleep. At approximately half past three in the morning a cry of anguish broke the stillness of the house. Everyone rushed to the patient's bedside, only to see him pass away quietly, almost imperceptibly, about five minutes later. Reporters who had been hovering near the house in defiance of the cold soon roused Madrid with special editions of their newspapers. By telegraph and cable the announcement was flashed across the world that Spain had lost one of her greatest figures.

* * * *

Lonely as Galdós was in his last years, out of contact with the masses whose warmth he had always craved, his death was in a sense his last and greatest popular triumph. The national government refused to accord him a state funeral on the ground that he had held no public office that entitled him to it, and for the same reason he was denied burial in the Panteón de Hombres Ilustres—a distinction which, incidentally, he had repeatedly requested to be spared. But the absence of official pomp and ceremony did not lessen the grief of the masses. The entire nation, shocked by his death, went into mourning. Somehow the rank and file had come to regard him as immortal, so long had he been a vital national force.

The morning of Galdós' death was raw and cold. At an early hour newsboys raced up and down the central streets, screaming the news. The front page of almost every paper was framed in heavy mourning and bore in sensationally tall letters the simple flash: "Galdós is Dead!" Before very long the neighborhood of the Galdós home was a solid mass of humanity—stunned, dazed, and grief-stricken. Messengers darted in and out of the house, delivering a steady stream of domestic and foreign telegrams. Oddly enough, many of the messages were addressed to Galdós personally, as if their senders refused to recognize the prerogatives of death over him.

As the morning advanced and the doors were opened, distinguished personages—artists, writers, actors, professional men, government officials, political leaders—began filing into the studio where the body lay and artists were making death masks and sketches. The royal palace was represented by the minister of public instruction. On their way out the callers signed their names in a book, and some of them added an appropriate sentiment. Gonzalo Cantó improvised the following striking lines:

En España ha habido dos
escritores brillantes:
el primero fué Cervantes,
el segundo fué Galdós.

(Spain has had two brilliant writers: one was Cervantes, the other Galdós.)

The steady procession of callers lasted most of the day. In vain did the family plead for a moment of privacy. Hundreds of unknown men and women humbly requested a last glimpse of Don Benito—their Don Benito. In the afternoon a young, distinguished-looking French woman asked permission to exchange a large, beautiful bouquet for one of the chrysanthemums on the casket. It was obvious that her grief was deep and sincere. She stood before the body with bowed head in silent prayer, and there were tears in her eyes when she left. A pall of mystery hung over the Galdós house. Was she an admirer, a friend, or someone more intimately related to the deceased?

Late in the afternoon, when the strain began to tell on the bereaved family, the city of Madrid announced that the remains would be removed early next morning to the crystal patio of the City Hall, where it would lie in state until the funeral. The municipal and national governments would take charge of all arrangements and defray all costs. After this announcement only Galdós' intimate friends were admitted into the house. Outside small crowds continued gathering, and on street corners, in cafés, clubs, casinos, and newspaper offices, groups spoke in hushed voices of their bereavement. Sunday night Madrid was silent: all the theaters cancelled their performances in tribute to the dramatist who had afforded the population of the capital so much entertainment.

The great capacity of the Spanish language for eulogistic expression was fully exemplified in the editorials and feature stories that appeared during the days following. These were not studied eulogies; they throbbed with genuine grief and dwelt on the thought that with the passing of Galdós an integral and intimate part of Spain, almost a vital organ, had ceased to exist. Even some of the Catholic papers feigned magnanimity and, as compensation for Galdós' falsely reported confession, glossed over momentarily what they regarded as his grievous errors. Conservative *El Debate* proclaimed in a banner headline that Galdós had died in the fold of the church. Only Carlist *El Siglo Futuro* refused to forgive and forget. At the same time that it called on its readers with unctuous piety to invoke heavenly mercy on Galdós' soul, it urged them to remember that all his life he had endeavored to undermine the religious faith of the nation. But it was the liberal press which expressed validly and adequately the full extent of the national loss: "Galdós is dying! These words sounded like the announcement of the end of an entire epoch. An entire century which had in him an historian and a poet was quaking before us when we heard them." [1]

The city of Madrid, which a few days before his death had been obliged by Galdós' condition to cancel a belatedly conceived tribute, expressed its sorrow in the following proclamation by Mayor Luis Garrido Jauristi:

> Madrilenians! Galdós is dead, the genius who brought glory to the literature of his age through the astounding creations of his pen.
>
> With his books he honored his country; with his life he honored himself. He was kind, pious, and the greatest worshipper of art and work.
>
> Those who admired him in his lifetime are asked to come to the City Hall to bid him a final farewell.
>
> Such a tribute of grief will please him because he always loved simplicity.

Actually, the people of Madrid did not wait for the mayor's exhortation. When, shortly after seven o'clock on Monday morning, the official hearse brought Galdós' body to the Ardent Chapel in the City Hall, the picturesque Plaza de la Villa was already crowded with humble men, women, and children, many of whom had been standing in line since dawn to be the first to bid Don Benito a painful *adiós*. Middle-class citizens were there too. It was a mixed crowd, well behaved, colorful—chastely Madrilenian—including a generous representation of old men and women and servant girls.

When the doors of the Ardent Chapel opened at about nine o'clock, the crowd began to file past the casket in a rapidly moving stream. No one was permitted to linger before the body, but many contrived to pause and pay their tribute in some personal, intimate way. Now and then a humble worker kneeled reverently and deposited a modest floral offering, perhaps purchased with his daily tobacco allowance. Women crossed themselves and muttered a prayer, the older ones invoking the Lord's merciful kindness in audible tones. In all some thirty thousand Spaniards thus paid their respects to Galdós in his home and in the City Hall.

Reverently and sorrowfully the people left the Plaza de la Villa to eat a hasty and frugal lunch. They would all be back for the funeral at three in the afternoon. Galdós was alone in the Ardent Chapel except for the rigidly pompous and formally mournful guard of honor in resplendent uniforms. There he lay, as one sleeping, draped in the national colors. Sickness had distorted his facial lines and once-energetic features. His hair had grown long, and his forelocks, fluffed out like the abundant locks of an hidalgo of former ages, were almost white. Shortly he would receive the plaudits of his public for the last time.

Before three o'clock Calle Mayor and Puerta del Sol were cleared of traffic. By the thousands the mourners streamed in from all directions. Flags were at half-mast, shop doors closed, window shutters pulled down. The day was bleak and cold and the sky threatening, but the crowd was oblivious. The funeral procession was forming. Government officials, educators, theater folk, newspaper men, representatives of civic and municipal organizations and of liberal and radical parties, members of workers' clubs and youth-movement societies—in short, a cross-section of Spain—were lining up behind the hearse to escort Galdós to the modest family plot in the Almudena Cemetery. Except for one incident everything proceeded in orderly fashion, and the masses behaved well, if not with the formal decorum demanded of them.

Official Spain, which had treated Galdós so shabbily, seemed desirous of making amends by participating in the funeral rites in accordance with prescribed etiquette. It reserved for itself a place directly behind the hearse and ordered that the masses be kept at a respectable distance. The people, however, insisting that a ceremonious procession solemnly pacing in well-kept lines would do violence to Don Benito's simple spirit, defied the attempts of the police to organize them according to a set pattern. They pressed close behind and up to the sides of the hearse, asserting their right to be close to Don Benito. A young student shouted fervently: *"Viva Galdós!"* A thunderous *"Viva!"* rumbled over the compact mass of forty thousand persons. When the police renewed their struggle to keep the marchers in orderly formation, they were met with the protest "Leave us alone! Galdós belongs to us!"[2] A contingent of some five hundred workers from the Casa del Pueblo, set on forcing its way to the funeral carriage, precipitated a mild riot which the authorities finally put down in front of the Madrid Casino on Calle Alcalá.

Barring these and other minor incidents, the procession moved more or less formally and laboriously up to the Plaza de la Independencia. There it halted. The official mourners had performed their duty and departed ceremoniously. Now the people took complete charge, and unofficially accompanied Don Benito to the very edge of his grave. It is a long distance from the Plaza de la Independencia to the Almudena Cemetery. To reach it, one must go by subway to the end of the line and there transfer to a taxicab for another sizable stretch. The crowd, however, defied fatigue and the stinging cold, and continued the procession solemnly and in orderly formation as official Spain returned to its warm living rooms, clubs, and cafés.

At a quarter before six o'clock, after a march of some three hours, the funeral cortège reached the cemetery. As the body of their beloved friend was lowered into the grave, the crowd pressed forward, standing silently with bowed, bared heads. For a long time no one moved. All seemed loath to leave their Don Benito alone. The cemetery attendants pleaded with them to clear the space near the grave, for the fast-descending darkness was making it impossible to see anything. Someone, as if awaking to a profound truth, exclaimed, "Gentlemen, it is impossible to see anything!" Just at that moment the moon pierced the thick patches of cloud overhead, and a diffuse, gray light outlined the grave and the sorrowing bystanders. A deep silence fell on the mourners as they stepped several paces back. A priest intoned the last response, and the first shovelful of earth was thrown over the earthly remains of Benito Pérez Galdós. The crowd returned to the city, silent, shivering, cold.[3]

*   *   *   *

Every year, on the fourth of January, the society of Los Amigos de Galdós invites the public of Madrid to a simple commemorative ceremony at the Galdós statue. As members of the family stay modestly in the background, writers and artists, actors and playwrights, many women and children, and humble residents of the Calle de Toledo district—the immortal setting of *Fortunata y Jacinta*—gather around the figure of Don Benito, deposit floral offerings in his lap and at his feet, and listen to a brief, heartfelt tribute to him. Troops of boy and girl scouts salute the kindly old man with the enigmatic expression and the blanket of cold stone over his lap. School children break the simple solemnity of the ceremony with a ringing *"Viva Galdós!"* The humble folk—the Calle de Toledo residents—stand silently apart from the small crowd in an attitude of worshipful communion with the spirit of the great artist who has immortalized them and their kin.

After the ceremony some linger to examine the soft simplicity of the statue and look up affectionately into the still eyes of the Homer-like figure. The rest stroll off, turning from time to time as if loath to leave their friendly Don Benito. They seem to hear the opaque voice of the pensive figure inviting them to return soon. Some do return—perhaps the very next day if the sun is bright and warm—to sit on the park bench before the statue. Sometimes they chat freely about the countless intimate, insignificant things that make their lives so tremendously complex. Don Benito listens. At other times they sit quietly listening to him, it would seem, as he meditates about the past and the present, finding between the two an indissoluble bond—the eternal features of Spanish life so faithfully traced in his novels and plays. Between Don Benito and the people there is a deep, sympathetic understanding which time will not erase.

Notes and References

Notes and References

THE SOURCES LISTED BELOW ARE limited to the more valuable published materials consulted in the preparation of this work. No attempt has been made to include a comprehensive bibliography on Galdós, since many of the general works that cover his life and writings contributed little to this specialized study, and even a partial listing of them would have had to be a matter of random selection.

In citing material derived from Spanish periodicals and reviews it has been impossible to avoid their almost chaotic method of entry. In every instance, however, sufficient information is furnished to permit identification of the source. Where the date, or even the title, of a periodical is omitted, the reference is to a clipping in the possession of Galdós' heirs. It would have been virtually impossible to identify these items more specifically.

CHAPTER ONE (pages 3–19)

NOTES

[1] Chaplain Domingo Pérez wrote a brief, delightful chronicle of the human experiences of the expedition, and his brother kept a strictly factual record of its military activity. The two documents constitute the only reliable source of information regarding the outstanding event in the life of Sebastián Pérez. They have been preserved in the Museo Canario of Las Palmas.

[2] These *datas* became in time the family country estate. Today it is the summer home of the Galdós survivors in Las Palmas.

[3] Don Sebastián must have influenced both sons: Ignacio directly, Benito indirectly. The central figure of the first ten *Episodios nacionales* presumably immortalizes the humble and modest Sebastián Pérez.

REFERENCES

García-Sánchiz, F., in *La República de las Letras*, 1:15 (July 22, 1907).
Marañón, Gregorio. "Galdós Intimo." *La Lectura*, vol. 20, no. 229 (1920).
Millares, Agustín. "Relación de los inquisidores." *Historia de la Inquisición en las Islas Canarias*, Vol. IV (Las Palmas, 1874).
Pérez Galdós, Benito. *Memorias* (Madrid, 1930), 224–226, 228–229.
Torre, Claudio de la. "Galdós en su tierra." *ABC*, April 5, 1931.

CHAPTER TWO (pages 20–40)

NOTES

[1] Domingo José Navarro, "Amigas," in *Recuerdos de un noventón*, 82–84 (Las Palmas, 1895).

[2] The preparatory course in the Colegio de San Agustín was organized as follows: *First Year:* Reading, English and Spanish Penmanship, Arithmetic, Christian Doctrine and Religion, Deportment, Castilian Grammar, Drawing. *Second Year:* Reading, English and Spanish Penmanship, Arithmetic, Christian Doctrine and Religion, Deportment, Castilian Grammar, Drawing, Rudiments of Agriculture, Industry and Commerce.

[3] The following is a transcript of Galdós' record at the Colegio de San Agustín:

1857–58: Latin and Spanish—Excellent
Preparatory Subjects—Excellent

1858–59: Second-year Latin and Spanish—Excellent
First-year French and Geography—Excellent
Christian Doctrine and Morals—Regular and Profitable Attendance

1859–60: First Course of Latin and Greek—Excellent
First Course of Mathematics—Excellent
First Course of French—Excellent
Natural History—Good
Doctrine—Attendance on Fourth Course

1860–61: Second Course of Latin and Greek—Good
Rhetoric and Poetics—Good
History—Good
Second Course of Mathematics—Excellent
Doctrine—Attendance on Fourth Course

1861–62: Psychology—Excellent
Logic—Excellent
Moral Philosophy—Excellent
Physics—Excellent
Chemistry—Excellent

[4] The results of Galdós' examination for the title of "Bachiller en Artes" were as follows:

September 3: Latin and Castilian, Greek and French—Excellent

September 4: Psychology, Logic, Moral Philosophy, Geography and History, Rhetoric, Poetics and Christian Doctrine, Church History (30 minutes)—Passed unanimously

September 5: Mathematics, Physics-Chemistry-Natural History—Passed unanimously

[5] Francisco Inglott, "Benito Pérez: Recuerdos," in *Diario de Las Palmas*, February 9, 1894.

[6] Berkowitz, H. Chonon, "The Youthful Writings of Pérez Galdós." *Hispanic Review* 1:102 (1933).

REFERENCES

Alcántara, Francisco. "Los Amigos de Galdós en Toledo—Historias galdosianas." *El Sol*, April 18, 1923.

Anonymous, *Memoria de la exposición*. Las Palmas, 1864.

Anonymous, "Benito Pérez Galdós." *Revista de las Canarias* (Havana), September 29, 1890.

Arunci. *"Quien mal hace, bien no espere*—Ensayo dramático en un acto y en verso, original de un estudiante llamado Benito Pérez Galdós, año 1861." *El Globo,* January 27, 1894.

Berkowitz, H. Chonon. "The Youthful Writings of Pérez Galdós." *Hispanic Review,* 1:91–121 (1933).

Latour, Tolosa (El Doctor Fausto). "Siluetas contemporáneas: Pérez Galdós." *La Epoca,* March 26, 1883.

Millares Cubas, Luis y Agustín. "Pérez Galdós: Recuerdos de su infancia en Las Palmas." *La Lectura,* vol. 20, no. 228, pp. 333–352 (1919).

Morales y Aguilar, Francisco. "Gloria de Las Palmas." *Diario de Las Palmas,* February 9, 1894.

Morote, Luis. "Los antepasados de Galdós." *La tierra de los Guanartemes,* 193–204. Paris, n.d.

Olmedilla, Juan G. "Paradoja de Galdós." *El Heraldo,* January 5, 1933.

Palacio Valdés, Armando. "Un estudiante de Canarias: Benito Pérez Galdós." *Diario de Las Palmas,* August 18, 1894.

Sarmiento, Miguel. "Pérez Galdós: Recuerdos de su vida." *Diario de Las Palmas,* January 5, 1920.

Viera y Viera, Isaac. "Don Benito Pérez Galdós." *Vidas ajenas,* Tenerife, 1888.

CHAPTER THREE (pages 41–73)

NOTES

[1] Unidentified clipping dealing with *La fontana de oro.*
[2] Benito Pérez Galdós, "Guía espiritual de España," in *La razón de la sinrazón,* 267 (Madrid, 1915).
[3] *Ibid.,* 259.
[4] F. García-Sánchiz, in *La República de las Letras,* 1:15 (July 22, 1907).
[5] Benito Pérez Galdós, *El doctor Centeno,* vol. 2 (Madrid, 1925), 38.

REFERENCES

Anonymous. "Benito Pérez Galdós." *Revista de las Canarias* (Havana), September 29, 1890.

————— "Pérez Galdós." *El Imparcial,* March 24, 1894.

————— "Un capricho de Galdós." *El Correo,* November 16, 1894.

————— "La vida del maestro," *El Sol,* January 4, 1920.

————— "El maestro Galdós." *Diario de Las Palmas,* special number, July, 1929.

El Bachiller Corchuelo. "Nuestros grandes prestigios: Benito Pérez Galdós." *Por Esos Mundos,* 11:27–56 (1910).

Balbín de Unquera, Antonio. "Novela y novelistas históricos en España." *Revista Contemporánea,* October, 1905, pp. 403–408.

Berkowitz, H. Chonon. "Galdós' Literary Apprenticeship." *Hispanic Review,* 3:1–22 (1935).

————— *"Un joven de provecho*: An Unpublished Play by Pérez Galdós." *Publications Modern Language Association,* 50:828–898 (1935).

Blasco, Eusebio. "Pérez Galdós." *Mis contemporáneos,* 49–51. Madrid, 1886.

González-Fiol, Enrique (El Bachiller Corchuelo). "Benito Pérez Galdós." *Nuevo Mundo,* January 19, 1913.

Gutiérrez-Gamero, Emiliano. _Mis primeros ochenta años._ Madrid, 1925.
Hartzenbusch, Juan Eugenio. _Apuntes para un catálogo de periódicos españoles desde el año 1661 a 1870._ Madrid, 1894.
Kasabal, "Galdós: _La de San Quintín._" _Nuevo Mundo,_ February 1, 1894.
Latour, Tolosa (El Doctor Fausto). "Siluetas contemporáneas: Pérez Galdós." _La Época,_ March 26, 1883.
Lustonó, Eduardo. "El primer drama de Galdós." _Nuestro Tiempo,_ 1:155–165 (1902).
Lyonnet, Henry. _Le théâtre en Espagne,_ 87–88. Paris, 1897.
Maura, Antonio. _Necrología de D. Benito Pérez Galdós._ Madrid, 1920.
Olmet, Luis Antón del, and Arturo García Carraffa. _Galdós._ Madrid, 1912.
Ortega Munilla, José. "Pérez Galdós." _El Imparcial,_ February 6, 1882.
Palacio Valdés, Armando. "Un estudiante de Canarias: Benito Pérez Galdós." _Diario de Las Palmas,_ August 18, 1894.
Pérez Galdós, Benito. _Arte y crítica,_ 38, 145–146, 147. Madrid, 1923.
———— _El doctor Centeno,_ Vol. 2. Madrid, 1925.
———— _Guía espiritual de España._ Madrid, 1915.
———— _Memorias._ Madrid, 1930.
———— _Prim._ Madrid, 1925.
Soriano, Rodrigo. "Galdós en la Academia." _El Imparcial,_ February 8, 1897.

CHAPTER FOUR (pages 74–89)

NOTES

[1] Benito Pérez Galdós, _Memorias,_ 36.
[2] _Ibid.,_ 41.
[3] This review, entitled "Un novelista español," was reprinted in Francisco Giner, _Estudios de literatura y arte_ (_Obras completas,_ vol. 3, Madrid, 1919), 303–306.
[4] Letter of Eugenio de Ochoa to editor in _La Ilustración de Madrid,_ September 30, 1871.

REFERENCES

Alcalá Galiano, José. "_La Fontana de Oro._" _Revista de España,_ 20:77 (1871).
Anonymous. "_La Fontana de Oro._" _Integridad Nacional,_ undated clipping.
———— Comments on Núñez de Arce's review of _La Fontana de Oro,_ in _La Verdad_ (Las Palmas), May 31, 1871.
———— "_La Fontana de Oro._" _La Política,_ September 4, 1871.
———— "Pérez Galdós." _El Imparcial,_ March 24, 1894.
Gutiérrez-Gamero, Emiliano. _Mis primeros ochenta años._ 87–98, 114–127. Madrid, 1919.
M. V. "_El audaz._" Unidentified clipping.
Núñez de Arce, Gaspar. Letter addressed to Galdós, in _El Debate._ Undated clipping.
Pérez Galdós, Benito. "_Cantares_ por Melchor Palau." _La Nación,_ February 25, 1866.
———— _La fontana de oro._ Madrid, 1921.
———— _Memorias,_ 36–37, 49–55.
———— _Prim._ Madrid, 1925.
———— Introduction to _La sombra._ Madrid, 1909.
R. M. "Variedades: _La Fontana de Oro._" _La Nación,_ May 16, 1871.
Silió, Evaristo. "_La Fontana de Oro._" Unidentified clipping.

CHAPTER FIVE (pages 90–103)

REFERENCES

Anonymous. *"La Guirnalda* en 1874." *La Guirnalda,* January 1, 1874.
———— "Don Benito Pérez Galdós." *La Ilustración de Canarias* (Santa Cruz), October 15, 1882.
————*Galería de españoles ilustres,* 1: 99–102. Buenos Aires, 1893.
———— "Benito Pérez Galdós." *El Noticiero Universal* (Barcelona), January 4, 1920.
Clarín (Leopoldo Alas). *Galdós,* 22, 30. Madrid.
Douesnel, Hélène. *"Electra." La Foi et la Vie,* April 1, 1901.
Huelin, Emilio. *"Episodios nacionales* por Benito Pérez Galdós: *Trafalgar." La Nación,* April 22, 1873.
———— *"Trafalgar." La Epoca,* April 23, 1873.
Latour, Tolosa (El Doctor Fausto). "Siluetas contemporáneas: Pérez Galdós." *La Epoca,* March 26, 1883.
Millares, Agustín. "Del naturalismo en la novela." *El Museo Canario,* May 22, 1882.
Ortega Munilla, José. "Rasgos de España: El triste narrador." *ABC,* January 4, 1920.
Pérez Galdós, Benito. *"La Arcadia moderna* por D. Ventura Ruiz de Aguilera." *La Nación,* January 9, 1868.
———— "Antes de *Trafalgar* (páginas de una novela)." *Revista de España,* no. 120, pp. 501–517 (1873).
———— *Memorias,* 54–56.
Rodríguez Correa, Ramón. *"Episodios nacionales* por Don Benito Pérez Galdós." *Revista de España,* no. 136, 1873.

CHAPTER SIX (pages 104–118)

NOTES

[1] A. F., "Revista de Madrid," in *Diario de Barcelona,* January 11, 1920.
[2] Manuel Linares Rivas, "Memorias de un hombre de teatro: Don *'Benoit'* Pérez Galdós," in *Blanco y Negro,* October 18, 1925.

REFERENCES

El Bachiller Corchuelo. "Nuestros grandes prestigios: Benito Pérez Galdós." *Por Esos Mundos,* 11:27–56 (1910).
Berkowitz, H. Chonon. "La biblioteca de Benito Pérez Galdós." *Boletín de la Biblioteca Menéndez y Pelayo,* 14:118–134 (1932).
———— "Galdós and Mesonero Romanos." *Romanic Review,* 23: 201–205 (1932).
———— "Gleanings from Galdós' Correspondence." *Hispania,* 16:249–290 (1933).
Bobadilla, Emilio. *"La loca de la casa." Solfeo,* 33–40. Madrid, 1893.
El Caballero Audaz. "La figura de la semana: Galdós." *Nuevo Mundo,* January 9, 1920.
Castell, Angel María. "Pérez Galdós y los *Episodios nacionales." ABC,* February 26, 1903.
Cubas, José de. "En casa de Galdós." *Blanco y Negro,* January 27, 1894.
El Chico del Escenario. "El maestro." *España Nueva,* December 10, 1913.
Doporto, S. "Hombres célebres: Benito Pérez Galdós." *Actualidad* (Colonia, Uruguay), March 20, 1914.

Espanueva. "Los proyectos de Galdós." *España Nueva,* November 25, 1907.

González Olmedilla, Juan. "Crónica de Madrid." *Ideas y Figuras,* May 1, 1918.

Hoyos Sáinz, L. de. "Galdós y su topografía madrileña." *Luz,* February 11, 1933.

Latour, Tolosa (El Doctor Fausto). "Siluetas contemporáneas: Pérez Galdós." *La Epoca,* March 26, 1883.

Martínez Olmedilla, Augusto. Galdós' answer to the question: "¿Cuál es mi obra predilecta?" *Por Esos Mundos,* February, 1907.

Morote, Luis. "Lo que dice Galdós." *El Heraldo,* August 31, 1903.

Navarro y Ledesma, Francisco. "Don Benito Pérez Galdós: Apuntes para un estudio." *Nuestro Tiempo,* 1:57–62 (1901).

Ortega Munilla, José. "Pérez Galdós." *El Imparcial,* February 6, 1882.

Pérez Galdós, Benito. Epilogue to illustrated edition of *Episodios nacionales,* iii–v. Madrid, 1885.

———— "Niñerías." *Memoranda,* 227–235. Madrid, 1906.

———— Prologue to E. Gómez Carrillo, *Campos de batalla y campos de ruinas.* Madrid, 1915.

———— "El crimen de la Calle de Fuencarral." *Cronicón,* 2: 124. Madrid, n.d.

———— *Memorias,* 71–72.

Romano, Julio. "Lo único que ha cambiado en las Cortes." *Luz,* May 9, 1934.

———— "Reportajes madrileños." *Luz,* December 14, 1933.

Ruiz de la Serna, Enrique. "Los personajes de Galdós." *Estampa,* October 22, 1929.

Ruiz de Velasco, Luis. "De literatura." *Madrid Cómico,* no. 789 (April 2, 1898).

Zamacois, E. "Figuras contemporáneas: Don Benito Pérez Galdós." *Alrededor del Mundo,* November 10, 1909.

CHAPTER SEVEN (pages 119–150)

NOTES

[1] Benito Pérez Galdós, *Cánovas* (Madrid, 1929), 274.
[2] *Ibid.,* 237.   [3] *Ibid.*
[4] Clarín (Leopoldo Alas), *Galdós* (Madrid), 308.
[5] Letter from José Hurtado de Mendoza to Galdós, dated Las Palmas, December 7, 1874.
[6] Arturo Mori, "María Guerrero y Fernando Díaz de Mendoza inauguran la temporada del Español con *Doña Perfecta* de Pérez Galdós," in *Informaciones,* October 31, 1924.
[7] Benito Pérez Galdós, *Doña Perfecta,* 202 (Madrid, 1927).
[8] ———— *Gloria,* 2:336–338 (Madrid, 1925).
[9] José María Pereda, *Discursos leídos ante la Real Academia Española,* 35 (Madrid, 1897).
[10] Benito Pérez Galdós, *Un faccioso más y algunos frailes menos,* 320–321 (Madrid, 1925).

REFERENCES

Alas, L. (Clarín). "*Gloria,* I." *Revista Europea,* no. 156, pp. 207-212 (1877).

———— "Nuestra literatura en 1879." *El Imparcial,* January 19, 1880.

Anonymous. "Libros nuevos: *Bailén*." *El Imparcial*, February 6, 1874.
———— "La novela española y la prensa inglesa." *El Imparcial*, March 26, 1883.
———— "Pérez Galdós." *El Liberal*, March 27, 1883.
———— "Pérez Galdós." *El Imparcial*, January 27, 1894.
Asís Pacheco, Francisco. "*Doña Perfecta*." *El Imparcial*, July 10, 1876.
———— "*Gloria*, I." *El Imparcial*, February 26, 1877.
Clarín (Leopoldo Alas). "Los *Episodios nacionales*." *Galdós*, 307–318.
Francos Rodríguez, J. "Fiestas de antaño." *La Esfera*, 1:28 (July 11, 1914).
Giner, Francisco. "Cartas literarias." *Boletín de la Institución*, 48–54 (January, 1920).
González Serrano, Urbano. "*Doña Perfecta*." *Ensayos de crítica y de filosofía*, 201–206. Madrid, 1881.
Huelin, Emilio. "*El 19 de marzo y el 2 de mayo*." *La Guirnalda*, November 1, 1873.
Latour, Tolosa (El Doctor Fausto). "Siluetas contemporáneas: Pérez Galdós." *La Época*, March 26, 1883.
Louis-Lande, L., "Le roman patriotique en Espagne." *Revue des Deux Mondes*, 14:934–945 (1876).
Millares Torres, Agustín. "*Gloria*." *La Prensa* (Las Palmas), July 17, 1877.
Múgica, Padre de, "Las novelas españolas modernas en Alemania," *España y América*, vol. 6, no. 2, pp. 323-325 (1908).
Palacio Valdés, A. "Pérez Galdós." *Revista Europea*, no. 112, pp. 335-339 (1878).
Pérez Galdós, Benito. "Observaciones sobre la novela contemporánea en España." *Revista de España*, vol. 15, no. 57, pp. 162–172 (1870).
———— *Cánovas*. Madrid, 1929. For historical background.
Revilla, Manuel. "*Zaragoza*." *El Imparcial*, June 8, 1874.
———— "*Doña Perfecta*," *Revista Contemporánea*, 4:15 (July 15, 1876).
———— "*Gloria*, I." *Revista Contemporánea*, 7:28 (January 30, 1877).
———— "*Los cien mil hijos de San Luis*." *Revista Contemporánea*, II–III: 8 (March 30, 1877).
———— "*El terror de 1824*." *Revista Contemporánea*, II–III:12 (December 15, 1877).
———— "*Marianela*." *Revista Contemporánea*, III–IV:14 (April 30, 1878).
———— "*La familia de León Roch*." *El Globo*, March 3, 1879.
———— *Obras*, 109–116. Madrid, 1883.
———— "*Cádiz*." *Críticas*, 2d series. Burgos, 1885.
Sánchez del Real, Andrés. "La quincena científica y literaria." *El Globo*, February 1, 1877.
Tenreiro, R. M. "Galdós novelista." *La Lectura*, vol. 20, no. 232, pp. 321–335 (1920).
Un Lunático. "Pérez Galdós (*Marianela*)." *El Imparcial*, April 8, 1878.

CHAPTER EIGHT (pages 151–173)

NOTES

[1] Benito Pérez Galdós," "Sobre *Los bocetos al temple* de Don José María de Pereda," *El Imparcial*, January 17, 1877.
[2] ———— *La desheredada*, I (Madrid, 1909), unnumbered page.
[3] Clarín (Leopoldo Alas), *Galdós*, 106–107 (Madrid).
[4] Rosario Acuña de Laiglesia, "*El amigo Manso*." *El Liberal*, July 10, 1882.

[5] *Ibid.*
[6] Clarín, *op. cit.*, 106–107.
[7] *El Imparcial,* March 4, 1883.
[8] Mariano de Cavia, "Crónicas momentáneas," in *El Liberal,* March 15, 1892.
[9] Anonymous, "El banquete a Pérez Galdós," in *El Globo,* March 27, 1883.
[10] ———— "El banquete a Pérez Galdós," in *La Epoca,* March 27, 1883.
[11] Viernes, "Banquete literario," in *La Correspondencia de España,* March 27, 1883.
[12] *Ibid.*
[13] Anonymous, "Manifestaciones en loor de Galdós," in *El Imparcial,* March 27, 1883.
[14] José Ortega Munilla, "Madrid," in *El Imparcial,* April 2, 1883.

REFERENCES

Alcázar Hernández, José. *"El amigo Manso."* Revista de España, 87:347 (1882).
Alfonso, Luis. *"La desheredada."* La Epoca, November 7, 1881.
Anonymous, Galdós' appointment as examiner at the University of Madrid. *El Imparcial,* January 22, 1882.
———— "Don Benito Pérez Galdós." *La Ilustración de Canarias* (Santa Cruz), October 15, 1882.
———— A letter protesting against Spanish indifference toward Galdós. *El Imparcial,* December 31, 1882.
———— "Pérez Galdós." *El Liberal,* March 27, 1883.
———— "El banquete a Pérez Galdós." *La Epoca,* March 27, 1883.
———— "Un banquete." *El Iris,* April 6, 1883.
El Bachiller Corchuelo. "Nuestros grandes prestigios: Benito Pérez Galdós." *Por Esos Mundos,* 11:27–56 (1910).
Blasco, Eusebio. "Pérez Galdós." *Mis contemporáneos,* chapter 3. Madrid, 1886.
Cabezas, Juan Antonio. *Clarín,* 62–83. Madrid, 1936.
Cossio, Manuel B. "Galdós y Giner: Una carta de Galdós." *Boletín de la Institución,* January, 1920, pp. 60–62.
Francos Rodríguez, José. "Fotografías olvidadas: Bilis Club." *Blanco y Negro,* February 23, 1919.
Luis y Yagüe, A. *"Episodios nacionales* por Benito Pérez Galdós. *Las Palmas,* 2:16 (April 27, 1876).
Nadie, Juan. "Un novelista español y un libro francés." *El Día,* March 26, 1883.
Ortega Munilla, José. "Madrid (novelas)." *El Imparcial,* June 26, 1882.
———— "Madrid." *El Imparcial,* February 1, 22, 1886.
Pérez Galdós, Benito. Letter to the president of the "Gabinete Instructivo" of Santa Cruz, dated May 15, 1883.
Viernes. "De los libros." *La Correspondencia de España,* July 8, 1881.

CHAPTER NINE (pages 174–195)

NOTES

[1] Benito Pérez Galdós, Prologue to Emilio Bobadilla, in *Viajando por España,* pp. v–vi (Madrid, 1912).
[2] *Memorias,* 187.
[3] Clarín, *Galdós,* 33.

⁴ Benito Pérez Galdós, *Memorias*, 213.
⁵ *Ibid.*   ⁶ *Ibid.*, 211.   ⁷ *Ibid.*, 212.   ⁸ *Ibid.*, 206.   ⁹ *Ibid.*, 213.
¹⁰ Benito Pérez Galdós, "La casa de Shakespeare," in *Memoranda*, 54 (Madrid, 1906).

REFERENCES

Anonymous.   Article about Galdós' fear of seasickness.   *El Heraldo*, October 10, 1894.
————— "Galdós por tierras de Castilla." *El Imparcial*, May 28, 1906.
Azorín.   "Veraneo sentimental—En San Quintín: Una tarde con Galdós." *España*, January 8, 1920.
Berkowitz, H. Chonon.   "Galdós' Literary Apprenticeship." *Hispanic Review*, 3:6 (1935).
————— "Gleanings from Galdós' Correspondence." *Hispania*, 16:249-290 (1933).
Ghiraldo, Alberto.   Prologue to Benito Pérez Galdós, *Viajes y fantasías*, 5. Madrid, 1928.
Maura, Antonio.   *Necrología de Don Benito Pérez Galdós*, 25.
Morote, Luis.   "Lo que dice Galdós." *El Heraldo*, August 31, 1903.
Ortega Munilla, José.   "Madrid (*Tormento*)." *El Imparcial*, March 17, 1884.
Pérez Galdós, Benito.   Prologue to Fernaflor. *Cuentos*, p. x. Madrid, 1904.
————— "La casa de Shakespeare." *Memoranda*, 35–57.
————— "Cuarenta leguas por Cantabria." *Memoranda*, 73–115.
————— Prologue to J. M. Salaverría. *Vieja España*. Madrid, 1907.
————— *Arte y crítica*. 51–63. Madrid, 1923.
————— *Fisonomías sociales*, 188–194. Madrid, 1923.
————— *Política española*, 1:255–262; 2:245–252. Madrid, 1923.
————— *Viajes y fantasías*, 11–160.
————— *Memorias*, 91–136.

CHAPTER TEN (pages 196–214)

NOTES

¹ Benito Pérez Galdós, *Política española*, 2:54.
² *Ibid.*, 12.   ³ *Ibid.*, 135–146.
⁴ *Política española*, 2:9.

REFERENCES

Anonymous.   "Don Benito Pérez Galdós." *La Epoca*, January 4, 1920.
A. F.   "Revista de Madrid." *Diario de Barcelona*, January 11, 1920.
Colorado, Vicente.   "La literatura española en 1886." *Revista de España*, vol. 114, no. 451, pp. 283–296 (1887).
Ortega Munilla, José.   "*Miau*." *El Imparcial*, June 18, 1888.
Pérez Galdós, Benito.   "Recuerdos de una fiesta." *La Nación*, September 13, 1868.
————— "El dos de mayo." *La Guirnalda*, May 1, 1874.
————— *Cánovas*.
————— "La cuestión social." *Cronicón*, 1:146-156. Madrid, n.d.
————— "El parlamentarista." "*Fisonomías sociales*, 209–230."
————— *Política española*. 2 vols.
See also the references for Chapter 17.

CHAPTER ELEVEN (pages 215–235)

NOTES

[1] Benito Pérez Galdós, *Lo prohibido*, 2:345–346 (Madrid, 1906).
[2] Clarín, *Galdós*, 168–169.
[3] Benito Pérez Galdós, *Fortunata y Jacinta*, 4:426 (Madrid, 1918).
[4] —— *Cronicón*, 2:124.
[5] Emilio Bobadilla. *Capirotazos*, 361 (Madrid, 1890).
[6] José Lázaro, "Revista general," in *España Moderna*, June, 1889, pp. 179–180.

REFERENCES

Alfonso, Luis. *"Tormento."* *La Epoca*, April 7, 1884.
———— *"La de Bringas."* *La Epoca*, July 21, 1884.
Anonymous. "La votación en la Academia." *El Imparcial*, January 17, 1889.
———— "En la Academia Española." *El Imparcial*, January 18, 1889.
———— "En la Academia Española: La recepción de Pérez Galdós." *El Liberal*, February 7, 1897.
———— "Recepción del Sr. Pérez Galdós." *La Epoca*, February 7, 1897.
———— Galdós, Portugal y España." *España*, 6:246 (1920).
Bishop, William Henry. "A Day in Literary Madrid." *A House-Hunter in Europe*, 157–162, New York, 1893.
Gómez de Baquero, E. "Crónica literaria: Pérez Galdós y Pereda en la Academia Española." *España Moderna*, vol. 20, no. 99, pp. 163–175 (1897).
Gutiérrez-Gamero, E. "La España de ayer: Pérez Galdós y Pereda en la Academia." *Libertad*, November 26, 1930.
Muñoz Peña, Pedro. *Juicio crítico de Fortunata y Jacinta*. Valladolid, 1888.
Orlando. *"Lo prohibido."* *Revista de España*, 104:414 (1885).
Ortega Munilla, José. *"Lo prohibido."* *El Imparcial*, May 11, 1885.
———— *"Fortunata y Jacinta."* *El Imparcial*, April 25, 1887.
———— *"Miau."* *El Imparcial*, June 18, 1888.
———— *"La incógnita."* *El Imparcial*, October 14, 1889.
———— *"Realidad."* *El Imparcial*, December 23, 1889.
Palau, Melchor de. *"La incógnita y Realidad."* *Revista Contemporánea*, 16:78 (May 30, 1890).
Pérez Galdós, Benito. Prologue to Francisco María Pinto, *Obras*, v–xii. Santa Cruz de Tenerife, 1888.
———— Preface to *La sombra*. Madrid, 1909. (The date of the preface is 1890).
———— *Discursos de la Real Academia Española*, 32–33. Madrid, 1897. (On the occasion of Pereda's inauguration.)
———— *La incógnita*, 83–85. Madrid, 1906.
———— "Zorrilla." *Arte y crítica*, 119–121.
———— "El crimen de la Calle de Fuencarral." *Cronicón*, 2:87–144.
Picón, J. O. *"La de Bringas."* *El Imparcial*, July 14, 1884.
Siles, José de. *"Crónica (Lo prohibido)."* *La Epoca*, May 11, 1885.
———— *"Fortunata y Jacinta."* *La Epoca*, August 4, 1887.
Zeda. "Galdós." *La Epoca*, February 8, 1897.

CHAPTER TWELVE (pages 236–261)

NOTES

[1] Vicente Blasco Ibáñez. *"El abuelo* de Galdós." *El Pueblo* (Valencia), n.d.

[2] Julio Burell, "La novela en el teatro: *Realidad* de Pérez Galdós," in *El Día,* January 13, 1892.

[3] Serafín and Joaquín Alvarez Quintero, "Intimidades del teatro," in *El Heraldo,* 1904.

[4] Emilia Pardo Bazán, *"Realidad,"* in *El Correo,* March 30, 1892.

[5] El Abate Pirracas, "La interpretación de *Realidad,"* in *El Heraldo,* March 17, 1892.

[6] P., *"Realidad,"* in *El País,* February 25, 1904.

[7] Benito Pérez Galdós, *Realidad,* 27 (Madrid, 1915).

REFERENCES

El Abate Pirracas. "La obra *(Realidad)."* *El Heraldo,* March 16, 1892.

Altamira y Crevea, Rafael. "El teatro de Pérez Galdós." *De historia y arte,* 275–314. Madrid, 1898.

Amaniel. *"Realidad."* *El Imparcial,* March 15, 1892.

Anonymous. *"Realidad."* *El País,* March 16, 1892.

———— "Anecdotario: El primer estreno." *Nuevo Mundo,* April 13, 1928.

Arimón, José. *"Realidad."* *El Liberal,* March 16, 1892.

Bobadilla, E. "Desde mi butaca: *Realidad."* *Triquitraques.* Madrid, 1892.

Bofill, Pedro. *"Realidad."* *La Epoca,* March 16, 1892.

Burell, Julio. *"Realidad."* *El Día,* March 16, 1892.

Calamocha. "Un acontecimiento literario: *Realidad."* *El Diario Español,* March 16, 1892.

Cavia, Mariano de. "Crónicas momentáneas." *El Liberal,* March 15, 1892.

Clarín. *"Realidad."* *La Correspondencia de España,* March 18, 1892.

———— *Galdós,* 231–232.

Contreras y Camargo, E. *"Realidad."* *El Teatro,* 5:42 (March, 1904).

Corral de la Pacheca, A. "Pérez Galdós en el Teatro de la Comedia." *El Movimiento Católico,* March 16, 1892.

Darío, Rubén. "Alrededor del teatro." *España contemporánea,* 201–202. Paris, 1901.

Guerra, Angel. *"Realidad."* *El Globo,* February 26, 1904.

Gutiérrez-Gamero, E. "Teatro de la Comedia: *Realidad."* *La Democracia de Madrid,* February 25, 1904.

L. B. *"Realidad."* *La Correspondencia de España,* March 16, 1892.

Martínez Barrionuevo, M. "¡15 de marzo! Pérez Galdós en la Comedia." *El Heraldo,* March 16, 1892.

Martínez Olmedilla, Augusto. "Nuestros ilustres contemporáneos: Don Benito Pérez Galdós." *ABC,* November 9, 1930.

Ortega Munilla, José. "La novela y el teatro." *El Imparcial,* April 4, 1892.

P. *"Realidad."* *El País,* February 25, 1904.

Palau, Melchor de. *"Realidad." Acontecimientos literarios.* Madrid, 1892.

Pardo Bazán, Emilia. *"Realidad." Nuestro Teatro Crítico,* vol. 2, no. 16, pp. 19–69 (1892).

París, Luis. "En la Comedia: *Realidad."* *España,* February 25, 1904.

Perera, Arturo. "Teatro de la Comedia: *Realidad."* *El Correo,* February 25, 1904.

Pérez Galdós, Benito. "Decadencia." *Nuestro teatro,* 151–198. Madrid, 1923.

Pérez Galdós, Benito. *Memorias*, 35–37, 59–60, 92, 165–176.

Picón, J. O. *"Realidad." El Correo*, March 16, 1892.

S. *"Realidad." El Correo Militar*, March 16, 1892.

Silvio. "En la Comedia: *Realidad." El Correo Español*, March 17, 1892.

Urrecha, F. "Madrid (*Realidad*)." *El Imparcial*, March 14, 1892.

———— "Madrid." *El Imparcial*, March 21, 1892.

Villegas, Francisco F. "Impresiones literarias: *Realidad." España Moderna*, vol. 4, no. 40, pp. 193–200 (1892).

Zeda. "La temporada teatral." *Revista de España*, 2:139 (1892).

———— *"Realidad." La Libertad*, March 16, 1892.

———— *"Realidad." La Epoca*, February 26, 1904.

CHAPTER THIRTEEN (pages 262–291)

NOTES

[1] G., *"Gerona,"* in *El Tiempo*, February 4, 1893.

[2] Alej., *"Gerona,"* in *El País*, February 4, 1893.

[3] Eduardo Casado Berbén, *"La de San Quintín,"* in *El Correo Militar*, January 29, 1894.

[4] O. M., "La obra de Galdós (*La de San Quintín*)," in *El Imparcial*, January 28, 1894.

[5] J. Arimón, *"La de San Quintín,"* in *El Liberal*, January 28, 1894.

[6] Matías Gómez Latorre, *"La de San Quintín,"* in *El Socialista*, March 2, 1894.

[7] El Abate Pirracas, "Telones y bambalinas," in *La Correspondencia de España*, December 19, 1894.

[8] José Cánovas y Vallejo, *"Los condenados,"* in *El Nacional*, December 12, 1894.

[9] A letter from Echegaray in the possession of the Galdós heirs.

[10] J. A., *"Voluntad,"* in *El Liberal*, December 21, 1895.

[11] Undated letter in the Galdós files.

[12] Manuel Bueno, "El triunfo de Galdós: *El abuelo,"* in *El Heraldo*, February 15, 1904.

[13] P. Mata, "Detrás del muerto," in *ABC*, January 10, 1920.

[14] Luis Doreste, "El padre Galdós," unidentified clipping.

[15] M. R. Blanco Belmonte, "Cosas de Don Benito," in *ABC*, January 5, 1920.

[16] M. R. Blanco Belmonte, "Galdós dramaturgo," *Fantoches*, n. d., probably after 1920.

[17] Salvador Canals, *"Voluntad,"* in *El Nacional*, December 21, 1895.

REFERENCES

Altamira, Rafael. "Pérez Galdós." *El Siglo* (Montevideo), January 26, 1916.

Amaniel. "En el escenario—En la calle (*La de San Quintín*)." *El Imparcial*, January 28, 1894.

Anonymous. "Pérez Galdós y la crítica teatral." *El Correo*, February 6, 1893.

———— "Otra comedia de Pérez Galdós (*Los condenados*)." *El Correo*, August 20, 1894.

———— "*Los condenados* del Sr. Galdós y el juicio de los críticos." *El Correo*, December 19, 1894.

Anonymous. "Pérez Galdós y la prensa (*Los condenados*)." *El Diario del Teatro*, January 16, 1895.

————— "*La fiera.*" *La Correspondencia de España*, December 23, 1896.

————— "El Rey y Galdós." *El Heraldo*, n.d. (1904?).

————— "Perfiles del día: Don Benito." *El Imparcial*, March 28, 1905.

J. A. "*Los condenados.*" *El Liberal*, December 14, 1894.

Arimón, José. "El prólogo de *Los condenados.*" *El Liberal*, January 8, 1895.

————— "*Casandra.*" *El Liberal*, March 1, 1910.

————— "*Celia en los infiernos.*" *El Liberal*, December 10, 1913.

Blasco, Eusebio. An open letter to Galdós about the prologue to *Los condenados*. *El Diario del Teatro*, January 17, 1895.

Bofill, Pedro. "*La loca de la casa.*" *La Epoca*, January 17, 1893.

El Caballero Audaz. *Lo que sé por mí*, 4th series, 25. Madrid, 1922.

Canals, Salvador. "*La fiera.*" *El Nacional*, December 24, 1896.

Castell, Angel María. "Pérez Galdós y los *Episodios nacionales.*" *ABC*, February 26, 1903.

Castro, Cristóbal de. "De *Chantecler* a *Casandra.*" *El Heraldo*, February 26, 1910.

Cavia, Mariano de. "Plato del día: Picadillo de Galdós." *El Liberal*, February 6, 1893.

————— "Epístola familiar." *El Liberal*, January 11, 1895.

El Chico del Escenario. "El maestro." *España Nueva*, December 10, 1913.

Diez Canedo, E. "*Pedro Minio.*" *El Globo*, December 16, 1908.

F. "El estreno de esta noche (*Amor y ciencia*)." *ABC*, November 7, 1905.

Fernández Shaw, C. "*La fiera.*" *La Epoca*, December 24, 1896.

Gil Blas de Santillana. "Críticas del mentidero: *La fiera.*" *El Día*, December 24, 1896.

Laserna, José de. "*Mariucha.*" *El Imparcial*, July 17, 1903.

————— "El prólogo de *Los condenados.*" *El Imparcial*, January 9, 1895.

Montemar, Felix de. "El año teatral (*Pedro Minio*)." *Nuestro Tiempo*, 2: 342–344 (1909).

Parmeno. "Galdós y Borrás." *El Heraldo*, January 6, 1910.

————— "El escudero de Galdós." *El Heraldo*, March 2, 1910.

Pepita Real. "Galdós." *Estudio* (Barcelona), vol. 19, no. 85, pp. 53–58 (1920).

Pérez Galdós, Benito. Prologue to *Los condenados*, 5–25. Madrid, 1920.

————— *Memorias*, 182–196.

Quijano, José de. "Rosario de Trastamara, Duquesa de San Quintín." *Blanco y Negro*, August 8, 1926.

S. "*Alma y vida;* Galdós y la Cobeña." *Alhambra*, 5:97 (January 15, 1902).

Urrecha, F. "Madrid (*La de San Quintín*)." *El Imparcial*, January 26, 1894.

————— "*Los condenados*, Galdós, algunos amigos y el que suscribe." *El Imparcial*, December 13, 1894.

————— "Madrid (*Los condenados*)." *El Imparcial*, December 17, 1894.

————— "*Voluntad.*" *El Heraldo*, December 21, 1895.

X. "*La fiera.*" *El Imparcial*, December 24, 1896.

Zeda. "*Los condenados.*" *La Epoca*, December 12, 1894.

————— "Las noches de estreno." *La Epoca*, February 4, 1896.

————— "Galdós." *La Epoca*, February 8, 1897.

————— "*Mariucha.*" *La Epoca*, n. d.

————— "*El tacaño Salomón.*" *La Epoca*, February 3, 1916.

Zamacois, Eduardo. "Figuras contemporáneas: Don Benito Pérez Galdós." *Alrededor del Mundo*, November 10, 1909.

CHAPTER FOURTEEN (pages 292–311)

NOTES

[1] Miguel Sarmiento, "Pérez Galdós: Recuerdos de su vida," in *Diario de Las Palmas*, January 5, 1920.

[2] Julián Cirilo Moreno, unpublished book entitled "Un libro más—Cosas de antaño" (Las Palmas, 1931).

[3] "Palabras de Galdós," in *Diario de Las Palmas*, special number, September, 1930.

REFERENCES

A. F. "Revista de Madrid." *Diario de Barcelona*, January 11, 1920.

Anonymous. "Pérez Galdós en Canarias." *El Correo*, November 1, 1894.

———— "Viaje de Galdós." *El Liberal*, November 14, 1894.

———— "Homenaje merecido." *Diario de Las Palmas*, February 17, 1897.

———— *Entre canarios: Homenaje a Benito Pérez Galdós.* Madrid, 1900.

———— "Galdós y Canarias." *La Acción*, January 5, 1920.

———— "El monumento a Galdós está arrinconado en un desván de Las Palmas." *Estampa*, January 22, 1929.

———— "El monumento a Don Benito Pérez Galdós." *El Sol*, September 30, 1930.

Batelori y Lorenzo, José. "Esbozando un artículo." *Canarias* (Buenos Aires), 13:204 (March, 1928).

Guerra, Angel. "Amor a la tierra." *Diario de Las Palmas*, January 24, 1900.

Mesa, Rafael de. "El Ayuntamiento de Las Palmas ha engañado a Don Benito Pérez Galdós." *El Tribuno* (Las Palmas), October 22, 1918.

Millares Cubas, Luis y Agustín. "Don Benito Pérez Galdós: Recuerdos de su infancia en Las Palmas." *La Lectura*, vol. 20, no. 228, pp. 333–352 (1919).

Torre, Claudio de la. "Galdós en su tierra." *ABC*, April 5, 1931.

La Voz Obrera (Las Palmas), 2:50 (January 4, 1931). Special edition.

Zamacois, Eduardo. "La roca de Pérez Galdós." *Nuevo Mundo*, October 6, 1922.

CHAPTER FIFTEEN (pages 312–345)

NOTES

[1] F. Urrecha, *"Angel Guerra"* in *El Imparcial*, June 29, 1891.

[2] The recent Spanish war has added a curious epilogue to Nazarín's career. Rafaela González, adopted daughter of Don José Hurtado de Mendoza, fled from Spain to Mexico and brought with her the treasured manuscript. Surprisingly enough, she permitted the Talleres Gráficos de la Nación of Mexico City to publish *Nazarín* in 1940 as a posthumous novel by Galdós, and it was reviewed and advertised as such. See M. M., "Libros y revistas: *Nazarín*," in *La Nación*, April 10, 1940.

[3] Benito Pérez Galdós, *Halma*, 144–145 (Madrid, 1913).

[4] *Ibid.*, 146.   [5] *Ibid.*, 149.

[6] M. R. Blanco Belmonte, "Cosas de Don Benito," in *ABC*, January 5, 1920.

[7] Florete, "Benito Pérez Galdós," in *Nuevo Mundo*, February 13, 1901.

[8] Clarín, *Galdós*, 320.

[9] E. Gómez de Baquero ("Andrenio"). "Crónica literaria," in *España Moderna*, vol. 11, no. 125, pp. 188–193 (1889).

[10] R[amiro] de M[aeztu], "Hacia otra España," in *La Vida Literaria*, vol. I, no. 9, pp. 151–152 (1889).

[11] Anonymous, "El papel vale más," in *Gedeón*, 9:379, February 27, 1903.

[12] Espanueva, *"España trágica,"* in *España Nueva*, April 21, 1909.

[13] R. M. Tenreiro, *"Amadeo I, La primera república,"* in *La Lectura*, vol. II, no. 129, pp. 63–66 (1911).

[14] Gregorio Marañón, "Galdós y la historia de España," in *Luz*, January 4, 1933.

REFERENCES

A. F. "Revista de Madrid." *Diario de Barcelona*, January 11, 1920.

Altamira, Rafael. "El teatro de Pérez Galdós." *De historia y arte*, 275–314. Madrid, 1898.

Bark, Ernesto. "El renacimiento literario." *Germinal*, 1:16 (August 20, 1897).

Berkowitz, H. Chonon. "Galdós and the Generation of 1898." *Philological Quarterly*, vol. 21, no. 1, pp. 107–120 (1942).

Burell, Julio. *"Mendizábal."* *El Heraldo*, November 20, 1898.

Gómez de Baquero, E. "La tercera serie de los *Episodios nacionales* de Don Benito Pérez Galdós: *Zumalacárregui*." *España Moderna*, vol. 10, no. 115, pp. 172–182 (1898).

Juan Parlante. "La literatura y los editores." *La Crónica* (Las Palmas), January 8, 1897.

Pérez Galdós, Benito. *Memorias*, 222.

Ruiz de Velasco, Luis. "De literatura." *Madrid Cómico*, April 2, 1898.

Sansón Carrasco. "Nuestros novelistas: Benito Pérez Galdós." *Blanco y Negro*, November 29, 1891.

Santaclara, A. "La crítica decadente." *Germinal*, 1:24 (October 15, 1897).

Uno. "Galdós editor." *Madrid Cómico*, February 26, 1898.

CHAPTER SIXTEEN (pages 346–382)

NOTES

[1] Del Olmet and García Carraffa, *Galdós*, 78.

[2] Anonymous article, "En casa de Galdós," in *Diario de Las Palmas*, February 7, 1901.

[3] A. Martínez Olmedilla, "Muertos ilustres contemporáneos: Don Benito Pérez Galdós," in *ABC*, November 9, 1930.

[4] Anonymous article, "El estreno de *Electra*," in *La Epoca*, January 31, 1901.

[5] Anonymous article, "Juicios de la prensa," in *El Correo*, January 31, 1901.

[6] See note 3 above.

[7] See note 2 above.

[8] Anonymous article, "El sainete de anoche," in *El Siglo Futuro*, February 2, 1901.

[9] Luis Taboada, "De todo un poco," in *Madrid Cómico*, February 9, 1901.

[10] Anonymous article, "Adivina, adivinaja," in *El Siglo Futuro*, February 2, 1901.

[11] José de Laserna, *"Electra,"* in *El Imparcial*, January 31, 1901.

[12] Andrés Ovejero, "Galdós en el teatro," in *El Globo*, January 31, 1901.

[13] José Martínez Ruiz, "Ciencia y fe," in *Madrid Cómico*, February 9, 1901.

[14] Pío Baroja, "Galdós vidente," in *El País*, January 30, 1913. This article appeared originally in the same paper on January 31, 1901.

[15] Anonymous article, "El crimen del día," in *El Siglo Futuro*, January 31, 1901.

[16] Paul Souday, *"Electra,"* in *Revue Universelle Larousse*, May, 1904.

[17] *El Sol*, October 24, 1924.

[18] *El Sol*, October 30, 1924.

[19] J[uan] Ch[abás], "¿Se representará *Electra?*" in *Luz*, March 29, 1933.

REFERENCES

The *Electra* bibliography is so extensive that only a highly selected sampling can be offered here.

Alsina, José. "Reaparición de *Electra.*" *El País*, January 31, 1913.

Anonymous. "El público y el drama." *El Liberal*, January 31, 1901.

—————— "El triunfo de Pérez Galdós." *El Correo*, February 1, 1901.

—————— "Tumulto en la Plaza de Santa Ana." *El Correo*, February 2, 1901.

—————— "Ante el Teatro Español: Atropellos de la policía." *El Imparcial*, February 2, 1901.

—————— "Homenaje a Pérez Galdós." *El Globo*, February 6, 1901.

—————— *"Electra."* *El Socialista*, February 8, 1901.

—————— "Petardo en casa de Galdós." *El Heraldo*, February 10, 1901.

—————— "La prohibición de *Electra.*" *El Correo*, March 21, 1901.

—————— "La estatua de Galdós." *Cosmopolita* (Las Palmas), May 12, 1901.

—————— "El acontecimiento artístico-político; *Electra* reaparece." *El País*, January 30, 1913.

—————— "El XXXIII aniversario del estreno de *Electra.*" *Luz*, January 30, 1934.

Araujo, Fernando. "Revista de revistas." *España Moderna*, July, 1901, pp. 155–156.

Bargiela, Camilo. "El público desde fuera." *El País*, January 30, 1913.

Becker, A. Henri. "L'*Electra* de Pérez Galdós." *Le Siècle*, April 4, 1901.

Berkowitz, H. Chonon. "Galdós' *Electra* in Paris." *Hispania*, vol. 22, no. 1, pp. 31–40 (1939).

Blanco García, Padre Francisco. "Cartas abiertas a Don Benito Pérez Galdós." *La Ciudad de Dios*, no. 64, pp. 31–39, 101–110.

Bobadilla, E. *Sintiéndome vivir.* 57–58, 205–206. Madrid, 1906.

Canals, Salvador. "De *Electra* a Sagasta." *Nuestro Tiempo*, 1:299–303 (1901).

—————— *"Electra."* *Nuestro Tiempo*, 1:210–218 (1901).

Caramanchel. "El ensayo general de *Electra.*" *La Correspondencia de España*, January 30, 1901.

J[uan] Ch[abás]. "El Teatro Escuela de Arte pone en escena *Electra.*" *Luz*, February 6, 1934.

D. L. de S. "¡Pobre Menéndez y Pelayo!" *El Siglo Futuro*, February 1, 1901.

Dicenta, Joaquín. "Crónica: Aire libre." *El Liberal*, January 19, 1904.

Frollo, Claudio. "Crónica." *Progreso*, February 7, 1901.

Gómez de Baquero, E. ("Andrenio"). "Crónica literaria: *Electra.*" *España Moderna*, 12:147 (March, 1901).

Hergoto. "Una obra, un homenaje, un hombre." *El Tribuno* (Las Palmas), February 23, 1934.

Licenciado Vidriera. "La señorita de Ubao." *El Heraldo*, February 1, 1901.

Maeztu, Ramiro de. "El público desde dentro." *El País*, January 30, 1913.

Martiartu, P. de L. de. "No lo ha querido." *El Siglo Futuro*, February 13, 1901.

Pérez Ferrero, Miguel. *Pío Baroja en su rincón*, 184–186, 198. Santiago de Chile, 1940.

Rojas, Ricardo. *"Electra." El alma española*, 89–106. Valencia, 1907 (?).

Suárez León, S. "Homenaje a Galdós." *La Aurora* (Puerto de Cabras, Fuerteventura), May 12, 1901.

Zeda. *"Electra." La Epoca*, February 2, 1901.

———— "Una representación de *Electra.*" *La Epoca*, February 28, 1901.

CHAPTER SEVENTEEN (pages 383–408)

NOTES

[1] *El Imparcial*, July 14, 1900.

[2] Anonymous article, "Galdós en Cartagena," in *El Correo*, October 12, 1903.

[3] J. López Pinillos, *"Casandra,"* in *El Liberal*, n.d.

[4] Eduardo Marquina, "El homenaje a Galdós," in *España Nueva*, November 16, 1906.

[5] Anonymous article, "El homenaje a Galdós," in *El Heraldo*, November 17, 1906.

[6] Anonymous article, "El mejor discurso," in *El País*, April 6, 1907.

[7] Anonymous article, "Discurso de Galdós," in *El País*, April 20, 1907.

[8] Anonymous article, "Discurso de Galdós," in *España Nueva*, April 19, 1907.

[9] Benito Pérez Galdós, "El primero de mayo," in *España Nueva*, May 1, 1907.

[10] Galdós, "¿Más paciencia?" in *España Nueva*, March 2, 1908.

[11] Del Olmet and García Carraffa, *Galdós*, 118–124.

[12] Benito Pérez Galdós, *Casandra* (Madrid, 1910).

[13] Anonymous article, "Anecdotario," in *Hoja Oficial del Lunes*, November 28, 1932.

[14] Anonymous article, "Pérez Galdós ante los Reyes," in *El Sol*, January 5, 1920.

[15] A. F. "Revista de Madrid," in *Diario de Barcelona*, January 11, 1920.

[16] Anonymous article, "Lo que hace Galdós en el Parlamento," in *La Epoca*, March 23, 1908.

REFERENCES

Andrenio, (E. Gómez de Baquero). "La carta de Don Benito." *La Epoca*, April 6, 1907.

Anonymous. "Pérez Galdós y *Le Temps.*" *La Epoca*, April 18, 1907.

———— "Discurso de Pérez Galdós." *España Nueva*, August 20, 1911.

———— "La protesta de la Conjunción." *El País*, December 1, 1911.

———— "Galdós." *El Ejército Español*, January 5, 1920.

El Bachiller Corchuelo. "Nuestros grandes prestigios: Benito Pérez Galdós." *Por Esos Mundos*, vol. 11, no. 185, pp. 791–807; no. 186, pp. 27–56 (1910).

Berkowitz, H. Chonon. "Unamuno's Relations with Galdós." *Hispanic Review*, 8:321–338 (1940).

Borges, França. "En la quinta de Galdós." *España Nueva*, August 29, 1910.

Bueno, Manuel. "El homenaje a Galdós." *El Liberal*, December 6, 1906.

E. D[iez] C[anedo]. "Tres hombres." *España*, October 17, 1918.

Espanueva. "Los proyectos de Galdós." *España Nueva*, November 25, 1907.

Gómez Carrillo, Enrique. "Galdós ante el Rey." *El Liberal*, January 10, 1914.

Montaner, Diego. "Habla Don Benito Pérez Galdós." *El Día Gráfico*, April 19, 1917.
Pardo Bazán, Emilia. "Un poco de crítica—Estatua en vida." *ABC*, January 27, 1919.
Parmeno. "*El caballero encantado.*" *El Heraldo*, January 15, 1910.
Pérez Galdós, Benito. "Al pueblo español." *España Nueva*, October 6, 1909.
———— Prologue to *Vulgarizaciones históricas* (*artículos publicados en El País*). Madrid, 1909.
Soriano, Rodrigo. "El buen Don Benito." *España Nueva*, May 27, 1909.
Torralva Beci, E. "Las tardes en San Quintín." *El Fígaro*, January 8, 1920.
Villa, Antonio de la. "Galdós político." *Diario de Las Palmas* (special edition), September, 1930.

CHAPTER EIGHTEEN (pages 409–431)

NOTES

[1] Un Lector, "El homenaje a Galdós," in *El Debate*, November 28, 1911.
[2] Anonymous article, "Homenajes," in *El Universo*, November 24, 1911.
[3] Anonymous article, "Homenaje inoportuno," in *La Época*, November 25, 1911.
[4] Y., "Junta Nacional de Homenaje a Galdós," in *El Siglo Futuro*, April 13, 1914.
[5] El Caballero Audaz, "Las migajas de una suscripción—Galdós acusa," in *El Día*, December 12, 1916.
[6] Tomás Romero, "El maestro ingrato," *El Liberal*, December 3, 1916.

REFERENCES

Andrenio (E. Gómez de Baquero). "El homenaje a Galdós." *Nuevo Mundo*, February 5, 1914.
Anonymous. "Galdós, el genio de la raza." *El Globo*, November 25, 1911.
———— "Galdós y los estudiantes." *El País*, November 26, 1911.
———— "Galdós y el premio Nobel." *El Imparcial*, February 14, 1912.
———— "Torquemada en el purgatorio." *España Nueva*, October 27, 1912.
———— "Don Benito Pérez Galdós." *ABC*, January 22, 1914.
———— "En honor de Galdós." *El Correo*, January 26, 1914.
———— "En favor de Galdós." *ABC*, January 28, 1914.
———— "De lo de Pérez Galdós." *El Universo*, January 31, 1914.
———— "En favor de Galdós: Seamos prácticos," *ABC*, February 2, 1914.
———— "La actualidad: El maestro Galdós." *Nuevo Mundo*, February 5, 1914.
———— "El caso Galdós." *ABC*, March 17, 1914.
———— "Junta Nacional del Homenaje a Galdós." *El Imparcial*, April 11, 1914.
El Bachiller Corchuelo. "El Obispo de Jaca y Pérez Galdós." *Nuevo Mundo*, February 1, 1912.
Benavente, Jacinto. "Acotaciones." *Nuevo Mundo*, December 7, 1911.
———— "Acotaciones." *Nuevo Mundo*, February 1, 1912.
Castrovido, Roberto. "Los que amaron a Galdós." *La Voz*, 1928.
Cavia, Mariano de. "Galdós Nobel." *El Imparcial*, January 21, 1912.
———— "Actualidad." *El Imparcial*, January 23, 1912.
———— "Entre Galdós y un Tití." *El Imparcial*, January 29, 1914.
———— "Los brindis de Don Benito." *El Imparcial*, April 17, 1914.

Dicenta, Joaquín. "El premio España." *El Liberal,* January 21, 1914.
Fra-Diávolo. "Una interviú sin palabras." *España Nueva,* July 14, 1912.
Fray Candil. "Baturrillo." *El Imparcial,* January 3, 1912.
García-Sanchiz, Federico. "El último retrato de Galdós." *El Liberal,* November 24, 1911.
Gil Asensio, Federico. "Hablando con Galdós." *Nuevo Mundo,* September 28, 1911.
Jerique, José. "Homenaje a Galdós." *España Nueva,* December 24, 1911.
López Alarcón, Enrique. "El patriarca y los fanfarrones." *La Acción,* March 13, 1916.
Pallot, Benigno. "Del premio España." *El Liberal,* January 24, 1914.
Répide, Pedro de. "Por percusión." *El Liberal,* December 3, 1911.
Rivas Cherif, C. "La obra de Benavente al fulgor del Premio Nobel." *La Pluma,* 3:31, December, 1922.
Sanz, T. "El premio Nobel y Galdós." *El País,* November 23, 1911.
Vergara, Gabriel María. "Homenaje nacional a Pérez Galdós." *El Globo,* December 14, 1911.

CHAPTER NINETEEN (pages 432–449)

NOTES

[1] Margarita Nelken, "Intimidades y recuerdos," in *El Sol,* January 4, 1923.

[2] *Ibid.*

[3] Mariano de Cavia, "Galdós y los Quinteros," in *El Imparcial,* October 13, 1916.

[4] Alejandro Pérez Lugín, "*Marianela* y Xirgu," in *El Heraldo,* October 17, 1916.

[5] Lugín, "Estreno de *Marianela,*" *in El Heraldo,* October 19, 1916.

[6] Anonymous article, "De la vida que pasa: Galdós, Unamuno, Cavia," in *La Esfera,* October 19, 1918.

[7] Cristóbal de Castro, "El monumento a Galdós," in *Nuevo Mundo,* March 1, 1918.

[8] E. Ramírez Angel, "Galdós íntimo: Los últimos años del maestro," in *ABC,* January 7, 1923; Marciano Zurita, "Los últimos años de Galdós," *ibid.,* January 5, 1920.

[9] E. Ramírez Angel, see the note above.

[10] Francisco Alcántara, "En la Rosaleda del Retiro," in *El Sol,* January 20, 1919.

[11] Anonymous article. "El monumento a Pérez Galdós," in *El Globo,* January 31, 1919.

[12] Rafael Domenech, "El monumento a Galdós," in *ABC,* February 3, 1919.

[12] Juan de la Encina, "El monumento a Galdós," in *España,* vol. 5, no. 200, p. 19 (1919).

REFERENCES

Alvarez Quintero, S. and J., Open letter about their dramatization of *Marianela. El Imparcial,* October 9, 1916.
Anonymous. "La religión y Pérez Galdós." *La Acción,* January 4, 1920.
Blanco Belmonte, M. R. "Galdós dramaturgo." *Fantoches* (after 1920).
Carrère, Emilio. "Por nuestro ciego glorioso." *Nuevo Mundo,* May 31, 1918.
Francés, José. "Un episodio nacional: Galdós." *Nuevo Mundo,* January 24, 1919.

Gómez Latorre, Matías. "Recuerdos de un ochentón." *La Voz Obrera,* 2:50 (January 4, 1931).

Martínez de la Riva, R. "Maestros y discípulos." *Blanco y Negro,* October 20, 1918.

Montañer, Joaquín. "Galdós." *El Sol,* January 5, 1920.

Ortega Munilla, José. "Rasgos de España: El triste narrador." *ABC,* January 4, 1920.

Doña Paz. "La última confidencia del maestro: Galdós como Balzac." *Hoy,* January 9, 1920.

Salado, José Luis. "La casa donde murió el autor de los *Episodios nacionales.*" *Diario de Las Palmas,* special edition, September, 1930.

————— "Cuando Galdós, con su criado Victoriano, nombraba ministros." *El Heraldo,* January 4, 1930.

Vegue y Goldoni, Angel. "El monumento a Galdós." *El Imparcial,* January 20, 1919.

CHAPTER TWENTY (pages 450–459)

NOTES

[1] *El Sol,* January 4, 1920.

[2] Angel Guerra, "Los dioses se van," in *El Diluvio* (Barcelona), January 14, 1920.

[3] J. Francos Rodríguez, "La vivienda de Galdós: Tributo debido," in *ABC,* October 4, 1927.

REFERENCES

Castell, Angel María. "Apuntes de la semana." *Blanco y Negro,* January 11, 1920.

Fernández-Florez, W. "Comentarios tímidos a propósito de la muerte de Galdós." *Blanco y Negro,* January 11, 1920.

San José, Diego. "El sudario del maestro." *La Esfera,* January 12, 1924.

The Published Works of Galdós

The works listed below include those published during Galdós' lifetime and the misnamed series of *Obras inéditas,* consisting of miscellaneous journalistic writings collected and edited after his death by Alberto Ghiraldo. The dates of composition accompany the titles; with few exceptions, they are also the dates of publication. The divisions are those established by Galdós himself.

I. Novelas de la Primera Epoca

La fontana de oro, 1867–68
La sombra, 1870.
El audaz, 1871.
Doña Perfecta, 1876.

Gloria, 2 vols., 1876–77.
Marianela, 1878.
La familia de León Roch, 3 vols., 1878.

II. Novelas Españolas Contemporáneas

La desheredada, 1881.
El amigo Manso, 1882.
El doctor Centeno, 2 vols., 1883.
Tormento, 1884.
La de Bringas, 1884.
Lo prohibido, 2 vols., 1884–85.
Fortunata y Jacinta, 4 vols., 1886–87.
Miau, 1888.
La incógnita, 1888-89.
Torquemada en la hoguera, 1889.
Realidad, 1889.
Angel Guerra, 3 vols., 1890-91.

Tristana, 1892.
La loca de la casa, 1892.
Torquemada en la Cruz, 1893.
Torquemada en el purgatorio, 1894.
Torquemada y San Pedro, 1895.
Nazarín, 1895.
Halma, 1895.
Misericordia, 1897.
El abuelo, 1897.
Casandra, 1905.
El caballero encantado, 1909.
La razón de la sinrazón, 1915.

III. Episodios Nacionales

First Series

Trafalgar, 1873.
La corte de Carlos IV, 1873.
El 19 de marzo y el 2 de mayo, 1873.
Bailén, 1873.
Napoleón en Chamartín, 1874.

Zaragoza, 1874.
Gerona, 1874.
Cádiz, 1874.
Juan Martín el Empecinado, 1874.
La batalla de los Arapiles, 1875.

Second Series

El equipaje del Rey José, 1875.
Memorias de un cortesano, 1875.
La segunda casaca, 1876.
El Grande Oriente, 1876.
El 7 de julio, 1876.
Los cien mil hijos de San Luis, 1877.

El terror de 1824, 1877.
Un voluntario realista, 1878.
Los apostólicos, 1879.
Un faccioso más y algunos frailes menos, 1879.

Third Series

Zumalacárregui, 1898.
Mendizábal, 1898.
De Oñate a la Granja, 1898.
Luchana, 1899.
La campaña del Maestrazgo, 1899.

La estafeta romántica, 1899.
Vergara, 1899.
Montes de Oca, 1900.
Los ayacuchos, 1900.
Bodas reales, 1900.

Fourth Series

Las tormentas del 48, 1902.
Narváez, 1902.
Los duendes de la camarilla, 1903.
La revolución de julio, 1903–04.
O'Donnell, 1904.
Aita Tettauen, 1904–1905.

Carlos VI en la Rápita, 1905.
La vuelta al mundo en la Numancia, 1906.
Prim, 1906.
La de los tristes destinos, 1907.

Final Series

España sin rey, 1907–08.
España trágica, 1909.
Amadeo I, 1910.

La primera república, 1911.
De Cartago a Sagunto, 1911.
Cánovas, 1912.

IV. Dramas y Comedias

Realidad, 1892.
La loca de la casa, 1893.
Gerona, 1893.
La de San Quintín, 1894.
Los condenados, 1894.
Voluntad, 1895.
Doña Perfecta, 1896.
La fiera, 1896.
Electra, 1901.
Alma y vida, 1902.
Mariucha, 1903.

El abuelo, 1904.
Bárbara, 1905.
Amor y ciencia, 1905.
Pedro Minio, 1908.
Casandra, 1910.
Celia en los infiernos, 1913.
Alceste, 1914.
Sor Simona, 1915.
El tacaño Salomón, 1916.
Santa Juana de Castilla, 1918.

V. Obras Varias

Discursos académicos, 1897.

Memoranda, 1906.

VI. Obras Inéditas

Fisonomías sociales, 1923.
Arte y crítica, 1923.
Política española, 2 vols., 1923.
Nuestro teatro, 1923.
Cronicón, 2 vols., n. d.

Toledo, 1924.
Viajes y fantasías, 1928.
Memorias, 1930.
Crónica de Madrid, 1933.

Index